D1528319

RULES, EXCEPTIONS, AND SOCIAL ORDER

RULES, EXCEPTIONS, AND SOCIAL ORDER

Robert B. Edgerton

UNIVERSITY OF CALIFORNIA PRESS
BERKELEY LOS ANGELES LONDON

University of California Press
Berkeley and Los Angeles, California

University of California Press, Ltd.
London, England

Copyright © 1985 by The Regents of the University of California

Library of Congress Cataloging in Publication Data

Edgerton, Robert B., 1931–
  Rules, exceptions, and social order.

Bibliography:
  Includes index.
  1. Social norms. 2. Deviant behavior. 3. Society, Primitive.
I. Title.
GN493.3.E33   1985   306   84–28134
ISBN 0–520–05481–4

Printed in the United States of America

1 2 3 4 5 6 7 8 9

To Christine
for all the usual reasons
and then some

Contents

Contents

Acknowledgments

This book has been so long in the making that many of the people and events that helped to get it started and keep it going are obscured by the gossamer clouds of forgetfulness. Thinking back, I would like to accuse all sorts of people of pushing me into the tar pit that this book became, but in reality most people tried to save me from this gooey fate. A wee nudge toward the pit came from Craig MacAndrew almost twenty years ago when we discussed excuses, or "time out," as we then said. Since that time, the ideas in this book were developed in various seminars at UCLA, where many students helped me in countless ways. Some of these students and many colleagues directed me to fugitive sources of ethnographic writing, where I rummaged to great profit. To the many ethnographers whose works I read for this book, I offer my sincere thanks. Complaints about the inadequacies of the ethnographic literature are more common than expressions of gratitude, but I feel a great debt to these ethnographers, whose work was never easy. I have done my best to report their materials accurately and to interpret them fairly. References to the Hehe, Akamba, Pokot, and Sebei, unless otherwise cited, refer to my own field research.

At the risk of slighting (or exonerating) those students and colleagues who helped me, I'll mention only those whose comments on an earlier draft particularly stick in my mind: Jorja Manos-Prover, Barbara Herr, L. L. Langness, John Kennedy, and Wally Goldschmidt. I am also grateful to Mervin Meggitt for his comments on my treatment of the Walbiri and to James Kubeck, sponsoring editor of the University of California Press, for his steadfast support. For various kinds of research assistance, I am indebted to Patti S. Hartmann, Marcia Gaston, and Barbara Herr. The manuscript was typed and retyped with care and good humor by Genevieve Gilbert-Rolfe, Martin Cohen, Lupe Montaño and Janell Demyan. Marcia Gaston provided all manner of bibliographic and editorial help, for which I am most grateful.

I gratefully acknowledge the support provided by NICHD Grants No. HD 09474–02, HD 11944–03, and HD 04612. For permission to reprint extracts from *Desert People* by M. J. Meggitt, I thank Angus and Robertson Publishers.

Introduction

What is it that every man seeks? To be secure, to be happy, to do
what he pleases without restraint and without compulsion.
                                                    —Epictetus

Not a gift of a cow, nor a gift of land, nor yet a gift of food, is so
important as the gift of safety, which is declared to be the greatest
gift among all gifts in this world.
                                                    —*Panchatantra*

In a particular time and place, freedom can seem to be the ultimate
human goal, as it did to Greek Stoic philosopher Epictetus in the first
century A.D.; in another time and place, such as fifth century India,
what matters most might be security, not freedom. Sometimes both
freedom and security are valued. When Rousseau wrote *The Social
Contract* in 1762, his fundamental concern was how people could live
in society without the loss of freedom. Throughout history it has been
written that the only way mankind can achieve freedom and security
is by following rules, laws, or moral precepts. Without rules, it has
often been said, human life would be chaotic, and no one could be
either free or safe. But here agreement stops. Are freedom and
security best achieved by rules that are flexible enough to accommodate the complexities of human living, or should rules be inflexible
and rigorously enforced? Philosophers, scholars, and theologians,
among others, have never ceased debating the proper place of rules
in human society, while practical men and women in all societies have
attempted to find rules that would allow them to cope with their
environments and one another. This book is about the kinds of rules
that men and women have developed. Why are some rules flexible
and others inflexible? When are people held strictly accountable for
following rules, and when are exemptions allowed?
   When Robert Burton wrote in *The Anatomy of Melancholy* that "No
rule is so general which admits not some exception," he was not
making an original observation. This idea was a truism in early seventeenth-century England and in many other countries both before and
since that time. Exceptions to rules—including important rules—are
commonplace. Why is this seemingly unremarkable phenomenon the

1

starting point for a book? Because, if rules are essential for the regulation of human affairs, if they are morally required or practically
necessary, then why should they have exceptions? Furthermore, if
"rules are made to be broken," as aphorists past and present have
said, why have rules at all?

But is it true that all rules have exceptions, or that rules are made
to be broken? Many scholars past and present have said that rules not
only do have exceptions but that they *must* have them. Yet it is undeniable that people in many societies—perhaps even all societies—have
taken some of their rules very seriously indeed. Men and women have
been so serious about some things—religion, adultery, money, and
honor, for instance—that the rules that have governed such matters
could be as serious as life or death. And they still are—a day seldom
passes without one group of people somewhere in the world killing
people of another group because of moral principles, religious convictions, or rules about honor, revenge, or justice.

THE THESIS

In most disciplines, there are antidisciplines, competing paradigms,
and complementary perspectives. The terms differ but the idea is the
same. A field of knowledge develops and a conventional conception
of reality takes hold. This conception is seldom without some visible
flaw, but it is usually not so palpably false that a better conception
quickly replaces it. This book is a reaction to the prevailing concept
of human rule use. This conventional way of looking at rules was a
useful corrective to an earlier conventional theory, which has been
called normative theory; this theory held that people everywhere not
only followed the rules of their societies—but also made these rules
a part of themselves and became, almost literally, inseparable from
them. This conception of rules had some usefulness in its time by
calling attention to the power of rules and to the need that people
had for rules in order to maintain secure, orderly lives and to find a
measure of autonomy within that order. But another theory arose to
account for the undeniable reality that people everywhere sometimes
failed to follow rules or to incorporate them and instead often used
rules for their own interests.

This new perspective—which I prefer to call strategic interactionism—was an important corrective, but I shall argue that as it grew
in acceptance and influence, the idea that rules sometimes constrained
people very strictly was lost. Yet the use of rules for self-interest could

only be a viable strategy if rules were themselves viable as governors of human conduct. Unless rules were considered important and were taken seriously and followed, it would make no sense to manipulate them for personal benefit. If many people did not believe that rules were legitimate and compelling, how could anyone use these rules for personal advantage?

Although all societies allow exceptions to many rules, all societies also enforce some rules for which there are no legitimate exceptions. The thesis of this book is that while societies differ markedly in the number of rules they enforce without exceptions, there are factors present in all societies that press strongly for exceptions. These factors include temporary conditions such as illness, intoxication, or emotional stress; more lasting circumstances such as age, sex, or physical disability; individual differences; and some aspects of human nature, as well as the nature of social context and of rules themselves. At the same time, conditions such as inequality, the need to cooperate, and the perception of grave danger appear to lead to the development of rules that permit no exceptions. The presence in all societies of rules without exceptions, whatever the precise reasons for their occurrence, calls for a reappraisal of those current social theories that conceive of social systems as being made up of rules that are flexible, negotiable, and subject to exceptions. Finally, I also suggest that to speak of rules as though they were all alike obscures the place of rules in creating or maintaining social order, and that in general, rules about exceptions to rules do not subvert social order but rather help to maintain it.

In chapter 1, the history of normative theory as well as of its corrective, strategic interactionism, is reviewed, and various issues about rules, exceptions, and strict liability are introduced. Chapter 2 introduces different types of rules and exceptions to rules. The remainder of the book is organized into three parts: Part I (chapters 3, 4, 5, and 6) describes some of the variety and nature of rules for breaking rules in societies in many parts of the world. Part II (chapters 7, 8, and 9) examines various societies that differ in the flexibility of their rules. Part III (chapters 10, 11, and 12) attempts to explain why certain types of rules are flexible and allow exceptions while others do not; also reviewed and discussed are the complexities that bedevil efforts to predict whether one type of society will have more or less flexible rules than will another type.

CHAPTER 1

Rules and Exceptions

The belief that rules are essential for human survival did not originate with Thomas Hobbes, but his spirited insistence that only rules in the form of the social contract could prevent man's egoism from leading to endless conflict became a landmark in the history of this idea. E. A. Hoebel, writing about the anthropology of law, caricatured the idea that rules arose to control conflict by imagining that (1954:276) "it is as though men were getting together and saying to each other, 'Look here! Let's have a little organization here, or we'll never get anywhere with this mess! Let's have a clear understanding of who's who, what we are to do, and how we are going to do it!' In its essence it is what the social-contract theorists recognized as the foundation of social order." It has, then, been generally thought that without rules, there could be no safety, security, or order for mankind. This is an enormous burden to place on rules, and, as we shall see, the idea is simplistic, but the belief that rules alone can control human conduct has been deeply embedded in Western thought from the days of Montesquieu, Vico, Rousseau, Ferguson, and many others of the past right up to the present day.[1]

Hobbes was born in 1588, the year that the Spanish Armada was defeated in the English Channel, and he lived through the turbulent and bloody civil wars between the supporters of the Stuarts and Cromwell, so he had reason to be concerned about conflict. Still, he should have known that there was social order *before* there was a social contract; Aristotle, among others, had pointed out that animals also lead orderly lives, so much so in fact that we now say of many of them that they are naturally "social." While animals other than man do not proclaim edicts or make laws, they do have implicit rules—just as humans do with regard to language or spatial relations—and these rules regulate not just aggression, mating, and social dominance but also many other activities that together contribute to an orderly society.[2] A. I. Hallowell (1976) referred to the primate pattern of implicit rules as "protoculture." Commenting on what man had to do to improve on this primate protoculture, anthropologist Elman Service (1962:42) wrote: "All that was necessary, then, was the symbolic ability to make some rules and values which would extend, intensify, and

4

regularize tendencies which already existed." These rules and values, especially those about sharing, Service thought, helped to establish alliances, inhibited conflict, and strengthened social solidarity.

But if Hobbes and others exaggerated the conflict and chaos of the imagined period before the "social contract" came into being, they may have been right in their belief in the importance of explicit rules for the survival of human society. Many great scholars have held this belief, and a great many contemporary social scientists still do. This line of thinking was summarized by sociologist Jack Douglas (1970a:vii):

> Shared rules are the most crucial meanings involved in constructing social order. Throughout human experience thus far, shared rules have proven to be a necessary ingredient in constructing any social order that was not merely transitory. Only shared rules, which are essentially prescriptions and proscriptions of typical actions in typical everyday situations supported by various internal commitments and external sanctions, have proven capable thus far of producing the degree of ordering of interactions which human beings have found necessary for existence and for the good life.

This declaration, or one very much like it, has been offered so often and so magisterially that it has become part of the catechism of social science, dutifully repeated in most textbooks.

Yet, as common as it has been to say that rules are vital for the construction of social order, it has been equally common to recognize that these rules not only do have exceptions but *must* have them. Once again, Jack Douglas (1970:20):

> Life is immensely too complex, too uncertain, too conflictful, and too changing for any set of abstract and predetermined rules to specify activities that will have results seen as adequate by the individual actors. Life itself would soon end if one tried to live in that way.

Assertions such as these by Douglas are based on abundant empirical evidence showing that all societies produce and enforce various kinds of rules that appear to contribute to social order and stability. But there is also abundant evidence that these same societies produce and sometimes enforce other rules that provide exceptions to these rules. Anthropologist Paul Bohannan said that (1965:35) "It is widely recognized that many peoples of the world can state more or less precise 'rules' which are, in fact, the norms in accordance with which they think they ought to judge their conduct. In all societies there are allowable lapses from such rules, and in most there are more or less precise rules (sometimes legal ones) for breaking rules." And, to repeat Douglas, these rules-for-breaking-rules, like the original rules, have their own "internal commitments and external sanctions."

It is important that we be clear about what is puzzling in the simultaneous presence of rules and rules for breaking rules. The point is not that conflict and deviance from rules occur in all known societies; it is obvious that people often break rules. Nor is the point that social rules are often ambiguous, uncertain, conflicting, and manipulable. That, too, is well-known. The paradox lies in the apparently contradictory reality that societies establish rules allowing at least some of their members to break rules, evading responsibility for conduct that would usually be seen as offensive, outrageous, or unthinkable. They do so not simply by turning a collective blind eye to misconduct or by squabbling about what is right and proper but instead by providing rules that prescribe exceptions to other rules. Most societies provide these exceptions by recognizing that there are temporary conditions, less temporary statuses, special occasions, and clearly defined settings that permit—and sometimes require—at least some persons in those societies to behave in ways that would ordinarily be prohibited and perhaps would even be unthinkable. It is probable that all societies have some socially accepted rules that provide exceptions to socially accepted rules. Some of these exceptions permit people to avoid obligations that would ordinarily be required of them, such as child care or economic productivity; others permit or reduce the seriousness of behavior that would ordinarily be horrifying, such as incest, rape, and even homicide. Sometimes escape from ordinary responsibility is possible because a rule is ambiguous, or because two rules conflict, but explicit rules often have equally explicit exceptions, just as Bohannan suggested. Still not all rules are like this. For some rules there are no exceptions at all.

The purpose of this book is to ask why some rules have exceptions and others do not. Like all difficult questions about humans and their social lives, this one will lead us into uncharted territory. There is no clearly marked path, and we will sometimes find ourselves moving through a hall of mirrors upon mirrors, and the reflected images of people and their rules will sometimes be difficult to discern or to separate. To prevent the questions that must be asked from becoming so ultimate that they can receive only the most banal of answers, or none at all, it will be necessary to simplify the search, at least at the outset. The basic questions are these: If rules are vital to social order, why should there be rules allowing exceptions to them? Does the presence of exceptions to rules indicate incomplete social organization, the unfinished business of history, or even social disorganization? Or are rules about exceptions to rules essential if people are to live with one another? And if this is so, why do some rules have no exceptions?

To begin, we need to look back at some of the beliefs and theories that have prefigured these questions yet have left them unanswered.

NORMATIVE THEORY: RULES ARE SOVEREIGN

When Bronislaw Malinowski wrote *Crime and Custom in Savage Society* (1926), he attempted to put to rest the scholarly opinion of the time that in primitive society "no one dreams of breaking the social rules," as Oxford anthropologist R. R. Marett (1912:182–183) put it. Malinowski effectively used his extensive knowledge of everyday life in the Trobriand Islands to demonstrate that "primitives" were not slavishly devoted to their rules but instead often used rules to their own advantage. But at the same time, Malinowski showed that the Trobriand Islanders did take many of their rules seriously and, for the most part, followed them. He also showed how Trobriand rule following was tied to a pattern of economic reciprocity in which everyone was dependent on someone else, with the collective well-being dependent on rules that defined those relationships (Mair 1965).

The first of Malinowski's points seemed to go unnoticed, while the second was affirmed by reports from many parts of the world. These reports eventually coalesced into conventional normative theory, which held that social order was the natural way of things everywhere, that this ubiquitous order was based on rules that were largely accepted and followed, and that exceptions to these rules, although sometimes present, were of little significance and probably resulted from the influence of external agents of change. This normative orthodoxy owed much to the ethnographic reports of many anthropologists, but many of the theoretical formalisms that gave it widespread legitimacy were authored by sociologists. It is tempting to suggest that this was so because sociologists lacked the firsthand research experience in small-scale societies that would help them to evaluate exceptions to rules, but the cause was more likely their penchant for grand theory, which was avoided by most anthropologists of that time. Whatever the reasons, the widespread acceptance of normative theory owes much to sociologists, beginning with the classic

work of Emile Durkheim and culminating in the theories of Talcott
Parsons and his Harvard circle. It is also important to recognize that
most anthropologists who *did* have firsthand field experience went
along with normative theory. A. R. Radcliffe-Brown, for example,
was one of its major proponents. Indeed, before World War II, the
ethnographic reports of life in small-scale societies by anthropologists
from both sides of the Atlantic typically concentrated on the rule-
governed character of social life. Society after society was depicted
primarily in terms of the consistency, regularity, and continuity of its
system of rules and of the power of these rules to bring about behavioral conformity. Exceptions to rules and exemptions from
punishment for rule breakers were sometimes noted, but the presence
of such phenomena was neither a central topic nor one of much
theoretical interest. Many ethnographers privately admitted that reducing real-life diversity to a neat normative model was no easy task,
but, easy or not, the task was accomplished over and over again.
Custom was king, and so was normative theory.

   Dissatisfaction with normative theory eventually crystallized, and
sociologist Dennis Wrong (1961) was speaking for many when he
criticized the prevailing theory as one in which it was incorrectly
assumed that people were easily socialized to follow the rules of their
cultures. As Wrong pointed out, normative theory assumed that
people everywhere "internalized" the rules of the culture into which
they were born, and as a result they were guided internally by what
was traditional and proper. This idea of internalization was central
to Parsons's theory of social action, just as it earlier had been central
to Durkheim's ideas of solidarity. People behaved correctly not only
because of "repression," as in the Freudian metaphor, but because
they incorporated rules of proper conduct. As a result, virtue became
its own reward. But people were also externally guided toward conformity with the rules of their society because of their desire for social
approval and acceptance. The more or less inevitable result of these
two phenomena was social order. This "conventional wisdom," as
Wrong mordantly referred to it, was criticized by him as being
founded on an "oversocialized view of man" and an "over-integrated
view of society." The history of normative theory is complex, and
Wrong's critique was incomplete (Blake and Davis 1964), but the
details of this history are not the issue here. It is enough for my
purposes to note that despite doctrinal disputes and dissatisfactions—
many of which were decidedly ill-tempered—one or another version
of this theory, usually linked to functionalism or social equilibrium
(Sztompka 1974), occupied a dominant position in sociological and

anthropological thought until sometime in the late 1950s or early 1960s.[3]

THE REACTION: STRATEGIC MANIPULATION OF RULES

Critics of the conventional normative model of society always existed in American anthropology, where the longstanding emphasis on individual action and psychological perspectives made some measure of dissent inevitable. Edward Sapir's many urgings to study individuals were particularly influential. Even so, little fundamental doubt was expressed about the power of "culture" to "mold" people to its rules. Deviance was sometimes reported and so was social disorder; the torment that some individuals suffered in trying to internalize or comply with the rules of their societies was also documented. But the molding force of rules was still taken for granted, and the central assumptions of the conventional, normative model held sway until well after World War II.

It is tempting to link the rejection of normative theory to the social and political upheavals of the 1960s, as Floyd Matson did in *The Idea of Man* (1976). These events surely had an impact, as did the intellectual interpreters of those events, such as Herbert Marcuse with his blend of Marx and Freud. But some of the most influential attacks on normative theory antedated the troubled decade of the 1960s. C. Wright Mills's book *The Sociological Imagination* (1959) was enormously influential, and so were the early works of Erving Goffman, such as *The Presentation of Self in Everyday Life* (1959). When anthropologists of that time engaged in field research or attempted to reanalyze old field notes, they often discovered troubling discrepancies between the inconsistent and contradictory social realities they observed and the normative theory they tried to make these realities fit.

Robert F. Murphy acknowledged all of these influences on his own thinking in his book *The Dialectics of Social Life* (1971), which soon became influential. Although other anthropologists of that time were not necessarily influenced in just the same ways that Murphy was, most came to share his revisionist view of rules (1971:52):

> Everybody understands, of course, that the norms are complex; they overlap each other; they are sometimes mutually contradictory; they pertain to differing segments of society; they do not at all elicit uniform response and acquiescence from all its members. The acceptance of

congruity between norm and behavior does not necessarily entail the notion that man is a totally passive victim of tradition—despite the fact that many sociologists still think this to be true of primitives. Each behavioral situation is understood to be unique, and each standard of conduct therefore applies to a multitude of possible interactions. There can be no exact conformity to norms because this is antithetical to the very nature of norms.

Revision of normative theory was not limited to American anthropology. In fact, an equally strong and even earlier protest had arisen among British social anthropologists, most of whom had been trained within the conventional, normative tradition of Durkheim and Radcliffe-Brown. Some signs of disagreement with normative theory were noticeable as early as the mid-1930s in Gregory Bateson's *Naven* (1958/1936), but Bateson's views were not taken very seriously in those days. An even earlier criticism of normative theory was published by Malinowski in 1934, and it too had little impact. Buried in an introduction to the doctoral dissertation of his student H. I. Hogbin, Malinowski anticipated Murphy's comments by more than three decades (1961/1934:xxlviii):

> . . . we find everywhere that rules of behaviour and principles of law, or call it custom if you like, cannot be rigid, since they act rather as elastic forces of which the tension decreases or increases; they cannot be absolute since they have always qualifications, codicils and riders; they cannot be automatic, since non-compliance with one rule can usually be justified by another rule of tribal law.

Despite Malinowski, it was not until the mid-1950s that British social anthropologists seriously began to ask themselves in print whether it might not be advisable to shift their analytic attention from elements of order, regularity, continuity, and consistency to such matters as ambiguity, inconsistency, conflict, and change. Max Gluckman, in his book *The Judicial Process Among the Barotse of Northern Rhodesia* (1967), continued to champion equilibrium theory, yet he made much of the uncertainty and flexibility of basic Barotse jural rules. And Victor Turner (1957), who, like Gluckman, did field research in Zambia (previously Northern Rhodesia), began a series of explorations into the inconsistencies and discrepancies in cultural principles and rules. When Australian anthropologist W. E. H. Stanner (1959:216) reviewed some of Turner's work among the Zambian Ndembu, he offered this soon to be widely approved comment:

It can be argued sensibly that it is precisely . . . the manipulative, bargaining, transactional approach to life, which *is* the system of their life. In other words . . . "endemic conflict" (including "exceptions" to the "rules") is not an upset or defect or an aberration or a fiction of some idealized or perfect system, but is *itself* the system.

There are many examples of a shift in orientation away from normative theory on the part of British anthropologists around this time. For example, Rodney Needham, known for his analyses of the rules of marriage, wrote the following in his introduction to Durkheim and Mauss's classic *Primitive Classification* (1963:xl):

If our first task as social anthropologists is to discern order and make it intelligible, our no less urgent duty is to make sense of those practically universal usages and beliefs by which people create disorder, i.e., turn their classifications upside down or disintegrate them entirely.

Needham did not emphasize the fact that usages and beliefs such as these are prescribed by rules, but he certainly caught the sense of paradox in a topsy-turvy world of social reality.

In his introduction to the 1964 reprinting of *Political Systems of Highland Burma*, Edmund Leach commented that his book (originally published in 1954) had marked the "beginning of a trend" against what he called "a crudely oversimplified set of equilibrium assumptions derived from the use of organic analogies for the structure of social systems (1964:ix)." Referring to the years before the original publication of this book, he added the following (1964:x):

When I wrote this book the general climate of anthropological thinking in England was that established by Radcliffe-Brown. Social systems were spoken of as if they were naturally existing real entities and the equilibrium inherent in such systems was intrinsic, a fact of nature.

Leach also scolded his colleagues, particularly Gluckman, for "mysticism" and "double-talk" in their continuing adherence to organic equilibrium concepts (1961). Instead of social systems in balance, with people governed by rules, Leach saw individuals making strategic choices among alternative rules in a quest for prestige or power. Leach recommended (1961:298) that rules, or "custom," as he preferred, should be seen "in terms of the private self-interest of the average man in that particular cultural situation."

Whether Leach initiated this way of thinking about rules in British social anthropology is not important for our purposes. He was very influential, but by his own admission he was not alone (Leach 1982). Victor Turner's contrast between the rule-governed nature of "structure" and the freedom of what he called "communitas" was surely influential, and many scholars in various countries contributed to the growing rejection of the earlier, "oversocialized" and "overintegrated" perspective. They were influenced by many social and intellectual currents, and while it is not necessary here to identify all of these influences, it is obvious that theories of conflict (Collins 1975), transaction (Barth 1966), and exchange (Kapferer 1976) played a role, as did developments in the study of communication, small groups, labeling, decision making, natural language, law, cognition, government, and many other subjects.[4]

Developments in the field of sociology were especially important. Beginning, it could be argued, with Niccolò Machiavelli's insight that all human life has the quality of a game in which how a person manages appearances in a particular situation is all-important, various philosophers, including Alfred Schutz and Ludwig Wittgenstein, examined rules from new perspectives in which context became central. In addition, sociologists from George Simmel to Erving Goffman developed their views of man as an actor, skillfully taking account of the social context in order to present himself to others in ways calculated to achieve personal advantage. Goffman's writings were especially influential. Normative theory was fundamentally moral, based on the belief that people in a society share common values. Goffman documented the constraints that rules impose on the strategic moves available to actors; he even noted that some rules were so "incorporated" into the person that they could not be broken, not even for strategic advantage (Goffman 1969). But he emphasized the manipulation of rules in an idiom of "moves," "ploys," "gambits," and "openings," using a game as his metaphor. As Alvin Gouldner put it (1970:383), for Goffman it was not "morality as a deeply internalized feeling of duty or obligation that holds things together"; rather, life was sustained by conventions that were no more serious than the rules of a game. In the growing professional and popular enthusiasm for this strategic interaction perspective (or "dramaturgical" model, as it came to be known), the fact that the strategic moves actors made were possible only because of the rules that ordered social relationships was often overlooked. Instead, rules were reduced to the status of tokens in the game of life.

From the slave of custom in the normative model, man came full circle to become the strategic master of rules—artful, dissembling, posing, deceiving, and calculating for his own advantage. Rules became resources, not constraints. Although later work in sociology, including that of Garfinkel, Cicourel, and others, tempered the dramaturgical solipsism of the strategic perspective somewhat, the sense remained that the essence of human life did not lie in following rules and in being rewarded by one's virtue but in making the best use of rules for one's own self-interest, depending on the situation.[5]

This emphasis on the strategic use of rules also influenced anthropologists interested in the most formal of rules, laws. No longer was it acceptable to study laws as abstract principles. Laws, like other rules, now came to be studied more and more as features of larger complexes of rules and motivational processes in which context was centrally important and strategic negotiation was highlighted (Comaroff and Roberts 1981; Gulliver 1979; Nader and Todd 1978). The study of disputes, or "trouble-cases," grew, and a well-established literature developed concerning the ways in which individuals *use* rules, including laws, to claim exemption from responsibility for what others might see as rule infractions. The claims and counterclaims in reference to rules were described as ubiquitous features of the disputes of everyday life (Scott and Lyman 1968) and were also found in moots, courts, and other means of adjudicating serious disputes. Among the Arusha of East Africa, for example, litigants regularly insisted that their conduct was justified by a rule; judges understood these claims as attempts to achieve advantage and made decisions accordingly (Gulliver 1963).

This revisionist shift from normative theory to strategic interaction can claim support in a growing body of empirical evidence from societies throughout the world. It is not only in the postindustrial West that Goffman-esque individuals manipulate flexible rules for their strategic purposes; they are reported to do so in societies of all sizes and degrees of social and technological complexity, as we shall see in subsequent chapters.[6]

In her important book *Law as Process*, anthropologist S. F. Moore reviewed many of these developments of roughly the past two decades, offering her own conclusion that "The making of rules and social and symbolic order is a human industry matched only by the manipulation, circumvention, remaking, replacing and unmaking of rules and symbols in which people seem almost equally engaged" (1978:1). Moore emphasized the "incomplete" or "unfinished" character of social order, writing that there appeared to be a "continuous struggle" between the pressures that work for order and regularity and those that work against it. "The strategies of individuals are seldom (if ever) consistently committed to reliance on rules and other regularities" (Moore 1978:39). Stressing the complexity of social living with its varieties of people, situations, and purposes, Moore added that "Established rules, customs, and symbolic frameworks exist, but they operate in the presence of areas of indeterminacy, or ambiguity, or uncertainty and manipulability. Order never fully takes over, nor could it" (1978:39).

Many came to share Moore's views—so many, in fact, that her ideas have become conventional, replacing the earlier ones that underlay normative theory. In most social theory today, rules are seen as ambiguous, flexible, contradictory, and inconsistent; they are said seldom to govern the actions of people, much less to mold these people by being internalized by them. Instead, they serve as resources for human strategies, strategies that vary from person to person and from situation to situation. In such a world, as Moore wrote, order is never complete and never can be. And in such a world, as Bohannan wrote earlier, exceptions to rules, and even to laws, are an ever-present part of social reality.

But while most rules are flexible—or are assumed to be so by most theories—some rules are not at all flexible or manipulable. For example, among the Tarahumara Indians of Northern Mexico, strategic bending of rules was commonplace in ordinary life; if a dispute reached court, however, rules were interpreted strictly and were enforced without exceptions (Fried 1953). Similarly, Harold Scheffler noted in his study of the Choiseulese of the Solomon Islands that many of their rules served as "strategic rhetorical resources" but others firmly guided behavior (1965). Walter Goldschmidt, writing of the Sebei of Uganda, emphasized the same point. For the Sebei, many rules—even seemingly important ones relating to incest and marriage—were flexible and negotiable (1969:180–181). Individuals among the Sebei redefined many rules, argued over them, and even made up new ones, all in the spirit of manipulating a situation for personal advantage. Yet not all Sebei rules were nonspecific and flexible (Goldschmidt 1969:181):

> In the face of such flexibility and uncertainty, there were other instances in which the rules were expressed with such rigidity as to make one start: the possessions of the deceased could not possibly be anointed with moykutwet root—it must be ram's fat; a funeral ram that had no horns could not be slaughtered. On such small matters—and, I daresay, on great ones too—there was no room for maneuver. I do not think that

the events gave us a basis for formulating any generalizations as to when to expect flexibility and when rigidity; both circumstances existed side by side.

That flexible rules and inflexible ones exist side by side is an ethnographic reality, one that will be illustrated in various societies in succeeding chapters. Yet in the strategic interaction perspective, the existence of rigid rules that must be followed without exceptions, without strategic maneuverability, has been typically ignored or denied. We have already heard from Murphy, Douglas, and others about the inevitable flexibility of rules, a view that Goffman strongly endorsed in perhaps his most mature book, *Frame Analysis* (1974). While he did give passing mention to rigid moral rules in his earlier work (mentioned earlier), in this later work (1974:269) Goffman insisted that rules were never so rigid that they constrained behavior completely (Fisher and Strauss 1978:480). Yet, rules that must be followed without exceptions do exist in many societies. Consider the following example from the Gusii people of Western Kenya as described by anthropologist Robert LeVine, whose field research among these people has spanned three decades (1982:32):[7]

> Thus, when a Gusii adult dies houseless, a ritual hut must be constructed on the spot where the house was or would have been, the corpse placed in it before burial, and rituals of fire and sacrifice performed to consecrate the hut as a symbolic house. This rule is invariant in its application and cannot be abrogated even when, as in the case described, the deceased is considered a witch and has not been the object of her children's affection. In that case, a good deal of money and effort were expended to give her a proper burial.

Just as people in all societies allow exceptions to many rules, in most—perhaps all—societies, people follow other rules strictly, allowing no exceptions. For example, the Siriono should not, and did not, eat raw meat, even when they faced starvation (Holmberg 1969:73). Iglulik Eskimo women with infant children were never allowed to share their cooking utensils with other women (Rasmussen 1929:15). Once a Taureg man from a noble tribe put on the veil that covered his face, he never removed it, not even in intimate moments with his wife or even, apparently, when he was alone (Fuchs 1955; Murphy 1963). This literature also reports that in some societies, such as the Tewa Pueblos, the fit between most rules and actual conduct was very close (Ortiz 1972:5), and that in others, such as the modern Hopi Indians,

members of the society continue to live by some rigidly inflexible rules
(Hall 1977:137).

None of this should be eye-opening for anthropologists, but with
the decline of normative theory, reports such as these are frequently
dismissed as statements of "ideal" rules that would not be borne out
by real behavior if the matter were investigated. Often the reports
are simply ignored. As a result, strict rules receive little attention in
modern social theory; it is far more likely that the flexibility and
intracultural diversity of rules will be emphasized.[8] Intracultural diversity and flexibility are universal realities, but so are strict rules,
which occur occasionally in all societies and very often in some. The
recognition that such rules are universal is essential if contemporary
social theory is to avoid going any further in the direction of reducing
rules to playthings, to rhetorical resources that are ambiguous at best
and impuissant in all cases. An important corrective to the strategic
interaction perspective is the recognition that rules sometimes have
great power to constrain behavior and sometimes are enforced without exceptions.

EXCEPTIONS TO RULES AND RULES
WITHOUT EXCEPTIONS

About 2,500 years ago in the villages and towns of feudal China,
harmony was the prevailing ethos. People sought to avoid social conflict because they believed that such conflict would endanger the
precarious balance among people, their environment, and the cosmos.
To prevent conflict and thus its potentially disastrous consequences,
the Chinese relied on the suasive power of their moral rules; they
attempted to prevent wrongdoing not so much by prescribing punishment for offenders as by guiding people toward conformity with what
was right. Many of the world's smaller societies still function like this,
but China changed. As time passed, a minority of the people who
held different moral beliefs seized power, established their authority
by force, and rapidly consolidated China into a great empire. The
centralized legal bureaucracy of this empire was based not on moral
principles calling for harmony but on clearly specified laws. The
penalties for violating these laws were severe, and there were no
exceptions for any reason. This period of stringent law and absolute
liability was, however, short-lived. It was replaced by a new government that restored the original emphasis on harmonious moral principles but combined these moral rules with laws which continued to

specify an exact penalty for each crime. These laws stipulated precisely a host of exceptions to rules based on people's social rank, relationships, and motivation as well as the circumstances surrounding the crime. As fabulous as this history may seem, it is not a fable or "just so" story about rules and exceptions. This system of law in imperial China was fabulous indeed but real nonetheless, and it endured for more than 2,000 years.

The historical record for this period is incomplete (Israeli scholar Ben-Ami Scharfstein [1974:79] complained that it sometimes resembled "a string of amputated citations joined together by clichés"), but it is clear enough to demonstrate that in pre-imperial China, law in the various warring feudal states of that period was based on Confucian moral principles, *li*. The li prescribed proper conduct based on one's age, sex, and rank within one's family and in society at large. They were founded on the idea that human nature was good, or that at least people could be guided toward goodness by good leaders and good government. The Confucian principles called for the li to be flexible for reasons summarized by Bodde and Morris (1967:21):

> A government based on *li* functions harmoniously because the *li*, being unwritten, can be flexibly interpreted to meet the exigencies of any particular situation. A government based on law creates contention because its people, knowing in advance what the written law is, can find means to circumvent it, and will rest their sophistical arguments on the letter rather than the spirit of the law.

Like natural law in European thought, the li reflected a moral consensus of Confucian beliefs (Needham 1951). How well these principles served as social control mechanisms cannot easily be inferred, but they must have been sorely tested, because forces for change were powerful in preimperial China. Economic and social change were accelerating, the slave-owning aristocracy had lost most of its power to newly rich commoner landowners, and war, intrigue, and rebellion were everywhere as feudal states jockeyed for advantage. Dozens of philosophical schools also vied for supremacy, with their scholarly disciples and political adherents traveling widely to spread their views (Bodde 1938). One of these schools, known as the legalists, rose to challenge Confucian ideals at about the same time that efficient and ruthless armies from the state of Ch'in in the far west of China defeated their opponents in bloody battles. Their leader, Ch'in Shih-huang, consolidated his power over all China and became its emperor. Ch'in Shih-huang and his advisors accepted the legalists' ideas and carried out a massive program of social change. As a result, the aristocracy was further stripped of its power (each noble had previously been a law unto himself), and an empire-wide bureaucracy was put in place by 221 B.C. In the process, they burned many Confucian books and also buried alive 460 Confucian scholars who opposed their rule (Li 1975).

The Ch'in legalists rejected the Confucian li with its many exceptions, including privileges for the nobles, in favor of a universal, impartial system of law (*fa*). In addition to creating universal laws, the legalists created the governmental, judicial, and penal apparatus to enforce them. Their reasoning, as abstracted by Bodde and Morris (1967:23–24), was a marked contrast to what had existed since at least the Chou period (1127 B.C.). First, they believed that no government based on li could be stable, because the li were unwritten, particular to every situation, and susceptible to arbitrary interpretation in granting exceptions. The legalists believed instead that laws must be impartial, with penalties applied irrespective of rank, privilege, or relationship. Because the legalists believed that very few people were naturally altruistic, they feared that the majority acted out of self-interest and must therefore be constrained by laws backed by severe punishments. Responsibility for obeying these laws should, they felt, be collective. This was done by dividing the population into units of five or ten families and by making every member of that unit "equally responsible for the wrongdoing of every other individual, and equally subject to punishment if he fails to inform the authorities of such wrongdoing" (Bodde and Morris 1967:24). Finally, the legalists believed that if laws were made severe enough, their mere existence would soon deter wrongdoing, allowing a reduction in governmental control and leaving society free of conflict.

How thoroughly the legalist program was put into effect is not known, but it is known that very stringent, even horrendous, punishments were inflicted for nonconformity with the new laws; it is known, for example, that the law specifying that anyone who spilled ashes in the street would have his hand cut off was enforced (Creel 1953). Collective liability was also enforced; according to the law, all relatives to the third degree had to be executed along with someone found guilty of many capital crimes (Bodde 1938:167). Many prominent citizens and their relatives were executed as a result of this law.

It is not clear to what extent the legalists' imposition of strict and collective liability led to the rapid fall of the Ch'in dynasty. Chinese historiography of this and other periods has been subjected to many reinterpretations—some of them frankly political—but it is apparent that one motive of the legalists was the protection of their new regime; justice for the many millions of people they had so recently conquered appears to have been a secondary consideration at best. Many of the conquered nobles were organizing insurrections to restore their power, and there is evidence that the common people were outraged by the severity of Ch'in punishments and also by excessive taxation and demands for corvée labor. The inflexibility of the law was also a problem, so much so that some legalist followers were led to defect, as did two officials who were leading corvée laborers to a work project and whose progress was slowed by heavy rains. According to the law, the penalty for their tardiness, which they saw would be unavoidable, was decapitation; no excuses would be possible. Instead of offering their heads to this inflexible and, in their minds, unjust law, these officials joined in a revolt against the empire. The revolt succeeded.

The Ch'in dynasty lasted for only fifteen years, and the succeeding Han dynasty leaders "Confucianized" the law, humanizing it greatly. Nevertheless, collective responsibility remained in force, as did the legalist formula that for every offense, civil or criminal, there must be a stipulated punishment. However, the legalist idea that the law would be blind to relationships, rank, or circumstance was abandoned. The imperial codes of law that resulted from Confucianization—and that endured for 2,000 years—attempted to anticipate every imaginable offense and to specify different punishments depending on the situation, the motivation of the offender, and, especially, the status of the offender and of the victim.

Who broke the law was all-important. For example, the codes allowed a parent to beat a son or a husband to beat a wife almost with impunity but specified severe punishment (e.g., decapitation or 100 blows with a heavy bamboo rod, respectively) if a son were to strike his father or a wife to strike her husband (Bodde and Morris 1967: 37). Age and degree of consanguinity also mattered. For example, an older brother could beat a younger one with no penalty at all, but if a younger brother beat an older one, the penalty was two and a half years of penal servitude plus ninety blows with a heavy bamboo rod, whether or not the blows had produced no injury (Bodde and Morris 1967:38). Because government officials were held to a code of *noblesse oblige* with respect to the law as well as to everyday life, sometimes the harsher penalities were applied to persons of higher rank. The situation and the offender's intent were usually taken into account, but sometimes (as in the case of a son's actions that had led to his father's injury or death) intent was considered irrelevant.

The code provided for appeals to higher authority, which included the highest judicial body, the Board of Punishment (*Hsing pu*), and the emperor. At every level of judicial review, the search was for the correct punishment as specified by the statutes, a punishment that had to fit all the circumstances in order to restore the balance of the universe. Magistrates and the Board of Punishment sometimes took special mitigating circumstances into account in imposing sentences, and emperors commonly granted amnesty (McKnight 1981); in principle, however (and for the most part, in fact), a magistrate's job was to find the correct statute and impose the sentence set by it. Despite a corpus of thousands of statutes covering every imaginable crime, gaps did exist, and magistrates sometimes resorted to analogies or to creative ad hoc solutions; this practice caused the Board of Punishments and the emperor to insist that all sentences be imposed *exactly* as specified by the laws and to warn that any magistrate failing to do so would be punished by thirty blows (Bodde and Morris 1967:516). By and large, over a period of twenty centuries, those who decided cases were literal in their application of the law.

What are we to learn from the Chinese attempt to write clear prohibitions, with equally clear penalties, for every conceivable variant of wrongdoing? First, it cannot be dismissed as merely a fool's errand, doomed to failure by the complexities of status, motivation, and situation, for this system of law lasted longer than any other yet developed on earth. However, we also cannot conclude that this system was an unqualified success in maintaining social order simply because it endured. The family, clan, guild, and community elders combined to create a powerful alternative system of social control that prevented much wrongdoing and that worked outside the penal system. Moreover, much of the power of the penal system to correct or deter wrongdoing lay in the severity of its *non*statutory penalties. Most people so feared the long and indefinite periods of incarceration and the brutal jailers they knew they would face while awaiting trial or appeal, as well as the threat of similar punishment for their family and kin, that they were careful to avoid any involvement with the Chinese imperial penal system.

How successful the Chinese approach to social order through the promulgation of a law for literally every occasion was, remains a vexed question that will probably always baffle historians (see Hulsewé 1955; Granet 1934). What is most relevant here is the dilemma that the system attempted to resolve. By recognizing a large but finite number of exceptions, Chinese law attempted a compromise between permitting personal and circumstantial mitigation for wrongdoing and imposing strict liability. It was an attempt to codify complexity—strictly. On a grand scale, over millennia, the Chinese system of law epitomized the fundamental opposition between strict rules as control mechanisms and the complexities of human living that seem to demand exceptions to those rules.

Thus, we have a historical drama, acted out over a span of centuries, about rules, exceptions to rules, and social order: Following a period during which rules were flexible and negotiable, a new government came into power which imposed inflexible rules that allowed no exceptions. This system of government was replaced by one that attempted a compromise, writing every conceivable legitimate exception involving age, gender, relationship, state of mind, and social circumstance into precisely stated laws that were strictly enforced.

CONCLUSION

In the development of sociological and anthropological theory, the earlier view of normative theory has been replaced by a perspective that emphasizes strategic interaction in which rules are used, not followed, and in which exceptions to rules are natural, even inevitable. As this perspective is commonly employed in anthropology and sociology today, the existence of rules without exceptions is often denied; if these inflexible rules are acknowledged at all, they are not accorded a prominent role in human affairs. A good summary of current thinking, one that is more sophisticated than most, is again provided by Moore (1978), who begins with the assumption that social reality is "fluid and indeterminate"; processes of "regularization" transform some of this fluidity into more fixed forms (rules, categories, customs, symbols, rituals, organizations, and the like), but countervailing "processes of situational adjustment" exploit available indeterminacy, maintaining "an element of plasticity in social arrangements" (1978: 50). Moore adds that people may resort to both processes—regularization and situational adjustment—in the very same situation, but she makes the importance of situational adjustment quite clear (1978: 4): "Yet, despite all the attempts to crystallize the rules, there invariably remains a certain range of maneuver, of openness, of choice, of interpretation, of alternation, of tampering, of reversing, of transforming."

Moore's model of social life as consisting of processes of rule making and rule unmaking taking place in a world of fluidity and indeterminacy accurately encapsulates what I believe are the essential presuppositions of most social theorists today. Yet, as clear and elegant as

Moore's description of this model is, I believe that it overstates the invariability of maneuver, openness, and the like. Some rules have exceptions galore, but other rules are fully "regularized—so much so, in fact, that they allow no exceptions.

If we are to take seriously the axiom that societies must regulate the most essential aspects of their members' conduct if they are to survive and that one of the ways of achieving that regulation is by creating various kinds of rules to guide or coerce proper conduct, then the apparent fact that seemingly important rules are so often conflicting, competing, ambiguous, and otherwise imperfect as regulatory mechanisms calls for an explanation. If, moreover, societies also create rules for breaking rules, as Bohannan put it, this state of affairs becomes still more paradoxical.

How paradoxical one finds these matters to be, or whether one sees a paradox at all, depends on one's theoretical perspective and reading of the evidence. Normative theorists, with their emphasis on rules as social control mechanisms, would presumably feel compelled to explain rules for breaking rules. In a fully integrated normative system, a true community of interest, such exceptions would seem to have no vital role; instead, they would more easily be accounted for as the product of social incompletion, change, diversity, or disorganization. Strategic interaction theorists, conversely, should have little concern about exceptions—the very stuff of strategic calculation—but they might well be perplexed by rules so strict that no exceptions are permitted. As we have seen, some scholars disavow any paradox by concluding that the simultaneous presence of strict rules and rules for breaking rules is the natural way of things in all societies, but they have not told us why.

I believe that rules for controlling human conduct and rules for breaking these rules do indeed coexist, but that this coexistence may constitute a true paradox: the presence in human affairs of phenomena that may be more contradictory than complementary.

CHAPTER 2

Rules, Responsibility, and Exceptions

The assertions cited in chapter 1 about the essential functions of rules or the need for exceptions to rules were written as though everyone knows what a rule is and, moreover, as though a rule were something singular. Most social scientists agree that rules regulate and control human behavior, but beyond that there is little agreement about the definition of the concept; it is obvious that "rule" (or "norm," as many prefer) is used to refer to quite different kinds of regularities, as Pierre Bourdieu (1977) noted in his criticism of normative theory. In this chapter, I shall discuss the concept of *rule* and the idea of responsibility for rule following. Types of exceptions to rules will be specified and will be related to different types of rules.

Since so many social scientists accord rules the central role in the achievement and maintenance of social order, it is perplexing that there is so little agreement about the nature of the concept. The historical development of the rule concept is both complex and muddled. One set of developments came from jurisprudence, including the studies of natural law; another set came from philosophers, including Aristotle, Kant, and Hume. Hobbes and Spencer made much of the governing power of rules in human affairs, as did the Prague School of Linguistics. In sociology, Durkheim and Weber emphasized the constraining power of rules, and later, the work of Chomsky, Wittgenstein, Lévi-Strauss, and others gave the rule concept great influence. As Peter Collett (1977) observed in his review of the concept, all of the social sciences now make rules part of their subject matter, although there is little agreement among disciplines concerning just what is meant by the term. *Rule* is often used in contemporary social theory as a gloss for a variety of related but by no means identical phenomena, including shared expectations, understandings, agreements, or regulations about how people should behave. Some related concepts include *norm, value, standard, blueprint, guide, regulation, law, custom,* and *code* (Cicourel 1972; Cancian 1975). A good discussion of these and related concepts has been provided by Susan Shimanoff (1980).

When I use the term *rule,* I refer to a shared understanding of how people ought to behave and of what should be done if someone behaves in a way that conflicts with that understanding. Rules, then, prescribe or proscribe behavior, and I reserve the use of the term for beliefs that have this regulatory sense. There are many other beliefs that people share that are simply existential—that the sun rises every day, that the gods are irascible, that a certain plant is poisonous, that $E = MC^2$. These beliefs (or scientific laws, if one prefers) are not rules in a regulatory sense, although they can become regulatory if people agree about what should or should not be done with regard to the sun, gods, plants, or energy. Used in this generic sense, all rules prescribe or proscribe human behavior, but they differ in many ways.

Philosopher Max Black (1962) and sociologists Richard T. Morris (1956) and Jack Gibbs (1965;1981), along with many others, have drawn our attention to some of the most relevant ways in which rules may differ. For example, rules may differ in the extent to which they are known, recognized, accepted as just or proper, and uniformly applied to members of the society. Rules may also vary in the severity of the sanctions that may be incurred by their violations as well as in their consistency of enforcement. They may vary in the degree to which they are internalized, in the mode of their transmission, and in the amount and kind of conformity they receive. It should also be reemphasized that some rules are relatively explicit while others are implicit, and some are clear while others are ambiguous. Some rules contradict others, while others stand for the most part unchallenged. Rules also differ in the extent to which they vary depending on the social context.

Many of the complexities of rules, from those governing communication to those that direct the inheritance of property, are not necessary for our purposes here, and thorough discussions are readily available (Collett 1977; Shimanoff 1980), but a few distinctions should be introduced. The first is between explicit rules (those that are articulated or articulable) and implicit rules (those that can only be inferred from behavioral regularities or from the reactions that occur after such rules have been broken). The second distinction is between rules that are intended to be universal in their application and those that are specific to particular situations.

Many rules, such as those of grammar, speaking distance, posture, and eye contact, are implicit. People ordinarily do not articulate such rules and, in many instances, cannot do so, yet implicit rules can be of fundamental importance. Ethnomethodologist Harold Garfinkel (1963) has shown that when such rules are broken, social interaction may break down, resulting in confusion or conflict. Modifying Kant's term Garfinkel calls implicit rules "constitutive," reflecting their basic importance for the maintenance of orderly social interaction. Emanuel Schegloff (1968) has nicely illustrated the importance of implicit rules in his analysis of telephone conversations; rules about who speaks first and how turns are to be taken are implicit, but they are crucial if a telephone conversation is to be conducted without confusion. Not all implicit rules are of fundamental social importance, of course, but some are vital to social order.

Explicit rules are clearly articulated, or at least they can be when the occasion calls for it; the penalty for violating such rules is often clearly articulated as well. In literate societies, we post signs prohibiting one behavior or another and also specifying the penalty; nonliterate societies can be every bit as clear about some rules. Every member of a society knows, for example, that eating a particular food is forbidden and that anyone who breaks this rule will fall ill and probably die. Whether one calls such rules taboos, regulations, injunctions, or laws, they are important because they explicitly prescribe or proscribe behavior. Some explicit rules may only set limits by indicating what is customary, traditional, or preferred, but others specify moral, supernatural, or legal imperatives. For instance, the Gusii funeral custom described by LeVine was an imperative.

There is a tendency for some Western scholars to assume that, like our morals or laws, rules vitally important for social living will be articulated. In many societies this is not the case. Implicit rules may be as imperative as explicit ones, and they may be every bit as vital to the establishment and maintenance of social order. For example, although there are no signs posted in most Catholic churches prohibiting roller skating or playing rock music on transistor radios during Mass, these behaviors would be seen as wrong (and, in fact, as downright outrageous and sacrilegious) by those attending the services. However, I once saw a badly weathered sign posted inconspicuously outside a mosque in a Cairo neighborhood far from the tourist trails. Written in French, it asked visitors to the mosque to remove their shoes before entering. A sign like this could only have been intended for strangers. Most Kyrenians do not read French, and Muslims in Cairo do not need signs to remind them to remove their footwear before entering a mosque any more than Italian women need to be reminded to cover their heads before entering a Catholic church. Small children need to be taught rules like these, often repeatedly and explicitly, but for adults they are implicit—at least until they are broken.

As we shall see, important rules of deference and demeanor are often implicit, as are some of the most important moral principles (for example, those that prevent or resolve conflict). Very general rules, or "meta"-rules (such as those that prescribe fairness, reciprocity, or reasonableness as right and their opposites as wrong) may also remain implicit. Such principles may underlie and prescribe other more explicit rules. In this sense, implicit rules, like rules of grammar, may be generative.

Like the distinction between implicit and explicit rules, the distinction between situationally specific rules and culturally universal ones meant to apply in all circumstances is also important. Many rules apply only in certain situations; more specifically, when a question or accusation about following or breaking a rule arises, the outcome is usually dependent on the individuals and circumstances involved. Which rule, if any, should apply *depends*. In our society, an adult is ordinarily never permitted to appear nude in a public place. But in some circumstances, such as a nude beach or a life-drawing class, nudity may be acceptable; in still other circumstances, such as bathing or lovemaking, nudity may be required. It is undeniable that context, or situation, can be all-important and that context is affected by the reputation—that is, the character—of the people involved. As Richard Brandt (1954) said of the Hopi, what a person ought to *be* is sometimes more important than what a person ought to *do*. As we will see later on, a person who is granted respect or honor can often break rules that less respected people must follow.[1]

Some rules do not depend on the situation but are expected to apply to everyone and in all situations. Even in our culturally heterogeneous society, there are universally enforceable rules. For example, the rule prohibiting mothers and sons from having sexual relations applies in all situations; although such behavior may occur, there is no rule that justifies or excuses its occurrence. A few men in our society may have sexual intercourse with very small children, but everyone in our society—even these men—would agree that this behavior is so terribly wrong that it can never be excused. In some small, more homogeneous societies, there are many rules that apply to everyone.

A rule that is intended to apply universally can be presumed to have great social, and often moral, significance. However, it is likely, and even probable, that no rule used by humans in their ordinary life activities is so explicitly formulated that it can apply unambiguously to *all* possible contingencies. Instead, rules tend to be vague around the edges. Garfinkel (1963:199) has insisted that all rules have an "et cetera" property—that is, even the most specific rules in our society, such as those for games or for legal contracts, do not cover all the problematic possibilities that could conceivably arise. All such codified rules have unstated terms, open-ended features, and unwritten codicils that form Garfinkel's "et cetera"; with ordinary social rules, this phenomenon is even more striking. Given this open-endedness, people may sometimes legitimately dispute what is meant by a rule or which rule applies when an unforeseen contingency arises. In our society, "et cetera" problems must sometimes be resolved by the Supreme Court; societies that lack courts or other adjudicative procedures must cope with such problems as a recurring feature of everyday living.

As Sir Henry Maine noted in *Ancient Law*, legalists deal with unforeseen circumstances by inventing fictions or analogies that allow problems not anticipated by the law to be resolved by rulings based on similar laws or principles. People in everyday life often deal with unforeseen contingencies by using social fictions that allow rules to be stretched, modified, or reinterpreted to fit particular needs. A person may be given a different status or a temporary identity, or the situation itself may be redefined. However, sometimes people simply act *as though* the rule covers any and all contingencies, instead of acknowledging that a rule does not cover a particular contingency, they insist that the rule *does* fit and demand that it be followed without exceptions and that any failure to do so be punished.[2] Sometimes contingencies do not matter, and an unclear rule can be treated as though it were categorical and enforced with the utmost severity; there is no room for maneuver and no mechanism for an appeal.

RESPONSIBILITY: STRICT OR NEGOTIABLE?

As children learn the rules of their society, they also learn what will happen if they break those rules. They learn when and to what extent they will be punished. They learn, then, to become responsible for their actions. The ideal for any society would be to so imbue its children with a sense of the moral imperativeness of following adult's rules that each generation would *want* to follow these rules, would punish themselves if for any reason they failed to do so, and would teach their own children to do the same. In fact, some societies have been reasonably successful in achieving this goal; the Mixtec Indians of Oaxaca are an example (Romney and Romney 1963) of people who have stressed the internal incorporation of rules and of penalties for breaking them.

Ethnographic literature reports that many societies have developed rules so powerful in their constraints that not only the men or women who violate them but also those who are the victims of such violations would rather kill themselves than live with their shame and humiliation. Samurai of the Tokugawa period in Japan were expected to prize their honor more than life; when honor was lost, they committed ritual suicide (*seppuku*) with such equanimity that Western eyewitnesses reported instances in which Samurai dissembowled themselves without flinching (Smith 1980). Loss of honor could lead to suicide in very small societies as well. Explorer David Thompson, who traveled among the Plains Indians from 1784 to 1812, witnessed the suicide of a Piegan woman whose husband, irritated by something, struck her "gently" with his riding quirt; this public rebuke was such an unlivable disgrace to this proud woman that, to Thompson's surprise and horror, she immediately stabbed herself to death (1916:356).

As noted, suicide can also result from the shame of one's own rule violation, as was the case with an Eskimo man who hanged himself after he was detected in an act of anal intercourse with his adopted son (Rasmussen 1931:197). And it is well-known that during times of starvation, aging Eskimo, as called for by an Eskimo moral rule, often killed themselves (or asked their relatives to help them do so) rather than prove a burden to others.[3]

Yet even though the internalization of rules by people who shared a community of interests was central to their theory (Parsons used the Freudian term *introjection*), even the most extreme advocates of the normative or "over-socialized" theory never asserted that societies could maintain social order solely by relying on the internalization of rules so that people would want to do, and actually *would* do, what they ought to do.[4] No society—at least, no society that survived long enough to become part of the historical or ethnographic record—has been able to rely solely on the internalization of rules for the maintenance of order. As powerful as feelings of virtue and guilt can be, they are never powerful enough to ensure rule compliance by everyone; and as potent as unconscious, implicit rules are, they never cover everything that needs regulation. Of necessity, then, all societies have also employed a repertoire of "external" means to ensure compliance with their rules—supernatural sanctions by spirits or gods, ridicule and gossip, sorcery and witchcraft, ostracism and exile, and the sanctioned use of force, among others. Hobbes wrote that the "source of conscience was the fear of death," and all societies use fear of human or supernatural sanctions to reinforce their rules.

Not all rule violations are seen as being equally serious, of course; some are trivial, funny, absurd, or merely annoying. The various external sanctions are employed, one must presume, because some of the rule violations that do occur are seen as being particularly objectionable, dangerous, or frightening. The control of some kinds of violence is important everywhere; so are at least some rules about incest and marriage. In most societies, rules about food sharing and other subsistence activities are also very important. In our society, we worry a great deal about people driving on the appropriate side of the road, and we have explicit rules concerning air traffic safety, the training of surgeons, and the safekeeping of nuclear missiles by the military. We take rules about these matters very seriously, and we would prefer to think that where these essential rules are concerned there will be no need for exceptions.

As we saw in chapter 1, however, it is sometimes anything but self-evident why some rules have exceptions while others do not. In some societies, rules about a ritual procedure, a food avoidance, or an act of deference may admit no exceptions, while a rule governing economic cooperation or incest may be a good deal more flexible. Why this may be so will be addressed in the final three chapters. What I want to emphasize here is that despite the apparent fact that strategic manipulation of rules takes place in all societies, not all rules are manipulable. People in all sorts of societies from our own to the smallest and simplest on record can and do hold one another very strictly responsible for following *some* rules. Philosopher Max Black (1962:129) has asked us to imagine the following:

> I imagine some tribe in which everyday conduct is found to be controlled by a strict penal code. The rules of conduct are stated in traditional formulas known verbatim by every member of the community. (We can imagine that the day begins with a formal recitation of the code on the part of each citizen.) Violations are invariably punished by flogging, and such punishment follows immediately a violation is detected, according to a graded schedule incorporated into the ritual statement of the laws. (The tribesmen chant 'I must not lay hands upon my brother's wife, on pain of fifty lashes' and so on.)

If there were such a society, and there is none quite like it (although some military organizations and the Chinese legalists have come close), it would epitomize strict liability—that is, liability with no exceptions.

Strict liability has a long, although poorly documented, history.[5] An ancient example may have been provided by the code of King Hammurabi of Babylon who, in ideal terms, at least (Yaron 1969), established a compilation of specific penalties for all manner of offenses, from failing to pay taxes to assisting runaway slaves (Burney 1977). Some versions of modern Islamic law incorporate strict liability, much like *lex talionis,* into their criminal law. Until recently, many Western students of law, including Henry Maine and Roscoe Pound, believed that non-Western societies regularly employed the principle of absolute liability, allowing no exceptions from the stipulated penalties for rule violations (Hart 1968; Moore 1978). Indeed, as recently as 1965, with his book *The Ideas in Barotse Jurisprudence,* Max Gluckman continued to accept the belief that strict liability was typical in African laws pertaining to personal injury, even though intention—presumed to be the motives a "reasonable man" would possess—was implicitly taken into account by the Barotse (Gluckman 1965:213).

Strict liability is also well-known in Western societies. Many so-called regulatory offenses, including such violations as misbranding whiskey, adulterating milk, or failing to follow certain motor vehicle or safety regulations, are punished without possibility of mitigation, as are some "status" offenses in which some characteristic of a person—such as age, sex, or marital status—is sufficient to bring about the prescribed penalty, again without the possibility of a mitigating defense. Statutory rape is one example of the latter; bigamy is another. As Colin Howard (1963:7) noted in his history of strict liability, of the 1,113 statutes creating criminal offenses in the state of Wisconsin in 1953, 660 used language that allowed the courts to impose strict liability. And some institutions, such as the U.S. Military Academy at West Point, have adopted strict liability wholeheartedly; the honor code at West Point, for example, not only punishes infractions of the code without exceptions but even punishes any known *intent* to break it (Galloway and Johnson 1973). Some non-Western societies in which witchcraft is particularly feared also punish evil intent alone.

Strict liability can be even more stringent if it applies to a collectivity of people rather than only to an individual. In the West, collective liability may apply to a family that is required to make compensation for some damage caused by their child; to all residents of a village, who must face a military firing squad because someone among them is thought to be guilty of killing an invading soldier; or to schoolboys who lose their privileges for a weekend because one of them has broken a rule. In each of these cases, the principle is the same, and it can be effective—all are responsible for the wrongdoing of one. As in the preceding examples, this principle has in fact been imposed on entire institutions: at the Japanese Naval Academy, Eta Jima, all plebes were lined up and struck in the face whenever any of them erred (Hara 1961); and in schools in the Soviet Union, children were collectively responsible for one another's misdeeds (Bronfenbrenner 1970).

The principle of rigid governance by rules is not confined to total institutions or to exceptional circumstances. As we saw earlier for China and as we shall also see in later chapters, it is known that there are entire societies both small and large in which, for example, everyone may suffer supernatural punishment for the taboo violation or sacrilege of one person; a close family member may be required to kill another who has sinned or brought dishonor to the family; an entire clan may be compelled to pay blood money because a clansman has killed someone; or many kinsmen must suffer physical punishment or even execution for the wrongdoing of a relative.[6]

But in the recent history of Western criminal law, more so than in that of its civil counterpart, exceptions to rules have played an increasingly important role. *Mens rea*, the intent or state of mind of the offender, is typically considered by Western legal systems in determining liability. When a specific state of mind is relevant in the determination of liability for a criminal offense, various legal jurisdictions often recognize that some people may be unable to form that state of mind and refer in such cases to "diminished capacity" or "partial insanity." Thus, killing may be seen as either justifiable or heinous; there may be a citation of merit for one act of homicide, a brief prison sentence for another, and capital punishment for other kinds of homicide. All Western systems of criminal law recognize mitigating conditions such as accident, coercion, duress, insanity, and even sleepwalking. Similarly, they recognize that the offender's intent may exacerbate his crime, as in the case of malicious, willful, or reckless actions. Oxford Professor of Jurisprudence H. L. A. Hart (1968) has shown that the offender's state of mind is considered relevant in many ways in Western law—in the initial decision to make a complaint to the police, in the decision of the district attorney to prosecute, during the trial itself, and in the judge's determination of the sentence. Moreover, as a succession of social scientists has demonstrated, the knowledge that certain conditions, including one's intent, may increase or decrease one's liability for misconduct can be an important consideration in the conduct of everyday life (Mills 1940; Scott and Lyman 1968).

The importance of exceptions is not confined to the postindustrial West. The former attorney general of Nigeria, T. O. Elias, listed many specific examples from African tribal societies in support of his contention that strict liability was *not* characteristic of African law (Elias 1956). The evidence used in support of arguments for the presence of strict liability in Africa was, as Elias noted, likely to ignore exceptions. In a widely referenced example, British administrative officer D. J. Penwill reported that the Akamba of Kenya set the fine, or "blood price," for homicide strictly. The penalty of eleven cows, two bulls, and a goat was said to have been imposed regardless of the intent of the killer or the circumstances of the death; according to Penwill, an accidental death and a premeditated murder brought the same fine. As an example, Penwill noted that the Akamba went so far as to demand the full blood money from a man who had killed a thief whom he had caught in the act of stealing. But in a separate passage, Penwill acknowledged that there was at least one exception: If a man killed his childless wife there was no penalty, because it was considered that it was the man who suffered most by his action (Penwill 1951:83). Earlier, another British administrator among the Akamba, Charles Dundas, had noted a number of conditions that mitigated the penalty for homicide; these included the case of accidents, which reduced compensation to half the amount exacted for intentional killing (Dundas 1921). Exceptions *did* exist. Indeed, a more recent investigator, anthropologist S. C. Oliver (1965:423), believed that the Akamba actually stressed flexibility in their rules: "There seems to be an almost conscious avoidance of *specificity* in many of the principles of Akamba culture. The rules are often vague and open-ended. They tend to be quite general, and a person is expected to make his own interpretation of them. The 'right thing' to do *should* emerge from argument and discussion, and the argument, though loosely structured, is by no means predetermined."

It is possible, of course, that some Akamba rules were categorical, while others were very flexible.[7] Such a state of affairs—one that has been reported for many societies in addition to the Sebei and Choiseulese societies mentioned earlier—forces us to return to the point made by Jack Douglas: If rules are mankind's most important means for the creation and maintenance of social order, why are some rules explicitly stated and rigidly followed but other rules are not? If rules are so vital, then why allow exceptions to them? Why not state them explicitly, unambiguously, and categorically, insist that everyone follow them, and penalize anyone who does not?

EXCEPTIONS AND EXEMPTIONS

Rules for breaking rules are universal. For convenience, I call these rules exceptions. An exception reduces or eliminates responsibility for not following a rule that would otherwise be enforced with some sort of penalty. There is extensive research in Western societies (Snyder, Higgins, and Stucky 1983) showing that exceptions may serve to exempt people from internal penalties such as guilt or a sense of personal inadequacy. Evidence for these kinds of exemptions in non-Western societies has not often been reported, but there is ample evidence from all kinds of societies showing that exemptions from external penalties are commonplace.

Exceptions to rules have a temporal dimension; they may vary from a brief period (a moment of rage, the time it takes for an accident to occur, or a few hours while one is drunk) to a lifetime (as sometimes happens when one suffers a permanent physical injury). Exceptions also differ in the degree to which individual choice is involved in qualifying for them. Illness, such as intoxication, may or may not be freely chosen or feigned, but others, such as serious physical injury, are usually not chosen by the victim (although even this sometimes happens—for example, a soldier shoots himself in the foot as a way of avoiding combat). On certain occasions or in certain settings, people may be *required* to break rules, and they may even be punished if they refuse to do so. The extent of exemption from responsibility may also vary from minimal reduction in accountability to total exoneration, including even justification or approbation. Some people may have their claim to an exception rejected altogether. Finally, rules that reduce responsibility vary in the generality of their applications. Some claims to exception, such as mild physical complaints, may only apply within one's own family, where a dizzy spell may temporarily excuse one from the tedium of housework; others, such as blindness, may apply almost anywhere.

It is possible to identify four general categories of rule exceptions that lead to reduced responsibility in most of the world's societies. First, there are exceptions based on *temporary conditions*, typically involving intoxication, spirit possession, illness, or strong emotions. Second, there are specific *statuses* that carry with them longer-lasting exceptions from certain kinds of responsibilities; statuses providing

such exceptions commonly include infancy, old age, political authority, and chronic mental or physical illness. Third, there are *special
occasions*, such as harvest or initiation rituals, funerals, and women's
protests; on these occasions, rules that ordinarily apply may be broken, and some *must* be. Finally, there are exceptions that apply only
in certain *settings*, such as sanctuaries, men's houses or barrooms.

Because each of these four types of exceptions is so widespread and
because each has importance for social theory, in the next four chapters each type will be examined in detail. However, before doing so
it is important to distinguish among types that differ with regard to
exceptions.

TYPES OF RULES AND EXCEPTIONS

Social theory has often been written about as though there were a
single category of phenomena that could be called "rules" or "norms."
So it is that rules are often described as ambiguous, contradictory,
inflexible, negotiable, or some other term said to be characteristic of
them. Certainly, it is often convenient to write as though rules have
a singular quality. It is undeniably tedious to qualify every reference
made to the concept when one is writing about general theoretical
matters, and I shall now and then refer to rules in the generic sense
when finer distinctions are not necessary. But when the nature of
rules is central to a theoretical point, it is impermissible to write as
though all rules were alike—and, as we saw in chapter 1, this does
happen. The failure to make distinctions among categories of rules
has limited the value of many theoretical essays, and some are flawed
beyond repair. When rules and exceptions to rules are the central
concern, as they are here, it is essential that some distinctions among
types of rules be made.

Among the different types of rules that exist in any culture, some
are likely to have rule-based exceptions and others are not. I shall
discuss five types of rules that differ in this way. Although other types
of rules exist, these five appear to be present in all societies: (1)
personal routines, (2) conventions, (3) secular regulations, (4) moral
rules, and (5) supernatural injunctions. Many other classifications of
rules have been proposed,[8] and each has some value for its purposes.
The typology I propose here has the sole purpose of distinguishing
among categories of rules that are more or less likely to allow exceptions in order that we may better understand why some rules allow
all sorts of exceptions and others allow none.

PERSONAL ROUTINES

Personal routines are practices that make up much of the taken-for-granted ways of everyday living; that is, much of human existence everywhere is made up of quotidian routines that almost seem to conduct themselves without any conscious awareness on the part of the actors. People get up, groom themselves, and otherwise busy themselves in more or less the same ways, day after day. They carry out many ordinary activities with little thought of rules; in fact, they are often bored, and their minds wander. If individuals can identify the rules that direct their routines—and often they cannot—they are likely to see most of these rules as being flexible, with many acceptable alternatives. We might refer to such behaviors as habits, things done automatically and repetitively, without thinking. Rules set some limits on the behavior that can become routinized and on the shape that routines may take, but the essence of these routines is the right of an individual to considerable choice among alternatives.[9]

Many routines are so individualized that they apply uniquely to a single individual—the practice of walking the dog each day at 5 P.M. and at no other time; always reading a particular part of the morning newspaper first; drinking two cups, and *only* two cups, of coffee with breakfast; and so on. These routines are the inventions, the rules, of one person; they are arbitrary choices about conduct that are not shared or endorsed by other people. They are not necessarily good nor bad; they are simply routinized ways of doing things that individuals have come to adopt as efficient or congenial means of dealing with some of the necessities of daily life (for example, feeding domestic animals, watering or weeding crops, fetching water, or gathering firewood).

Sometimes, personal routines can change. Someone who has "always" put his right shoe on before his left one can, if challenged to do so, reverse the routine. When any routine is challenged, the actor may become aware that what he has so long done unreflectively has been guided by a rule—an arbitrary rule, granted, but a rule nonetheless. Some personal routines (e.g., in our society, diet, dress, or exercise) may be quite conscious and may take on such strong regulatory or even moral shadings that a person may feel uneasy, disoriented, or at fault if the routine is not followed. Sometimes, a routine may be obsessively followed; evening prayers, morning meditation, a healthy diet, and daily aerobic exercise are familiar examples in our society. Exceptions can become relevant for this kind of personal routine, and these exceptions can be justified in terms of a rule: one should not have to exercise on Sunday, one should be able to eat dessert on special occasions, and so on. In general, exceptions to a personal routine are as personal as the routine itself, but if the routine becomes annoying to another person, rules and exceptions may become central subjects of ensuing disputes. Usually, however, personal routines exist in a zone of freedom from shared rules, a domain of indeterminacy about matters of right and wrong. In the routines and habits of life, humans usually have little conscious concern with rules or with exceptions.

CONVENTIONS

Very little has been written about personal routines in small non-Western societies, even though it is probable that much of what people do everywhere consists of routines. But in all societies there are other kinds of rules that impose far greater constraint on the ways people can behave without penalty, and more has been written about these rules. Conventions, whether implicit or explicit, are widely shared within a population, and they are usually followed closely. Breaches of these rules are annoying or strange, and they can be discrediting, wrong, or even dangerous. Implicit conventional rules direct the ways that people speak, make eye contact, conceive of time, and walk; they define certain smells, bodily warmth, physical closeness, and speaking volume as normal and desirable while designating others as alien, hostile, or even wicked. Rules like these are often neglected in ordinary ethnographic reports, but enough details are available that we can be certain that implicit conventions are universal.[10] Even though they are usually unconscious—Edward T. Hall (1977) termed them "hidden" culture—they control behavior so powerfully that there is little deviation from them. Hall (1966;1977), who is probably the leading anthropological student of rules like these, believes that they constrain our behavior much more effectively than do any explicit rules.

In fact, we follow conventions so unreflectively that we are seldom aware of implicit conventions as rules until they are broken; when they are breached, however, the flow of ordinary life can be disrupted, and people may experience confusion, consternation, anger, or even outrage, as Harold Garfinkel (1963) and his students have demonstrated in a number of ingenious experiments designed to break implicit conventions. What is more, experimenters who were asked to breach such rules often themselves experienced anxiety and dread

(Gregory 1982). In addition to these artificial experiments, there are reports of naturally occurring breaches of implicit conventions in the accounts of early explorers, contemporary international businessmen, and foreign students (Hall 1977). As a spate of literature on invasions of private territory have so richly documented,[11] the experience of having someone stand too close, speak too loudly, make eye contact too directly, or touch in unexpected ways can be disturbing and can lead the offended person to flee in confusion or anger. A woman whose personal space is invaded by a man may even be quite frightened (Fisher and Byrne 1975). In the West, however, when an implicit convention is broken, the breach can be normalized, explained away, or exempted as caused by a stranger's ignorance, a madman's insanity, a drunkard's lack of control, the uninformed foolishness of a small child, or a joke.[12] Anyone who breaks an implicit convention, it is reasoned, must either not know the rule or be temporarily unable to follow it.

These rules are important because they allow any member of a culture to predict how others will behave and to assign meaning to this behavior. They also define what is normal and even what is human. Breaches of conventions have the quality of being senseless, anomalous, or meaningless. Exceptions to implicit rules, then, would probably seldom confer strategic advantage. Someone wishing to feign mental illness might choose to break these rules, and comedians may do so with hilarious effect, but in general, people are much more likely to seek exceptions to explicit rules than to implicit ones.

It is unfortunate that most theoretical discussions of rule-based social control usually mention implicit conventions only in passing, if at all, because so much of the rule-based predictability, order, and meaning in human societies is provided by these kinds of rules. We know very little about how people may try to use them for personal advantage, but there is a reason in addition to inattention why explicit rules, and not tacit ones, have received so much attention from social theorists. Tacit rules are truly hidden culture, constraining us but taken for granted. It is explicit rules that we and people everywhere most often discuss, unmake, evade, ignore, resent, modify, and manipulate. Because explicit rules prescribe or proscribe behavior, either specifically or in general, they are perceived to be social regulators. They may be talked about a great deal or not much at all, but they *can* be talked about, and if they are broken, a common result is fear of the consequences and a search for exemptions.

Many conventions are explicit.[13] Where one must sit in public, how to offer a greeting, when one may speak, and how one should eat are a few examples. Conventions, manners, etiquette—that is, rules of public decorum—are important partly because they define a person as worthy but even more because they show respect for others and for social relationships. Some explicit conventions can literally be seen as matters of life and death. For example, Captain R. S. Rattray (1929:372–373) offered this account of what happened when a rule of etiquette was broken among the Ashanti of West Africa:

> During the visit of a person of considerable importance, who was much beloved by the loyal and generous-hearted Ashanti, the Chief and Elders of a remote province, in common with many others, had come to do him honour. When it came to the turn of a certain old man to be presented, in bending forward to do obeisance, he, unnoticed by all but his immediate followers, inadvertently broke wind. Within an hour of the termination of the ceremony he had gone and hanged himself. He had 'disgraced' himself and his following. The universal comment in Ashanti among his fellow countrymen was that he had done the only right thing under the circumstances. He could never have lived down the ridicule which he might otherwise have incurred.

Raymond Firth (1961) reported a suicide that took place for similar reasons among the Tikopia of the Solomon Islands.

Not every explicit convention is taken this seriously, of course, but any breach of an explicit convention can give offense; even if it does not lead to supernatural retaliation, it can shatter a relationship and leave people resentful, mistrusting, and embittered. Simmel's (1950: 400) famous example of the dangers of failing to greet an acquaintance on the street emphasized this point: "Greeting someone on the street proves no esteem whatever, but failure to do so conclusively proves the opposite. The forms of courtesy fail as symbols of positive, inner attitudes, but they are most useful in documenting negative ones, since even the slightest omission can radically and definitely alter our relation to a person."

People may grumble about some of these conventional rules, finding them burdensome or silly, but they *do* follow them, and any failure to do so must be justified by a rule. In our society, as seemingly unserious a matter as responding to a dinner invitation is bound by strict rules. If the invitation cannot be accepted, an explanation must be given. If one fails to respond, or declines with no good reason, the offense may be lasting, and if the response is to say bluntly that one does not wish to accept, the offense given may be irreparable. In his various chronicles of deference and decorum in our society, Goffman gave many examples of the maneuvers by which people use these kinds of rules to advantage; at the same time, he documented the force of such conventions.

As constraining as these explicit conventions can be, there are many kinds of equally explicit rules that provide exceptions to them. The very young or the very old, the ill, or the physically handicapped are often exempt in various ways, and there are both places and occasions where and when many of these rules may be ignored with impunity or may even be parodied. To break such a rule without a rule-justified exception, however, can evoke ridicule or contempt. With few exceptions, people are afraid to break an explicit convention unless an explicit, acceptable rule allows them an exemption. The penalties for breaking explicit conventions are usually not as severe as those for breaking the rules we shall consider next, but they can be unpleasant enough to be avoided.

I have called these rules conventions because they are traditional and customary; very often, people cannot recall when or why a particular convention originated. Conventions are distinguished from another type of rule that usually *does* have a known origin, a known originator, and a reason for its enforcement. I call these rules *secular regulations*.

SECULAR REGULATIONS

Secular rules that regulate certain behaviors are common in stratified societies, particularly in those with more developed political and jural systems. We have seen examples of the development and enforcement of secular regulations earlier in the legal code of imperial China, and in subsequent chapters, I shall discuss England's Black Laws, medieval efforts to control fire, and regulations on warships at sea. In small societies that lack political and legal institutions, many rules that regulate behavior are not wholly secular but are suffused with moral and supernatural meaning. Even in these societies, however, there are some rules that regulate on a purely secular basis and others that very nearly do so. The hunting and gathering San of the Kalahari desert and the Mbuti of the Ituri forest regulated the handling of their deadly poisoned arrows very strictly and secularly. For example, when a married San woman was found guilty of breaking the rules for keeping poisoned arrows away from children, she was beaten severely and accused of negligence but not of immorality or of offending any supernatural power (Shostak 1981:76).

Secular regulations may be imposed on special occasions, such as on military forays, when otherwise unruly Jivaro warriors were required to obey the commands of an ad hoc leader (Turney-High 1971), or during special activities, such as the communal hunts of the Plains Indians, during which they made widespread use of warrior societies as police. The Cheyenne Indians of the Plains, whom I shall examine at length in chapter 7, were heavily committed to moral and supernatural sanctions in support of their rules, but some of their rules were altogether secular. For example, they invented purely secular rules as needed, such as one that prohibited anyone from borrowing another man's horse without his permission. The Mbuti, too, made secular rules when necessary. Some of these regulations had moral and supernatural overtones, such as the one invented on the spot by an elder who was sick and tired of all the quarreling that resulted from a man's insistence on sleeping with the latest, youngest, and prettiest of his three wives to the total neglect of the other two. The elder declared that this conduct was so wrong that, if it continued, the forest would be so displeased that it would kill their children (Turnbull 1965*b*:209). On another occasion, however, Mbuti elders agreed that it was wrong for young people to sleep together each night yet refuse to marry. They insisted that such couples henceforth would have to declare their intention to marry or stop sleeping together. The rule was secular, without clear moral or supernatural underpinnings, yet it held; all the couples stopped sleeping together (Turnbull 1965*b*:205).

Although secular regulations do occur in egalitarian societies, they are most often associated with inequality in power. Some states attempt to regulate many of the actions of all citizens; those states lacking the enforcement mechanisms to attempt this kind of regulation may yet do so within certain unequal relationships. In all societies, parents impose secular rules on their children, as do older siblings on younger ones when they can. Husbands often regulate the conduct of their wives in this way, or at least try to do so. Various persons with a degree of power may make and enforce secular regulations on persons of lesser power, knowledge, and skills. This is true of warriors, senior wives, elders, great hunters, dance leaders, and many others who may decree certain rules that regulate specific activities.

Because secular regulations restrict or forbid behaviors which people otherwise enjoy, or have at least grown accustomed to, these rules are likely to create resentment. Even when everyone can see the need for a particular regulation and can agree that it should be enforced absolutely, the rule may still be difficult to follow. If this were not so, there would be no need for a regulation. Because people are likely to find it difficult or unpleasant to comply with secular regulations, these rules are enforced by explicit social sanctions. And because these regulations usually lack moral or supernatural support, unless enforcement procedures are particularly strict, people are very likely to employ various tactics to evade, modify, or remake rules of this kind. We recognize that our failure to obey traffic laws may endanger our lives and that police detection may lead to fines or imprisonment, yet we often break traffic laws when we are inattentive, in a hurry, or simply think that it is safe to do so. So it is, I believe, with many secular regulations in all societies. Secular regulations restrict and constrain, and people may be resentful, especially because secular regulations are transparently "man-made"; as Mary Douglas has noted (1966), when the human authorship of rules is obvious, they lose some of their authority. The same point was made by a sixth-century Confucian scholar who wrote that a ruler was most effective when he relied on the force of moral rules. When a ruler imposed secular regulations, he encouraged people to seek loopholes in them and to become litigious (Li 1978:25). The next two categories of rules—moral rules and supernatural injunctions—lose no power or authority because of their human origins. These rules are not believed to be of human manufacture, and they are not for humans to remake.

MORAL RULES

In 1934, Malinowski wrote that "rules of conduct are safeguarded not merely by penalties. They are invariably baited with inducements" (1961/1934:lxv). As we have seen, not all rules have positive inducements, but moral rules usually do. Sometimes we are not at all certain why we follow certain rules; we simply feel that it would somehow be wrong to do otherwise. As British philosopher Martin Hollis (1977: 136) commented, people (himself included) sometimes feel obligated to vote even when there is no instrumental reason for voting and no penalty for not doing so.

   All human societies acknowledge moral rules, rules that are right, imperative, and unchangeable.[14] Some societies have more moral rules than others, but all societies have some. These rules, like secular regulations, may be difficult to follow, because they proscribe what comes easily to people—aggression, lust, envy, greed, hatred, lying, adultery, quarreling, and laziness—but unlike secular regulations, they also define and reward virtue. A person who can avoid doing what is wrong becomes a good person, and a good person is praised and celebrated (and sometimes exempted from punishment). For the

Chinese, filial piety was a moral rule, right and imperative. To display filial piety could be taxing, calling for self-control and sacrifice, but a son or daughter who displayed these moral virtues to follow the rule not only earned the respect of others but also gained *self*-respect. By following a moral rule well and truly, we can think well of ourselves, and, as Mervyn Meggitt observed of the Walbiri of Central Australia (chapter 8), most people want to think well of themselves. Moral rules may constrain us, but, supreme among rules, they can also reward and even ennoble us. Obeying the rules of filial piety could reward a Chinese. Following the Ten Commandments can assure a Christian's virtue, and when done with exceptional dutifulness and grace, it may even sanctify. The Cheyennes had moral rules about male bravery and female chastity; the Mbuti credited their forest with immanent morality.

Moral rules are usually categorical, allowing exceptions only under the most unusual circumstances. To violate a moral rule is often so unnatural, so wrong, and so unthinkable that a person accused of breaking a moral rule is likely to deny that the offense took place—something else was done, something less grievous and perhaps even commendable.

Even though moral rules are usually categorical, they are often stated in such general terms that they are open to interpretation; as a result, it is sometimes possible to evade responsibility for a moral breach by claiming that another moral rule (ideally, more important) was being followed. Ambrose Bierce wrote in *The Devil's Dictionary* (1911) that responsibility was "a detachable burden easily shifted to the shoulders of God, Fate, Fortune, Luck, or one's neighbor." Where moral rules are concerned, responsibility is not so easily evaded. It can be done, but not too often or too blatantly. As Jerry Jacobs has pointed out (1962), it may even happen that someone may succeed in justifying his behavior to others but may fail in self-justification. And when responsibility cannot be shifted, it can weigh so heavily that a moral offender may choose to commit suicide rather than to live without the respect of others and of oneself.[15] In some societies, the search for moral justification can be ceaseless.

Moral rules, then, can build self-esteem when they are followed consistently, but when they are broken, the result can be self-loathing. It goes without saying that if individuals do not usually seek exceptions to moral rules for themselves, neither do they usually allow them for others. Even psychopaths who break moral rules and do not truly *feel* them as moral imperatives often acknowledge the legitimacy and authority of these rules.[16]

The requiredness of moral rules is often buttressed by supernatural authority. This is common in European societies in which moral rules have often been defined as divinely ordered, "natural" laws; much early law was attributed, at least indirectly, to "divine law givers" (Robson 1935).[17] As I have said earlier and as we shall see often in later chapters, in some societies any separation of moral rules from supernatural ones is arbitrary. But in some societies, moral rules do not involve supernatural justification, nor do moral violations bring supernatural sanctions. Moreover, many supernatural rules that *are* enforced by pollution, defilement, illness, or death are not moral rules.[18]

SUPERNATURAL INJUNCTIONS

There are various kinds of rules that are believed to be ordered or enforced through the basilisk eyes of supernatural powers such as high gods, lesser gods, spirits of all kinds, and sacred entities and essences of such things as streams, mountains, and forests. Some supernatural injunctions are believed to be moral. As we shall see in chapter 7, a Cheyenne who committed murder was considered guilty not only of a profound moral wrong that required exile from society but also of a supernatural offense that polluted both the individual and the tribe as a whole. It was felt that the entire society would be in danger until it was purified. Some of our own laws are sacred as well as moral, and many Mbuti rules were both moral and supernatural; for example, the Mbuti believed that someone who violated their moral rule against incest would contract leprosy as supernatural punishment. To the Australian Walbiri, who will be discussed in chapter 8, *all* law was inseparably moral and sacred.

Many supernatural injunctions, however, have nothing to do with morality. Often called taboos, these are simply fear-provoking rules that must be followed or else the supernaturally caused consequences will be dreadful and automatic (Radcliffe-Brown 1939). Rules of this kind are as universal (they continue to exist even in the postindustrial West) as they are enigmatic. They often have no known or even putative historical origin and no justification except fear; not to obey them is dangerous.

Sometimes taboos prescribe activities whose routines must be followed. The Mbuti, as we shall see, believed that they had to wash every time they crossed a stream; sometimes a prayer had to be said or a ritual act performed. For some East African peoples, crossroads were places of supernatural danger, and anyone coming to such a place was obliged to make a propitiatory sign to ward off the unseen dangers. In 1961, I observed people making such signs. Even my acculturated Akamba interpreter did so, although he sometimes tried to hide it from me because he had told me that he did not believe in superstitions. When he fell gravely ill, he confessed that he was being punished for a single occasion when he had inadvertently failed to perform the prescribed propitiatory action at a crossroads. Some in our society may feel the same way about knocking on wood or throwing spilled salt over one's shoulder.

Other taboos prohibit actions such as approaching certain places or eating particular foods. A !Kung San woman was certain that her son had died because he had eaten some honey that was taboo to him (Shostak 1981:313–314).

In many societies, taboos may number in the hundreds, with some enforced automatically by gods or spirits and others enforced by the magical power of a chief or religious specialist. The Iglulik Eskimo of Central Canada had many taboos and lived in dread of them. Knud Rasmussen (1929) once asked a knowledgeable Iglulik man, Aua, about his people's taboos. Aua replied that the Iglulik did not explain their taboos, they *feared* them. Other Iglulik men agreed, saying that they lived in perpetual fear of breaking certain rules and thereby giving offense to the souls of animals or of people, to the spirits of the weather and the sea, or to various forces in the universe. Rasmussen was left with no doubt that these people were truly terrified of breaking supernatural injunctions.

There are seldom any rule-based exceptions to supernatural injunctions, although some taboos apply only to certain categories of people, such as women or hunters, and some apply only to a single individual. For example, the famous Cheyenne warrior Roman Nose was required by a taboo never to eat food taken from a container with any iron implement; if he did so, he would lose his protection against bullets and be killed in battle. Someone who did not know about this taboo once used an iron fork to serve food to him. Although Roman Nose was not aware of it at the time, when he learned about it later he refused at first to take part in a battle that was under way; eventually, however, as the fighting grew more severe, he felt honor-bound to enter the battle and was killed (Grinnell 1915:276–277). Instead of rule-based exceptions to supernatural rules based on temporary condition, status, occasion, or setting, humans have sought supernatural protection through the use of amulets, ritual precautions, or magical procedures. Among the Thonga of Mozambique, as described by Junod (1962), people were able to defend themselves against many of the hundreds of fearsome taboos that plagued them by purchasing the supernatural powers of certain specialists; some Thonga chiefs also possessed the supernatural ability to suspend or cancel certain taboos. This was a contest of one supernatural power against another, not of rule against rule.

Among the Iglulik Eskimo, if anyone broke a taboo, everyone was endangered. When a person fell ill, it was assumed that he had violated a taboo; to protect everyone else, a shaman was required to purge the sufferer of pollution by inducing him to confess to all manner of taboo violations, recent and past. Led by the shaman, the community joined in a chorus to ask the offended supernatural powers to forgive the sufferer and thus the community as a whole (Rasmussen 1929:131ff). The point here is that they asked forgiveness rather than claiming immunity based on another rule. Sometimes, ritual purification (like that of high-caste Hindus or of the Cheyenne or like the public confession of the Eskimo) was successful in counteracting the supernatural penalties that a breach was expected to bring, but these counteractive measures were themselves suffused with fear. When some supernatural rules were broken, people vented their own wrath on the wrongdoers without waiting for the offended gods, spirits, or ancestors to punish all of them indiscriminately. The terror felt by someone who had violated a sacred "law" was perhaps great enough to bring about his death—as seems to have been the case for the luckless Maisie, an Australian aborigine, whom we shall discuss in chapter 8—but others may sometimes have helped the process along by withholding water, thus speeding up the dehydration that helps to cause so-called voodoo death.[19] The Chetris of Nepal were so concerned about violations of supernatural rules that could pollute them all that they sometimes took harsh steps to discredit and punish persons who were only rumored to have broken pollution rules (Fürer-Haimendorf 1967:170).

Some supernatural injunctions may have arisen in response to environmental hazards such as dangerous foods, plants, animals or activities, but the adaptive significance of most rules of this kind is anything but obvious.[20] To be sure, some of these rules support the authority of a chief or a shaman. Also, like witchcraft beliefs, they may help to explain the occurrence of misfortune, illness, or injury, deflecting the agency of misfortune from malevolent humans to malevolent spirits, gods, or ancestors. Whether these rules reduce anxiety or social conflict by redirecting hostility from humans to supernaturals remains an open question, however. What is obvious and inescapable is that these rules create and perpetuate fear.[21] People follow them strictly not because it is right or useful or conventional to do so but because it would be too dangerous not to do so.

RULES AND EXCEPTIONS

The typology of rules I have introduced here is not exhaustive of rule types, nor are the types necessarily mutually exclusive. I have chosen these types to show that the various conditions and predilections that press for exceptions to rules affect some types of rules more than others and that the same thing is true of the conditions that contribute to the development of rules without exceptions. Where routines, as I have called them, are concerned, exceptions are largely irrelevant, as they are where most implicit conventions are concerned. Explicit conventions do have exceptions, as do secular regulations; the press for exceptions, however, is likely to be much greater with secular regulations than with explicit conventions. Moral rules are a very different matter, because people are positively motivated to comply with them; there can be exceptions, even startling ones, but very often people seem most concerned about the opportunity to justify whatever they do under one or another moral rule. Supernatural rules that are not moral are different still. There are few exceptions to these rules, only protective and remedial actions that avoid or mitigate their harmful sanctions.

It is likely that all societies have all these kinds of rules (and some undoubtedly have other kinds as well), but the proportions of these rules probably differ from one society to the next. To my knowledge, no one has examined this question, but it seems plausible that all societies have a large core of routines and conventions and that the proportions of secular regulations, moral rules, and supernatural injunctions may vary. As a result, the overall appearance of flexibility may differ from society to society. Reasons for exceptions to rules exist in all societies, as chapter 10 will show, but whether these reasons will result in rule-based exceptions to rules depends in large part on the balance of types of rules in a particular society. A society with a preponderance of secular regulations, like our own, will be more likely to recognize exceptions than one whose rules are largely moral and supernatural.

PART I

RULES ABOUT EXCEPTIONS TO RULES

CHAPTER 3

Conditions That
Temporarily Exempt

In all societies, people are expected to follow many important rules *unless* some condition or circumstance temporarily reduces or eliminates their responsibility for doing so. People everywhere become ill or experience extreme emotions, and many become intoxicated or possessed as natural and inevitable accompaniments of life; sometimes these conditions are irrelevant to someone's responsibility for following a rule, but often they exempt one partially or even wholly. Sometimes, as we shall see, the conditions may become named, ritualized, or otherwise symbolically set apart as sufficient reason for suspending ordinary liability for rule following. Many conditions are culturally recognized and named as brief periods during which the temporarily ill, intoxicated, bereaved or possessed person is expected to behave in ways that would ordinarily be prohibited. There are clear limits to the behavior that will be excepted, of course, but as long as the behavior remains within these limits, the essential question is entitlement to the condition. Was someone really possessed, truly drunk, honestly grief-stricken?

As we shall see, entitlement is sometimes challenged. Not all temporary conditions that *can* exempt someone have clear criteria for entitlement, nor is there always a clear understanding of what rules one is permitted to break if one is entitled to a temporarily exempting condition. Sometimes, these claims and understandings must be negotiated when someone accused of wrongdoing insists that what he did was accidental or unavoidable due to illness or to the influence of some external power such as a spirit, god, or demon.

Some temporary conditions permit one actively to break ordinary rules, even moral rules. Being drunk is one such condition. Other conditions allow one to escape onerous duties. *Susto* and other forms of illness often do this. In either case, it is understood that for a time, but only for a limited period of time, the individual is not responsible for certain of his actions. It is also understood that when the condition ends, the person will once again be fully responsible, just as he was before it occurred.

Some of these temporary exceptions can be the result of an affirmative act. For instance, the use of intoxicants (alcohol, marijuana, cocaine, qat, or some of the sundry medically prescribed drugs such as Valium that are so conspicuously consumed in the United States) is usually a volitional act. But responsibility-exempting conditions may also happen to people in nonvolitional ways, such as when they are in trance states brought about by spirit possession, certain illnesses, or profound emotions. And while it is probable that temporary exceptions frequently involve personal routines and explicit conventions, many of which relate to household duties or to interpersonal relationships, some temporary exceptions involve important secular regulations as well as moral and supernatural rules.

For example, in Western societies, few acts have been regarded with greater horror than cannibalism, and as Westerners extended their influence and political control over much of the world, they made the eradication of cannibalistic practices a moral, legal, and religious imperative. In all Western societies, the eating of human flesh is not only prohibited by law, it is so morally repellent that many people cannot even discuss cannibalism without experiencing physical revulsion (Sagan 1974). It is no wonder, then, that when the Uruguayan survivors of a plane crash ate the bodies of passengers who had died, it became front-page news around the world. Yet when the cannibalistic survivors were rescued and returned to Uruguay, they were absolved of wrongdoing by officials of the Catholic church. Affirming the views of other Uruguayan theologians, the archbishop of Montevideo said, "Morally, I see no objection, since it was a question of survival. It is always necessary to eat whatever is at hand, in spite of the repugnance it may evoke" (Read 1974:308). In this case cannibalism was not only forgiven, it was morally justified and even considered to have been "necessary."

Why was cannibalism, so abhorrent under ordinary circumstances, found to have been "necessary" in this instance? The reason is that the circumstances were temporary and were anything but ordinary. In October 1972, an airplane carrying forty-five people (the members of a rugby team, their friends and relatives, and the crew) crashed in the Andes at an altitude of 11,500 feet. Thirty-two people survived the crash, but several of these were badly injured. Except for a few tins of food, some candy, and some liquor, there was nothing in the wreckage for the survivors to eat, and the snowscape around them offered no food of any kind. After ten days, twenty-seven people were still alive, but they were desperately hungry and weak. Realizing that their rescue might not be imminent and that they could not survive much longer without food, the survivors held a meeting to discuss the legitimacy of eating the flesh of the bodies lying preserved in the snow. Their decision to engage in cannibalism was not furtive, and there was nothing impulsive, irreverent, or orgiastic about it. They met, all together, and heard the strong opinion of some of the young men among them that their survival of the crash must have been God's will, and that since God had willed them to survive, it was their Christian duty to survive by the only means available to them—eating the bodies of those who had not survived. It was also suggested by them that eating the bodies was equivalent to taking Holy Communion. None of the survivors found it easy to eat human flesh at first, and some took days to overcome their revulsion; eventually, however, all of them ate human flesh and organs. Yet some rules remained. Out of consideration for the feelings of some survivors, certain bodies (those of one survivor's wife and another's mother and sister) were not eaten.

It was over two months before rescue finally came; by that time there were only sixteen survivors, all of whom owed their lives to their regular diet of human flesh. When they were rescued, some of the survivors who feared the moral and legal consequences of what they had done tried to hide evidence of their cannibalism and to deny that it had taken place, but a few were candid, justifying their actions as necessary and morally right because they were obeying a moral and religious rule to survive. Some of the rescuers were appalled, as were some of the families of crash victims who later learned that their loved ones had been eaten. Yet most forgave the survivors, the Catholic church absolved them of wrongdoing, *and* the Uruguayan public made them celebrities of heroic stature in Uruguay (Read 1974).

And so a profoundly moral rule against cannibalism was set aside because, under the circumstances, an even more fundamental moral rule temporarily came into effect—the Christian duty to survive. However, another, even more fundamental, moral rule remained very much in force throughout this terrible ordeal: no one was murdered. Despite injury, disease, cold, altitude sickness, lack of privacy, and constant fear, all of which contributed to suspicion, hostility, bickering, and open quarrels, there was no killing. But suppose that the rescue had been delayed by another month, or even longer, and that all the bodies had already been consumed? Under such circumstances, it is possible that one or more of the survivors would have been killed and eaten. If this had happened, we might feel sympathy for the human beings who were subjected to such dreadful conditions, but we would probably be safe in assuming that if the survivors had killed one another for food, neither religious nor secular authorities would have absolved them. Breaking this rule would not have been justifiable.

The events surrounding this tragic crash illustrate the central concern of this book. There can be legitimate, even necessary, exceptions to rules, including important moral rules. These exceptions are rules, just like the ones they temporarily supersede. Rules like these—rules for breaking rules—occur in all societies, but not all rules have exceptions. Some rules must never be broken; if they are, there can be no legitimate excuses.

TEMPORARY EXEMPTING CONDITIONS: A REVIEW

Some temporary exceptions can be the result of strong emotions, such as sexual passion, rage, depression, hysteria, or grief.[1] For example, among the 3,500 Ilongots who live in the forests of Luzon in the Philippines, peoples' responsibility was very much affected by their emotional states—so much so, in fact, that even murderous acts could be excused. Men in this society, for example, are expected to succeed at head-hunting before they marry, but successful head-hunting calls for an emotional state called *liget,* which is something like an amalgam of passion, anger, and energy. But unless liget is counterbalanced by *beya,* knowledge, the result is likely to be antisocial violence. So it was when a young man named Burer, filled with the spirit of liget but lacking beya, one day slashed the ropes of a footbridge over a deep chasm. His aunt had to cross this bridge in order to fetch water, Luckily, she did not step on the bridge before the damage was discovered, but she was mightily upset and had reason to be because, as anthropologist Michelle Rosaldo (1980) reported, everyone knew that Burer clearly intended to do her harm. Nevertheless, his emotional state of liget without beya had caused him to be temporarily deranged, and his hostile act was excused without any punishment. Because of his emotional condition, the ordinary rules did not apply. Our distinction between crimes of "passion" and those committed in "cold blood" may be similar, with the former more likely to be excused than the latter. In everyday life, a person who is "depressed" may be excused from many obligations at work and home and may be treated with unusual sympathy by family and friends (Coyne 1976); and "emotional shock" has been recognized as a possible criminal defense by courts in the United States, the United Kingdom, and Canada (Taylor and Dalton 1983).

Perhaps the condition that most compellingly demands the suspension of liability for following *any* rule is unconsciousness, the absence of any emotion or cognition. Although a person might well be blamed for what led up to unconsciousness, such as falling asleep on guard duty or negligently bumping one's head in a manner that exposed others to danger, once someone is unconscious—whether from exhaustion or from a blow to the head—he can hardly be held responsible for failing to follow rules such as maintaining vigilance on guard duty or showing proper respect or deference to a superior who happens by. For example, in Western law a person who is unconscious cannot usually be held responsible for a crime, and more remarkable, one may even be absolved of responsibility for a crime committed while sleepwalking. H. L. A. Hart (1964:21) provided this striking example, taken from *The Times* (London), 18 February 1961:

> A man may cause very great harm, may even kill another person, and under the present law neither be punished for it nor subjected to any compulsory medical treatment or supervision. This happened, for example, three years ago when a United States Air Force sergeant, after a drunken party, killed a girl, according to his own story, in his sleep. He was tried for murder but the jury were not persuaded by the prosecution on whom the legal burden of proof rests that the sergeant's story was false and he was accordingly acquitted and discharged altogether. It is worth observing that in recent years in cases of dangerous driving where the accused claims that he suffered from "automatism" or a sudden lapse of consciousness, the courts have striven very hard to narrow the scope of this defense because of the obvious social dangers of an acquittal of such persons unaccompanied by any order of compulsory treatment.

"Social dangers," indeed! A sudden lapse of consciousness would be a convenient excuse for many rule violations.

As we shall see in later chapters, not all societies recognize one's intent in determining responsibility, but trauma-induced unconsciousness—that is, the absolute lack of intent of any sort—poses an interesting dilemma for any society. Should a temporarily unconscious person be absolved of all responsibility for otherwise prohibited behavior? How can authentic unconsciousness be distinguished from a feigned condition? Sleepwalking is even more problematic. We in our society might accept the reality of somnambulism, but in many societies, such as that of the Hehe of Tanzania, someone walking around at night—however "asleep" they might appear—would not be seen as a nonvolitional "sleepwalker." The nocturnal stroller among the Hehe would be suspected of malevolent doings and most likely dealt with as a witch or an adulterer.

Whether societies hold people responsible for the content of their dreams provides another example of a temporary condition that can be exempting. When a dreamer is thought to be responsible for the content of his dreams, he might not wish to mention forbidden dream content to others. We, for example, would probably be reluctant to tell anyone (except, perhaps, a psychotherapist) that we have dreamed about killing someone we love or having incestuous sexual relationships. The Senoi of Malaya took a very different approach to dreams. As described by Kilton Stewart, who studied them in 1934, the Senoi are said to have encouraged one another to dream about certain kinds of prohibited behavior and then to tell others about it. For example, the Senoi were told that if they dreamed about sexual intercourse with someone who "looked like" a brother or sister, they should continue the dream to orgasm and then tell others about it; no incest taboo was violated because the dream image of a brother or sister was a disguise (Stewart 1969:165)—shades of Don Quixote's "enchanted" world! In a more remarkable shift of responsibility, when a Senoi dreamed that a friend harmed him, he told his attacker, who was required to exhibit "friendly social intercourse" to repair his damaged dream image (Stewart 1969:166). Although we may not routinely exempt dream content from ordinary accountability, we do sometimes allow people to make strategic use of dreams. For example, a young man too shy to express his romantic interest in a young woman directly may do so indirectly by mentioning a dream to her in which something romantic took place. The woman may or may not choose to hold the dreamer responsible for his dream or for the decision to tell her about it.[2]

Temporary exceptions to rules have probably achieved their greatest attention in discussions of the "sick role." Talcott Parsons (1953) was one of several prominent social scientists who noted that illness may be a socially sanctioned way of evading the demands and stresses of everyday responsibility. When someone is sick, the rules are different. The ways in which intoxication may serve to absolve "drunken" or "high" offenders from ordinary standards of responsibility are similarly well known. Drunken mayhem on the highways may lead to public outrage and severe penalties not just in the United States and most of Western Europe but in many parts of the Third World as well, yet in certain social circumstances drunken indiscretion or physical aggression—particularly if it is sublethal—is often winked at or even excused.

When these kinds of temporary conditions, especially illness, emotional extremes, and some forms of intoxication, are socially accepted as exemptions from responsibility, it is because they offer rule-based exceptions to ordinary rules: when someone has a high fever, he or she need not clean house, and when someone is drunk, how can he or she be blamed for being a little risqué? Everyone understands, that is, that a sick or intoxicated person is responsible in some ways but not in others. Not all the rules change, only some, and almost everyone knows which ones change and which ones do not. Almost everyone also knows that entitlement to reduced responsibility under these changed rules can be falsely claimed. Someone skilled at strategic manipulation of rules may successfully exaggerate the extent to which he is ill, emotionally distraught, or intoxicated in order to claim the exemptions from responsibility that these conditions can provide. A slight fever may become a disease requiring three days of bed rest; a minor depression can become a life-threatening condition calling for sympathy, attention, and indulgence; and being high on alcohol can become out-of-control drunkenness during the course of which the drunkard cannot be held fully responsible for any hostile behavior.

Some people may attempt not simply to exaggerate these temporary conditions but instead to fake them altogether. Sometimes, as Scott and Lyman (1968) have illustrated in their discussions of the "accounts" people offer to avoid the full consequences of their misbehavior, these people succeed because they are skillful and judicious about invoking temporary conditions as reasons why they should not be held responsible for a rule violation; sometimes, however, others may accept these claims not because they believe them but because they wish to avoid confrontation and further trouble (Howard 1974). At other times these claims are rejected as "mere excuses." As we shall see later, the cumulative effect of exaggerated or fraudulent claims, of too often inventing excuses, can damage a person's reputation.

To return to sickness as a common temporarily exempting condition, it is obvious that societies differ in the extent to which they allow their sick members any relief from ordinary responsibility. According to Arthur Kleinman (1980), a psychiatrist with anthropological training, the Chinese in Taiwan are more willing than Americans to exempt the sick from responsibility, *but* it is only the young and the old who are exempted; anyone else is much less likely to receive any relief from work or household chores. Some societies do not indulge the sick. Among the Sarakatsani shepherds of Greece, married women had to be strong and robust; for these women, to be sick for more than a brief spell was inexcusable (Campbell, 1964). Among some migratory hunting and gathering societies, such as that of the Siriono of the tropical forest in eastern Bolivia, during times of food shortage anyone too ill to travel with the band was left behind to die. Anthropologist Allan Holmberg (1969:225) has given us a poignant firsthand account of a middle-aged woman who was too ill to travel and was left behind when her band moved; unwilling to be left for dead, she crawled after the band as long as she could before succumbing. Her bones were later found on the trail.

Among modern Westerners, there are also marked differences in rules about exemptions for the ill. Mark Zborowski (1952) conducted a classic study of such differences among Jews, Italians, and "Old Americans" in New York City. The differences in responses to pain in these patient populations led some doctors to believe that Jews and Italians must have lower pain thresholds than did Old Americans. But as Zborowski (1952:262) pointed out, the differences were cultural; unlike Old Americans, Jews and Italians freely accepted expression of feelings and emotions: ". . . both the Italians and Jews feel free to talk about their pain, complain about it and manifest their suffering by groaning, moaning, crying, etc. They are not ashamed of this expression. They admit willingly that when they are in pain they do complain a great deal, call for help and expect sympathy and assistance from other members of their immediate social environment."

In 1929, the German medical historian Henry Sigerist clearly outlined the exempting characteristics of being sick in Western society (1977:393):

> Illness releases. It releases from many of the obligations of society, first, from school attendance, and generally from work duties. The sick person is relieved from many important concerns with which society demands that the healthy busy themselves. Yes, the sick man even becomes the object of duties, the recipient of special attention. Illness frees a man also from the performance of many occupations. It also lessens the degree of responsibility or removes it entirely, a viewpoint which has revolutionized the penal law from its foundations.

Sigerist also observed that the sick role was so appealing to some that they might be tempted to seek it out voluntarily instead of waiting for real illness. Such strategic opportunism is hardly confined to the urban West. It was also known, for example, in the Oaxaca Valley of

Mexico in the form of *susto,* or fright sickness, among the Zapotec Indians. Douglas Uzzell (1974) suggested that for the Zapotec, adopting a sick role was a conscious choice made to escape more onerous aspects of everyday life. A Zapotec who suffered from susto withdrew from relationships with others and from ordinary responsibilities. Perhaps because it was believed that susto could be fatal, the sufferer, the *asustado,* was permitted to behave almost as he or she wished. As Uzzell (1974:373) reported:

> However, the *asustado* is allowed to do things with impunity that in other contexts would destroy interactions, give offense, and perhaps even invite physical punishment. It appears reasonable, then, to think of the playing of the role of *asustado* by one participant in an interaction in such a way that his coparticipants recognize that he is playing that role, as establishing a context in which the *asustado's* otherwise deviant acts not only become nondeviant, but are even required for maintenance of the interaction.

Uzzell (1974:374) concluded that the role of asustado, which was usually assumed by a woman, was often preferable to ordinary life, which included being beaten by her husband. As a named and acceptable role, then, susto allowed a person temporarily to behave in a fashion that would otherwise be unacceptable. It was an ideal opportunity for strategic interaction, and it was by no means a trivial one. The exemptions provided by the sick role in Oaxaca and elsewhere can permit someone who is ill to ignore or violate some basic secular and moral rules and may often do so not only without penalty but also without visible resentment.

Temporary exemptions from responsibility, such as susto, sometimes appear to be granted in an attempt to avoid conflict between people who are in important relationships with one another. An example from Japan illustrates the lengths to which people will sometimes go in devising rules that excuse irresponsible conduct in the service of community harmony. As described by anthropologist Hiroshi Wagatsuma, the Japanese are able to avoid holding someone responsible for misconduct, and hence to avoid confrontation, by attributing the cause of misbehavior to a worm, *mushi,* that has entered his body (1970:58):

> When one is depressed, one may be described as "possessed by *fusagi no mushi,* or worm of depression." When a person is still angry, the worm in his abdomen is not calmed down. When a man suddenly desires an

extramarital affair, his behavior may be explained as the result of his being possessed by the worm of fickleness.

According to Wagatsuma, if someone dislikes another person, it is actually because his worm dislikes them. Wagatsuma speculates that the Japanese attribute misconduct to an external agent in order to avoid the necessity of holding an individual responsible for "impulsive" behavior. Because it is not the individual but an external agent who is responsible, the individual may still have a chance for acceptance. Wagatsuma (1970:58) concluded that "when an individual's impulsive behavior becomes too abnormal and aberrant to be explained away as the worm's doing, such behavior is often explained as the consequence of possession of a more serious kind, such as by a fox or dog, that has to be driven out by magic and rituals ('*kitsune tsuki*')."

Attributing untoward behavior to the invasion of an external agent, whether worm or demon, is a widespread phenomenon. For example, a lawyer in Danbury, Connecticut, recently attempted to use demonic possession as a defense for murder, offering to call Roman Catholic priests to testify on his client's behalf; the court refused to admit the plea.[3] Possession by demons of devils, once so familiar in the West, is but one version of the near-universal phenomenon of possession by spirits. And when spirits possess someone, the rules change dramatically. As I. M. Lewis (1971) and P. J. Wilson (1967) have noted, it is most often women who experience spirit possession; while possessed, it is common for them to behave without penalty in ways that would otherwise be unacceptable and punishable. Examples of spirit possession offering exceptions to ordinary rules about propriety are not only numerous but also go back at least to biblical times (Bourgignon 1976).[4] A more modern example has been provided by C. W. Hobley (1922), a scholarly British administrator in Kenya, who witnessed an "epidemic" of spirit possession among the Akamba of the remote Kitui District in 1911. In this "epidemic," only women were possessed by *Ngai*, a high god. Possessed women danced in a "frenzy," and onlookers joined in the excitement. The leader of the possession dance—a woman who translated the wishes of *Ngai*—demanded beer, a bullock, and a goat, all of which the Akamba men were obliged to provide. In addition, everyone at the possession dance was required to give each possessed woman some money.

Hobley's account (1922:256–257) continues: "The elders do not approve of these dances, but are generally too frightened to intervene. The reason for their disapproval is not far to seek; every woman who becomes possessed is told to demand something from her husband or the mania will not leave her." Likening these behaviors to ancient accounts of demonic possession or to a form of possession called *Bonda* in Abyssinia, Hobley (1922:257–258) went on to add that "these mysteries work the credulous and susceptible women into a state of frenzy, when they cease to be responsible for their actions. One chief, with some pathos, stated that women who have been to one of these dances often go back home and beat their husbands." In ordinary life, it was Akamba men who dominated, and sometimes beat, their wives, while the women were required to be inordinately deferential toward men, a pattern that has persisted into very recent times (Edgerton 1976).

More recently, in her description of the Taita of Kenya, a society located near the Akamba, anthropologist Grace Harris (1957) recorded a similar example of spirit possession as a temporary condition during which rules are broken with remarkable impunity. Like Akamba women, Taita women were dominated by their husbands. Perhaps as a result, Taita women often became possessed by spirits, and when possessed they danced, had convulsions, spoke in tongues, and otherwise appeared to be in a dissociated state of consciousness. Taita women who were possessed not only demanded material goods from their husbands but also dressed and danced as men, temporarily taking on the male role. Husbands indulged them in this behavior and in their material demands because it was believed that failure to do so could result in death for the women (an outcome that meant clear economic loss for the husbands). Harris reported that some possessed women appeared to be genuinely dissociated; however, other possessed women appeared to be shamming in order to take advantage of this privileged condition. That some people may fake an exempting condition is, of course, common knowledge, but unless there are others who are seen as being genuinely entitled to the condition, fraud is unlikely to be successful. Many Taita women were thought to be genuinely possessed.[5]

Spirit possession by women has also been common in the New World. Weston LaBarre's well-known description of a Southern snake-handling cult (1969) is but one example of a phenomenon seen in Pentecostal and revivalistic churches in many parts of the United States. Because spirit possession is so widespread, it may be worthwhile to examine another example in more detail. A description of spirit possession in Trinidad by Walter and Frances Mischel (1958) is especially valuable as an illustration of the multiple ways in which being possessed can provide exemptions from everyday responsibilities. The Afro-Trinidadians studied by the Mischels were possessed by a spirit related to Shango, a deity among the Yoruba people of West Africa. Women made up 75 percent not only of the Trinidadians who became possessed but also of the audiences who witnessed the trances. The possession trance was apparently induced by drumming, dancing, singing, candlelight, and other dramatic alterations of the everyday environment. As their possession took power over them, the women underwent dramatic changes, vibrating, standing stiffly, convulsing, and uttering grunts and groans; they also took on a fiercely masculine expression and manner, and their eyes dilated and stared ahead fixedly. Some possessed women danced in stereotypical ways, while others were hurled to the ground by their possessing spirits and writhed violently. It seemed to the Mischels that some trances were far "deeper" than others, yet they observed that even persons who lost motor control and lapsed into unconsciousness did not inflict any injury to themselves or to others, which suggests that they were never fully out of conscious control.

Mischel and Mischel (1958:254) hypothesized that spirit possession "permits the sanctioned expression of behaviors which are otherwise socially unacceptable or unavailable." One dramatic fact is that the possessed person was in almost absolute control of the onlookers. Her slightest wish—whether for rum, food, or merely silence—was carried out with awe and respect and even with fear. Mischel and Mischel (1958:255) analyzed this transformation as follows:

> The domestic who thirty minutes earlier was submissive to the whims of her British mistress is, under possession, transformed into a god; the unemployed laborer is master of an audience of several hundred people. The transition is often an almost direct role reversal—from passive impotence to central importance, dominance, power, and recognition, which appear to be the major reinforcements obtained through this behavior pattern.

In addition, the possessed person in Trinidad was able to behave in a sexually free manner with persons in the audience or to express aggression. For example, the possessed person could push or even lash someone in the audience with whom a much more restrained or deferential relationship was ordinarily required. Possessed persons could also behave with complete abandon, rolling and writhing, or they might "regress" to childish behaviors. These behaviors, which would ordinarily be seen as quite bizarre, served to authenticate the state of possession for onlookers, but they may also have been intrinsically rewarding for some possessed persons. As Mischel and Mischel pointed out, however, not every claimant to this role was accepted; some were ridiculed, and their efforts to claim reduced responsibility were rejected. Dramatic exemptions were reserved for the truly possessed.

Spirit possession provides an opportunity for status-deprived, powerless, or subordinate persons—usually women—to enjoy advantages otherwise denied them. They do so by claiming to be under the sway of an external agent, a powerful religious spirit. But other external agents, such as intoxicants, can bring about similar exemptions. Alcohol has been one of the world's most popular intoxicants for centuries. MacAndrew and Edgerton (1969) have argued that many societies permit people who are culturally defined as drunk to behave in ways that would ordinarily be highly improper, yet suffer few undesirable consequences. That is so because "drunken" persons are thought to be temporarily "under the influence" of a substance, alcohol, whose toxic properties chemically deprive them of the capacity to exercise self-control. In many societies, then, it is alcohol that receives the blame; the person who drank it is thought to be partially or completely blameless for violating rules. In these societies, the opportunity to drink alcohol in order to take advantage of the excuse it provides is obviously available. In our own society, for example, conduct that would be an outrageous offense by a sober person may be taken lightly or excused altogether if the offender is drunk; wife-beating is one example among many (Snyder, Higgins, and Stucky 1983).

MacAndrew and Edgerton (1969) described various societies around the world in which serious offenses (including violence and sexual transgressions) committed under the influence of alcohol were considered to be less serious than they would have been if the offenders had been sober. Why this was so was illustrated by the seventeenth-century Jesuit missionary Father LeJeune (Thwaites 1896, 17:231), who reported that he received this reaction from a Huron Indian when he questioned him about a drunken murder: "'Put thy wine and thy brandy in prison,' they say: 'It is thy drinks that do all the evil, and not we.' They believe themselves to be entirely excused from crimes they commit, when they say that they were drunk."

The transfer of responsibility for offenses from the intoxicated individual to alcohol is not confined to any specific part of the world. In his review of drinking behavior in fifty-six societies around the world, Horton (1943:255) concluded: "Smaller fines, a shorter jail sentence, or some other moderation of punishment is often characteristic of the attitude toward drunken aggression. The drunken man is not held strictly accountable for his actions." In a subsequent survey of sixteen societies, Washburne (1961:262) agreed: "A person is not punished as severely for doing forbidden things while drunk." He added this significant observation (Washburne 1961:262): "The feeling is nurtured that the best time to do such things is when drinking."

Supporting this observation that strategic uses of drunkenness to excuse rule violation was common, MacAndrew and Edgerton (1969) reported evidence from various societies showing that persons often feigned drunkenness in order to escape full responsibility for their actions. A very early example was provided by the French merchant Nicholas Denys who wrote about his experiences in Canada in 1633 (Denys, 1908:449):

> In addition to all the wickedness of which I have spoken, the [French] fisherman have taught them [the Indians] to take advantage upon one another. He who may desire ill to his companion, will make him drink in company so much that it makes him drunk, during which time he holds himself in restraint. He acts as if he were drunk as the others, and makes a quarrel. The fight being commenced, he has an axe or other weapon, which he had hidden before the drinking; this he draws and with it kills his man. He continues to make a drunken orgie, and he is the last to awaken. The next day he is told that it is he who has killed the other man, at which he expresses regrets, and says that he was drunk.

A French priest writing in 1659 (Thwaites 1896, 46:105) added that since any crime committed while drunk was excused, "those that have any quarrels pretend to be intoxicated in order to wreak vengeance with impunity." Examples of feigning drunkenness are also available from other continents. Paul Bohannan (1960), in discussing the statistical relationship between homicide and drunkenness in Africa, noted that some tribes took advantage of the fact that courts were inclined to excuse killings that took place during drunken brawls.

The argument that drunkenness excuses otherwise punishable behavior and that people sometimes take advantage of this state of affairs by pretending to be drunk is given increased credibility by the realization that people can drink, and drink heavily, without necessarily being deprived of their sense of propriety or responsibility. For example, the Camba Indians of Bolivia, as described by anthropologist Dwight Heath (1958), drank an alcoholic beverage approximately twice as potent as Scotch whiskey, and they drank it in substantial

quantities, undiluted. Indeed, they often drank to the point of unconsciousness, slept for a while, then began drinking all over again. The
next day, they arose and worked in their fields under the hot sun;
their sweat reeked of alcohol. Yet at no time during these epic drinking bouts did the Camba behave in any way that was objectionable.
There was no drunken aggression, sexual license, or obscene joking,
not even "maudlin sentimentality, clowning, boasting or 'baring of
souls'" (Heath 1958:501).

Another example comes from Japan, where even very heavy drinking among groups of men was seldom associated with violence. However, the normally very strict Japanese implicit conventions about
avoiding physical closeness and maintaining dignified posture were
regularly broken without any disapproval (Benedict 1946:189): ". . .
relaxation of the strict rules of Japanese posture and gestures is
universal. At urban *sake* parties men like to sit in each other's laps."
A similar pattern of exemption for men hugging one another after
drinking also occurred in rural areas (Norbeck 1954). In many
societies, being drunk is a common temporary exemption for breaking
implicit conventions.

It is essential to realize that here, as in previous examples, we are
dealing with rules. Even when drunkenness is associated with mayhem
or debauchery, this drunken misconduct follows culturally defined
rules. When some drunken offenses are excused but others are not,
it is no surprise that inexcusable offenses rarely occur. For example,
Dwight Heath (1964:131) observed 405 Navaho drinking occasions,
noting that while fighting was the "normally expected" outcome and
that serious violence in the form of shootings or knifings was not
uncommon, fights between cross-cousins or biological brothers *never*
occurred, even though such men often drank together. When Siriono
men in the Bolivian forest were drunk, it was permissible for them
to wrestle, but it was not permitted for them to fight with weapons
or even with their fists (Holmberg 1950:62). Anthropologist Mac
Marshall (1979:53) reported that the Trukese of Micronesia believed
that "when one ingests an alcoholic beverage in whatever amount and
of whatever sort, he is drunk and no longer entirely responsible for
his words or deeds." For the Trukese, being drunk was a condition
that temporarily permitted otherwise prohibited behavior, especially
aggressive behavior. But the kinds of aggressive behaviors that were
excused were clearly defined by rules. Drunken young men who
physically attacked their siblings of either sex—a behavior that was
ordinarily forbidden by a moral rule—were excused. They were also

permitted to scream their anger at older men, but they could not attack them physically; and some people, such as children and the elderly, "were absolutely off limits" (1979:122–123).[6]

Noting that legal drinking began only in 1971 among Australian aborigines (who had no alcohol before European contact), Australian anthropologist Lee Sackett pointed out that aggression that occurred between drunken men was completely "forgiven and forgotten" because "they were all 'full drunk,' i.e., not in control of themselves" (Sackett 1977:93). Yet Sackett also noted that this was so only if the rules of proper drunken combat were observed; for example, it was permissible to hit an opponent with a beer bottle, but it was not permissible to break the bottle first. Moreover, drunkenness did not excuse some things at all. If a drunken man uttered certain secret terms in the presence of women or the uninitiated or intruded on sober men who were performing a sacred ritual, the drunken person would not be exempted from ordinary responsibility. As Sackett put it (1977:95), "Both offenses cause great consternation among the non-drunks and have been known to lead to bloodshed."

Alcohol, like many psychoactive drugs, does have demonstrable effects on the central and autonomic nervous systems, although the "disinhibited" behavior changes that are associated with alcohol are more likely to be the result of the setting and the drinker's expectations than of the toxic effects of alcohol (Marlatt and Rohsenow 1980).[7] But the effects of almost all psychoactive drugs can be influenced at least to some degree by expectations and overridden by human "will," and as a result more drugs can be manipulated by those who desire to take advantage of the possibilities offered by intoxication. Others, probably the majority, may have no interest in perpetrating fraud and may indeed never have even considered such a thing as a possibility, but they can still profit indirectly by their unquestioning acceptance of a cultural belief system that treats drunken offenses as less serious than sober ones. Presumably, comparable opportunities obtain for persons who are intoxicated by other drugs, such as marijuana, heroin, cocaine, or PCP.

For example, John Kennedy reports that the amphetamine-like drug qat, which is commonly chewed in Yemen to enhance conversation and sociality, is seldom accompanied by untoward behavior. Qat is legal and is a major drug in Yemen, whereas alcohol, which many qat chewers must drink before going to sleep to counteract the exhilarating effects of qat, is illegal (Kennedy, Teague, and Fairbanks 1980). Despite the Yemeni cultural definition of qat as a trouble-free drug, it sometimes happens that excessive use of qat is blamed for serious misbehavior. Kennedy describes the case of a Yemeni policeman who was caught stealing. The ordinary penalty for this offense would be the loss of a hand, but when the defendant explained to the judge that he had chewed such an enormous amount of qat that he did not know what he was doing, his hand was spared and he was only fined a small amount of money.[8]

The use of marijuana (*Cannabis sativa*), whether used by itself or with alcohol, raises other issues concerning the role of drugs in temporarily reducing responsibility. *Cannabis sativa* is a complex drug containing over 400 chemical compounds, of which the isomer Delta-9 tetrahydrocannabinol (THC) produces the primary psychoactivity. Despite its widespread use today and in antiquity, there is a good deal less ethnographic detail available concerning the use of cannabis than of alcohol; nevertheless, enough is known to make several points. First, as with alcohol, the subjective experience and behavioral consequences of using cannabis are influenced by both the psychological set of the user and the sociocultural setting in which the drug is used (Weil 1972), as some experimental research has confirmed (Jones 1971; Smith 1978). In natural settings, these effects can be complicated by the many ways in which cannabis is ingested (it is smoked, drunk in teas and soups, smeared on the body in pastes and ointments, and contained in various foods) and by the varying amounts of THC that these preparations contain.

The effects that cannabis is expected to produce vary as much as the ways in which it is taken. The Mbuti pygmies of Zaire sometimes used it to enhance their courage, skill, and religious power when hunting dangerous animals such as elephants (Schebesta 1933). Members of the growing Rastafarian political and religious sect that originated in Jamaica in the 1930s use cannabis as a sacred "herb" through which they establish communion with God (Kitsinger 1971). In various parts of Muslim North Africa, men carry four grades of cannabis (which they call *kif*) around with them in special pouches, offering it to persons they meet; the grade offered indicates the intended degree of friendship and esteem. Some homes there have special rooms set aside in which family groups gather to smoke kif, sing, dance, and recite poetry or ancient traditions (Bowles 1962; Joseph 1975). Cannabis is socially accepted and integrated into many aspects of life in some Muslim countries, but it has achieved perhaps its greatest social and cultural integration in Hindu India. Thought of as sacred, cannabis is consumed in religious ceremonies, weddings, and festivals as well as in everyday secular life to promote health, achieve euphoria, remain alert, or reinforce social ties. It is smoked, drunk in soups, and eaten in sweetmeats and even ice cream. Most important, it is typically taken in a social setting, often that of the family (Hasan 1975). Cannabis is legal in India and, while the government controls the manufacture and sale of cannabis resin, most people simply grow the plant themselves.

Obviously, then, some societies take a positive view of cannabis, making its use socially approved, legal, and even required. Use of cannabis begins in childhood and continues throughout life; the goals of its use are socially and psychologically positive and include good health, mental clarity, strength, relaxation, and euphoria. In these societies, cannabis is not associated with rule breaking. The dosage is socially determined and controlled, with appropriate sanctions or antidotes for overindulgence. Persons who behave inappropriately under its influence may or may not be excused, but they are often socially eased out of its use. Socially positive consequences of cannabis (or hashish) consumption have long been reported in many countries (Emboden 1972). For example, accounts from twelfth- and thirteenth-century Egypt attributed the following behavioral changes to the consumption of cannabis (Khalifa 1975:199): "euphoria, acquiescence, sociability, carefreeness, feelings of importance, meditativeness, activation of intelligence, jocularity, and amiability." A similar view has been common in Cambodia and other parts of Southeast Asia in modern times, where cannabis is not only used for the treatment of most physical ailments but also taken with friends to enhance sociability. Although the Western-educated elite in Southeast Asia may disparage cannabis or legislate against it, the majority of the population uses cannabis widely, almost always in group settings. While some ill effects of heavy usage are noted, the typical consequences of consumption are seen as being socially beneficial (Martin 1975). Research in Pakistan, where cannabis is also socially accepted, has reported no physical or mental ill effects nor socially disfavored behavior among a sample of seventy men who had been using cannabis for twenty years (Khan, Abbas, and Jensen 1975). In societies such as these, there is no need to consider temporary exemptions for misconduct by cannabis users.

But not all non-Western societies report such a positive experience with cannabis. Indeed, in several societies it is believed that cannabis produces socially disruptive violence. Although cannabis has seldom been associated with violence in recent U.S. history (Tinklenberg et al. 1977)—and is, in fact, commonly thought to bring about nonviolent moods—in some societies, interpersonal violence is considered to be the natural and even inevitable outcome of cannabis consumption.

For example, cannabis-"caused" violence is said to be common in East Africa, in areas from Réunion Island to the highlands of Ruanda. Anthropologist Helen Codere (1975:222) wrote this comment about the cannabis (*injaga*) smoking of the Twa people of Ruanda:

> A number of individuals who claim to have been eye-witnesses report that the usual outcome of *injaga* smoking is that the smoker becomes physically violent toward others. Acts of violence are described as wild, mindlessly fearless of receiving any hurts in the fights that ensued, and wholly undiscriminating in their object which might be a wife, a friend, a Tutsi protector and patron, or whoever was about.

Codere does not say to what extent Twa cannabis smokers were held to be responsible for these violent assaults. However, the same sort of cannabis-related violence occurred in East Africa where cannabis (*bhang*) users were characterized as *kali* (fierce). Such persons were avoided and feared, but their aggressive actions often went unreported and unpunished. In my research in East Africa,[9] I met several "bhang men" whose reputation for ferocity was so great that they were able to intimidate other people, who hastily granted their demands for food, beer, and women rather than risk giving offense. Because of the bhang, these men were incapable of self-control; they were avoided, and no one tried to hold them responsible for offenses they committed while intoxicated.

Cannabis has also been thought to lead to violence in parts of Mexico. In some Mexican communities, such as the town of Juxtlahuaca in Oaxaca, alcohol was not believed to be capable of causing violent behavior, but marijuana *was* (Romney and Romney 1963). Moreover, while violence was feared and deplored, it was the marijuana that was blamed and not the person, whose actions were largely excused. The belief that marijuana caused violent behavior was widespread among Mexican-Americans of the southwestern United States in the early years of this century. As Bonnie and Whitebread (1974:33) noted, a common Mexican folk saying of that time stressed the idea that three puffs of a marijuana cigarette would make the smoker oblivious to danger, supernaturally strong, quarrelsome, and destructive. The effects of cannabis on Mexican soldiers were said to be particularly alarming, leading to crimes committed in violent frenzies. This Mexican view of the violent criminogenic properties of cannabis spread into the United States with Mexican immigrants and contributed to the overstatements of the now notorious Anslinger report (Bonnie and Whitebread 1974:36). However much the Anslinger report exaggerated the dangers of cannabis, it is the case that cultures as widely separated as those of Mexico and East Africa developed exceedingly negative beliefs about the consequences of ingesting cannabis, beliefs that have been confirmed by the actual behavior of at least some members of those societies. Sometimes cannabis intoxication served to excuse violence, as it did in East Africa; but often it did not, especially in Mexico, where laws against marijuana have long been harsh.

And this illustrates an important point. Some rules—secular, moral, and supernatural—are so universal that they apply to everyone at all times, but others have much more limited application. For example, in all societies, especially the more complex, socially stratified ones, there are some rule systems that vary relative to one's family, lineage, village, neighborhood, caste, ethnic group, or religion.[10] Conflict among these rule systems can occur when marriage or property rights are involved or where drugs are concerned. In many parts of the world, Western-produced alcoholic beverages are the drug of choice for those able to afford them, while the cheaper drug—cannabis—is consumed by poor and socially stigmatized classes, castes, religious, ethnic, or racial groupings whose use of the drug is often regarded by others as morally depraved or politically dangerous (Beaubrun 1975).

This contrast is sharply drawn in Jamaica, where those who can afford to do so drink Scotch whiskey, while the many poor, working-class people consume cannabis (*ganja*) daily, in considerable amounts (Dreher 1982). Cannabis was introduced to Jamaica in the nineteenth century by Indian laborers. Its use, along with the religious and cultural beliefs that supported that use, spread to Jamaica's poor, most of whom were descendants of former slaves. The British planters and their colonial government became alarmed and enacted secular regulations in the form of anti-cannabis laws. This pattern of legislation, begun before World War I, continued after political independence in 1962, when the emergent Jamaican middle class joined the Jamaican elite in decrying the evils of ganja. Frightened by lurid press reports of violence set off by ganja, these respectable alcohol-consuming Jamaicans enacted ever-stricter laws against the drug (Fraser 1974). Those who committed offenses while under the influence of "the weed," as ganja was also called, were not excused—indeed, they were punished more severely than were offenders who had been drunk.

This pattern of denying cannabis intoxication any excusing properties grew over the years, even though there was no sound evidence to support the belief that users of ganja were more dangerous than anyone else. Indeed, as Rubin and Comitas (1976) determined, Jamaican users of cannabis were no more likely—and perhaps were somewhat *less* likely—to be violent or otherwise socially disruptive than were nonusers. Those Jamaicans who used ganja did not believe that the drug led to violence, pointing instead to what they saw as self-evident—namely, that only persons with a predisposition to violence became violent after smoking ganja. What is more, they took steps to convince such persons that they had "no head for it" and urged them to give up ganja before serious trouble ensued (Beaubrun 1975; Rubin and Comitas 1976). Reminiscent of Carstair's research in India, where there were similar disputes between alcohol and cannabis users (1954), these Jamaican cannabis users insisted that it was alcohol and not cannabis that led to antisocial behavor.

Recently, Jamaica relaxed its laws against cannabis somewhat (Nettleford 1978), but—to underscore the point about multiple sources of rules—this relaxation came about not as a result of any conviction that ganja was a socially positive drug, but rather because the straitened economic conditions in Jamaica during the late 1970s and early 1980s made the value of cannabis as an export crop all too clear, even though cannabis was illegal in the countries to which it was transported.[11]

Various drugs, including alcohol and cannabis, can be culturally accepted as intoxicants capable of depriving users of their ability or will to follow rules. Intoxicated persons are considered to be "out" of their minds. In some societies, intoxication can temporarily exempt someone of responsibility for important moral and supernatural rules, while in others, only weak exemptions, or none at all, are allowed. Sometimes, as among Australian aborigines, this is because sacrilege is so feared; in other societies, it is because an elite class or caste fears drug-related "crimes" by other classes or castes.

MORE LASTING EXEMPTING CONDITIONS

Some exempting conditions that are usually temporary may persist and become long-term conditions; they may even become statuses. An illness may be brief, or it may be chronic; it may even last a lifetime. Drunkenness may occur only on Saturday nights, but it may also be a perpetual feature of an "alcoholic" status. Mental illness is another example. The various behaviors that are construed by different cultures as evidence of mental illness may be chronic, or they may appear only for a period of days or even hours, perhaps recurring at widely spaced intervals. The Ashanti King, Osai Yao, is said—although probably apocryphally—to have rejected mental illness as an excusing condition when he had both a drunken man and a madman placed in a burning hut and only the madman fled for his life. Even if this did take place, Ashanti law paid little heed; a drunkard was not held responsible for any crime except that of homicide or of cursing the king, whereas mental illness exempted a criminal from any of the usual penalties for any crime. However, an insane criminal was ordered to be chained to a tree or a log; some were fed by their families, but for others the order could be a death sentence (Rattray 1929). Western law, with its emphasis on intent, has long agreed that a mentally ill person is not responsible for a criminal act (Fingarette and Hasse, 1979). Insanity as an excuse was recognized in the Roman Empire as early as the third century A.D. and in England by the thirteenth century (Alexander and Selesnick 1966), and it has come to be widely accepted in modern Anglo-American and Continental law (Morris 1976).

Mental illness, in its various forms and intensities, may excuse all sorts of misconduct. There is nothing automatic about the excuse, however; attitudes toward mentally ill persons and their behavior are often complex and ambivalent. Nancy Scheper-Hughes (1979) sensitively portrayed the existence of this ambivalence in rural Ireland, where psychotic persons were sometimes treated with unusual kindness but more often were feared and rejected. Drunkenness, on the other hand, excused a great deal that would ordinarily be intolerable: "A certain amount of mental illness and 'abnormal' behavior (by village standards) is tolerated when disguised in the cloak of alcohol" (Scheper-Hughes 1979:83).

A mentally ill person in the contemporary United States may also be stigmatized, and experience social rejection; the suffering many such persons have endured has been amply and painfully documented, as in the recent account of deinstitutionalized mentally ill persons by Sue Estroff (1981). Yet, as Estroff also pointed out, being mentally ill can have strategic advantages too—for example, it can provide an excuse for failure and dependency, allow otherwise unacceptable behavior, or entitle one to a guaranteed income (e.g., Supplemental Security Income). George Devereux (1963) noted that people may simulate a psychosis for advantage, such as the evasion of military service, something Snyder, Higgins and Stucky (1983) also documented. In many societies, persons defined as being mentally ill can use "crazy" behavior to manipulate others for their own self-interest.

Ludwig (1971:17) said this about mentally ill persons in the United States: "Not only does it [mental illness] provide a convenient vehicle and ready-made excuse for the expression of otherwise taboo feelings, thoughts and behaviors, but it also guarantees them a kind of special attention and concerned care that they would not receive while behaving sanely."

Small, non-Western societies differ in the extent to which they absolve mentally ill persons of responsibility for their actions, but the condition of mental illness can sometimes excuse a great deal. The Konyak Nagas of India's northeast frontier punished arsonists by exile unless the incendiary was "insane," in which case there was neither banishment nor punishment (Fürer-Haimendorf 1979). In traditional Malay society, both men and women ordinarily carefully followed very strict rules of public deference and decorum. Yet sometimes both men and women broke these rules dramatically without being thought responsible or held accountable. A Malay man might suffer an attack of *amok,* flying into a violent rage and attacking anyone he met; a woman who was overcome by *latah* might shout obscenely, eliminate publicly, or fall into a trance. Since these conditions were thought to be caused by evil spirits, the person was considered to have been temporarily irresponsible and not liable for following ordinary conventions, secular regulations, or moral rules (Ackerman and Lee 1981).

William A. Lessa (1966:47) reported that the people of a much smaller society, tiny Ulithi Atoll in the Caroline Islands, likewise did not hold the mentally ill responsible for following some important rules, including moral ones:

> While on the atoll, I was deeply impressed by the solicitude with which the people treated a young manic who damaged property, refused to work, struck his father, pursued women threateningly, and menaced small children with fishing spears. They tolerated an old woman who was accustomed to steal, spread falsehoods, hoard food, and shirk communal chores. These psychotics were shown every consideration and sympathy. Effort was made to draw them and others like them into the pattern of daily life.

Edgerton (1969) reported similar indulgence of certain mentally ill persons in various East African tribal societies. Although, unlike on Ulithi, psychotic behavior involving violence or property destruction was not excused and could lead to harsh social sanctions, some psychotics in these societies were able to commit homicide and then succeed in pleading that their mental illness should mitigate their offense (Edgerton 1969). In other instances, it was family members or fellow clansmen who insisted on the exemption; when liability is collective, as it was there, the interests of many persons can be at stake in negotiating entitlement to an exemption.

This introduction to some varieties of rule-based temporary exemptions for responsibility has necessarily skirted many of the complexities of real life, where people who claim exemption from responsibility by referring to a temporary condition have that claim honored or rejected in an interchange that takes into account inferred intent, past conduct, present relationships, and future possibilities. Illness, for example, may stigmatize more than it exempts. For instance, in our contemporary society a person with genital herpes must take on more social responsibility in sexual conduct than must uninfected persons. And even with our cultural emphasis on an individual locus of responsibility, mental illness may nevertheless stigmatize kinsmen as well as the afflicted individual. In other societies where there is more widespread collective responsibility, an entire family or lineage may be thought guilty of bringing on an illness, and they may share responsibility for the afflicted person's actions or omissions. The resulting social negotiations can be Byzantine in their complexity (Edgerton 1971a).

Sometimes, because a rule is explicit and no exceptions to it are allowed, people may manage to use it to escape from onerous responsibility. An example is provided by John G. Kennedy (1967) in his discussion of taboos among the Nubians of Egypt. The Nubians recognized taboos that, if broken, would supernaturally bring serious harm to persons undergoing such crises as birth, circumcision, or marriage. These taboos called for the strict avoidance of many substances (such as blood, knives, or eggplant) as well as activities (such as visiting a market or crossing the Nile or one of its inlets). At the time of a birth or marriage, all relatives and fellow villagers were obligated to visit the vulnerable person, an obligation that obviously was time-consuming and which some Nubians felt was burdensome. Anyone who wished to avoid this obligation needed only to announce that they had crossed the Nile, seen blood, or broken some other taboo (Kennedy 1967:699). Hence, the very clarity and strictness of these taboos allowed an overburdened Nubian successfully to evade social responsibility. If someone had visited a market, that person *was* polluted, at least temporarily, and could not visit the vulnerable person. There could be no arguments and no recriminations—unless, of course, someone became polluted too often to avoid the obligation of visiting. An inflexible rule, like flexible ones, can be manipulated for personal advantage, but only when the manipulation follows other rules.

Old exemptions may lose their force, but new ones come into being. In recent years, courts in the United States and United Kingdom have considered that culpability for criminal offenses might be mitigated by disorders such as epilepsy and diabetic hypoglycemia (Taylor and Dalton 1983). And in 1980 and 1981, two women accused of murder or threats to commit murder successfully claimed diminished responsibility before British criminal courts on the grounds of premenstrual tension, or premenstrual syndrome (PMS), as it has come to be known (Press 1983). One of the women had driven her car into her lover after an argument, killing him; the other woman (who had nearly thirty previous convictions for violent offenses) had stabbed her lover and threatened to kill a police officer. Their successful defenses were based on medical evidence that both suffered from a neuroendocrine disorder that led to exceptional premenstrual hormonal changes; these were said to transform them into "raging animals" who were not responsible for their aggressive acts because hormonal influences diminished their capacity to judge the wrongfulness of their acts or to control their conduct (*New York Times,* January 10, 1982). The future of this defense, like so many others now before courts throughout much of the world, must remain in doubt.[12]

The rules that define and circumscribe temporarily exempting conditions are as clear and as explicit as those that obtain under ordinary circumstances. This does not mean that such rules are posted, like "No Trespassing" signs, or published in decrees or, as M. Black (1962) asked us to imagine, recited every morning. Instead, people come to understand how someone can be expected to behave when sick, drunk, possessed, or depressed in the same ways that they come to understand how people can be expected to behave under ordinary conditions. The rules about appearing to be ill or grief-stricken, like the rules concerning exemption from certain responsibilities but not others as a result of illness or grief, may be either clear or ambiguous—but they are still rules.

Sometimes the rules are clear and are known to everyone, but sometimes they are ambiguous, contradictory, or disputed. Certain conditions, such as spirit possession, provide a virtual script for performing rule-breaking behavior with impunity; as long as the possessed person stays within the script, responsibility is suspended as a matter of course. Other conditions, such as many illnesses, are not so clearly scripted; these conditions may be argued about, and the outcome is not predetermined.

This raises an important point. As much as temporary exemptions from responsibility may benefit the exempted person, they may cause others distress, fear, or anger. When a possessed wife beats her husband with impunity or demands goods or services that he must provide, the husband is unlikely to be pleased. Among the Akamba of Kenya, where a temporary exemption of this kind was available to women, men were *anything* but pleased; they were angry, and they often complained into the night about the indignities visited upon them by their possessed wives. But they complied, because the rules of the culture gave them no choice; as one man said, shrugging, "It has always been this way; what can we do?" Temporary conditions can permit behaviors that disturb or frighten many people; drunken insults can be unpleasant, and drunken violence can result in serious injury and even death. But when the rules about temporary exemptions are clear—as they usually are about possession and intoxication—people are governed by them. Temporarily, they must make the best of an unpleasant situation. When the rules are ambiguous, as they may be where some illnesses are concerned, people may grant exemptions reluctantly or not at all.

Temporary exceptions may recur; a person is not limited to one illness or one drunken rampage. These are exempting conditions that people in societies must learn to live with, but they are not exemptions that the few claim from a long-suffering majority. While some temporary conditions are reserved for children or women, some are available to all. They may "happen" to people in the normal course of events, or they may be simulated for personal advantage. Many of these conditions—grief, illness, intoxication, and spirit possession, for example—can readily be exaggerated, prolonged, or faked altogether, but this is possible only because these rules for reducing responsibility have power. A claim to an exemption for being ill, drunk, possessed, or whatever may be rejected, and the claimant may suffer various sanctions as a result, not the least of which is ridicule.

Many people undoubtedly believe that under certain temporary conditions they would not be able to behave responsibly and should not, therefore, be held accountable. Unless these beliefs were held by most people in a society and unless they were based on shared rules, there would be no point in anyone trying to turn these rules to his or her own advantage.

CHAPTER 4

Statuses That Exempt

In addition to the temporary conditions that provide various degrees of exemption from ordinary responsibility, it is common for societies to establish longer-lasting, even lifelong, statuses that offer certain exemptions. This type of exception defines certain types of people as wholly or partially free from the responsibilities that bind most members of their society. This does *not* mean that some kinds of people are simply more entitled than others to claim temporary exemptions (although this also happens). What it does mean is that certain social categories of people may break some rules that others must follow; sometimes, responsibility for their rule violations is shifted to someone else. For example, in many societies, children, women, and slaves have had no legal responsibility for their acts; their parents, husbands, or masters were held responsible for what they did.[1] Lloyd Fallers (1969) reported that among the Busoga of Uganda, only men could be held legally responsible for adultery, because legally a wife was a man's property. As a Busoga chief explained (Fallers 1969:101), "You ask why the woman is never accused in adultery cases. But if someone were to steal your shoes, would you accuse the shoes?" Sometimes, types of persons exempted from responsibility for breaking some rules are held more responsible than most people for following other rules. So, in many societies, men may be free to commit adultery with impunity while women are strictly denied the right to any similar indiscretion, and slaves may be punished harshly for something that routinely goes unnoticed among free persons.

There are so many statuses in the world's societies which offer significant, rule-defined exemption from responsibility that even a very partial catalog of them would fill countless pages. Instead of attempting a listing of these, I shall suggest that exempting statuses can meaningfully be divided into two groups: (1) those that are, or are thought to be, more or less a product of biological constraints and (2) those that seem to have little to do with biological restrictions but everything to do with cultural ones.[2]

STATUSES INFLUENCED BY BIOLOGICAL CONSTRAINTS

In all societies, the ability of some persons to participate fully in their social and cultural world is limited by aspects of their own biology. The biological conditions that may reduce full responsibility for following the rules of one's culture can be relatively minor, as is the case with epilepsy, reduced motor coordination, or various injuries, but the constraints that some biological factors set may be quite limiting, as is the case with severe mental retardation, paraplegia, or blindness. Yet cultures differ markedly in the extent to which they prescribe rules allowing such biological limitations to reduce responsibility.

The very young and the very old provide cases in point. While no society could reasonably expect an infant or a senile octogenarian to be a fully responsible, rule-following citizen, what societies do expect of relatively small children and elderly persons varies greatly. As Margaret Mead (1937) pointed out, Zuni Indian parents reproached their children if they behaved in a childish way, while Samoan parents reproached theirs if they behaved as responsible adults. Over the course of European history, expectations for childhood responsibility have changed. In the middle of the eighteenth century in England, it was not uncommon for children under the age of ten to be hanged; as recently as 1831, a boy of nine was hanged at Chelmsford (Laurence 1960).[3] Such severity might not have surprised French historian Philippe Ariès (1965), who asserted that it was characteristic of medieval child-rearing to impose adult expectations on children who were barely out of infancy. While Ariès's account of such an early induction into a world of full responsibility has been questioned (Hunt 1970), it nevertheless contrasts sharply with the practice of prolonging childhood nonresponsibility well into adolescence that has characterized postindustrial society, particularly in middle-class America. Perhaps most extreme is the Irish pattern described by Arensberg (1959) and Scheper-Hughes (1979), in which a male could remain culturally a "boy," without full responsibility, until his marriage, which was often delayed until he was more than forty years of age.

Treatment of the elderly also varies. They are often granted no exemption from responsibility. They may be abandoned to die, as occurred in times of hardship in various hunting and gathering societies, or they may simply be "put away," as so frequently occurs in the contemporary United States (Laird 1979). The elderly may also not fare well in some tribal societies, such as that of the Thonga of southern Mozambique, who often abandoned their elderly to a solitary fate, reviling them all the while (Junod 1962:I, 132). Among the

Eskimo of western Greenland, "Old age, after a life of labor, brought no rewards. An old woman might be branded a witch and stoned to death, thrown into the sea, or cut to pieces" (Oswalt 1979:103). But other societies, such as the Kirghiz of Afghanistan (Sharani 1981), have indulged and honored the elderly, freeing them from many of life's responsibilities. In many tribal societies, women past childbearing age are allowed to act ribaldly. For the traditional Japanese, old age was considered to be a period of freedom and permissiveness. This was a significant exemption, because the Japanese were as concerned with conformity to rules of proper conduct as any people known. To maintain respect, the Japanese people meticulously followed many categorical rules, most of which were so moral that failure to obey them meant shame—something to be avoided at any cost. Yet, as Ruth Benedict pointed out in *The Chrysanthemum and the Sword* (1946), people aged sixty or older, like children under the age of 6 or 7, were indulged and allowed to act "without shame."

The Nigerian jurist T. O. Elias puckishly observed that age defined the extent of an individual's responsibility not just in the so-called age-graded societies of Africa or Australia but also in modern England (1956:105):

One does not often realise how important age is in English law, for example, until one looks at some such facts as these:
(a) Three-year-olds must be paid for on public transport.
(b) Five-year-olds must go to school.
(c) Eight-year-olds may now be prosecuted for crimes.

Elias went on to note that English fourteen-year-olds were permitted to enter a "public house" but could not drink alcohol in it; fifteen-year-olds were permitted to leave school; sixteen-year-olds were permitted to marry, subject to parental consent, and to smoke in public; seventeen-year-olds could drive a motor car and be tried as adults for crimes; eighteen-year-olds could drink in public, be conscripted into the armed forces, and be hanged for treason or murder; full legal capacity, including the right to marry without parents' consent and to vote, along with the obligation to be responsible for one's own debts, was finally achieved at age twenty-one. Most of these age distinctions, obviously, have nothing to do with biological incapacity.

But sometimes biological factors can play a role. The birth of intersexual children—or hermaphrodites, as they were formerly called—provides an instructive example of cultural variation in rule-reduced responsibility for persons with biological anomalies. It is probably a universal assumption that the world consists of only two biological sexes and that this is the natural and necessary way of things. It is understood that biological women may fail to behave in ways appropriate to their sex—they may act too masculine or too feminine or may even become transvestites, as European women did rather freely in medieval times (Bullough 1974)—but such persons are nevertheless known to be biological women. It is expected that people will be born with male *or* female bodies and that, despite a lifetime of acts that compromise or even reverse normal sex-role expectations, everyone will continue to live in the body of either a man or a woman.[4] Occasionally, however, children are born with bodies that are neither male nor female. These are the cases of intersexuality—that is, of individuals possessing some degree of anatomical or physiological sexual ambiguity often involving their external genital morphology.

Despite a growing underground demand in some of the larger cities in the United States for transvestite prostitutes—a few of whom have had their genitals altered surgically in order to increase their appeal—the prevailing attitude toward intersexual persons has clearly been one of aversion, so much so that such persons have often felt compelled to seek surgery in an effort to be transformed into an unambiguous gender, either male or female (Green 1974). The Pokot of Kenya also expressed profound aversion for intersexual persons. In Pokot culture, with its stress on sexuality, marriage, and reproduction, intersexual children were seen as a liability; those who survived did so by a combination of chance and of the willing adoption of a life of hard work with few pleasures (Edgerton 1964). Intersexual persons in Pokot society were not allowed significant rule-based exceptions to the demands of ordinary responsibility and propriety; indeed, they were held more responsible than others for following their society's rules. The Romans, too, provided no exemptions for such persons; intersexual infants were put to death because of a belief that they were auguries of divine displeasure that could lead to national disaster. The ancient Greeks, however, were tolerant of intersexual persons, permitting them to live full lives free of stigma and of some of the demands put on ordinary citizens (Cawadias 1943).

An even more indulgent view was taken by the Navaho Indians of the southwestern United States. As described by anthropologist W. W. Hill (1935), the Navaho offered intersexual persons a favored position in life.[5] Such persons were believed to be the supernaturally designated custodians of wealth, and any family with an intersexual child born to it had its future wealth and success assured. Parents were required to take special care with such children, who were "afforded favoritism not shown to other children of the family" (Hill 1935:274). As these children grew older, this special care changed to respect and virtual reverence, not only from the "favored" family but also from the community at large. Dressed as women, they generally acted as head of the family, with control over all property, and they were free to have sexual relations with men. One intersexual person told Hill (1935:278) of having had sexual relations with more than one hundred men, which would ordinarily have been a shocking violation of moral rules.

Hill (1935:274) was impressed with the Navaho respect for those who were intersexual:

> They were never made fun of and their abnormalities were never mentioned to them or by themselves. This respect verges almost on reverence in many cases. A few quotations from various informants will serve to make this attitude clearer. One states, "They know everything. They can do both the work of a man and a woman. I think when all the *nadle* [intersexuals] are gone that it will be the end of the Navaho." Another says, "If there were no *nadle,* the country would change. They are responsible for all wealth in the country. If there were no more left, the horses, sheep, and Navaho would all go. They are leaders just like President Roosevelt." A third says, "A *nadle* around the hogan will bring good luck and riches." A fourth that "They have charge of all the riches. It does a great deal for the country if you have a *nadle* around." And a fifth, "You must respect a *nadle.* They are, somehow, sacred and holy."

Depending on the society in which they live, persons who are blind, like those who are intersexual, may or may not be granted exemptions from ordinary responsibility for proper conduct. Intersexual persons present an anomaly that can be interpreted as a sign of divine displeasure or delight, but in most societies, these people can be economically productive. Blind persons, however, are an economic liability in many societies. It is not surprising, then, that there are many societies in which blind persons receive no exemptions. As we noted before, some Eskimo bands lived so close to the margin of survival that on many occasions they left behind their old and infirm, some of whom, at least, readily acquiesced in seeking death so that the rest of the band could hunt more efficiently and thus, perhaps, survive (Stefansson 1951).[6] In that harsh environment, the nonproductive person, such as a blind man, had no chance, as Bilby (1923:150) illustrated with his account of a man named Nandla: "The inexorable law of the wild left one handicapped as Nandla with no choice. The man was comparatively young, but by reason of his blindness useless to himself and a burden upon others. In a hungry land, where every extra mouth to be filled represents a problem, there is no room for one who cannot provide for himself." During a long period of scarcity, Nandla's fellow Eskimo one day led him to a gaping seal hole in the ice into which he unseeingly stepped and drowned.

The Marsh Arabs, who lived at the confluence of the Tigris and Euphrates rivers in Iraq, also had periods of food shortage, yet, as explorer Wilfred Thesiger (1964:168) reported, they protected and indulged the blind: "The tribesmen were especially kind to the afflicted, and among them a major physical disability was perhaps less of a handicap than in some parts of the world. . . . A boy, though born blind, moved freely about in the village, and even went out a short way by himself in a canoe to collect hashish."

In his book *The Making of Blind Men,* sociologist Robert A. Scott (1969) described differences in the extent to which blind persons are exempted from responsibility in various Western countries, including the United States. Anthropologist John L. Gwaltney (1970), himself blind, described blindness as an exempting status in the small village of San Pedro Xolox in Oaxaca, Mexico. As a result of the blindness-causing disease, onchocerciasis, San Pedro Xolox had the largest blind population—twenty-one persons—of any village in the infected zone of Oaxaca. These twenty-one persons, most of whom were elderly, imposed a heavy economic burden on their households and relatives, since they were unable to contribute to their families' subsistence. Gwaltney (1970:105) quoted a villager as saying, "Everyone's blindness is a cross which he and his kin must carry alone."

Nevertheless, the blind of San Pedro Xolox were not only exempted from the necessity of making any economic contributions but were thoroughly indulged. For example, young children led blind persons around the village "out of love," they said, and in general the blind were accorded public courtesy. Moreover, as Gwaltney (1970:110–111) noted, their rule violations were largely excused:

> There is a pronounced decrease in malicious gossip about blind persons and their public "abuses" are treated with far less severity than the same offenses committed by sighted villagers: "When Don Rafael made himself drunk after much drinking and abused some of the people with many hard words and even struck some with his sticks, it was a bad thing. But the authority did not make him pay a *multa* [fine] as they would if he were a sound man. They spoke mildly to him and he answered them softly and no one spoke of it very much after that for we were all ashamed."

As noted in the last chapter, exhibiting symptoms of mental illness may or may not provide exemption from responsibility. In some societies, such as Micronesian Ulithi, mentally ill persons may destroy property and assault others with impunity; in others, such conduct results in harsh penalties. But this societal variation in according exemptions for the mentally ill should not be surprising. Mental illness comes in a multiplicity of forms, and even the most severe psychoses may manifest themselves only episodically. What is more, most mental illness does not occur until late adolescence or adulthood, after a more or less normal earlier life during which a network of concerned or obligated parents, kinsmen, spouses, or children may have been established. When mental illness occurs, then, it often does so after a history of social participation and worth.

The severely mentally retarded—"idiots," in earlier language—have no such history. Such persons are usually born with visible physical stigmata, and it is apparent early in life that their capacity to learn rules and follow them is dramatically impaired. Such persons have so little prospect of establishing social relationships or social value that one might reasonably expect societal reaction to be anything but indulgent. And so it is, or was, in many of the world's societies, where these children were killed or were left exposed to die; the Northern Saulteaux Indians, for example, burned them alive (Skinner 1912). But this was not always their fate; severely retarded children, including microcephalics, survived in a number of the world's small-scale, remote societies (Edgerton 1970), and in some they were not simply tolerated but were also given a favored and exempted status. C. H. Hawes (1903) wrote about a retarded man named Oto among the Gilyak, a Siberian people who regarded retardates as having sacred religious powers. Oto was not required to work for his subsistence; all his needs were supplied by others, "for they regarded him as a kind of sacred person singled out or set apart by the unseen powers" (Hawes 1903:251). Similar examples have been reported from Cambodia, pre-Soviet peasant Russia, central Asia, Nepal, India, and various parts of the Islamic world (Edgerton 1970).

Because of the extent of their intellectual disability, severely mentally retarded persons are unable to comprehend or follow most of their culture's rules, from implicit conventions to moral and supernatural rules. As a result, these persons require—and sometimes receive—almost total exemption from responsibility. In societies where a breach of a supernatural rule or injunction can pollute or otherwise endanger others, we might surmise that severely mentally retarded persons would require close supervision or that their

breaches would be culturally discounted as meaningless and inconsequential.[7]

CULTURALLY DEFINED EXEMPTING STATUSES

Statuses that confer exemption from ordinary responsibility sometimes do so because persons are biologically limited in their ability to
learn or to follow the rules of their society or to participate in valued
social activities. The severely mentally retarded are an example and
young children are another. But, as we have noted, many societies
allow—or require—the young and the very old to escape full responsibility for following various kinds of rules. The same phenomenon
can be illustrated by the various ways in which societies exempt
another category of persons who do not know how to conduct themselves properly. This category includes strangers (traders, war captives, refugees, shipwrecked sailors, conquering soldiers, tourists, and
so on), who often do not know the rules of the alien societies in which
they suddenly find themselves. Often strangers are feared or detested
and are put to death before responsibility for rule-following can
become an issue; sometimes, however, strangers are tolerated or wel-
comed, and, as with tourists in many countries today, a great number
of their rule violations may be overlooked.[8]

In all probability, most exempting statuses have nothing whatever
to do with biological limitations. For example, most socially stratified
societies have granted some degree of exemption to persons in positions of political power, although a few have insisted on *noblesse oblige*.
Kings, dictators, political leaders, and the very wealthy have been
granted such exemption—or have arrogated it unto themselves—in
most Western societies. Indeed, many continue today to have at least
partial immunity from prosecution. In earlier times, such exemptions
could be extraordinary. In his review of the history of criminal law
in England, Sir James Fitzjames Stephen (1883) noted numerous
statuses that were exempt from ordinary legal sanctions.[9] The clergy,
for example, had many exemptions—so many, in fact, that at least
until 1779, "benefit of clergy" had a literal meaning. Indeed, Stephen
(1883:463) observed with undisguised disfavor that the privileges of
clergy had brought the administration of justice in England "to a sort
of farce." He continued (1883:463–464):

> Till 1487 any one who knew how to read might commit murder as often
> as he pleased, with no other result than that of being delivered to the

ordinary to make his purgation, with the chance of being delivered to him "absque purgatione." That this should have been the law for several centuries seems hardly credible, but there is no doubt that it was. Even after 1487 a man who could read could commit murder once with no other punishment than that of having M branded on the brawn of his left thumb, and if he was a clerk in orders he could till 1547 commit any number of murders apparently without being branded more than once.

Exemptions for the wealthy or influential have occurred—and continue to occur—not only in societies with well-defined statuses of political authority but also in societies in which authority roles are weakly defined. For example, the Akamba of Kenya had no clear status that conferred political authority, but they did allow one category of person—rich men, especially rich elders—to break rules that others were compelled to follow strictly (Edgerton 1971*b*). Like many societies, the Akamba had a very clear and strictly enforced rule requiring a man to avoid his mother-in-law. This explicit rule, called *ndoni*, required a man to go to such extreme and unpleasant lengths to avoid his mother-in-law that if the two met on a narrow path and no other means of avoiding each another existed, the son-in-law was obliged to dive off the path, even if the only available landing place was in a thornbush. Ndoni was as categorical as a rule could be. Nevertheless, the Swedish anthropologist Gerhard Lindblom (1920:91) recorded the following episode:

> Kisese, an elderly man living north of Machakos, took part in a drinking-bout close to his mother-in-law's village. When very drunk and incapable of recognizing people, he went to her hut in the evening, where he crept into the *we* [sleeping place] and went to sleep, not waking until the following morning. The consternation of the people at this event was indescribable, and even Kisese must have felt sheepish at first. Having been a leader in the time of the wars, however, he was equal to the occasion. He at once sent a messenger home for a fat ox and some goats, which he presented to his mother-in-law, saying "From this time forth all *ndoni* is over between us two." If he had been a youth, it would probably have cost him dear, but as he was a rich and influential man, he got his own way.

There are many other societies that lack formal authority statuses yet allow some wealthy and influential men to achieve exemption from rules that bind lesser men. A well-known example comes from the Kapauku of the highlands of Papua New Guinea. As described by anthropologist Leo Pospisil (1971), the Kapauku recognized neither chiefs nor formal leaders, but they did have a status called *tonowi*, which literally means "wealthy man." Pospisil (1971) described the actions of a Kapauku headman, Awaiitigaaj, who decided to violate one of his culture's most important rules. The results included changes that affected an entire confederacy of people. Pospisil reported that Awaiitigaaj was so enthusiastic about feminine charms that he had already acquired no fewer than ten of the most comely women in the area as wives, when he encountered an eleventh whose beauty was too great for him to resist. If the mere fact of having ten wives was not enough to give Awaiitigaaj pause, the fact that the clan membership of the eleventh beauty made marriage to her a serious breach of the Kapauku law forbidding incest should have been enough. Indeed, the prescribed penalty for breaking this law was death. Undaunted, Awaiitigaaj married her, then fled to avoid execution at the hands of outraged villagers and kinsmen. After much complicated legal maneuvering, the eleventh wife's kinsmen made a tactical error that compelled the community to accept the marriage as a *fait accompli*.

This dramatic episode should not be put aside as simply an epic example of human lust or arrogance in a social system where a clever and audacious headman was sometimes able to break rules without accountability. Subsequent acts by Awaiitigaaj made it clear that he was no mere lecher. He used every opportunity to transform his "crime" into a morally justifiable and socially desirable exception to the incest rule. For example, when Pospisil asked him in public about his motives in this extraordinary saga of incest and marriage, Awaiitigaaj offered this explanation (1958*b*:833): "To marry [a girl of the same sib and generation] is good as long as she is a second paternal parallel cousin. In the old days people did not think of this possibility, but now it is permissible. . . . To marry [such a girl] is not bad, indeed it is nice; in this way one becomes rich." Awaiitigaaj, then, claimed to have found a rule that made his misconduct acceptable, and he actually referred to this new rule he had discovered as a law. But when Pospisil (1958*b*:834) questioned Awaiitigaaj in private, his response was different and cynical, to say the least: "I think whoever likes any girl should be able to marry her. I set up the new taboo only in order to break down the old restrictions. The people are like that. One has to tell them lies."

Awaiitigaaj's tactics are revealing of the power that Kapauku rules could have. When he first plotted his strategy, he assumed that by playing for time (hiding in the bush after the marriage so that his bride's relatives could not find him), he would give the girl's father further time to realize that his own self-interest did not lie in outraged morality that would lead him to kill the girl or Awaiitigaaj and thereby lose the still unpaid bride price due him. This appears to have been exactly what happened. The girl's father eventually tempered his initial demands for mayhem and sent go-betweens to Awaiitigaaj's relatives to arrange for payment of the bride wealth. This act was an implicit recognition of the incestuous marriage. It was also recognition on the part of the girl's relatives that there were clear advantages to a marriage to someone as wealthy, clever, and powerful as Awaiitigaaj. Unfortunately, their best-laid plans went awry when Awaiitigaaj's relatives were successful in their plan to provoke the girl's relatives into violence. By Kapauku law, such a display of violence both cemented the marriage and absolved Awaiitigaaj's relatives from the obligation to pay the bride price (Pospisil 1971:216–217). By calculating the relative power of Kapauku laws and by exploiting his own power, Awaiitigaaj won.

Pospisil concluded his account of Awaiitigaaj's use of privilege and power as follows (1971:218):

> The happiest man, of course, was Awaiitigaaj, whose scheming genius had accomplished the seemingly impossible. Not only did he manage to go unpunished and keep his incestuous bride as his wife, but he was also absolved from the usually onerous payment of the bride price, for which his patrilineal relatives had to pay with bleeding scalps, a couple of fractured noses, and bruised bodies. Although they were beaten, and the girl's father suffered the loss of the bride price, Awaiitigaaj gained the woman, was absolved from the payment for her, and successfully broke an established taboo.

In Awaiitigaaj's case, the accomplishments and the absolutions could only have been achieved by a man of wealth and power, but they also required unusual intelligence and strong nerves and, as Pospisil emphasized, a knowledge of Kapauku rules and laws and of how to use them.

Sometimes, however, a man who occupies a potentially exempting status may attempt to bend rules to his advantage only to suffer a surprising comedown. A. J. F. Köbben (1979) described such an occurrence among the Djuka, a Maroon society of Surinam, where an important elder who was serving as temporary headman of his village broke the rules of clan incest by impregnating a young woman of his own clan. Köbben said that such a matter would ordinarily have been settled quickly by sanctioning a normal marriage ritual but that in this case the presumptuous headman was tried, punished, and subjected to public humiliation by the priests. Commenting on the headman's failed maneuver, Köbben made this observation (1979:334):

> It should be noted that this punishment by the priests was also a political maneuver. They did not want the man in question to become village headman, and this affair gave them an opportunity to campaign against him.

Sometimes, as among the Amazonian Kagwahiv, the rules relating to the behavior of leaders are purposefully ambiguous, allowing such men great freedom in using these rules to justify their actions. Waud Kracke describes how one leader, Jovenil, was accepted by his followers, while another man, Homero, was rejected (1978:68):

> Homero lost his followers' support by transgressing the norms of Kagwahiv leadership style, demanding more from his followers than was acceptable, claiming extranormative privileges, and giving commands in a way that is not simply not done.

Yet, as Kracke learned, Jovenil, the successful leader, behaved in very much the same ways as Homero. What is more, the complaints about Homero were clearly contradictory. Kracke's (1978:69) conclusion repeated what we have learned from many societies, not excluding our own, and this is that one man's violation of a rule may be justified by his status, another's may be overlooked, and still another's may be exaggerated and used against him.

In the rough-and-tumble world of strategic interaction in small societies, it is no doubt typical that claimants to special privilege fail at least as often as they succeed and that those who do succeed may lose their exemptions as quickly as they achieved them. Shamans, prophets, and rainmakers, for example, may quickly gain unusual privileges to break social rules for their own advantage by virtue of their successful exploits, but when their cures fail, their predictions are unfulfilled, or the rains do not materialize, they may just as quickly lose their privileged statuses and sometimes even their lives.

Still, persons in statuses such as these may be permitted to violate rules with extraordinary impunity—at least for a while—and some may do so throughout life. For example, the Netsilik Eskimo of Greenland were horrified by incest, especially that between parents and children, and according to Knud Rasmussen (1931), violations of incest rules were "exceedingly rare." Nevertheless, a Netsilik shaman was permitted to violate these and other rules of proper sexual conduct with impunity. Rasmussen (1931:198) reported that a shaman named Quvloruarneq became "very great" and "famous" because he had sexual relations with his mother—with impunity.

Other statuses exist that allow people to escape the burdens of everyday economic, military, or sexual responsibilities. In our society, for example, a conscientious objector need not serve in military combat, an alcoholic may be shielded from many of the stresses of everyday life, and a schizophrenic may receive a stipend from the government that relieves him of all economic duties. Such statuses are socially stigmatized, but for a person who finds ordinary accountability too burdensome, they may be desirable nonetheless. The extent to which volition is involved in "choosing" a status such as this varies, of course; some people who drink heavily may try to avoid being labeled an alcoholic, while others may welcome the label and the idea that they suffer from a disease (Snyder, Higgins and Stucky 1983).

Non-Western societies frequently offer similar options. Perhaps the best-known example of an "escape hatch" status that may be chosen consciously is the so-called *berdache* status that was available in many warlike North American Indian societies. Young men in such societies could avoid duties as warriors, as well as those as husbands, by assuming the dress and social role of females (Jacobs 1968).[10] In Hindu India, a similar kind of escape from social stresses and obligations could be obtained by renouncing worldly life and becoming a wandering ascetic or joining a monastic order (Dumont 1960). Describing the monks and monasteries of Bhubaneswar, Miller and Wertz (1976) found that many who had chosen the monastic life had done so as an escape from economic or marital failures. Others, seeing the poverty of their parents, had chosen monastic life early in their youth.

Anthropologist Gerald Berreman, who has written extensively about inequality in India, described the feelings of almost intolerable oppression and despair experienced by many stigmatized, low-caste persons, the so-called untouchables. Berreman (1979) pointed out that despite formidable obstacles, some untouchables continually attempted to escape their degraded status by whatever means were available to them. Writing of a small Indian village named Sirkanda, Berreman described the lives of several untouchables and their efforts to escape their status as blacksmiths, among the most stigmatized of the castes. One man succeeded by virtue of becoming possessed by a deity so powerful that he was able to become an extraordinarily successful shaman who was "an exalted, awe-inspiring figure, rewarded with money and food as well as respect and deference—but required to abstain from many worldly pursuits in order to retain this status" (Berreman 1979:172). The new status was regarded as an involuntary consequence of divine forces; to what extent this man manipulated his apparent supernatural possession for his own advantage, we do not know.

Another blacksmith escaped by simulating the behavior of a psychotic, also a traditionally recognized status that set one free from caste restrictions (Berreman 1979:171):

> He had severed all ties to the village, and now made his meagre living collecting wood and other forest products for sale in the market. He lived wherever he wished, moving from place to place unencumbered and accountable to no one. He had become a social deviant, but in no sense that I or my assistant could detect, was he mentally deranged. He rejoiced in his freedom from the constraints of untouchable life in a small and tightly bounded village. He had escaped his birth-ascribed status at the cost of economic security, family life and stability—a price he was willing to pay for freedom. No sanctions were brought against him because his was regarded as a malady brought on by fate rather than choice.

Anthropologist P. L. Newman (1964) described a man who was unable to cope with mounting economic burdens among the Gururumba of the Papua New Guinea highlands; he escaped these obligations by exhibiting "wild man" behavior and, while he lost a measure of social respect as a result, he achieved a status that required far less of him. The Gururumba emphasized economic exchange, and most Gururumba found great psychological (and material) satisfaction in these exciting and potentially enriching exchanges. But some Gururumba did not share these feelings. Newman described a man named Gambiri who was in his mid-thirties, married, with one child and with another on the way. Like most young Gururumba men, Gambiri was indebted to his kinsmen and villagers for the food and other wealth that he had to acquire in order to pay for his bride. The pressure to repay all these people was intense, and Gambiri apparently could not cope with it. Newman (1964:96–97) summarized Gambiri's reaction:

> One day Gambiri began exhibiting the behavior the Gururumba describe as "being a wild pig." For three days he roamed about the village and its environs attacking people, bursting into houses and stealing things. His actions had all the classic signs of anxiety hysteria: his speech and

hearing were partially blocked, he had lost full motor control, he behaved irrationally, and when he did speak it was either in the form of commands or blatantly false statements. The onset of this attack was sudden and when it was over, he claimed no memory of it.

The result was a little like declaring bankruptcy; the economic pressure was reduced. Newman concluded that as a result of this episode people made fewer demands on Gambiri to enter into exchange relationships. Of course, there is nothing inherently exempting about wild-man behavior. Quite similar behavior occurred in other Papua New Guinea highland societies without its leading to a reduction in responsibility (Langness 1965).

Escape-hatch statuses such as those described by Newman and Berreman do allow certain individuals to avoid some kinds of responsibilities, but it is always at a social price. However, in most—perhaps all—societies, there are other statuses that *require* people to behave in ways that would ordinarily be highly offensive, yet this misconduct carries with it no social penalties. For example, rules that require people to make public expressions of disrespect for one another are widespread. A. R. Radcliffe-Brown (1940) was among the first to focus attention on such rules, observing that cross-cousins, in-laws, or even neighboring tribesmen were permitted or required to tease, ridicule, or insult one another while the victims of this uncharacteristic abuse or raillery were required not to take offense. These insults or acts of ridicule took place in public and usually evoked great hilarity on the part of the onlookers. Radcliffe-Brown referred to these exchanges as "joking relationships."

Writing of the Tarahumara Indians of northern Mexico, John G. Kennedy noted that while joking relationships often involved young people of the same sex, such as siblings-in-law or cross-cousins they also involved people of different sexes and generations. He described grandmothers and grandfathers rolling on the ground and pretending to copulate with one another, while the audience howled with glee (1970:42). Kennedy also recorded the still more remarkable phenomenon of cross-sex, alternate-generation joking relationships (1970:42):

> In one typical incident, an old man held a corn cob in a manner simulating a penis as he laughingly chased his granddaughters of about sixteen and nineteen years, attempting to raise their skirts. The girls responded by trying to lift his loincloth and by deprecating his sexual ability. In another situation a boy of about seventeen was observed to make rough

sexual overtures to a classificatory grandmother. She showed annoyance and discomfort, but permitted his advance, disengaging herself as soon as was expedient.

Persons who shared a joking relationship among the Tarahumara, like people in Africa and elsewhere, were also required to make lewd jokes and gestures while disposing of a deceased relative. Only they could handle the deceased's possessions and the corpse itself without danger, and they did so with the utmost disrespect—laughing, making outrageous jokes, and insulting or threatening the corpse or a simulation of it (Kennedy 1970:41).

Sometimes, license to joke or to insult others was not only available to persons who stood in a particular relationship to one another but became the full-time right of someone in a particular status. In medieval times in Europe, the status of the fool provided license to escape the full measure of the law, even though it was the powerful persons at court who most keenly felt the sting of the fool's mockery. Members of medieval societies of fools were able to claim similar license for briefer periods by donning the motley dress of the fool (Welsford, 1936). A comparable status has existed in many societies. Junod (1962) described a kind of court jester whom he referred to as "the public vituperator" among the Thonga of Mozambique. This person's position, *shitale*, was officially recognized and was hereditary; no Thonga, not even the chief, was safe from the insults and accusations of the vituperator, who enjoyed complete immunity from punishment. Junod (1962:428–429) quoted a Thonga informant as follows:

> "Just see him arriving in your village," said Tobane to me, in his picturesque language. "He begins shouting out the most frightful things. He accuses you of incest, of taking your own sisters as wives! Even if he sees you talking to your 'great sister-in-law,' whom your wife's brother married with your oxen, whom you treat with the greatest respect, he will not hesitate to pass remarks which will make you blush with shame! . . . once he begins to rattle off his vituperations, beware! Nothing will stop him! He respects nothing, human or divine!"

Like the vituperator among the Thonga, clowns in many societies had license for outrageous conduct. In modern Samoa, as anthropologist Bradd Shore (1978:178) described, they were free to speak openly about socially sensitive matters because they were thought to be possessed by ghosts:

Comedy and satirical skits were traditionally a high-point of the festivities put on by travelling parties in Samoa. The social licence permitted to the clowns was, and remains, extraordinary, particularly given the normal Samoan emphasis on tact, propriety and etiquette in most public performances. . . . The most common objects of the ridicule are the high, the respected, those most clearly in authority, to whom one must normally show elaborate deference. Pastors, the elderly, Europeans, chiefs and political leaders all become the objects of wild, mocking laughter.

A similar pattern of license existed on the nearby island of Tokelau (Huntsman and Hooper 1975).[11]

A related, and even more extreme, example of social license occurred in pre-Christian Tahiti. The *'arioi* organization, or sect, formed what Robert Levy (1973:469) has called a privileged, institutionalized antistructure "which violated many of the taboos and proprieties of old Tahiti." Dedicated to the god Oro, members of the 'arioi were found in all districts of Tahiti, sometimes in substantial numbers. Most members were unmarried men, but there were seven or eight classes of membership, so that even men of old age still belonged. So did some women, although their role in the sect is not clearly understood (Oliver 1974:III, 1107). The 'arioi were exempt from most requirements for proper conduct. For example, they were free to ridicule or lampoon priests and chiefs, conduct that was likely to result in death for other Tahitians (Oliver 1974:III, 1054; Ellis 1829:I, 317). Moreover, they could apparently demand any personal property they wished and could not be denied it. They were even immune to the otherwise murderous attacks of masked mourners who, following the death of a prominent person, armed themselves with clubs and spears and attacked with impunity anyone they met, even chiefs. Only the 'arioi were safe from these attacks.

The 'arioi also had license to engage in extraordinary sexual promiscuity. James Morrison (1935:234), who arrived aboard the *Bounty* in 1792, described the 'arioi as a "set of young men of wild, amorous, and volatile dispositions who from their infancy devoted the youthful part of their lives to roving pleasure and debauchery." The extent to which members of the 'arioi had license to violate the customary Tahitian reserve and sexual decorum can be seen in the following description of a public performance given by some male members of the 'arioi as described by Captain Bligh of the *Bounty* (1937:II, 35):

The men now began their performance, which of all things that was ever beheld I imagine was the most uncommon and detestable. They suddenly took off what clothing they had about their hips and appeared quite naked. One of the men was prepared for his part, for the whole business now became the power and capability of distorting the penis and testicles, making at the same time wanton and lascivious motions. The person who was ready to begin had his penis swelled and distorted out into an erection by having a severe twine ligature close up to the *os pubis* applied so tight that the penis was apparently almost cut through. The second brought his stones to the head of the penis and with a small cloth bandage he wrapped them round and round, up towards the belly, stretching them at the same time very violently until they were near a foot in length which the bandage kept them erect at, the stones and head of the penis being like three small balls at the extremity. The third person was more horrible than the other two, for with both hands seizing the extremity of the scrotum, he pulled it out with such force that the penis went in totally out of sight and the scrotum became shockingly distended. In this manner they danced about the ring for a few minutes when I desired them to desist and the Heivah ended. It however afforded much laughter among the spectators.

The 'arioi sect was unusual not only in the extent to which its members might break important rules with impunity but also because a substantial number of persons enjoyed these extraordinary exemptions for a large portion of their lives. More typical of the world's societies were more episodic exemptions, such as those enjoyed by clowns in North American Indian societies. Among these peoples—from the Iroquois "false faces" and the Plains Indian "contraries" to the Northwest Coast Kwakiutl "fool dancers"—clowns, often masked, from time to time behaved in unnatural and outrageous ways (Ray 1945). For example, clowning was well developed among the Zuni Indians, where members of the *Koyemshi* society had important duties in the sacred ritual cycle, among which was the right and obligation to serve as masked clowns who amused, frightened, and shocked their audiences. Because the Koyemshi clowns were defined socially as children, they were not responsible for their actions, which included obscene dances, scatological acts, outrageous speeches, and shameless female impersonation. As Ruth Bunzel (1929/30:521) wrote, "The sacred clowns are privileged to mock anything, and to indulge in any obscenity." Although these men acquired their status as clowns through membership in an exclusive society, they performed as clowns only at certain times of the year as determined by the Zuni ritual cycle. Their social right to break rules, then, derived in part from their status and in part from the special occasions in which they participated. This pattern was common (Crumrine 1969; Ortiz 1972) not only for North American Indian clowns but also for many others who, because of their status, were free to break the rules of their societies, at least for a time.

All societies must deal with the dilemma posed by children and by those adults who are unable to be fully productive because of developmental disabilities, illness, or injury. Whether a society responds by offering a favored, indulged status or by abandoning such persons depends on a multitude of economic factors, supernatural beliefs, the interests of corporate groups, and, not inconsiderably, the affection felt toward an afflicted person.[12] In addition to these kinds of statuses, most societies (and perhaps all) allow special persons such as headmen, clowns, shamans, ascetics, and transvestites to violate many rules with remarkable impunity. Because of their special social identity, such persons may literally get away with murder, may break incest rules, or may ridicule and revile the most powerful members of their societies.

Although the right of these persons to break important rules, including moral and supernatural ones, is usually clearly understood to be prescribed by rules that define the rights of persons in a particular status, there is often a social price to be paid for these "rights." Sometimes the person—the ascetic, psychotic or berdache—surrenders economic privileges, access to women, and rights to participate in various kinds of pleasurable social exchanges. Such persons may be forced to live in social isolation and to feel contempt. Moreover, some special statuses, such as those of shaman, vituperator, or headman, may generate envy and resentment—so much so, indeed, that ordinary people may take every opportunity to remove such a person from their indulged status. The status itself will probably survive, but its recent incumbent may not. Those who use rules to break rules may miscalculate and may be broken themselves by still other rules.

In this chapter, the place of status—both temporary and permanent—in reducing responsibility has been highlighted. In the following chapter, we turn to special occasions during which people may be allowed or required to violate fundamental rules with immunity from sanctions.

CHAPTER 5

Occasions That Exempt

Few aspects of human affairs have attracted more attention than have ritual events. These rituals, often called ceremonies and variously defined, are unchallenged as the most visible and exciting occasions for the display of rule-based exemptions from ordinary propriety.[1] Edward Norbeck (1974:50) offered this concise description:

> Ritual behavior of any kind is always somehow extraordinary, and hundreds of societies have hit upon the idea of doing as ritual acts things that reverse or oppose normal procedures and normal values. The customs of reversal are, of course, themselves norms; their special nature is that they oppose the norms applying at other times. Reversals may be only small elements of rites of any class or kind, or they may be the guiding theme of grand festivals. They are included in rites as diverse as funerals, weddings, initiation ceremonies and other rites of passage, cyclic rites, witchcraft, rain ceremonies, and rites propitiating ancestral spirits.

Many of these ritual occasions not only allow aggression, obscenity, indecency, sacrilege, theft, and the destruction of property, they often *demand* that these violations of propriety, values, and law take place.

Why ritual occasions should so often upset or reverse the rules of ordinary life has fascinated scholars from many disciplines. Between the time of Arnold Van Gennep's (1909) portrayal of ceremonies in terms of separation, liminality, and reaggregation and Victor Turner's (1974) elaboration of the idea of liminality and his notion of "communitas," many distinguished scholars have offered influential theories about the nature and function of ceremonies and the rule reversals they so often include. Emile Durkheim emphasized the idea that ceremonies brought about social solidarity; E. E. Evans-Pritchard's (1929) analysis of collective expressions of obscenity is less well-known but no less important. Evans-Pritchard emphasized the role of ritual obscenities in dramatizing the social importance of the activity being focused on, such as collective labor, as well as the capacity of these rituals to channel dangerous emotions into prescribed activities. These views presaged later, more complex formulations by Max Gluckman (1954,1959), Monica Wilson (1959), Edward Norbeck

(1963), Victor Turner (1969), and many others. In another genre, scholars such as Gregory Bateson (1958), Alfred Schutz (1967), Erving Goffman (1974), and Erik Erikson (1977) called attention to various devices that people use to shift from "ordinary" or "serious" reality to play, dreams, or theater—that is, to nonserious or extraordinary occasions when the rules are changed so that the unusual or outrageous becomes acceptable and expected.

There is little agreement about the alleged functions of ceremonies—whether their purpose is to resolve conflict, create social solidarity, maintain authority, or support a system of values—but one thing is clear: the rules of everyday life are often violated during ceremonies, and sometimes they *must* be. What is more, these rules are violated with impunity, because other rules—rules that apply with great force—take over on ceremonial occasions. There are many types of rituals, both religious and secular,[2] but for our purposes here, examples of three general types of ritual occasions will be sufficient: (1) cyclical-calendrical rites; (2) status change, "life crisis," or initiation ceremonies; and (3) rituals of "women's rights." The first two are well-known, but the third is much less so.

CYCLICAL-CALENDRICAL RITES

Examples of exemptions from conventions, moral rules, taboos, and even laws during cyclical or calendrical rites can be provided from virtually every part of the world. While such rites sometimes occur among hunting and gathering peoples, they are more common and elaborate among more settled horticultural people (Eliade 1958), and they persist in such contemporary ceremonies as the Mardi Gras of New Orleans and the carnivals of Brazil and Trinidad. Edward Norbeck, who reviewed cyclical rituals throughout Africa, reached the following conclusion (1963:1272):

> The rites reviewed here make it clear that African customs allow periodic freedom from restraints of many kinds. At the same sorts of occasions and often the identical times that one is allowed to 'speak out,' he is often also freed from other normal restraints. He may violate rules of sexual behavior, indulge in lewdness and obscenity, commit theft, and take many other liberties.

As Norbeck also noted (1963:1267), not only are these rule violations shocking to the ethnographers who report them but such dramatic

violations of propriety or law are also often shocking to the participants themselves.

So it was, for example, during Han dynasty times, when the Chinese
celebrated the end of the agricultural year with a thanksgiving festival
called *cha*. This festival featured, among other forms of license, sexual
orgies (Bodde 1975:71):

> . . . the festival had the characteristics of an orgy, with much eating and
> drinking, music, dancing, and ceremonial masquerades, "in which the
> people of the entire state appeared as if mad."

The Iroquois Indians of the northeastern United States celebrated
a midwinter ceremony called *ononhara*, which combined aspects of
curing, dream guessing, and thanksgiving feasting (Tooker 1970).
Like *cha*, it involved a period of dramatic license. Father LeJeune
witnessed a portion of the *ononhara* ceremony concerned with curing
(Thwaites 1896:Vol.17:179):

> The third [portion of the ceremony] followed, which, according to forms
> and customs, consists in a general mania of all the people of the village,
> who—except, perhaps, a few Old Men—undertake to run wherever the
> sick woman has passed, adorned or daubed in their fashion, vying with
> one another in the frightful contortions of their faces—making
> everywhere such a din, and indulging in such extravagance, that, to
> explain them and make them better understood, I do not know if I
> ought not to compare them, either to the most extravagant of our
> maskers that one has ever heard of, or the bacchantes of the ancients,
> or rather to the furies of Hell. They enter, then, everywhere, and have
> during the time of the feast, in all the evenings and nights of the three
> days that it lasts, liberty to do anything, and no one dares say a word to
> them. If they find kettles over the fire, they upset them; they break the
> earthen pots, knock down the logs, throw fire and ashes everywhere, so
> thoroughly that often the cabins and entire villages burn down.

Sometimes, ritual license was so extreme that the most fundamental
moral and supernatural rules were broken. During the Hindu ceremony *Sakti-puja*, as it was performed by the followers of Vishnu,
the rules that ordinarily strictly required caste avoidances could be
violated without fear of ritual pollution (Dubois 1897:286–287):

> People of all castes, from the Brahmin to the Pariah, are invited to
> attend. When the company are assembled, all kinds of meat, including
> beef, are placed before the idol of *Vishnu*. Afterwards the *pujari*, or
> sacrificer, who is generally a Brahmin, first of all tastes the various kinds

of meats and liquors himself, and then gives the others permission to devour the rest. Men and women thereupon begin to eat greedily, the same piece of meat passing from mouth to mouth, each person taking a bite, until it is finished. Then they start afresh on another joint, which they gnaw in the same manner, tearing the meat out of each other's mouths. When all the meat has been consumed, intoxicating liquors are passed round, every one drinking without repugnance out of the same cup. Opium and other drugs disappear in a similar fashion. Men persuade themselves that under these circumstances they do not contract impurity by eating and drinking in so revolting a manner. When they are all completely intoxicated, men and women no longer keep apart, but pass the rest of the night together, giving themselves up without any risk of disagreeable consequences. A husband who sees his wife in another man's arms cannot recall her, nor has he the right to complain; for at those times every woman becomes common property. Perfect equality exists among all castes, and the Brahmin is not of higher caste than the Pariah.

Although intoxication undoubtedly helped to define this ceremony as a time for extraordinary exemptions (a role played by intoxication in many ceremonies), we should recall that dramatic rule violations— such as passing meat from the mouths of pariahs to the mouths of Brahmins—took place *before* anyone had consumed intoxicating substances.

The varieties of ceremonies that take place on a calendrical or cyclical basis are too many to summarize, but one extremely widespread form of ceremony in which rule reversals take place occurs at year's end. In various parts of the world from ancient Babylon to the modern United States, the year's end is as Theodore Gaster (1955:15) put it in his book *New Year*, turned topsy-turvy: "Public offices cease to function; slaves are permitted to lord it over their masters; and a spirit of license and revelry prevails." For example, the traditional Buddhist celebration of the new year in northern Thailand was marked by intoxication, aggression, and sexual license (Preuss 1979). So it was also during the Scottish "Daft Days," the German "Fastnacht," and the English *Fasten's E'en*. In Christian societies, during the twelve days from Christmas to Shrove Tuesday a common pattern arose involving masked and otherwise disguised strangers who engaged in various forms of license while others attempted to guess their identity. Occurring in places as disparate as Quito, Ecuador, and Tolstoyan Russia, these practices were also well known in the English-speaking world, where they were often called "mumming." As described by Halpert (1969:34), mumming includes such contemporary phenomena as the Philadelphia Mummers' Parade, the New Orleans Mardi Gras, the North of England Sword dance, the St. Stephen's Day Wren-boys, the Shetland "skaklers," the "belsnickles" from German tradition in Nova Scotia, Pennsylvania, Virginia, and West Virginia, medieval and Renaissance pageants, the court masque of England, the *perchtenlauf* of Austria, and the folk plays of Thrace.

J. C. Faris (1969:132) offered this account of the license involved in mumming in a Newfoundland fishing village:

> Once the mummers are admitted, people say, "Anything can happen." They mean just that, for the role deviation sanctioned by the "false face" is practically unlimited. . . . The behaviour of mummers today is quite uninhibited. I witnessed a mummer (a female disguised in male clothing) engage in mock copulation with one hostess. . . .
>
> Although undisguised females are largely the "victims" of the mummers' antics, the mummers themselves are by no means the only ones allowed license. In determining the identity of the mummers, the hosts are sometimes allowed to explore with their hands the upper torso, head, and face of mummers in an effort to "find them out." Undisguised men, for example, often single out an obviously female mummer and proceed to dance a few steps with her, then "feel her up." It is said that this "feeling up" must always be "above the waist."

Here, as elsewhere, some rules change during ceremonies, but others remain very much in force.

In many parts of the world, mummers also organized parades, as did celebrants of the pre-Lenten festival, carnival. Wearing masks, carnival paraders often indulged not just in boisterous and obscene antics but also became violent, leading some of the more austere and propertied members of these societies to object and to undertake protective measures. In an effort to control violence, masked paraders were banned in London as early as the fourteenth century (Story 1969:176); indeed, around the year 1400, Henry IV was very nearly assassinated by noblemen who were masked as Christmas mummers (Salusbury-Jones 1939). Several edicts banning masked revelry in Trinidad were enacted by the British colonial government of that West Indian island (Hill 1972).

Indeed, the license allowed or taken by slaves in the West Indies at these times was so extreme that authorities, while indulgently suffering certain indignities at the hands of slaves, nevertheless routinely declared martial law at year's end. Many slave revolts were planned and actually carried out at these times (Dirks 1978). To control possible insurrections, it was a policy in the British West Indies to call the militia to active service from Christmas Eve until after New Year's Day.

In many societies, the social tension and the contagion of license created by masked revelers was so alarming that efforts to suppress masked celebrants continued into recent times, as Charles Welch (1966:533) reported:

> ... the violence and disrespect for authority concomitant to the reversal of rules common to masking by "the lower orders," whether at Carnival or Christmas seasons, disturbed the dominant, well-to-do middle class, who succeeded in having masking officially banned. ... Today we have the phenomenon whereby an originally spontaneous folk tradition is present in Trinidad, Philadelphia, and New Orleans on civic sufferance, and subject to civic censorship.

These examples emphasize the obvious fact that ceremonial license is clearly defined by rules. Some rules are changed drastically, but others remain intact and extraordinary control measures may be employed to ensure that they are followed.

An example of the threat that masked revelers and their ritual rule reversals can pose to social order can be taken from *Carnival in Romans*, a detailed account by the French historian Emmanuel LeRoy Ladurie (1979) of the role of carnival in a French town in the year 1580. The people of Romans staged two carnivals: one by rich nobles, another by poor commoners. The nobles marched in elegant costumes, guarded by well-armed soldiers; reversals were dramatized, not just in male and female roles, but in all domains of life (e.g., roosters laying eggs, the cart coming before the horse, etc.). As staged by the nobility, these reversals were not subversions of the social order; they were amusing and absurd devices for reinforcing order. As LeRoy Ladurie put it (1979:192), "If men exchanged roles during Carnival, it was only to reaffirm the strength and permanence of the social hierarchy."

But the carnival staged by the poor in Romans was something far more than this. It celebrated the sins of the flesh and allowed considerable sexual license, which was sometimes directed against the women of the nobility; it also featured symbols of death and cannibalism and enacted martial virtues. This exalting of pagan excess can be construed in classical Van Gennepian terms: a preliminal period of masquerade, a magical world of reversals, then reintegration in which order is restored and the proprieties of everyday life are reinstituted and reinforced. At the same time, however, it is clear that the commoners' carnival in Romans had elements of serious and rebellious social protest. For one thing, the poor challenged the right of the rich to their wealth (nobles and clergy were tax-exempt, while commoners were impoverished by rising taxation).

The nobles perceived the threat of carnival clearly. One of their leaders, Antoine Guerin, said this about the poor people's carnival (LeRoy Ladurie 1979:162): "The poor want to take all our earthly goods and our women, too; they want to kill us, perhaps even eat our flesh." According to Guerin, poor men took sexual liberties with upper-class women at a fancy dress ball during carnival. While LeRoy Ladurie (1979:223) believed that Guerin and the upper-class men may have used this charge of sexual assault as a pretext for political retaliation and repression, he also noted that young men of the lower classes were in fact given to sexual violence, including gang rape, and that these young men may well have taken advantage of the license offered by carnival to make sexual advances toward the nobles' women; if so, they were not excused. This emphasizes again that in a class-stratified society, ceremonial license may be claimed by the poor and powerless against the rich and powerful who, in turn, may attempt to outlaw such behavior by socially "dangerous" persons. Historian Natalie Zemon Davis (1975), who also studied the aggressive misrule of young men in sixteenth-century French towns and cities, suggested that the ceremonials of these youth groups both reinforced the social order and posed political challenges to it.

In tribal societies, shocking forms of ritual criticism of authority also take place, but with far less subversive effect (Turner 1978). Max Gluckman (1954), for example, called the annual ceremonies of the Zulu and Swazi of South Africa "rituals of rebellion" because of the abuse and denunciations that warriors heaped upon their king on these occasions. Gluckman interpreted these reversals of ordinary propriety as cathartic acts that served to reaffirm social solidarity. In Australia, during the Gunabibi ceremony of the Murngin, an aboriginal people of Arnhem Land, ceremonial license was required as a kind of societal "safety valve" intended to reduce social conflict. Like many Australian peoples, the Murngin gathered together from all over their vast territory to celebrate their great totemic ceremonies.[3]

These ceremonies had profound religious significance relating to the welfare of the Murngin, including the continuance of their food supply, but they also had the explicitly recognized purpose of bringing peace to the conflict-wracked people. For various reasons, including the many incest regulations deriving from their complex kinship system, there was a marked scarcity of marriageable women among the Murngin. The competition among Murngin men for the few available women often led to open combat, which sometimes culminated in homicide. Because of the obligations among relatives in the Murngin system of reciprocally obligated clans, homicide could easily lead to widely proliferated feuding: "An isolated killing, owing to the strength of the kinship structure, usually results in the whole of northeastern Arnhem Land becoming a battleground at fairly frequent intervals" (Warner 1937:156). However, while the Gunabibi ceremony was in process, the rule was that all fighting must cease; if it did not, the ceremony was terminated.

As Warner reported (1937:157), the ceremony was intended to extend the social solidarity of the clan to the tribe as a whole, and since the principal cause of divisiveness among the Murngin was conflict over women, it is not surprising that the ceremony accorded special significance to sexual relations between men and women. The grand finale of the Gunabibi ceremony was a ritual exchange of wives that involved sexual intercourse. This exchange was conducted with many formal ritual precautions, since such "adulterous" intercourse was a dangerous violation of the ordinarily prevailing concepts of sexual exclusiveness and fidelity in marriage.

Although ceremonial sexual partners were not supposed to have intercourse until the final day of the Gunabibi, some partners met clandestinely for sexual liaisons earlier in the ceremony. Others, however, were extremely reluctant to carry out this ceremonial obligation at all—young men were sometimes shy, and women sometimes were fearful of their husbands or found their partners unappealing. In such instances the reluctant partner was told by a ceremonial leader that sexual intercourse must take place or both partners would become ill, perhaps fatally so. When the unwilling partner had finally been persuaded or coerced, intercourse did occur, but a special position was required and the sweat of the husband had to be rubbed on the body of the man having intercourse with the wife.

Warner (1937:307) reported that the Murngin often told him that the sexual exchange was purifying: "'This makes everybody clean. It makes everyone's body good until next dry season.'" And one man, described by Warner as the oldest leader of the Gunabibi ceremony in that area, was explicit in saying that the function of sexual freedom during Gunabibi was to prevent sexual conflict. Attributing his words to the Murngin creation myth, he said: "It is better that everybody comes with their women and all meet together at a Gunabibi and play with each other, and then nobody will start having sweethearts the rest of the time (Warner 1937:308)."

This explanation of ceremonial sexual license as a safety-valve mechanism is unusual in that it was not provided by the anthropologist but by a leader of the ceremony in question. Yet, however much the Murngin may have wanted the Gunabibi to prevent sexual conflict, conflict over women continued at a high rate. Still, the audacity of this ceremony was remarkable. Ordinarily, adultery would result in combat and possibly death, but during this ceremony—and only during this ceremony—adultery was compulsory.

RITES OF STATUS CHANGE OR LIFE CRISIS

License to break otherwise important rules with impunity is also common in ceremonies that mark transitions from one status of life to another. In many parts of the world, as Van Gennep (1909) and others noted long ago, these ceremonies not only permit behavior that reverses propriety, they sometimes *require* behavior that violates deeply held supernatural or moral rules. In most foraging societies, adolescent initiation ceremonies centered around girls rather than boys (Schlegel and Barry 1980). However, the Selk'nam (or Ona), a small hunting-and-fishing society of Tierra del Fuego, conducted an elaborate ceremony—the *Hain*—to initiate young men and also to bring men who were enemies together in a spirit of harmony. The ceremony featured some extreme forms of sexual license, many of which involved women or female spirits; there were also offensive clowns who engaged in extraordinary aggression against women, tempered somewhat by comic sexual antics (Chapman 1982).

For more detailed examples of ceremonies that mark transitions, let us consider some ceremonial practices of the Kikuyu[4] who were involved in the Mau Mau rebellion, and the initiation ceremonies of the Akamba, a neighboring society in Kenya. The Kikuyu-led Mau Mau movement swept Kenya in the early 1950s, leading to a declaration of a state of emergency by the British government of Kenya in 1952 and the eventual use of thousands of British troops equipped with aircraft and sophisticated weaponry before the rebels were subdued. Induction into the Mau Mau movement involved ceremonies that combined oaths and ritual acts. The oaths, which ranged from pledges to support the Mau Mau movement to promises to kill, were based on the Kikuyu belief in the power of a sacred oath to kill anyone who violated it. The accompanying rituals, like the oaths, varied in their level of seriousness. The first-level rituals began with traditional Kikuyu symbolism and ritual practices but escalated to include practices that Kenyan Europeans and British authorities denounced as "bestial," "barbaric," and "unthinkable." These rituals involved such practices as eating feces and drinking urine, eating or licking the penis of a ram that had previously been inserted into the vagina of a menstruating prostitute, having public intercourse with a sheep or a prostitute, and eating the brains of a dead man.

So ghastly and unspeakable were these practices to most Europeans that they were commonly likened to black magic or thought to be the products of "diseased" or "depraved" minds. L. S. B. Leakey (1954), perhaps to protect the reputation of the Kikuyu people for whom he had such affection and respect, insisted that these "bestial" practices had nothing to do with Kikuyu tradition. According to Leakey (1954:86), these acts were so vile that initiates who had undergone them probably could never be "cleansed" and return to normal life; to him, they were forever beyond the pale of ordinary society.

Mau Mau initiates themselves, however, often told another story. Although they universally reported that the oaths and rituals were "horrible," they regarded them as "typically Kikuyu" in character (Barnett and Njama 1966; Muriithi and Ndoria 1971). These acts and symbols were violations of deeply held and felt Kikuyu moral rules; the Kikuyu widely believed that the more repulsive or terrible the ritual rule violation, the more powerful and binding the effect of the oath. For the Mau Mau, terrifying ritual reversals of ordinary morality were employed to strengthen the power of oaths intended to bind initiates to their promises to obey, including killing, if need be.

It is difficult to determine to what extent the Kikuyu utilized similar ritual reversals in other ceremonies,[5] but evidence from a related and neighboring society will allow us to examine further the uses to which ceremonial license may be put. The Akamba, a society of more than one million people which adjoins that of the Kikuyu to the southeast, are culturally quite similar to them. As described by Hobley (1922), Lindblom (1920), Jacobs (1961), Muthiani (1973), Ndeti (1972), and Oliver (1982) and supplemented by my own field research, the general outlines of Akamba initiation ceremonies are well known. The Akamba circumcised both males and females. The ages at which children were circumcised varied greatly, usually depending on the ability and desire of their fathers to pay for the ceremony. After the circumcision surgery had been performed, there was public dancing, some of which was erotic; the fathers of children who had already

been circumcised drank beer, sang, and sometimes spoke in a sala-
cious way. In general, however, this first ceremony was primarily
surgical, lacking any clear sense of the sacred or the profane, and few
ritual rule violations were allowed.

The second, or "great," ceremony had elements of both the sacred
and the profane. Every young man and woman had to take part in
this ceremony in order to attain adulthood. Most initiates varied in
age from eight to twelve, but some were older. The initiates were
completely naked, a dramatic change from ordinary modesty. Boys
and girls alternated in singing songs, many which were remarkably
obscene by Akamba standards. However, sexual intercourse, which
was ordinarily freely available to the young, was now prohibited. The
initiates were also presented with various puzzles which they were
required to solve. Some of these required solutions that would ordinarily be improper or indecent. For example, Lindblom (1920:53)
reported that one puzzle could only be solved by the male initiate's
inserting his penis into the vagina of a woman of his mother's generation, a shocking violation of Akamba incest rules. The initiates were
also required to steal sugarcane and prepare beer from it. Nevertheless, in comparison to the third ceremony, the second resembled a
lighthearted spree far more than it did a life-changing experience.

The third circumcision ceremony, practiced only in some parts of
Akamba territory, was sacred and secret. It took place irregularly,
perhaps every three to five years. Only men were involved, and the
seriousness of the proceedings was unquestionable. It is likely that no
European has ever witnessed these ceremonies[6] and even mentioning
them to a noninitiated man could result in serious sanctions. As
recently as 1962, when I was first told about these ceremonies by a
few Akamba, the conversation was guarded, and the men were tense.

The ostensible purpose of the ceremony was to transform "unfinished" young men into "men of reputation"—that is, fully entitled
men of Akamba society. A full description of this protracted, complex
ceremony is not relevant here. What matters for our purposes is the
occurrence of a series of startling breaches of moral propriety.

The naked initiates, referred to as "animals," were subjected to
many trials, from sucking up sand through a straw to uttering rev-
erential replies when older men broke wind. They were also forced
to swallow lumps of human feces and were prohibited from expelling
these by vomiting. And although the initiates were physically mature
young men, they were exhausted by the painful and tiring physical
ordeals that were also inflicted on them. For example, they had to
roll across stone-strewn ground without using their hands; if they

were not sufficiently swift in their progress, they were beaten. They were also required to pull a wooden peg out of hard ground with their teeth or, again, be beaten. They also ran a gauntlet of initiated warriors who beat them—sometimes viciously—with long wooden clubs. According to Lindblom (1920:65), a disliked initiate might even be beaten to death. In addition to these and other physical ordeals, sexually obscene trials were imposed. The young Akamba men, who were every bit as imbued with values of sexual modesty as the Kikuyu, were required to induce erections with lumps of wood tied to their erect penes, and then, were required to march before a hilarious audience. More shocking still, each initiate was forced to copulate to ejaculation with a hole that was scooped out of the sand and filled with water; initiates also had to perform sexual acts with one another to demonstrate their copulatory skill.

Following a forty-eight-hour period of isolation in a remote place, the initiates marched home, singing outrageously obscene songs. When they finally arrived at their homes, they were slapped or punched. They were also compelled to express reverence while they watched initiated men defecate. Perhaps most horrifying of all in terms of Akamba culture, each initiate was required to place his penis in his father's ear; refusal to do so resulted in a beating and a fine of a bull.

After a night during which the initiates slept at home, there began a five- or six-day period of exceptional license to commit violence. The initiates carried long, heavy sticks with which they beat anyone they met who had not undergone the third circumcision; the initiates, who were still referred to as "animals," also raped younger women (it is not clear exactly how incest prohibitions applied here, although there is evidence that they were suspended to some extent). Lindblom (1920:66) reported that Europeans would "probably" be immune from attack by the initiates, but an African of any tribe would be attacked. If a man could not identify himself by making a secret sign indicating that he had passed the third circumcision, he was subject to violent attack. However, if an intended victim killed an initiate in self-defense, it was said that he had killed a "baboon," and he was not subject to any punishment for homicide. This exemption is especially remarkable because, as we saw earlier, Akamba law recognized few exemptions from responsibility for homicide in ordinary life. Similarly, should an initiate kill a victim, he too was not held responsible.

It is not possible to say how often homicide actually occurred during this period of license (although I was told of five alleged instances between World War II and 1962), but it is clear that the Akamba took the threat very seriously, moving themselves and their families as far away from the initiation area as possible to avoid the danger. Jan Vansina (1955) has warned that African men may exaggerate the rigors of their initiation ordeals in order to impress women or un- initiated males. This is probably so, but I have no reason to doubt the authenticity of these Akamba practices. Similar ceremonial practices have been described by Evans-Pritchard (1929) and summarized by Norbeck (1963).

Why do such extreme exemptions from normal accountability occur on these ceremonial occasions? During the second initiation, the physical ordeals and sexual trials are like those that accompanied the Mau Mau oaths. Yet these experiences, which Akamba men and women alike described as physically painful and emotionally shocking, were required of the Akamba in order to establish full citizenship in their society (Nida 1962). For the third circumcision, male initiates not only violated rules of incest and moral decency but also committed assault, rape, and even homicide in order to escape their "animal" status and become fully entitled men in Akamba society. Why should these acts—which one could argue went beyond those utilized in all but the most extreme Mau Mau ceremonies—achieve the goals of male status transition? Akamba men who were queried in 1962 about the reasons for the third circumcision (at that time, the ceremony was still being practiced) either could not or would not adduce any expla- nations for the ceremony except to repeat that it was necessary for the achievement of manhood.

Rules may be reversed, suspended, or otherwise violated with equal impunity at many other times of life change or crisis. Funerals are one example of such occasions. From Japan to Africa, behavior during funerals has typically been the reverse of what would be considered normal, often including expressions of joy and hilarity rather than of grief (Norbeck 1974; Huntington and Metcalf 1979). At times, funerals called for what appeared to be almost complete license. So it was in Tahiti (Oliver 1974) and Hawaii. The following account by the missionary J. J. Jarves, despite the morally indignant language, appears to be an accurate enough description of a Hawaiian version of a widespread Polynesian pattern (1847:34):

> But these usages, however shocking they may appear, were innocent, compared with the horrid saturnalia which immediately followed the death of a chief of the highest rank. Then the most unbounded license prevailed; law and restraint were cast aside, and the whole people appeared more like demons than human beings. Every vice and crime

was allowed. Property was destroyed, houses fired, and old feuds revived and revenged. Gambling, thefts and murder were as open as the day; clothing was cast aside as a useless incumbrance; drunkenness and promiscuous prostitution prevailed throughout the land, no women, excepting the widows of the deceased, being exempt from the grossest violation. There was no passion, however lewd, or desire, however wicked, but could be gratified with impunity, during the continuance of this period, which happily from its own violence, soon spent itself. No other nation was ever witness to a custom, which so entirely threw off all moral and legal restraints, and incited the evil passion to unresisted riot and wanton debauchery.

Extraordinary, to be sure—but we should take note that even at such times, some rules continued to prevail strictly; for example, "widows of the deceased" were "exempt from violation," and so were the 'arioi in Tahiti, as we saw in the last chapter.

RITUALS OF WOMEN'S RIGHTS

The collective retaliation of women against men who are thought to have violated their rights may also involve the "throwing off of moral and legal restraints." The right of women to take such collective action against men who ordinarily possess both de facto and de jure power over them has not received much recognition. For example, Marvin Harris (1977:85) observed that women "seldom ritually menace" men, referring to the absence of female counterparts to the bullroarers, masks, and clubhouses that men sometimes use to menace, intimidate, or dominate women. Yet, in 1949, Max Gluckman reported that women among the Wiko of Africa "rebelled" against the female role during initiation ceremonies; in striking contrast to their ordinary conduct, they directed lewd and abusive behavior toward men. The same observation was made in Africa by many other writers both before and after Gluckman's report (Norbeck 1963). Similar behaviors have been reported from non-African societies, too, as in the song contests of the Eskimo or the *hamath* of the Micronesians of Ulithi (Lessa 1966).

Even in societies in which men possess profound power over women, women may sometimes take collective action against men with full exemption from male retaliation. And, what is more, this collective action need not occur during prescribed ceremonial occasions. An example can be taken from the Akamba, some of whose ceremonial practices we have just examined. Both recently and in the past, Akamba men dominated women (Edgerton 1971*b*). Not only did the men sometimes speak of and treat their wives as chattel, they were fully responsible before the law for any transgressions by their wives, since women, like children, did not own any property with which they could pay a fine. Lindblom (1920:180) characterized Akamba women, their docility and their collective rights as follows: "On the whole, the Akamba woman goes through life calmly and quietly, doing her duty and suitably subservient to her husband." Yet, as Lindblom (1920:80) went on to say, when something happened that the women saw as a threat to their crops or to village life itself and they felt that men had done too little to rectify matters, the women would "conspire together to enforce their views by their own efforts—and they generally succeed[ed]."

In support of this assertion, Lindblom cited an instance which is worth presenting in full. As apparently happened often, a man lent a field which he did not need to another man. When he wanted it back later, the wife of the other man refused to return it. She was exhorted to give in, but she refused; the dispute became heated. According to the women of the neighborhood, the controversy would bring bad luck to the crops of all the neighboring fields, since it might cause the rains to fail. Therefore, even though disputes of this kind among the Akamba should have been settled by an all-male council of elders, the women decided to take the matter into their own hands. First, they urged the husband of the obstinate woman to provide a goat so that the fields might be cleansed, but he refused. Lindblom (1920:181) continued the account:

> Then the women beat their big drums and met in council. A deputation of two old women was sent to the refractory man to demand the immediate presentation of a goat. He still refused, and the women became furious, and went in a body to let him hear—in none too mild language—their opinion of his behavior. . . .
>
> If anyone persists in his defiance, the women strew leaves in front of the entrance to his hut, and then the owner cannot enter until he has submitted.
>
> When the women come thus in a body, beating their drums and carrying boughs in their hands, the men try to keep out of the way as much as possible. Anyone coming across their path is showered with derisive and insulting epithets; and in the district of Kitui it is even said to have happened that the men have been assaulted and maltreated. Only the oldest *atumia* (elders) escape unmolested, but even they hide their faces in their blankets while the crowd of women is passing.

It may be maintained that, by such behavior, the women interfere in a way in the administration of justice, desiring to get a dispute which is injurious to the community settled more quickly than it would be *if the law took its normal course* [emphasis added]. Seen from another point of view, their conduct bears a religious stamp, since the spirits [*aima*] are thought to be incensed at such disputes.

Lindblom (1920:182) concluded his remarks on this remarkable form of female vigilantism in a male-dominant society thus: "It is interesting to observe the submissive attitude of the men when such proceedings take place. The reason is perhaps a tacit recognition of the justice of the women's demands." Interesting indeed. The law has *not* taken its normal course; instead, another set of rules has come into play, allowing women an extraordinary coercive power. And, while the actions are accompanied by religious ritual, they also have a secular quality, and they occur ad hoc rather than as part of a ceremonial cycle or event.

The Akamba are not alone as a society in which men dominate and abuse women as a matter of routine yet occasionally accord women the right to take remarkably harsh collective action against a man who somehow goes too far. Women among the Igbo of Nigeria could behave similarly, "sitting on" an offending man by

> gathering at his compound, sometimes late at night, dancing, singing scurrilous songs which detailed the women's grievances against him and often called his manhood into question, banging on his hut with the pestles women used for pounding yams, and perhaps demolishing his hut or plastering it with mud and roughing him up a bit. A man might be sanctioned in this way for mistreating his wife, for violating the women's market rules, or for letting his cows eat the women's crops. The women would stay at his hut throughout the day, and late into the night, if necessary, until he repented and promised to mend his ways (Van Allen 1972:169).

Women among the Samburu of Kenya (Spencer 1965:228–229) behaved in a similar way, and among the nearby Pokot of Kenya, female vigilantism went beyond that permitted by the Akamba, Igbo, or Samburu. Edgerton and Conant (1964) described a practice the Pokot called *kilapat* (something organized secretly). Although men might utilize kilapat against women, it was usually undertaken by women against an errant husband. Pokot men arrogantly and capriciously flaunted their power over women, often punctuating their dominance by inflicting severe beatings on their wives for little apparent cause. Yet when a husband's misconduct became too outrageous, an aggrieved Pokot wife could legitimately organize other women to "shame" her husband in kilapat. In so doing, the women had full exemption to ridicule him, revile him obscenely, expose their genitals to him, beat him, defecate and urinate on him, and, finally, to slaughter his favorite ox. These acts violated some of the most fundamental rules of Pokot culture, yet men meekly accepted them.

A woman who took part in kilapat described what happened when a man was "shamed" by his wife (Edgerton and Conant 1964:404–405). This particular man was abusive to his wife who became very unhappy. He drank excessively and kicked and beat his wife every day. After beating her, he would go to sleep without having sexual intercourse with her. His wife grew increasingly unhappy and complained to her father and her brothers, but they told her to be quiet and be a good wife. Since her husband was a rich man, they did not want her to leave him. They took no action, and he continued to mistreat her.

Finally, the wife took matters into her own hands. One night she collected seven or eight women who lived nearby, and together they seized the man as he lay sleeping in his usual alcoholic stupor. They tied him up before he awakened, then dragged him out of the house and tied him to a tree in a sitting position. He cried in pain and argued with them, threatening to beat them all, but they only laughed at him derisively. Then the women began to sing an abusive song, which among various insults, accused him of committing incest, or its equivalent, and referred to him as a dog, something filthy and not human. They also sang obscenely about his drunkenness and his impotence; then they laughed and laughed, mockingly.

While they were abusing him, they danced around him and, in a shocking violation of Pokot morality, they pushed their naked vulvas into his face. Some of the women also urinated on him. Women sometimes even defecated upon a man during kilapat, but this time they stopped short of that. For several hours they laughed at him and sang more songs to him that repeated all his failings. Next, some of the women began to hit his genitals with some small sticks. They did not hit him very hard, but it was hard enough that the effect was painful as well as humiliating. One woman sang a song that asked why he needed testicles, since he had proven that he was not a man. They all laughed at this display of wit.

After several hours of this, they demanded that he slaughter an ox for them, saying that they would keep him tied and would beat him until he agreed. He said that if they would let him go he would slaughter an ox in a few days. The women laughed at this feeble maneuver and insisted that it be done right away. The husband still refused, so the women cut larger sticks in order to beat him more severely. When they began to beat him, his wife suddenly intervened, saying that even though he had wronged her, she could not let the women kill him. The other women grudgingly agreed, but emphasized that they were doing so only because the wife had spoken for him. However, they insisted that they would not release him until he agreed to slaughter an ox for them. And it could not be just any ox—it had to be his favorite one, the ox that he thought was the most beautiful and that he sang songs about. After more abuse, he agreed, and the ox was slaughtered. He was then untied, and he left as hurriedly as his battered body and pride would allow. The women sang happily and danced until the meat was all eaten or divided up. The woman who recounted this episode added that the husband had not abused his wife again.

Recently, Shirley Ardener (1973) recorded examples of similar, although more restrained, female vigilantism in several African societies. One example will suffice to demonstrate the similarity. Among the Bakweri of West Cameroon, if a man insulted a woman by making an offensive remark, the women were not only entitled, but obliged, to retaliate (Ardener 1973:422–423):

> The insult is typically envisaged in the form of an accusation that the sexual parts of women smell. If such an insult has been uttered to a Bakweri woman before a witness, she is supposed immediately to call out all the other women of the village. The circumstances having been recounted, the women then run and pluck vegetation from the surrounding bush, which they tie around their waist. Converging again upon the offender they demand immediate recantation and a recompense. If their demands are not met they all proceed to the house of the village head. The culprit will be brought forward, and the charges laid. If the insult is proved to have taken place, he will be fined a pig of a certain size for distribution to the group of women, or its money equivalent plus something extra, possibly salt, a fowl or money, for the woman who has been directly insulted. The women then surround him and sing songs accompanied by obscene gestures. All the other men beat a hasty retreat, since it is expected that they will be ashamed to stay and watch while their wives, sisters, sisters-in-law and old women join the dance. The culprit must stay, but he will try to hide his eyes. Finally, the women retire victoriously to divide the pig between them.

It is apparent that collective expressions of female wrath like these occur widely in Africa and elsewhere (Hogbin 1961); while they contain ritual elements, they occur spontaneously like vigilante justice. The rules they violate range from implicit conventions to moral rules and secular laws; the rules that women follow at these times are clear, and they are known and accepted by men as well as women.

In the preceding discussions, we have examined various kinds of ceremonies or ritually tinged actions in which socially sanctioned rule violations occur. We have also mentioned some of the many explanations that have been offered for ceremonial license. It is doubtful that any one reason can explain the widespread occurrence of occasions on which ordinarily enforced rules may be, or must be, shattered without penalty. On some occasions, it seems that participants willingly violate such rules for pleasure, revenge, or strategic advantage; in other ceremonies, participants are forced to violate rules, however distasteful it may be for them to do so, or they are obliged to remain passive while others violate rules. We should also emphasize that while many of these occasions occur only infrequently and at well-known and prescribed times, others may occur in response to a specific event. The presence of what I have here called female vigilantism is one example of this latter phenomenon; funeral practices such as those in Hawaii are another.

In reviewing the ethnographic literature, one can hardly escape the conclusion that human beings have been generous in providing themselves with occasions during which they either *may* or *must* violate ordinarily important rules. But we should not lose sight of the fact that however dramatic the license may be during ceremonials, some rules remain strictly inviolable. Given the potential for contagious rule-breaking when groups of people, sometimes intoxicated, often excited, "behave as if mad," "throwing off all moral restraint," it is indeed remarkable that ceremonial conduct follows rules so faithfully. Ceremonial occasions actually dramatize the power of rules; some rules remain in force no matter what, while other rules, ones that reverse ordinary morality, are enforced strictly despite the horror of many people who are compelled to behave as these rules prescribe. Ceremonies are displays of rules and of rules for breaking rules. Above all, they demonstrate the constraining power that both kinds of rules can exert over people.

CHAPTER 6

Settings That Exempt

Since the meaning of human behavior is invariably influenced by the context in which that behavior occurs, it is hardly remarkable that some physically defined settings provide exemption from all sorts of ordinarily applicable rules. The definition of what is correct, acceptable, or forgivable varies in all societies, depending not only on the occasion (some are solemn, some joyous), the activity itself (games and wars have rules that are not present in many other activities), and who is present (what is good conduct in the company of one's peers may not be acceptable in the presence of one's mother-in-law) but also on the culturally defined setting (acceptable behavior in public places often differs from that which is acceptable in settings defined as private).

The ways in which people construct, define, and maintain the meaning—the "reality"—of various situations, contexts, or settings have long occupied the attention of social scientists (McHugh 1968). Ecological or environmental psychologists such as Egon Brunswick, Roger Barker, and Albert Mehrabian (1976) as well as ethnomethodologists such as Harold Garfinkel (1967) have analyzed the properties of settings and the processes by which they create, sustain, and convey meaning.[1] Erving Goffman (1963) has also identified certain features of settings that are related to exemptions from ordinary responsibility for misconduct. For example, Goffman distinguished between settings that were "serious" and those that were "unserious," with the latter being places where what one does becomes relatively inconsequential. As Sherri Cavan (1966) has shown in her research on bar behavior in the United States, many bars are places where the conventional consequentiality of actions is suspended. Much of what happens in bars, even if it is aggressive, sexual, silly, or maudlin, does not *really* count; it does not have the same seriousness that it would elsewhere.

Cavan (1966:68) provided an account of an episode she witnessed in a bar that had a young, middle-class clientele:

A young man and a young woman had been sitting together chatting and occasionally dancing for about an hour and a half. Suddenly the man hit the girl in the face, knocking her from the bar stool onto the

113

floor. The general hum of conversation that had been going on among the eight or ten people in the bar stopped for about thirty seconds, during which time the man walked out. No one made any attempt to stop him. One patron quite casually went over to the girl to help her and the bartender held out a damp towel for her to put to her face. The rest of the patrons went back to their conversations as though nothing had happened. The girl got up, said something to the bartender, and then went to the bathroom. She came out, about ten minutes later, her face back in order, and sat down at the bar, where she remained for about fifteen minutes longer. No one made any further comment on the scene. After she had left, P. C. asked one of the patrons sitting next to him about it and was told, "They've been living together for months. That happens all the time."

Cavan also noted that overt sexual behavior may take place in bars without evoking censure; she said that it was common to see couples dancing very closely and women sitting on the laps of their companions. Couples at the bar were also permitted to hold hands, rest their heads on one another's shoulders, and hug or kiss. They might also fondle each other more intimately (Cavan 1966:71): "A couple in their mid-thirties were sitting along the bar, just to the right of me. They had been talking softly and holding hands when we got there, but soon he was fondling her breasts and kissing her—all quite openly."

Needless to say, bars differ in the extent to which ordinarily prohibited behavior will be accepted. The bizarre entertainment, sexual hustling, "drag queens," and occasional violence of the working-class male homosexual bar described by K. E. Read (1980) would be totally out of place in a heterosexual college-student bar such as the one studied by James Spradley and Brenda Mann (1975). The older Portuguese-American men who regularly visited a private "social club" bar in a southeastern New England city ordinarily would not engage in homosexual horseplay with one another. However, when they visited the social club they regularly did so, grabbing at one another's crotches or feigning sodomy. Moreover, this behavior took place *before* the men had become intoxicated; *after* they had been drinking, their conduct returned to its ordinary dignified restraint (Cabral 1930). The availability of alcohol and marijuana in the social club no doubt helped to define it as a place where behavior could be out of the ordinary, but it was primarily the setting, not the drugs, that justified the behavior.

Many other physically delimited, culturally defined settings in the United States—brothels, psychiatrists' offices, automobiles, and beaches, for example—offer opportunities for otherwise prohibited behavior to take place without negative consequences. In brothels, it is commonplace for married men to engage in forms of sexual conduct that would be unacceptable to their wives (Castle 1974). A patient in a psychiatrist's office may weep or reveal secrets, and patients in group therapy may be required both to suffer and to deliver verbal attacks. Automobile drivers may express verbal aggression or callous disregard for others with little concern for the consequences. Beaches are settings where men and women may strip down to skimpy bathing suits (Edgerton 1979), and on nude beaches one may freely remove *all* clothing, and may also engage—albeit discreetly—in sexual behavior (Douglas et al. 1977). Yet in many nudist colonies, one must remove all clothing, but sexual behavior is absolutely prohibited; it is even wrong for one's eyes to stray (Weinberg 1970). In these settings and in many others like them, rules allow or require persons to behave in ways that in most settings would be reprehensible, discrediting, or punishable.

Although much more attention has been paid to setting-specific behaviors in the urban West than in non-Western tribal societies, these societies also contain settings in which otherwise unacceptable behavior goes unpunished. All societies—even those with such simple material cultures that members can carry with them everything they possess—use physical settings to define what is proper. For example, people use huts, windbreaks, mats, blankets, hammocks, streambeds, bushy areas, trees, or rocks to define settings that regulate such behaviors as eating, sleeping, defecating, giving birth, menstruating, copulating, divining, or propitiating deities. The rules about where such activities may take place are often quite explicit and categorical.

Some societies utilize portable material objects to change the setting and the conventional rules of conduct. We have already discussed the use of masks in this regard; a mask or costume not only obscures the identity of the person but also changes the definition of the setting. For example, among the Kwakiutl Indians of the northwest coast of North America, a "speaking mouth"—looking very much like a set of wooden false teeth—allowed its owner the privilege of publicly criticizing others. Since the person who wore the mouth (*heygukhsti*) could not easily articulate anything, the actual criticism was made by someone standing next to the mouth wearer. The important thing about this "portable setting" is that no one was permitted to take offense to the remarks, no matter how cutting or scandalous they might be (Holm 1972).

As we have seen, much that is prohibited in ordinary life becomes acceptable or even required during certain special occasions. For example, homosexual relations between males (and perhaps females as well) during rituals of initiation have been reported to take place in a number of societies, including several in Melanesia (Keesing 1982).

According to anthropologist Gilbert Herdt (1981), however, ordinarily prohibited homosexual behavior could be *required* of men and boys not just during a brief ritual period but for many years of their lives. This behavior was required, and acceptable, in only one setting—the men's clubhouse. Writing about the pseudonymous Sambia of highland Papua New Guinea, Herdt reported that men vigorously insisted to outsiders that homosexuality among Sambia males did not exist. They were so secretive about this practice that Herdt had lived with the Sambia for five months, including two weeks in the men's clubhouse, before he learned that all Sambia males spent many years of their lives in the daily practice of fellatio. Sambia boys aged seven to ten were initiated into the practice of homosexuality by being forced to fellate older men during a secret ritual. For the next ten to fifteen years of their lives they took part in acts of fellatio every day; first, they were the fellators of older males, then when they had grown older they were fellated by new cohorts of novices. Because it took place only in the strict secrecy of the men's clubhouse, this behavior remained unknown to all women and to younger boys. When young men married and moved out of the clubhouse to live with their wives, they became exclusively heterosexual. To continue male homosexuality after marriage was morally wrong, and Herdt believed that it happened very rarely.

The practice of male homosexuality among the Sambia was made necessary by a complex of beliefs calling for semen to be ingested daily if biological maleness and masculine virtues were to be developed (Herdt 1981:2). Reasons for the secrecy of the practice and its confinement to a single setting were related to a larger pattern of rules that defined correct conduct in various spatial settings (Herdt 1981:75):

> A cultural mosaic of spatial taboos and architectural designs separate women from men inside the hamlet. Its narrow confines are sexually segregated into men's spaces and women's spaces. Zones of female movement become polluted, according to male dogma, and since no area is immune to this contagion, persons must be restricted by taboos. A startling assortment of such taboos and avoidance rules curtail the movements of women, initiates, and men.

One of these taboos denied women any access to the men's clubhouse, a rule which Herdt believed was never broken. As Herdt wrote (1981:34), "Concerns about female pollution and the superiority of their domain prompt men to enforce these restrictions. But another hidden motive is far more powerful: this is men's smug and fervent complicity as secret sharers in a tradition of institutionalized homosexuality." Whatever the motives, the rule was clear: male homosexual behavior *must* take place in the men's clubhouse, and it must never occur outside of it.

Even in caste-stratified India where, as was mentioned in earlier chapters, rules of acceptable conduct are clearly defined by caste membership and violations of these rules can lead to dangerous pollution and social conflict, there are settings in which these rules may be loosened or overlooked altogether. Gerald Berreman (1962) described the many caste rules and avoidances—of food and physical contact, among others—that so oppressed lower-caste people in the Indian village of Sirkanda. Yet Berreman noted that when Sirkanda villagers went to larger towns, they did not follow the rules of pollution carefully. For example, high-caste men ate in public places with people whose caste they did not know, and they even ate with low-caste people from their own village. Caste restrictions were also ignored in houses of prostitution, where men of both high and low caste knowingly patronized the same prostitutes (Berreman 1962:236). In the village itself, while high-caste people would never visit the homes of low-caste people nor allow low-caste people into the cooking areas of their houses, the verandas of high-caste houses were settings where high- and low-caste people mingled, drank alcohol, and even shared certain foods. From the interior of a house to its veranda was only a few steps, but in terms of rules they were worlds apart.

Caste rules were usually followed rigidly in the small tribal village of Dhanaura in Uttar Pradesh. As in Sirkanda, low-caste people could not enter the houses of high-caste people, and people of the lowest castes were required not only to avoid physical contact with high-caste persons but also to avoid even close proximity. According to L. M. Sankhdher (1974) these rules were usually followed quite strictly. However, certain ceremonies allowed some of these rules to be relaxed, and, in at least one setting, the rules were set aside completely. The Adalti Panchayat was a village court that dealt with all criminal and civil cases, and which met in a temple (Sankhdher 1974:37):

> One thing very important is to note that no caste discrimination is made at the meetings of the Adalti Panchayat where people from different

communities sit together close to each other. Even more remarkable than sitting together is that people from all communities, tribal, Hindu and Muslim get entry into the temple of Panchdev without any hesitation. Not only the members of Panchayat but other people also may enter the temple with their shoes off and sit down on the floor.

SANCTUARY

In addition to settings where otherwise forbidden behavior may or sometimes must take place, without the usual sanctions being applied, there are other settings—asylums or sanctuaries—where persons who have committed serious offenses or crimes may temporarily or permanently escape responsibility for these acts.

The concept of sanctuary has long been known in the Judeo-Christian world. The six Levitical "cities of refuge" in Israel were apparently established in an effort to reduce the dangers of feuding following homicide; if an offender could reach a sanctuary, feuding was preempted. A person who fled to a city of refuge did not escape judgment, however. The priests and judges of the city investigated the crime, and if the person was found guilty he was returned to his own city for punishment. Those found to be innocent could remain safely within the city of refuge until the death of the high priest of the land, after which time they were free to leave the city in safety. The Greeks also created sanctuaries, such as the famous asylum of Diana of Ephesus, as did the Romans, with temples, statues, and other places. Babylon, too, had its sanctuaries (Eliade 1958;1959).

Early Christian churches offered criminals and other fugitives protection from the cruel secular punishments at least as early as A.D. 303, when Constantine's Edict of Toleration came into being. When Christianity became the state religion of most of Europe, its church-based sanctuaries superseded the older system of asylum in temples, statues, or sacred trees.[2] As medieval times approached, the availability of sanctuary on Christian church grounds (not in the churches themselves) proliferated, and this served to mute—and sometimes to challenge—the sanctions of secular law.

Like the Levitical cities of refuge, the Christian churches did not provide total immunity from punishment (Stephen 1883). In his review of the history of Christian sanctuary, A. S. Diamond (1951) noted that many who sought asylum in churches were fleeing from death at the hands of a king or his agents. The idea that a church could provide asylum was based on the concept of sacredness, but this concept was potentially in conflict with secular law (Diamond 1951:161): "The Church could not allow the sanctuary to be violated by the pursuers; and, on the other hand, it could not allow the privilege of sanctuary to be abused."

As historian John Bellamy (1973) described medieval England, famine, plague, and the erosion of the feudal order brought about by the widespread social and economic changes of the fourteenth and fifteenth centuries made the preservation of public order a particularly difficult task for the English kings of that time. Crimes of all sorts, including crimes of violence, were widespread, and yet so was the opportunity for sanctuary, since the privilege of affording sanctuary was possessed by every parish church or its churchyard (Bellamy 1973:106). But if places of sanctuary were numerous, so were the types of individuals who were denied safety within them (Bellamy 1973:107):

> Those excluded from the privilege were common or notorious offenders (men in modern parlance with a criminal record), suspected or indicted traitors, heretics, and those who dabbled in sorcery, clerks, those who were believed to have committed a felony in a church, and those originally caught in the act. Nor were men who had committed only a minor offence against the king's peace, which did not involve the danger of loss of life or limb, afforded any protection. No man could have sanctuary if he had already been convicted of the offence, either by judgment in court or by outlawry.

Just as many rules regulated the search for asylum, once the fugitive was inside a sanctuary, he was forced to follow many more rules, both secular and ecclesiastic. Even then the fugitive might not be safe for long unless he agreed to "abjure the realm" and leave England. Sometimes both kings and church authorities ordered sanctuaries to be invaded, but this was apparently done only with good cause, such as the removal of a criminal who was not entitled to asylum. Bellamy emphasized the great reluctance of any king to disregard the wishes of the church concerning the privileges of sanctuary; the anathemas of church authorities were not to be taken lightly. Bellamy offered the following example as a case in point (1973:109):

> There was a notable case in 1378. An esquire called Robert Haulay, who had sought sanctuary on breaking out of captivity in the Tower of London, was slain together with a sacristan in the abbey church at Westminster. The offence seemed the more outrageous for being committed in front of the prior's stall, by a large number of armed men led

by the constable of the Tower, when high mass was being celebrated at the high altar. The case aroused great public interest and undermined the authority of the government. Those who committed the murders were excommunicated and had to pay a large fine to the abbey.

This sort of conflict between church and state over the rules of sanctuary continued until Henry VIII finally abolished church-based sanctuary, establishing instead seven cities of refuge, including Westminster, York, and Manchester.

The concept of asylum remains today, in the supposed inviolability of diplomatic personnel and especially of the grounds of their embassies, which, in principle, may not be entered by the police forces of the host country without permission and where all manner of political refugees may seek asylum.[3] It is also found in many children's games (Opie and Opie 1969).

The provision of places of sanctuary is not confined to Europe or to the Judeo-Christian world. It was known among North American Indians, including the Cheyennes (whom we shall discuss in the next chapter), and among the Australian aborigines[4] (Spencer and Gillen 1927). It was widespread among the Bedouin, where sanctuary took many forms but was often associated with the sanctity of women, and among the Eskimo, where a man's house provided asylum.[5] Anthropologist Sulayman Khalaf indicated that among the Bedouin in Syria, every Bedouin tent became a sanctuary, with the section of the tent reserved for women (the *mharam*) being the most powerful and sacred sanctuary. Khalaf also wrote that a man was duty-bound to receive any fugitive who asked for protection:

> Even his own enemy can demand sanctuary of him, and rest assured of protection against himself, since his obligation to respect the sanctity of his own home takes precedence over the right and the temptation for vengeance. A man may enter the house of the brother of a man he has killed. If he demands *dakhala* (sanctuary) he is safe for three days, after that time, he must say where he wants to go, and he will be seen safely to his destination. When this is done, the brother of the man he has killed is free to resume his blood vengeance. It should be noted, however, that the sacredness of the home makes it a sanctuary only to the stranger, not to the fellow kinsman of one's own community.[6]

Among other Bedouin groups, equally absolute sanctuary might be granted for as long as a year (Dickson 1949).

Although there was some tribal variation in this regard (Musil 1928), Khalaf used the following personal reminiscence of his own

Bedouin boyhood to emphasize the power of Arab women to confer sanctuary:

> A girl cutting firewood in the desert or her mother spinning outside the tent alone can offer protection to a man who is being followed by his enemies. I recall when we were young and would find ourselves in fights or just rough play, the defeated boy would seek "dakhala" in the Prophet Mohammed. This move may not help him much. Then he would say, "*Ana dakhl 'ind Allah*," meaning—I beg dakhala in Allah. Again if his begging is not heard he would resort to the most forceful of all and say to his opponent who may still be beating him up on the head: "*Ana dakhl 'ala daid'ummak*,"—I seek dakhala in your mother's milk. At this point the boy is invoking the strongest of all bonds, the bond of brotherhood captured and lived in the milk of the mother.[7]

The Bedouin could also extend sanctuary in the symbolic form of the cane of their shaikh. According to Dickson (1949:134), a man carrying such a cane could travel safely throughout the shaikh's tribal territory, even though persons in the tribe might have a blood feud with him. Australian aborigines also had a form of safe conduct based upon the possession of sacred materials, and North American Indians of the Eastern woodlands used their calumet, or peace pipe, not only to achieve peaceful settlements of conflicts within their tribes but also to guarantee safe passage (Underhill 1953:121):

> A calumet was not only a sign of alliance, like the signature on a treaty, but also a passport. "Carry it about with you and show it," said Father Dablon, "and you can march fearlessly amid enemies who even in the heat of battle, lay down their arms when it is shown." Marquette was given a calumet by the Illinois and, by grace of it, passed the whole Mississippi River in safety.

Sanctuary was also widespread in tribal Africa. For example, among the Pokot, *sintagh* was the first of a series of ceremonies that celebrated the summer solstice. One feature of sintagh was the practice of *kicitit*, a form of marriage by capture, which included abduction, confinement, and forcible sexual intercourse, sometimes involving torture. But sanctuary was available. Francis Conant (1966), who witnessed kicitit in 1962, described it as ranging from playing with words having sexual innuendo to pitched battles that were waged either to carry out or to prevent rape and abduction. In its mildest form, the atmosphere was one of permissiveness, like an "art students' ball" or a Mardi Gras. Conant added (1966:514):

In its more violent aspects, kicitit frequently took the form of a young man's attempt to catch the hand or arm of a girl in the dance line at the Mwina grove and then to drag her off into the near-by bushes. Most frequently, after a brief scuffle, the girl would break free and either disappear into the crowd of dancers or make a run for *kokwa-munung* ("meeting-place of youngsters"), the rocks which are considered as sanctuary for girls and women.

Conant pointed out that the violence surrounding kicitit could result in serious injury to a woman who was raped (one woman had her hip dislocated), and it might also lead to a general affray; this was avoided in part because the Pokot clearly recognized sanctuary. Conant (1966:516) reported that it was a rule that the rock ledge of kokwa-munung was acknowledged as "an area of sanctuary within which women and girls may not be violated."

In other African societies, various kinds of offenders could achieve a degree of safety, or complete absolution, by reaching a sacred rock or tree, by touching a king's person or entering his homestead or that of his counselor or, among some tribes (such as the Barotse), by fleeing to a village of refuge. Among the Kikuyu of Kenya, as among many of their neighbors, if someone who committed a serious offense, including murder, was able to flee to a sacred place—usually a sacred fig tree—he was safe from retaliation. Once safely at such a place, he was taken away by the elders, who put him through various rituals of purification. Although the offender's relatives had to pay blood money, the offender was saved and rehabilitated (Hobley 1922). This pattern was known in many societies, but Hobley (1922:48) reported another form of sanctuary among the Kikuyu that was less common:

> If, again, a man should kill a tribesman, he can run to the house of his victim's father and, by confessing his crime, obtain sanctuary there. The father will then kill a ram and place a strip of skin on the right wrist of the homicide, who must have his head shaved and ceremonially purified by a medicine man—*tahikia*, as it is termed. He will henceforth become as a son of the deceased's father.

Whether these practices permanently avoided feud or merely drove animosities beneath the surface of life where they would smolder, later to break out again, is not known. But this latter pattern did exist, as was illustrated by Evans-Pritchard in his discussion of feud among the Nuer of the Sudan (1940:152–153):

> As soon as a man slays another he hastens to the home of a leopard-skin
> chief to cleanse himself from the blood he has spilt and to seek sanctuary
> from the retaliation he has incurred.

Although the killer was safe while he remained in the leopard-skin
chief's household, the possibility of blood vengeance by the deceased's
kinsmen remained; indeed, they were obligated to seek vengeance.
They lurked outside the chief's homestead, hoping to spear the killer
should he leave that sanctuary. If no opportunity to use their spears
arose, they then rejected the chief's attempts to negotiate a *wergild*
settlement in cattle. As many as forty or fifty cattle might finally
be agreed upon, but until the full price was paid—and this might
take years—the killer and his agnatic kinsmen were vulnerable to
vengeance.

A more highly institutionalized and absolute form of sanctuary was
developed in Polynesia, particularly Hawaii. Various kinds of sanctuaries were known in Polynesia; some, like caves and hilltops, offered
safety only because they were easily defended positions, but others
were centered around sacred places, usually shrines, and some of
these offered rule violators both inviolate protection from punishment and complete absolution for their offenses. For example, in
Tahiti during the late eighteenth century, any fugitive except a person
already chosen to be sacrificed could achieve refuge if he could reach
a *marae* (sacred shrine). Although details of this Tahitian form of
sanctuary are sketchy,[8] the following comments from European visitors were typical:

> Their *morais* are a kind of refuge for criminals of every kind; they fly
> to them when in any imminent danger, and according to the custom of
> the country, must not be taken from thence (Turnbull 1813:366).

> The sacred ground around the morais affords a sanctuary for criminals.
> Thither, on any apprehension of danger, they flee, especially when
> numerous sacrifices are expected, and cannot thence be taken by force,
> though they are sometimes seduced to quit their asylum (Wilson 1799:
> 339).

More is known about sanctuaries in Hawaii. Precontact Hawaiian
society maintained many *kapus* (taboos) that were rigidly enforced.
When a kapu was broken, whether it entailed an affront to a chief or
a violation of food preparation, the penalty was usually death.
Hawaiians of those times were not only constrained by many such

kapus but were also often caught up in warfare. Since even noncombatants in these wars were likely to be killed, many who were not involved in the fighting sought sanctuary along with defeated warriors. If a violator of a kapu, a noncombatant in a war, a defeated warrior, or even someone who had committed a serious crime could reach the sacred grounds of a sanctuary, that person was safe from further pursuit and punishment. Within the inviolable sanctuary, there was no trial or judgment; a ceremony of absolution was performed by a priest, and the offender was free to return home with complete immunity. Unlike Christian sanctuaries, where offenders were often required to live for years before their crimes were forgiven—if they ever were—Hawaiian offenders often received absolution overnight, and sometimes even in a matter of a few hours. Jarves (1847:33–34) provided this description:

> Those who fled from an enemy, the manslayer, those who had transgressed taboo, the thief, and even the vilest criminal, if they could reach their precincts, were in an inviolable sanctuary. They were free to all of every tribe, or condition, though the flying party could be pursued to their very gates, which were perpetually open. The rescued party repaired immediately to the idol, and offered a thanksgiving for his escape.
>
> They also afforded safe retreats during war. All the non-combatants of the neighboring districts, men, women, and children, flocked into them, and there awaited the issue of the struggle. To them also the vanquished fled. If they could reach a spot, a short distance outside the walls, where, during war, a white banner was displayed, they were safe. Should a victorious warrior venture further they would be put to death by the attendant priests and their adherents. Those once within the pale of the sanctuary, were under the protection of *Keave,* the tutelar deity of the enclosure. Houses were erected for the accommodation of all within their walls. After a short period, they were permitted to return unmolested to their homes, the divine protection being supposed still to abide with them.

There were not just one or two such sanctuaries in Hawaii, but at least one in each district of each island.[9] Therefore, the opportunity for sanctuary was apparently widely available. It must be said that we do not know how accessible these Hawaiian sanctuaries were in terms of actual proximity, nor do we know what social factors may have prevented successful flight to one; we also do not know whether someone who was purified and absolved in such a sanctuary suffered any negative social consequences as a result. We can only see the outlines of the institution, but it appears to have been a remarkable one: total amnesty for anyone who could reach a sanctuary, with no questions asked—no compensation, no contingencies, not even an inquiry.

Such a singular pattern of forgiveness calls for a closer look. It is clear that elements of sanctuary that were known elsewhere in the world were established in Polynesia before the advent of the Hawaiian system. The system rested on a belief in *mana* (and, to a lesser extent, secular power) as it resided in chiefs. Chiefs in Hawaii appear to have achieved total power over their subjects, including the power to excuse anyone for any misdeed; this power inhered in their bones, which after a chief's death were buried and deified in the shrines around which sanctuaries were built. There is some evidence that chiefs were pleased when their subjects requested sanctuary from them because this was an affirmation of their power. Chiefs supported the sanctuary system by requiring that priests in a sanctuary kill any persons who attempted to violate the sacred area.[10]

For example, Dorothy Barrere (1957) cites a legendary source in an account of two brothers who had violated a kapu and then tried to talk their way out of arrest and subsequent trial, but who failed to convince the chief's guards. The brothers had to fight their way free and run for the sanctuary. The chief sent his executive officer and his warriors after them, but the brothers reached the sanctuary ahead of them. The chief's men demanded the release of the kapu violators but were told by the priest of the sanctuary that the brothers were in a sacred refuge. The chief's officer then threatened to take the brothers by force, but the priest reminded him, none too gently, that such an affront to the sanctity of the refuge would bring down the wrath of the gods on all of them, a terrible fact well known to all. The chief's men withdrew, and the priest invoked the names of many gods ancestral to the chief and protective of the refuge in order to carry out absolution for the two kapu violators. If this account, which is consistent with other evidence, is accurate, it supports the idea that Hawaiian places of refuge did offer inviolable sanctuary to criminals and that in so doing they reinforced the sanctity of the chief's ancestors and, of course, of the chief himself.

There is no doubt that warfare in Hawaii was ruthless, especially during the expansionist wars of King Kamehameha, which were still taking place at the time of the first Western knowledge of the sanctuary system. Horrible deaths were meted out more than generously. Also, violations of the many kapus were met with horrible punishments, as Jarves (1847:33) described:

Unless powerful friends interfered, the slightest breach of any of its requisitions, however absurd or artificial, was punished with death. Some were burnt, others strangled, despatched with clubs or stones within the temples, or sacrificed in a more lingering and dreadful manner. Eyes were scooped out, limbs broken, and the most exquisite tortures inflicted for several days, before the final stroke was given.

Hawaii also had its share of secular criminals. It is possible to speculate that so great an abundance of people in fear of their lives led to the development of a sanctuary system, especially when chiefs with the power of life and death were competing with one another for territory or followers. This analysis is not altogether convincing, however, for we know too little about Hawaii to be certain of the facts, and we must also acknowledge that people in many other societies—in Europe, Asia, and Mesoamerica—endured a similar set of circumstances without developing the institution of sanctuary to a comparable degree.

CONCLUSION

This review of settings has identified additional kinds of exempting phenomena. First, many societies—perhaps all—set aside certain physically bounded and culturally defined places (I have called them settings) where people may without penalty behave in ways that would ordinarily be objectionable and punishable. The rules that may be violated with impunity include moral and supernatural rules, as we saw in the examples from India. Sometimes, very important rules must be broken, as illustrated by the example of the Sambia. Second, we have seen that many societies also provide settings that temporarily or permanently absolve wrongdoers of blame for their offenses committed elsewhere. The constraining power of rules (and of rules for breaking rules) is highlighted in the concept of sanctuary: someone who breaches a law or even a supernatural rule could escape punishment by the relatively simple expedient of flight to a "sacred" setting. Those who were offended against, including kings, were powerless against the rules that provided safety and absolution.

PART II

CONTRASTS IN RULE SYSTEMS: FLEXIBLE AND INFLEXIBLE

Introduction

The purpose of Part I was to introduce four types of rule-based exceptions to important rules that are common throughout the world. Many more examples could have been presented, but those offered in the last four chapters should be adequate to indicate that many compelling options exist for claiming rule-based exceptions to rules. To this extent, the evidence supports the strategic interaction perspective.

But something else emerged from the same evidence: not all rules have exceptions, and neither rules nor their rule-based exceptions are *merely* rhetorical or strategic devices which people manipulate for self-interest. Some rules are quite inflexible, and so are some rules-for-breaking-rules; often, these rules allow little room for strategic maneuvering and instead exert great power over people, guiding, governing, or coercing their behavior. People conform to these rules, feeling that it is right or necessary to do so, and they punish those who do not conform to the rules.

This returns us to the puzzle mentioned in the first chapter: Why are some rules flexible and others very inflexible? But we cannot come to an understanding of the conditions that underlie rule flexibility on the one hand or inflexibility on the other without examining rules and exceptions to rules in their larger social and cultural contexts. This is the task of the three chapters that make up Part II.

CHAPTER 7

A Societal Contrast in Rules and Responsibility

It is not difficult to conceive of a continuum of societies that differ in the relative flexibility of their rules. At one extreme we can imagine societies in which rules are largely implicit; such rules would be largely taken for granted until they were breached, and the ensuing argument might or might not clarify matters. In such a society some explicit rules would exist, but they would be flexible; an offender might or might not be held liable, depending on the circumstances. In a society where rules are this flexible, rules about exceptions from rules would be flexible, too. Individual restitution or compensation for wrongdoing would be less important than conciliation and the return of social harmony. Such a system need not be prototypically Durkheimian, with shared goals and a harmony of interests—there *would* be disagreement, grievance, and conflict. But the rules that would guide everyday life, control conflict, and restore peace would be either implicit, loosely phrased, or both. Thus, although such a system would not lack rules, these rules would be elastic and negotiable. Strict liability could not exist; exceptions, alternatives, and negotiation would be the very nature of the system. It would be an arena for strategic interaction.

At the opposite extreme would be a society like the one imagined by Max Black in chapter 2. Such a society would not be quite so extreme as the one T. H. White (1965:122) imagined in describing a sign that might be posted outside an ant colony: "Everything not forbidden is compulsory." Its members, though, would have clearly articulated, categorical rules, would share knowledge of the penalties that specific rule violations would incur, and would typically enforce many of their rules absolutely, allowing no excuses to mitigate liability. In such a society, wrongdoers would suffer physical punishment or destruction of property or be banished from the society altogether. Some explicit rules providing exceptions to rules might be recognized, but in general the rules and their enforcement would be inflexible.

Do societies actually exist at either of the extremes of this idealized continuum? We have known for many years that societies have been said to differ considerably in the flexibility of their rules and in the strictness with which they hold their members accountable for wrongdoing, as the following remarks, made by Ralph Linton (1949:123) at a conference in 1947, illustrate:

> Different cultures show a tremendous amount of difference in the degree to which their patterns are consciously formalized. My experiences with Polynesians and Comanches illustrate this: Polynesians can give you practically an Emily Post statement of what proper behavior should be on all occasions, whereas Comanches, when asked how they do anything, immediately answer, "Well, that depends."

As we shall see in this and in the next two chapters, many societies have been characterized as either flexible or inflexible in their approach to rules.[1] In this chapter we will examine two societies that have been said to differ in this way, the Mbuti Pygmies of Zaire and the Cheyenne Indians of the North American plains. The Mbuti have been said to possess a highly flexible form of rule system (Gardner 1966); in contrast, the Cheyenne political and legal system has been described as highly developed (Eggan 1937; Hoebel 1960). As we shall see, these characterizations are only partly accurate; the Mbuti hold one another strictly to account for some of their rules, and the Cheyennes permit some legitimate exceptions to theirs.

THE MBUTI

The Mbuti pygmies of the Ituri forest in Zaire have been characterized by anthropologist Colin Turnbull as people who maintain themselves without reliance on explicit rules or the attribution of personal blame. For example, Turnbull (1961:83) wrote: "The Pygmies seemed bound by few set rules." He added (1961:118): "Disputes were usually settled with little reference to the alleged rights and wrongs of the case, but chiefly with the intention of restoring peace to the community." Turnbull also noted that even on those few occasions when serious instances of misconduct led to a public thrashing, the destruction of property, or temporary ostracism, the wrongdoer was not made of suffer lasting blame. In an environment where cooperative net hunting was essential, the Mbuti seem to have achieved a measure of intraband harmony by avoiding both explicit rules and the imposition of strict liability for the violation of rules. The Mbuti stand in marked contrast to the Cheyennes and, as we shall see in the next chapter, to several other societies in which individuals are strictly responsible for following set rules and may incur lasting blame for wrongdoing.

While there is a large inventory of commentaries on the Mbuti, few have ethnographic value. Patrick Putnam wrote very little before the loss of his field notes and his death, and Father Paul Schebesta, despite considerable firsthand knowledge, was often surprisingly insensitive and unsympathetic. As Turnbull (1965b) observed, despite Schebesta's extensive contact with the Mbuti, he traveled with his own entourage, lived apart from their camps, and sometimes took it upon himself to resolve their disputes, applying force when he was so disposed. He also referred to them in less than endearing terms. In his first popular book (1933:25), he referred to them variously as "appallingly ugly" and "loathsome," adding that he found them "indescribably repulsive, many so hideous that they make me shudder." He was also arrantly ethnocentric. For these reasons, many of his judgments and interpretations are highly suspect. Even his descriptive passages must be viewed with caution. And recent ecologically oriented research by Harako (1976) and Tanno (1976) typically lacks relevant detail.[2]

As a result, we rely primarily on the work of Colin Turnbull for our knowledge of Mbuti rules and exemptions. While some questions about accountability in Mbuti culture necessarily remain unanswered, Turnbull's writings provide considerable information about Mbuti life during the 1950s. The Mbuti described by Turnbull were gatherers and net hunters in a forest environment that was remarkably benign.[3] There were no extremes of climate, few malignant diseases, and only occasional dangers from animals, such as leopards, that were known to attack people in their camps (Putnam 1954). Hunger was rare, and starvation was unknown (Turnbull 1965b:128). There were some 35,000 or 40,000 Mbuti in all, but they lived in small bands of twenty or thirty households, seldom comprising more than one hundred people. There were few occasions when bands came together. The Mbuti bands that exploited this forest world had no persons of lasting authority, no chiefs or councils, no elders or "big men"; yet the Mbuti had to cooperate to hunt and to live, and when disputes arose that threatened band harmony, order and cooperation somehow had to be restored.

Although the Mbuti recognized that cooperation in the hunt was a necessity, disagreement about most things was nevertheless almost continual. Schebesta (1933:95) wrote that the Mbuti were "explosive" and "quarrelsome," and he complained about the "infernal din and clamorous wrangling" of camp life. For once, Schebesta understated matters. The Mbuti loved a good argument, especially at another's expense, and they were seldom without a lively quarrel to overhear, laugh at, comment upon, and, sometimes, join. Few of these daily broils led to more than heated words and a good sulk for a few hours. Most died down of inanition, but a few were cooled down by a peacemaking rule, such as one specifying that a woman who sat straight up and still was so displeased that she should be left strictly alone. But some quarrels did not wear themselves out, nor were they readily settled (Turnbull reported 124 serious disputes during his stay with one band), and these could lead to kicks, punches, and blows with clubs or even with logs dragged out of the fire. Injuries were usually minor, although teeth were sometimes knocked out, but the potential danger to the harmony of the band was serious indeed. With their explosive tempers, a fight among the Mbuti might even involve weapons despite strict rules against their use; even without injury, a fight could leave such lasting hostility that cooperative hunting was impossible. The band might even break up, leaving too few people for effective net hunting.[4]

Although Mbuti life often appeared to be anarchic, even chaotic, Turnbull (1965*b*:216) cautioned that "despite its unformalized nature and the absence of political or legal systems," there were strong forces for social order in Mbuti society. For example, to avoid social disruptions—especially to hunting, on which so much depended—major disputes were likely to be reacted to with ridicule or mime or, in more severe instances, with ostracism or exile. Of course, the Mbuti sought to avoid disharmony for the usual reasons, too, including those of public opinion and of the very real affection that many people felt for one another. And, perhaps most importantly, there was the forest. For the Mbuti, the forest *was* morality; it acted as the ultimate arbiter of right and wrong. "If you ask a Pygmy why his people have no chiefs, no lawgivers, no councils, or no leaders, he will answer with misleading simplicity, 'Because we are the people of the forest.' The forest, the great provider, is the one standard by which all deeds and thoughts are judged; it is the chief, the lawgiver, the leader, and the final arbitrator" (Turnbull 1961:125). The forest was believed to be good, but if it were displeased by the Mbuti, it might punish them by causing storms, trees to fall, ill health, and poor hunting. What displeased the forest was "noise"—trouble, dispute, or discontent. Some fundamental sources of noise were laziness, aggressiveness, or disputatiousness, but any conflict that threatened harmony and, therefore, economic cooperation was dangerous. If the forest were to remain beneficent, the Mbuti believed, they had to avoid conflict—noise—and restore peace and harmony as rapidly as possible. In the view of the Mbuti, to dwell upon individual blame was not only secondary to the maintenance of harmony but could also be counterproductive, deflecting people from their most vital task: living in harmony with their forest.

Turnbull's portrait of Mbuti life, which was seemingly so free of explicit rules and lasting blame, was in stark contrast with his picture of the neighboring BaBira and BaNgwana African villagers, with whom the Mbuti had enduring economic and ritual ties. The BaBira and BaNgwana lived in a world dominated by explicit rules, including strict taboos that had to be followed on pain of harsh supernatural punishments. They also emphasized individual accountability for rule violations (Turnbull 1961, 1965*b*). As good pragmatists, the Mbuti paid necessary lip service to this rule-governed world when they lived among the villagers, even seeming to accept their ideas of individual responsibility for taboo violation, sorcery, and witchcraft; when the Pygmies left the villages to return to the forest, however, they left behind the governance of rules and chiefs as well as, we are told, any question of determining individual responsibility for wrongdoing or misfortune.[5]

There may be reason for caution about some aspects of this depiction of Mbuti life, as we shall see. But there is no reason to doubt that relative to many societies, including those of the neighboring African villagers, the Mbuti relied less on explicit rules than on adherence to general moral or supernatural principles, or meta-rules, and that they preferred to resolve conflict without holding persons lastingly responsible for wrongdoing.

Turnbull repeatedly stressed that Mbuti behavior was consistently guided—but not rigidly constrained— by moral principles such as the conviction that cooperation was right while laziness, aggressiveness, and argumentativeness were wrong (Turnbull 1965*b*:278). But, although Turnbull did not stress this, the Mbuti also had some quite explicit secular rules that were often invoked in preventing or resolving disputes about such matters as incest, theft, and violence, to mention but a few of the more important and potentially disruptive problems of their life. Still, some apparently important rules were not always followed. For example, Turnbull (1965*b*:120) noted that the rule requiring food from the hunt to be shared within the band was important, and that "everybody" knew the rules that stated how meat was to be divided; nevertheless, these rules were routinely broken by women who furtively concealed meat in pots or under the leaves on their roofs rather than sharing it.[6]

Turnbull also found it curious that seemingly important matters such as birth and marriage were so poorly defined by clear rules (apparently, such events were considered to be important only for the nuclear family rather than for the band), while some seemingly far less consequential matters required conformity by the entire band (1965*b*:118): "This pattern is sometimes most plain in matters that seem most trivial, such as the insistence that embers that fall from the fire should not simply be scooped or pushed back but should be picked up and placed on top of the fire; [and] the feeling that anyone passing through a stream should wash himself, or at least a part of himself, even if he [had] crossed another turn of the stream a few yards back." As Goldschmidt observed of the Sebei (chapter 1), it is not always the most obviously important rules (to the ethnographer's eyes, that is) that are the most strictly insisted on.

As one continues to read Turnbull's various reports about the Mbuti, more and more explicit rules turn up. Some were conventions, others were secular regulations. What is more, some were scrupulously followed. For example, despite the cooperative emphasis among the Mbuti, individual rights to honey trees were clear and enforced, as were rules of band territory and trespass (1965*b*:96); unmarried youths had considerable sexual freedom, but the girl was always required to give her permission, and no violations of this rule were known (1965*b*:96); and homosexuality, which was repellent, apparently did not occur (1965*b*:122). There was also a clear rule that forbade nursing mothers from engaging in extramarital sexual intercourse; as far as Turnbull could learn, this rule, too, was never broken (1981:215). Members of the same sex derived mild sexual satisfaction from sleeping together, but the Mbuti "state very carefully rules as to how to lie, with legs thrown backwards around the other's legs, or even around his hips or waist, and they say one may entwine legs while lying front to front, though it is not considered good to hold each other too closely with the arms" (Turnbull 1965*b*:122).

We also learn that the umbilical cord of a newborn had to be cut by an arrow blade of its father, that neither parent could eat meat until the child was old enough to crawl, that only children could eat fish, that there were mandatory terms of address, and—very puzzling, given the importance of hunting—that children were required to light a fire in a certain way that gave off smoke just so, or the hunters could not, and *would* not, leave camp to hunt (1978:191, 1983:51). And we learn that among children as young as four, a child who teased another so harshly that the victim cried was ostracized by the other children.

These rules, among a good many others, make it clear that the Mbuti—children as well as adults—did have explicit rules of various types that were taken so seriously that they were followed without apparent exception. One of these rules specified procedures for keeping their deadly poisoned arrows out of harm's way. Yet it remains true that other rules were anything but clear and were not often adhered to. This was especially obvious during disputes, when various rules were dredged up and argued over until the reason for the argument appeared to be forgotten. It was the conventions and secular regulations of the Mbuti that were categorical; the moral and supernatural rules were often much more open to interpretation.

It is also true that while the Mbuti blamed one another for just about everything, employing the most colorful and wounding insults in the process, they usually avoided imposing long lasting blame in the form of pejorative labels, stigmatized statuses, or persisting sanctions. For example, a young man who was caught committing incest with his cousin (thus breaking a moral and supernatural rule) was chased out of the camp into the forest by young men and girls wielding knives and spears. He was exiled to "live alone forever" for having committed so shameful an act. One man said to Turnbull, "Nobody will accept him into their group after what he has done. And he will die, because he cannot live alone in the forest. The forest will kill him. And if it does not kill him, he will die of leprosy" (1961:112). The camp made a great to-do about the shameful event, with copious tears, angry accusations, and dire threats. Yet it was plain that everyone had known about the incest for months. Incest with one's cousin was wrong—the Mbuti seemed unanimous about this—but it was not until the incest became indiscreet that it required action. When the time came, that action was dramatic enough, and when the young man fled into the forest he was plainly frightened. But three days after he began his exile "for life," he emerged from the forest and, although he was rudely ignored at first, he was soon accepted. Five years later, Turnbull said (1961:114), this young man was one of the best liked and most respected hunters in the band. He did not have leprosy (the automatic sanction imposed by the forest), but he did not repeat the incest either. Thus, the rule about incest was enforced, but without lasting blame.

Yet sometimes blame *was* insisted on, and the wrongdoer was painfully reviled and then compelled to apologize and make restitution before he was forgiven and peace was restored. This happened when a man named Cephu surreptitiously placed his hunting net in front of those of the others and was caught red-handed. Cephu tried every imaginable moral justification, but Turnbull's (1961) long account of what he referred to as this "crime" made it clear that Cephu's act was not excused, and was in fact inexcusable, even though his contrition and restitution led to a dramatic and sudden return of harmony to the camp. It is unlikely that what Cephu did was ever truly forgotten, much less forgiven. It was simply put in the past so that the harmony of the camp and the tranquility of the forest could be restored.

On another occasion, the nephew of an esteemed member of the camp offended Mbuti moral rules by loudly claiming personal authority in the hunt. He was harshly criticized for his actions, and a senior hunter insultingly called him a "completely bad man." Eventually, all the senior hunters agreed, in what was a de facto legal action, that the offender must leave the band, and he did so. But while the Mbuti could impose lasting blame and even physical exile in extreme cases, they preferred to deflect blame from an individual by a variety of tactics. These included the intervention of a camp clown who, it seems, willingly served as a scapegoat (Turnbull 1981:210), as well as the ever-present, highly approved expedient of blaming the villagers for many of the problems that arose (Turnbull 1965*b*:214).

The Mbuti were also exquisitely skilled in the art of diverting public attention away from their own wrongdoing by calling attention to the allegedly greater wrongdoing of others. Strategic interaction at its best! For example, a man was accused of "offending the forest" by hoarding the surplus honey on "his" territory and denying access to others, even though they too claimed rights to the territory through official ties. The man was, according to Turnbull (1965*b*:194), "very much in the wrong," but when he quickly pointed out that another man was engaged in a "major crime" (secretly trading meat to the village outside of approved trading relationships), he effectively shifted attention from himself to another. On other occasions, however, someone who was clearly wronged so revelled in the offender's guilt that public opinion turned against him and he was shamed into silence (1961:118). Strategic interaction gone wrong!

What use, then, did the Mbuti make of rules? On a few occasions they held individuals strictly accountable, but most times they shifted the blame or else "forgot" the trouble after a few hours or days. In such a flexible system of assigning fault, did the Mbuti acknowledge rule-based exemptions, or did they, as Turnbull suggested, simply argue back and forth until the original rule violation was forgotten? The answer is not completely clear, but it appears that most of the time, rule-based exceptions to rules were less important than were strategic *uses* of flexible rules. For example, temporary conditions such as those brought on by cannabis or alcohol intoxication or by strong emotion were apparently not accepted as mitigating pleas, or at least not consistently. Serious illness might allow someone to escape ordinary responsibility without blame and to receive solicitous concern and care, but a physically impaired person who could not hunt effectively could not marry and, in some circumstances, might not even survive (Turnbull 1961:41).[7] The idea of "accident" could also mitigate; it was invoked as an excuse in the serious rule violation of Cephu when he was caught surreptitiously putting his hunting net up in front of the nets of others. When confronted, he insisted that, among other things, he had done so "by accident." His excuse was rejected out of hand in this case, but despite the apparent fact that personal intent was typically of little relevance in dispute settlement, and despite Turnbull's report that the Mbuti rarely admitted that they were wrong (Turnbull 1961:133), it is obvious that the concept of "accident" as a means of claiming absence of intent did exist and might sometimes serve as a mitigating plea.

There are few indications in Turnbull's publications that any status except being elderly provided reduced responsibility. For example, although children were loved, even toddlers were often held very strictly accountable and were readily slapped if they endangered themselves or annoyed someone; they were also expected to take on adult duties very early in life (1961:127; 1978:177). But the very old were treated with respect, were mourned at death, and were exempted from many everyday responsibilities (Harako 1976). They were also immune to physical assault when, as often happened, disputes turned into general affrays. A male elder who was a noted hunter might be able to exercise more authority than others. And elderly women, alone among the Mbuti, were able to successfully voice explicit criticism in the middle of the camp; these old women were heeded, while male elders could only grumble or complain and were likely to be ignored (Turnbull 1981:211). As mentioned earlier, one special status was that of camp clown. Apparently someone in a Mbuti band was available to play the role of clown and scapegoat when a dispute occurred (Turnbull 1965b:189):

> Rather than attempt a probably impossible reconciliation of the excited participants, the rest of the band joins in an effort to divert attention away from the actual cause of the dispute. If this fails, they attempt to dissipate the blame by raising all sorts of minor but associated disputes, so that a number of people become involved. If blame still seems inescapable, the camp clown is likely to try and take it on himself, or else it will

be put upon him by the others. The disputants, in my experience, accept this device as a genuine solution.

It appears that the role of camp clown was reserved for men who suffered from some disability that prevented them from hunting effectively (Turnbull himself was assigned this role), but whether the role carried with it any exemption from responsibility as compensation for serving as a scapegoat is unclear.

Although the Mbuti had many rules about what behaviors were acceptable only in the privacy of a hut or of the forest, there is little evidence that any setting in the forest environment regularly served as a place where normal responsibility could be reduced. However, the nearby horticultural villages fringing the forest served this function, at least to some degree. When the Mbuti were in these villages, where they occupied rather ambiguous roles as ritual clients and trading partners of the villagers, they suspended many of the rules that ordinarily obtained in the forest. They accepted laziness, violated food taboos, suspended the rules concerning the sexual division of labor, relaxed some sexual rules, and ignored cooperation except within the nuclear family (Turnbull 1965*b*:85–86).

Some ceremonies served as occasions when otherwise objectionable behavior had to be accepted. For example, during the *elima* ceremony (a girls' puberty festival), adolescent girls could attack males of all ages, switching them painfully and drawing blood, a clear violation of the otherwise important moral rule that one Mbuti should never spill the blood of another. During the same ceremony, unmarried girls were free to have open sexual relations, including intercourse, with certain boys of their choice, although other boys remained strictly off-limits. A girl might also have sexual intercourse in the presence of her brother, something that would otherwise be decidedly improper. In the *molimo mangbo* ceremony, a dramatic reenactment of the potential conflict between individual self-interest and the social good, Mbuti youths were responsible for restoring harmonious cooperation, and they took vigorous punitive action against adults thought guilty of wrongdoing. During the exhausting course of the ceremony, adult men were held strictly responsible for staying awake and singing well, but others were less responsible (Turnbull 1978:217):

Some laxity is allowed the elders, youths, females and children; but if an adult male as much as nods during the long nights of *molimo* singing he is threatened with death. The intensity of his singing, equally, must be greater than that of any of the others.

Usually, women were forbidden to see the molimo ceremony, and they locked themselves in their huts to avoid doing so. There was, according to Anne Putnam (1954:60)—who was terrified of the molimo herself—real fear on the part of women. The Mbuti said to Putnam, with all seriousness, that a woman who inadvertently saw the molimo would die within two days.

The Mbuti also performed a ritual of "reversal"—or "transvestite dance," as Turnbull characterized it (1983:58)—called the *ekokomea*, in which "the sex norms are all cast aside, reversed, and ridiculed. Alternative modes of behavior are experimented with and tested by mime and ridicule. In particular, both as individuals and as groups, women and men are able to ridicule the opposite sex, most often in terms of sexual behavior and cleanliness" (1978:215). Improper forms of sexual behavior were graphically burlesqued by, as Turnbull delicately put it, drawing attention to "the less usual apertures" (1965:250). The ceremony evoked great hilarity and was followed by the resumption of ordinary sex roles and sexual behaviors.

What are we to make of the Mbuti pattern of rule-based exemptions? The most obvious conclusion is that while the Mbuti allowed some exceptions based on status or temporary conditions, except during ceremonial periods, rule-defined exemptions from responsibility were relatively few and were restricted in scope. Instead of allowing exceptions to rules based on temporary conditions, statuses, settings, or occasions, the Mbuti seemed more likely to refer to a calculus of rules in which more imperative rules took precedence over less imperative ones.

Public opinion was all-important in determining which rule was the more imperative; it was rare for disputes among the Mbuti not to elicit diverse opinions, always offered with enthusiasm. Sometimes consensus was achieved by forceful appeal to a moral and supernatural rule. These rules often had a decidedly ad hoc quality, because the judge of what was moral was the forest, with its abhorrence of "noise." A senior man or woman could sometimes mobilize public opinion into a moral consensus as much by the force of his or her reputation as by reference to a rule as such. Turnbull (1965*b*:205) offered examples of the process of achieving moral consensus, including on one occasion consensus about the moral unacceptability of a person who was declared persona non grata and forced to leave the band permanently. As we have seen, others were exiled briefly, returning after a few chastening days of forest solitude.

Let us look at an example of Mbuti rule calculation more closely. Turnbull reported that the Mbuti believed that it was terribly wrong to draw blood in a dispute or to hit someone on the head, especially on the forehead (1965b:188–189). The case material he presented indicates that the Mbuti took this moral rule seriously, with the dramatic exception of the previously mentioned elima ceremony, during which girls drew blood by whipping boys. Yet there was at least one circumstance when it was fitting and proper to hit someone on the head until they were good and bloody.

When the Mbuti married, they paid little mind to ritual niceties and also did not pay bride price, but they did recognize the necessity of exchanging wives, whereby a group who gave a wife to another group would receive another wife—and her vital economic services— in return. This was a secular rule, but a strong one, and without such an exchange, no marriage could take place. In an instance recorded in detail by Turnbull (1961:206), one confirmed bachelor, Kenge, finally fell very much in love and wanted to marry. His sister was an obvious candidate for exchange, being of appropriate age and much desired by several men, but she refused to marry. After much delay, Kenge accused his sister of every conceivable moral defect and de- manded that she, as an eligible bride, stop being lazy and do her duty by marrying. She refused with brio, which Kenge matched, then pummeled her and left her bleeding, scratched, and bruised (1965b:208). When she still refused to marry, their mother joined in and beat her repeatedly.

Turnbull (1965b:208) picked up the narrative: "That evening the old men discussed the case by the central fire, with the women throw- ing in remarks from the huts all around. They were unanimous in believing that Kenge had done the only thing he could have done." This sort of flexibility in which action is justified by reference to a hierarchy of rules based on seriousness and urgency was typical of much of Pygmy life. One should not draw blood, *unless* the reason was good enough. In this case, the rule that it was necessary to exchange wives in order to marry was good enough.

It might be concluded that the Mbuti were more likely to manipu- late their rules than they were to follow them strictly. For the most part, they decided what was important and what must be done in order to be consistent with their moral and supernatural meta-rules, and they found the rule that fitted the need. They did not lack rules, but they were usually flexible in selecting among them to accomplish their purposes. They found the villagers' reliance on rules, no matter what the circumstances might be, to be a foreign way. The pitting of one rule against another in search of a compromise is no doubt known in all societies, but for the Mbuti it was not just an occasional practice nor one confined to smoke-filled rooms; instead, it was basic to their way of life. The Cheyennes would probably have found this way foreign and distasteful, just as the African villagers did.

THE CHEYENNES

The Cheyenne Indians of the Great Plains of North America were a small, largely egalitarian society that developed a remarkable concern—one might even say obsession—for law and governance. They specified strict rules, some of which were created on the spur of the moment, and they held one another rigorously accountable for following these rules. In the explicitness of their rules and the clarity of the penalties for violation of them, the Cheyennes seem to have tried to create a social order based on strict liability, while at the same time recognizing the need for some mitigating conditions. As a result, they afford us a fascinating example of a small society whose members sought to live by explicit rules and *almost* enforced them strictly.

Although the Cheyennes suffered military defeat against the U.S. Cavalry late in the nineteenth century and were confined to reservation life before they could be studied by anthropologists, many relevant aspects of their prereservation culture, including its law, have been recorded. Accounts of Cheyenne life before their confinement are available in the writings of various French, Canadian, Mexican, and American trappers, hunters, priests, traders, explorers, and military men,[8] as well as in the personal documents of Cheyennes and part-Cheyennes.[9] In addition, an astute and scholarly observer, George Bird Grinnell (1915, 1923), studied the Cheyennes intensively from 1885 to 1910. This was a period when many salient aspects of Cheyenne culture had not yet changed very much and when most Cheyennes still retained vivid memories of earlier times. Anthropologists James Mooney (1907) and George A. Dorsey (1905) also studied the Cheyennes around this time, as did the Swiss missionary Rudolphe Petter (1907), among others.

Aspects of Cheyenne culture and history have recently been reviewed and analyzed,[10] adding new information to the valuable research of E. A. Hoebel (1960) and Karl N. Llewellyn (Llewellyn and Hoebel 1941), who, based on field research in the 1930s, together provided a rich corpus of case materials and insightful analyses concerning both the principles of Cheyenne law and the actualities of Cheyenne behavior when trouble erupted in everyday life.

Some of the accounts of Cheyenne life, including those of Grinnell, and Llewellyn and Hoebel, relied on high-status Indians for information and may have idealized Cheyenne culture somewhat as a result. Nevertheless, there is enough information available for us to be able to identify these biases.[11]

Like many other of the Indians of the Great Plains, the Cheyennes came to rely on horses in their nomadic pursuit of buffalo and other game. Also like these other peoples, they had entered the Great Plains from another area, bringing with them cultural features from their earlier, partly horticultural life in the woodlands of the Great Lakes region. The Cheyennes had acquired enough horses to become fully committed to a life of nomadic hunting and warfare in the early years of the nineteenth century; the apex of their cultural commitment to this mode of life occurred in the years between about 1820 and 1879. After 1879 most Cheyennes were forced to accept confinement on reservations. The following discussion refers to their culture as it existed during the apogee of their independent life on the plains of Wyoming, Colorado, and Oklahoma and of neighboring territories and states.

The Cheyennes were a small society. In the period referred to, there were only between 3,000 and 4,000 Cheyennes, organized in ten main nomadic bands and some smaller ones. Each band was composed of one or more closely related kindred. These bands were united into a tribe by common language, sacred rituals, political organizations, and a sense of the Cheyennes as one people. During the summer months, all or most of the Cheyennes camped together, renewing their social ties and carrying out their sacred ceremonies. Warfare had a central place in Cheyenne life, as illustrated by the fact that almost all Cheyenne men belonged to one of six or seven military societies (Peterson 1964). In addition to providing war leaders, these societies provided police during major tribal ceremonies, migrations, and buffalo hunts, at which times these police had the obligation and absolute authority to enforce rules; they also shared legislative power with a tribal council of forty-four tribal or "peace" chiefs. These forty-four chiefs were chosen by the warrior societies for a ten-year term and were the principal legislative and judicial body of Cheyenne society. These men not only led by example but also had recognized authority to enact laws and to determine punishment for wrongdoers; also, along with the military societies, the chiefs decided matters of war and peace. But the leaders of the military societies also enacted rules, some of which had nothing to do with warfare, and the power of these societies grew during the nineteenth century (Hoebel 1954).

The contrast between the total absence of formal government

among many small societies and the emphasis on formal governing bodies among the Cheyennes could hardly be more dramatic. For example, there were no positions of socially sanctioned authority among the Mbuti, but the Cheyennes elected four leaders for each military society and chose forty-four men to serve on the tribal council as lawmakers and judges. The Cheyennes also had many priests; five of these were also secular chiefs and had the authority to enforce and modify many of the rules that governed the essential supernatural activities of the Cheyennes, including many aspects of warfare.

Since the Cheyenne population during this period was never more than 4,000, this means that at any given time, one out of every hundred persons in the society was a member of the supreme governing body. More astonishing, one out of every dozen or so men of appropriate age served on this council (Llewellyn and Hoebel 1941: 269). In 1891, every man over the age of fifty was either a priest or a council chief (Moore 1974:91–92). This representation was one indication of the Cheyennes' preeminent concern with rules and their enforcement (Hoig 1980).

An early example of a chief's authority comes from 1820, when Dr. Say of the Long expedition described the powers of the Cheyenne chief of a band they encountered as "exacting," saying that he was "a man born to command . . . capable of inflicting exemplary punishment upon anyone who should dare to disobey his orders" (James 1823, vol. 2:186). Later, Grinnell (1962, vol. 2:349) would say this:

> Public opinion was the law of the camp, and few were bold enough and reckless enough to fly in the face of it. Conformity to the rules of conduct established by custom and enforced by the chiefs was insisted on, and infractions were punished with a severity measured by the injury done, or likely to be done, to the community by violating these laws.

So taken were Llewellyn and Hoebel (1941:337) by this emphasis on law that they concluded that the Cheyennes possessed a "legal genius unique among primitives."

Whatever the truth may be about their uniqueness, there can be little question that the Cheyennes made clear rules, knew them well, and expected them to be followed. A man named Wooden Leg recalled how everyday life was regulated within the lodge by an old woman (Marquis 1931:76–77):

> This old woman saw that each occupant of the lodge used only his or her own proper bed or place of waking repose. She compelled each to

keep his or her personal belongings beside or at the head of the owner's assigned space. She was at the same time the household police man, the night watchman and the drudge. Ordinarily her badge of office was a club. She was conceded the authority to use this club in enforcing the rules of the lodge.

While admitting that the Cheyennes did sometimes break their moral rules as well as their secular laws, Hoebel concluded that "the Cheyennes as a group have an unusually strong sense of proper form, and they are not prone to let misconduct pass lightly" (1960:26).

The Cheyennes recognized many quite explicit supernatural injunctions that strictly regulated many ritual activities (Powell 1969; Hoebel 1960). A violation brought bad luck or supernatural punishments. Other supernatural rules, such as those regulating conduct during or prior to sacred ceremonies, were strictly enforced by police societies (Llewellyn and Hoebel 1941). For example, only the bravest warriors were permitted to wear "war shirts," painted with sacred symbols to protect them in battle. Any man who wore a war shirt was strictly bound by several rules that allowed no exceptions. One of these rules specified that if the wife of an owner of a war shirt ran away with another man (a problem that worried the Cheyennes greatly), the husband could take none of the actions ordinarily approved, such as taking possession of the horses of the runaway wife's lover. George Bent (Hyde 1968:207) recalled this instance: "I remember the case of a friend of mine, a Northern Cheyenne, still living, who had a war shirt made for him those days. The same day that the shirt was completed, my friend's wife ran off with a young man, and nothing could be done about it. . . . This rule was one of the main reasons why very few men wore those shirts."

Explicit conventions could be equally categorical and just as strictly enforced. For example, the right of a brother to dispose of his sister in marriage was clearly understood and enforced. Menstrual avoidances were strictly followed, as was the rule that prohibited a young man from speaking to his adult sister (Grinnell 1923: vol. 1, 155); when old men were smoking, no one was permitted to make any noise or to walk between the smokers and the fire (Grinnell 1923: vol. 1, 75). There were also many secular regulations enacted for specific purposes by the legislative declaration of a police society (Hyde 1968). Like martial law proclamations, such new rules were formulated on the spot, announced by a crier, and immediately enforced. Llewellyn and Hoebel 1941:127–128) reported the formulation of such a rule that forbade the borrowing of horses without the owner's permission, a practice that was previously permitted but that had been creating conflict:

> Now we shall make a new rule. There shall be no more borrowing of horses without asking. If any man takes another's goods without asking, we will go over and get them back for him. More than that, if the taker tries to keep them, we will give him a whipping.

Some moral rules were seen as being especially important. One of these was the rule calling for women to be chaste before marriage, and the consensus of all who knew the Cheyennes was that this rule was rarely broken. Although Cheyenne men have been characterized as sexually "repressed" (Gladwin 1957; Hoebel 1960), there is abundant evidence that the success women had in remaining chaste had nothing to do with lack of either sexual ardor or effort by Cheyenne males, as various contemporary observers noted (Collins 1928; Garrard 1955). Wooden Leg (Marquis 1931) recalled his own sexual awakening as well as the amatory adventures of other men, young and not so young. Some Cheyenne men not only raped captive women and miscreant wives, they engaged in a relentless if not quite reckless pursuit of Cheyenne girls and married women, as one Cheyenne woman remembered vividly (Michelson 1932). The rule requiring chastity was moral, but it still needed tough enforcement, and it got it in part through the Cheyennes' practice of requiring every girl to wear a chastity belt from the time of her first menses until marriage; even after marriage, a woman was required to wear it whenever her husband was away. In spite of the aggressiveness and guile of Cheyenne men as well as the amorous attentions of sundry trappers, traders, hunters, and cavalrymen, the rule was followed remarkably well. An occasional girl strayed and was subjected to public humiliation, but as Lt. W. P. Clark and Col. Richard Dodge, among others, agreed, Cheyenne girls and wives were remarkably chaste (Powell 1969; Berthrong 1963; Limbaugh 1973). This was so much the case that a Cheyenne bride boasted of her virginity and might continue to wear her chastity belt for ten to fifteen days after marriage before finally yielding to her husband (Grinnell 1902). A man who attempted to touch or remove a woman's belt would be attacked by the girl and her mother. Hoebel (1960:79) reported a case in which this happened; the guilty man made no resistance and was stoned so severely that he was left for dead. Although a wise man might look the other way at the indiscretions of his wife, other men could become violent (Sandoz

1953), and one outcome (which apparently horrified many Cheyennes) was to arrange for the errant wife to be gang raped.

The rule demanding fidelity, then, was clearly a strict one, and violations of it were harshly punished. Nevertheless, there were at least two kinds of ceremonial exceptions. First, during several sacred ceremonies, the wife of the man who pledged the ceremony was expected to have sexual intercourse with the priest instructor. This breach of morality was so profoundly felt that the Cheyennes were seldom willing to discuss it (Powell 1969, 2:443). Another exemption was allowed to men who vowed to die in the next battle. These so-called suicide warriors had a special dance called the "Dying Dance" or, ironically "Old Man's Charm" (Powell 1969, 1:112). Men who took this vow were expected to fight bravely in the next battle until they were killed, although if the warrior fought with exceptional courage and yet somehow survived, he might be accepted back into the tribe and his vow canceled. Suicide warriors like these were known in many Plains Indian societies, and they may have played an important part in the destruction of Custer's command at the battle of the Little Bighorn (Stands-in-Timber and Liberty 1967:61). The vow to become a suicide warrior might also excuse otherwise prohibited sexual conduct.

On one occasion, a band of Arapaho Indians was camped next to some Cheyennes with whom they were generally friendly and, on this occasion, allied with for war against the Kiowa. A young Arapaho man named Flat-War-Club took a vow to die in the next fight. He then announced that since he would soon die, he would like permission to "talk to" (the Cheyenne euphemism for sexual intercourse) Cheyenne girls and married women. On the face of it, this was a stupefyingly outrageous request; nevertheless, the Cheyenne chiefs met and decided to honor his request, perhaps to affirm their traditional alliance with the Arapaho, but also because his vow of valor allowed him a dying request. They ordered the Cheyenne men not to interfere with Flat-War-Club's license to have sexual relations with whomever he wished. George Bent, a half-Cheyenne, half-Caucasian American, who was one of the few men to live as a Cheyenne before their warlike and nomadic life was destroyed and then to write about it, tells the rest of the story (Hyde 1968:76):

> During the rest of the march [to war against the Kiowa], Flat-War-Club enjoyed himself. Every day he painted himself up, put on fine clothes, mounted a special war horse and rode around inside the Cheyenne

camp circle, with his flat war club in his hand, singing his death song as he went. After this parade he would dismount and go down to the stream and stand beside the water trail along which the women and girls came through the thickets to get water at the creek. Whenever he saw a pretty girl or married woman he would stop her and "talk to" her. No one interfered with him. Some old women are yet living who were "talked to" by Flat-War-Club, and they tell the story with pride. My step-mother, who was only a young girl at that time, used to tell us how Flat-War-Club talked to her, in the camp on Crooked Creek.

As vowed, Flat-War-Club fought with conspicuous courage and was killed in the battle with the Kiowa. It is remarkable that a request like his, which ran counter to such basic rules of Cheyenne sexual conduct, was accepted by the Cheyennes, and it is especially so since Flat-War-Club was neither a chief nor a famous warrior but simply, as George Bent said, "a handsome young dandy" (and an Arapaho at that). His handsomeness may have added to his attraction for the Cheyenne women, who had temporary license for lovemaking, but it must have done little to assuage the anger of jealous Cheyenne lovers and husbands. This episode dramatizes the extraordinary force of Cheyenne rules, including rules that were exceptions to everything that was ordinarily held to be morally imperative.

There were other possible exceptions to clear and important rules or roles. Like many Plains Indians, the Cheyennes had two formally defined statuses that may have provided alternatives for Cheyenne men who had difficulty coping with the stresses of ordinary male role expectations. These alternative statuses were those of the "contrary" (an exaggeration of the male role) and of the "half-men half-women" (transvestites). Other statuses, such as those of the practical joker (Grinnell 1923, 1:124) and the psychotic (Strauss 1977:343), provided many exemptions from everyday propriety.

Cheyenne law also recognized at least one *setting* that clearly served to absolve wrongdoers. It was a classic form of sanctuary. The two most sacred materials and concepts of the Cheyennes were the Medicine Arrows (*Mahuts*) and the Sacred Hat (*Is'siwun*). The sacred materials—a bundle of four arrows in the former case, a buffalo hat in the latter—were kept in separate, sacred lodges. The importance of these materials and their associated rituals for the well-being of the Cheyennes was inestimable (Hoebel 1960; Powell 1981); nothing, literally nothing, was more important to these people. In Cheyenne law, any enemy warrior would be granted sanctuary and safe conduct if he could take shelter in either lodge (Hoebel 1960).

It is not clear to what extent these two sacred lodges also provided asylum for Cheyenne criminals. For example, there is no direct evidence that Cheyenne criminals attempted to reach one of these lodges in order to escape punishment. There was an episode, however, in which the Sacred Hat lodge was created symbolically in order to save a young woman from a man's rage; she fled from him toward the wife of the Sacred Hat keeper, who was carrying the Sacred Hat bundle on her back while the band was on the march. As her pursuer approached, the young woman screamed for asylum; the wife of the Sacred Hat keeper made a symbolic lodge by forming a circle around the young woman with her arms and holding a stick from the sacred bundle. The sanctuary was respected, albeit reluctantly. Another form of sanctuary was sometimes available in the hospitality of the neighboring tribes, especially the Arapaho and Dakota, with whom the Cheyennes usually had friendly relations. When a murderer was banished from Cheyenne society, he sometimes lived alone, following a Cheyenne camp at a proper distance until his exile was commuted, usually after a period of four to ten years. But some murderers moved in with the Arapaho or Dakota, who apparently welcomed them with no questions asked (Llewellyn and Hoebel 1941:133).

The Cheyennes also had a ceremony that included role reversals, license, and bizarre behavior. The *Massaum* ceremony (also known as the "Crazy Dance" or "Foolish Dance") was apparently intended to assure ample subsistence for the entire tribe. This four-day-long ceremony was quite complex, but on the final day it featured clowns (members of a society that, like contraries, did things in reverse) who behaved eccentrically, reversing normal roles and behaviors, to the vast enjoyment of the audience (Grinnell 1923, 2:329).

There were, then, some kinds of exceptions for the Cheyennes, but what about their most basic rules? In addition to the moral rule requiring female chastity and those supernatural rules defining the sacredness of their Medicine Arrows and Sacred Hat, two rules stood out as being fundamental and were apparently intended to be followed without exceptions. The first of these was a purely secular regulation: no one was permitted to violate the regulations established by a duly authorized military society, especially regulations governing communal buffalo hunts. Second, no Cheyenne was permitted to kill another, not even a fetus (Llewellyn and Hoebel 1941:118–119); this rule, uniquely for the Cheyennes, was supernatural as well as moral. Liability for each law was supposed to be categorical, enforced with no exceptions.

When the tribal council of forty-four appointed one of the military societies to establish and enforce regulations on certain occasions, the chiefs delegated to members of the military society police—or "soldiers," as they were often called—the authority to punish offenders in almost any way short of death. In fact, offenders were whipped or clubbed with heavy horsewhips, and they might also have their weapons smashed, blankets cut to shreds, lodges destroyed, and horses killed. A serious offender might be left on the prairie far from the nearest Cheyenne camp, brutally beaten, without clothing, horse, or weapons (Grinnell 1962, 1:232). According to Hoebel, the Cheyennes were "inflexible" about this law (1960:54).

Remembering his years of life with the Cheyennes, George Bent recalled that one of the reasons the village of his uncle, Chief Dull Knife, was successfully attacked by the U.S. Cavalry in November 1876 (the defeat of Custer's troops had taken place in June) was that a Fox military society rule forbade anyone's leaving the camp. Despite the fears of many Cheyennes that the camp was vulnerable to attack, the Fox society enforced their "law" so absolutely that "people were so cowed that no one dared suggest moving, and so the village was taken at a disadvantage and destroyed and many people were killed" (Hyde 1968:336).

The military society police were kept busy patrolling the camp and punishing offenders, especially during large communal buffalo hunts of the summer, when it was important that all men hunt in a coordinated way to avoid frightening away the herd before a large number of animals could be killed. Yet the lure and excitement of such a hunt were great, and the volatile, competitive Cheyenne men sometimes went off on their own. When an offender was caught, he was often beaten as the law prescribed, but not always. He could often reduce the punishment he received if he quickly expressed submission to the police, confessed his wrongdoing, apologized, and offered his property for destruction (Llewellyn and Hoebel 1941:113; Marquis 1931:69). Another means of lessening one's punishment was to turn "state's evidence" by informing on others to the police; on at least one occasion, a guilty person who informed on others was excused completely, while those on whom he informed were whipped "unmercifully" (Grinnell 1923, 2:54).

The offender's status might also mitigate his punishment. For example, the status of "child" could provide considerable exemption. In general, children, especially boys, were indulged in many ways and were never subjected to physical punishment, because the Cheyennes said that whipping a boy would break his spirit and make him unfit to become a warrior. Although children early undertook adult economic and even military roles, they sometimes continued to enjoy an exempted status. For example, when Wooden Leg was sixteen years old, he broke the laws established for moving camp and rode ahead of the warrior society police, thus potentially endangering the security of the band. He was discovered and caught by the police (Marquis 1931:65–66):

> I was frightened to distraction, but my mind was made up to take bravely whatever punishment they might inflict. Nevertheless, I became mentally upset when four determined-looking Fox warrior policemen dashed up to me. "Do not whip me," I begged. "Kill my horse. You may have all of my clothing. Here—take my gun and break it to pieces." But after a talk among themselves they decided not to do any of these penal acts. They scolded me and said I was a foolish little boy. They asked me my name, and I told them. That was the last time I ever flagrantly violated any of the laws of travel or the hunt.

When this incident occurred, Wooden Leg had been a member of a warrior society himself for two years and stood six feet two inches. Two years later he was to fight with distinction against Custer's troops on the Little Bighorn, killing at least one soldier and capturing a rifle in hand-to-hand fighting. Not exactly a "little boy," one would think, but he was excused on this occasion nonetheless.

Being considered a child certainly did not excuse everyone, because another juvenile, who was considered an "incorrigible" delinquent (Hoebel 1960:56), was beaten severely by the police. What often mattered most in determining punishment was a person's reputation—for virtue, bravery, or other indicators of good character. There are many examples of this. For instance, when a man named Old Bear was caught butchering buffalo while a no-hunting decree was in effect, the police whipped him but did not kill his horse or destroy his property, because he was considered to be one of the bravest men in the tribe (Llewellyn and Hoebel 1941:89,115). The police possessed full authority to enforce rules, and the penalties for rule violation *could* be harsh. Yet liability was not absolute; the severity of punishment depended on situational and reputational factors, among others. In fact, police control over buffalo hunts was hardly unique to the Cheyennes, nor were their penalties as harsh or as strictly applied as those of some other Plains tribes. The establishment of police authority to control buffalo hunts was reported for the Dakota around 1680 (MacLeod 1937), *before* these Indians had left the woodlands for the

Plains, and the same role of police was witnessed among the Illinois about the same time (Pease and Werner 1934:309). By the nineteenth century, all of the Plains tribes authorized warrior societies to police collective buffalo hunts, and several of these societies imposed far stricter penalties than the Cheyennes did (Lowie 1954:126, Ewers 1955:164).

Then what about the most basic fear of the Cheyennes—homicide? In a society in which males were trained from early childhood to excel at war, to exhibit bravery, and to compete with one another for martial glory and for women, including other men's wives, the potential for explosive violence and resulting intratribal conflict was great. As Mari Sandoz, among others, observed, the Cheyennes were quarrelsome and quick to anger, and serious trouble could quickly erupt, even out of play (1953:154). The prevention of homicide and thus of the retaliation that could lead to a feud was essential to Cheyenne survival, as a small society divided by internal strife could hardly hope to stand against its many and more numerous enemies. It is not surprising, then, that killing another Cheyenne was not only a sin that polluted the killer and called for ceremonial action in which the sacred arrows were cleansed and renewed but was also a crime against society. Murder, the Cheyennes believed, would put them in great supernatural danger—hunting would fail, enemies would triumph, the world would be unsettled.

As a result, Cheyenne law called for every murderer to be banished from the tribe, immediately and without exception. He could not be killed, nor could a fine be imposed, but he must be banished. Only years later might circumstances allow the council of chiefs to consider commutation of this sentence. The law was clear, and it was supposed to be inflexible. In their review of sixteen cases of homicide known to have occurred between 1835 and 1879, Llewellyn and Hoebel (1941) concluded that the law was usually strictly enforced. Indeed, one murderer was banished for four years as late as 1890, well after the reservation period had begun (Limbaugh 1973:54).

The strictness of enforcement was sometimes remarkable. When two women beat their daughters, itself an offense in Cheyenne law, the two girls committed suicide; both women were beaten severely before being exiled as murderers (Llewellyn and Hoebel 1941:161–162). However, Llewellyn and Hoebel also concluded that homicide was occasionally justifiable, as in self-defense against incestuous rape or in the removal of a homicidal recidivist. For example, a young Cheyenne woman disemboweled her father with a knife when he attempted to rape her. Rape was a heinous crime for the Cheyennes, and incestuous rape was unthinkable. The daughter was not banished, nor was she considered to be polluted—her patricide was justified.

There were other categories of justifiable homicide not recognized by Llewellyn and Hoebel. On one occasion a man became insanely violent, severely beating members of his family. As Wooden Leg recalled:

> One case was where a man who had become angered to craziness about something went at beating his whole family. He clubbed every one of them he could reach. All of them were put into an insane fright. An adult daughter, screaming and struggling to get away from him, stabbed him with her sheath-knife. He let loose of her, walked away staggering, and soon fell dead. The young woman was in great grief because of her having killed her own father. The chiefs and all of the people sympathized with her. She was not punished (Marquis 1931:327).

Madness did not excuse the father's mayhem, but his daughter was completely exonerated despite her patricide.

Similarly, Col. Richard Dodge, who spent considerable time with various Cheyenne bands during his thirty-three years of military service, reported three murders by women, all of whom went unpunished (1882:79–81). He may have been wrong in his facts (he sometimes was on other topics), but if he was right, then some homicides—at least some committed by women—may have been completely excused or justified. We do know that Cheyenne men ignored, or even enjoyed, brawls among women (Limbaugh 1973:41). Accident could also excuse homicide altogether, especially within the family, while both provocation and drunkenness mitigated the offense.

Drunkenness did not excuse homicide among the Cheyennes as it did for so many American Indian societies (MacAndrew and Edgerton 1969), where murder was commonly dismissed by saying that it was the whiskey, not the individual, that was to blame. It was not that the Cheyennes were uniquely abstemious—various sources agree that the Cheyennes had become enamored of whiskey by the 1830s, and in the next decade, many writers referred to them as "a tribe of drunkards" (Berthrong 1963). From time to time, whole camps of Cheyennes were so intoxicated that they were unable to obtain food (Powell 1969, 1:84), and sometimes warriors were so drunk that they had to be tied to their horses so that an endangered camp could escape from a threatened attack by the U.S. Cavalry (Hyde 1968:271–272). Not surprisingly, Cheyenne drunkenness was sometimes accompanied by mayhem. Berthrong (1963:90–92) cited reports of eleven Cheyennes killed in drunken brawls in 1842–43; these homicides apparently were not included in the sixteen cases reported to Llewellyn and Hoebel.

The best evidence that the Cheyennes might consider drunkenness as a mitigating condition in the way that so many other Indian tribes did was the case of Little Wolf, a very prominent, highly respected tribal chief who was also the keeper of the sacred bundle of Sweet Medicine; the latter was one of the two most important religious roles in the society. One day while drunk, Little Wolf shot and killed Famished Elk, whom he had long suspected of being intimate with his daughter and his two wives. Without waiting for action to be taken against him, Little Wolf went into self-imposed exile and suffered ritual humiliation. Yet he did not surrender his office as chief, nor did all Cheyennes shun him, as the law called for them to do. As Wooden Leg recalled (Marquis 1931:347), "Even the nearest relatives of Famished Elk never kept bad hearts against Little Wolf. At different times I have heard talk of him from Bald Eagle, a brother of the young man killed. Bald Eagle said: 'Little Wolf did not kill my brother. It was the white man whisky that did it.'"

Nevertheless, Little Wolf's crime was only *lessened* by his drunkenness (as well as by his status as a great chief and keeper of the sacred medicine), not fully excused. As Llewellyn and Hoebel (1941:85–86) put it: "To him the murderer's stigma stuck, nevertheless, and because of it he could not touch his lip to the pipe with other men. From the fatal day on, he did not eat from other men's bowls. The greatest man of all the Cheyennes, the hero of his people, a chief to the end of his term, because a chief could not be deposed, was yet a man apart." The case of Little Wolf was unusual not just because he was drunk— or, as he himself said, "crazy"—when he fired the fatal shot (Marquis 1931:346) but because he was also a great chief and the custodian of sacred material.

Ordinarily, drunkenness might lessen the seriousness of homicide, leading to a reduced period of banishment, only if it was clear that the killing was an accident—that is, that no possible malice could be discovered. But this was granting drunkenness no special power as a mitigating condition, because "accident" in general mitigated homicide (Llewellyn and Hoebel 1941:1968). In fact, when accidental homicide occurred within a family, it appears that it could be excused completely, presumably because there was no danger of retaliation in such instances (Marquis 1931:111). It is not clear how the Cheyennes dealt with homicide when both the assailant and the victim were drunk, as in the "drunken orgies" reported by traders, military officers, and the Cheyennes themselves.

What conclusions can we draw from all this? First, the Cheyennes developed an elaborate system of government dedicated to the formation, promulgation, and enforcement of explicit rules and laws. These rules and laws were known and accepted, as were the penalties for their infraction. In retrospect, there can be little doubt that the Cheyennes were determined to create and enforce rules as though they were *laws* and to hold one another accountable for any violation of them—although in some important aspects of Cheyenne culture, such as the control of warriors in the perpetual and vital battles that controlled Cheyenne destiny, the rules were surprisingly vague and weakly enforced. For the Cheyennes, unlike so many other peoples whom we shall discuss later, there was no glossing over who was at fault in the service of achieving a compromise or restoring harmony. That often came later, by commutation of a sentence or by rehabilitation, but the question of *fault* was not evaded. Cheyenne law was constituted to determine personal blame and to impose penalties accordingly. Yet accountability was tempered by many considerations, including lack of intent, temporary conditions, status, ceremonial occasions, and even setting. Hoebel never backed away from his many assertions that the Cheyennes were uniquely concerned with rule governance, but he commented that their law was "kept flexible by a continuous concern for individualism" (1954:176). Still, compared to their Plains-dwelling neighbors and, in fact, to most small-scale societies that lived by hunting and gathering, the Cheyennes had extraordinarily categorical rules and laws as well as strict enforcement procedures.

CONCLUSION

What should we conclude from this comparison of rules among the Mbuti and the Cheyennes? First, there can be very little doubt that these societies differed dramatically in the flexibility of their rules. The Mbuti on one hand preferred to subordinate their rules to a strategy of "negotiation," in Philip Gulliver's (1979) term, or "situational adjustment," to borrow Sally Moore's (1978) phrase. The Cheyennes, on the other hand, lived by categorical rules which they made, followed, and enforced with awesome seriousness. Yet each system contained its countervailing dynamic, or, in more theory-laden language, its dialectic. The Mbuti could sometimes be very explicit about rules and tough about enforcing them; the Cheyennes allowed various exemptions. Before we conclude that every rule system generates an antisystem, we need to look further at the ethnographic record. Specifically, are there societies that go beyond the Cheyennes in demanding strict liability for rule violation and others that go beyond the Mbuti in their situational adaptability without strict rules? The answer in both cases, detailed in the next two chapters, is yes.

Do societies that impose strict liability nevertheless allow exceptions? Similarly, do societies with highly flexible rules sometimes impose strict liability? The answers to these questions are more equivocal.

CHAPTER 8

Explicit Rules, Strictly Enforced

As we saw in Part I, exceptions to rules are many and varied. Some exceptions appear to be nothing more remarkable than alternative versions of rules that were flexible and negotiable to begin with. Others are manipulated as rhetorical resources for accusing someone of wrongdoing, for justifying one's own conduct, or for negotiating a settlement. But sometimes there are startling or outrageous exceptions to rules that are ordinarily treated as being inviolable. These are not merely contingent or alternate rules, they are special exceptions. And it also appears to be the case that even societies with flexible rules, such as the Mbuti, have some categorical rules that are rarely or never violated. (This last assertion will probably raise few, if any, eyebrows, and if it does, then a reading of chapter 9 should help to lower them.)

But it is one thing for a society to have an occasional rule that is followed and enforced strictly; it is quite another for a society to treat many or most of its rules in this way. Next we ask whether there are other societies like the Cheyennes. Are there, perhaps, others that have gone even farther than the Cheyennes in adopting a large number of rigidly categorical rules and enforcing them strictly, even absolutely? Is it possible for humans to live together under such inflexible rules, or will people who formulate strict rules be forced to allow exceptions to them?

CONTEMPORARY VIEWS OF STRICT LIABILITY

In chapter 1, I cited Jack Douglas's opinion that life is too complex for "abstract, predetermined" rules to be seen as adequate by "individual actors." Douglas said (1970:20): "Life itself would soon end if one tried to live it that way." The idea that no society could live entirely, or even primarily, by strict rules has been widely shared for a good many years, and not only by scholars whose theoretical perspectives belong to what I have called the strategic interactionist position.[1] Many anthropologists would agree with what Ethel Albert (1963:181–182) wrote two decades ago:

157

A society would be crushed by the weight of its own rules, if each infraction were punished strictly according to prescribed sanctions and if all the formal norms were always respected. To be a part of a society is to know which of its rules prescribe or prohibit absolutely or conditionally; whether a particular action which is not forbidden is nevertheless something that is simply "not done"; whether human beings, always imperfect, must in any particular case actually be punished or whether the offence should be blinked.

However much it seems intuitively correct that no society could hold every one of its members strictly responsible for following all of its various kinds of rules, the Cheyennes punished infractions of *many* of their rules strictly. We do not yet know how many rules of various types can be enforced strictly before a society is "crushed." Secular regulations may be felt as burdensome long before moral ones, and implicit conventions may not be felt at all unless they are broken.

Formulations like the one by Albert are consistent with the new conventional theories of strategic interaction in which the manipulation of flexible rules is taken for granted; this may account for part of the intuitive appeal of such formulations. But they are also in agreement with the views of many scholars, including legal scholars, who have linked the growth of modern civilization and humanism to the decline of strict liability (Pound 1921; Hart 1961, 1968). Earlier in this century, Western scholars interested in jurisprudence had no difficulty believing that strict liability characterized earlier and "less civilized" societies (Maitland 1911). They found evidence for their convictions in early law, including the Code of Hammurabi, which proved, they believed, that early law was originally absolute, with no exceptions (Moore 1972). This interpretation of early law was eventually challenged by archeological data (Diamond 1957). For example, Rueven Yaron (1969) analyzed publications excavated from the city of Eshnunna (conquered by Hammurabi) showing that early law was much more flexible in its recognition of exceptions than was the more "civilized" law that replaced it.

Reports from non-Western societies, like that of the Akamba of Kenya (mentioned in chapter 1), apparently attested to the presence of absolute liability, but further evidence showed that some exceptions were allowed, sometimes due to the connivance of lineage members who might otherwise be liable for damages (Edgerton 1969). And when scholars such as T. O. Elias (1956) and Max Gluckman (1965) independently reviewed much of the evidence asserting the presence of strict and collective responsibility in various societies, they concluded that categorical rules and strict liability were found in many societies but that various circumstances also existed which could either mitigate or exacerbate an offense (Gluckman 1972:234). P. P. Howell's (1954) analysis of Nuer law is a good example. A British administrator among the Nuer of the Sudan, Howell noted that these tribesmen stated their law absolutely, with a fixed payment of compensation stipulated for an offense regardless of the offender's intent. In reality, however, the amount of compensation required was modified by the offender's intent as well as by the status of the victim (Howell 1954).

The Yurok Indians of the northern coast of California are another well-known example of a people who stated their laws categorically. A. L. Kroeber, a longtime student of the Yurok, reported that intent played no part whatsoever in their law (1925:20): "Intent or ignorance, malice or negligence, are never a factor. The fact and amount of damage are alone considered. The psychological attitude is as if intent were always involved." Indeed, the Yurok even held one another responsible for hostile intent without any act.[2] Moreover, malicious intent could increase the penalty imposed. The Yurok were obsessed by the accumulation of wealth and by litigation in pursuit of wealth, but their system of strict liability was not enforceable because they lacked any political institutions that could arbitrate disputes or enforce penalties. As a result, the resolution of a dispute was dependent on negotiation rather than on strict rule following and the force of law (Kroeber 1925:338):

> Yurok procedure is simplicity itself. Each side to an issue presses and resists vigorously, exacts all it can, yields when it has to, continues the controversy when continuance promises to be profitable or settlement is clearly suicidal, and usually ends in compromising more or less. Power, resolution, and wealth give great advantages; justice is not always done; but what people can say otherwise of its practices?

This widely referenced example lent further support to the conviction that, in actuality, strict liability was an ideal that was always compromised in real life.

Various Mediterranean societies were also reported to compromise their avowed principles of strict and collective liability. The Sarakatsani shepherds of a remote mountainous region of Greece shared in the widespread Mediterranean emphasis on honor, insisting that both men and women follow various rigid rules in order to avoid the loss of honor. When J. K. Campbell studied the Sarakatsani in the early 1960s, he confirmed that many of these rules were never broken. Yet sometimes the Sarakatsani failed to take prescribed action even though their honor was clearly compromised (Campbell 1964). So it was, and probably still is, among the Bedouin in Israel and in many other parts of the Arab world. For these honor-sensitive people, it was a strict rule that an unmarried woman who had sexual intercourse or a married woman who had intercourse with someone other than her husband must be killed by a member of her family to restore the family's honor. This punishment was said to be imperative irrespective of the woman's intent, so much so, indeed, that it had to be imposed even if the woman had been raped (Kessel 1981). Kessel reported many cases in which such family-honor homicides were in fact carried out despite the clear threat of legal sanctions by the Israeli police. However, as several commentators, among them Joseph Ginat and Emanuel Marx, have noted, in many parts of the Arab world women have premarital and extramarital sexual affairs that become common knowledge without their leading to retributive killing (Kessel 1981). Before a killing for honor would occur, it seems, common knowledge had to turn into a public challenge or complaint.[3]

On the basis of examples such as these, various scholars concluded that strict liability was a "now you see it, now you don't" phenomenon. Max Gluckman, for one, came to doubt that any society ever imposed absolute liability without concern for extenuating circumstances (1972:209). In Gluckman's analysis of Barotse law, he observed that liability for some wrongs was absolute, but that for others, intent was a central consideration; in all instances, social circumstances were relevant (1972:234). He concluded that the more socially distant the relationship between parties to an offense, the more absolute the liability, because the assumption of guilty intent was more likely among relative strangers.

It was with this general understanding that the matter apparently came to rest in the mid-1960s. With the growing interest in the flexibility of rule systems and in the strategic use of rules for self-interest, categorical rules and absolute liability were increasingly neglected. While both were acknowledged to exist, it was almost as oddities or anachronisms and always as "ideal" phenomena that were hedged around by "real life" exceptions. The strict rules and behavioral conformity of some societies (the Japanese, many of the Pueblo Indians, and some Australian aborigines, among others) were also acknowledged, but usually with no more than a passing comment. Most ethnographic reports had little to say about either categorical rules or strict responsibility, and those few that did seem to have had little impact on the ways that rules and responsibility were construed in social theory, even though some societies were described in which most rules were categorical and responsibility for following them was strict and collective. Two examples of this type of society are the Jalé of Papua New Guinea and the Walbiri of Australia.

THE JALÉ

From 1964 to 1966, when they were studied by anthropologist Klaus-Friedrich Koch, some 10,000 people known as the Jalé were living in a remote mountain valley of the western highlands of New Guinea (now the Indonesian province of Irian Jaya) where their way of life was largely unaffected by European contact or influence, so much so that they still engaged in intertribal warfare and practiced cannibalism. As recently as 1968, they were reported to have killed and eaten two white missionaries (Koch 1974*b*).

The Jalé recognized many categorical rules of all types, involving the utterance of personal names, the ceremonial use of pig's fat, inheritance of property, postpartum sex taboos, and the exclusiveness of the men's house, to mention a few. These rules seem to have been taken quite seriously, and some were enforced without apparent exception (for example, that against negligence in daily work duties on the part of young boys). Rules about matters such as theft or adultery that could lead to violent conflict were enforced with exceptional seriousness. When a member of an agnatic descent group killed or injured an outsider, the entire kin group was liable. Because the Jalé lacked the political organization to mediate a dispute effectively or to intervene if necessary, any serious offense that had the potential for violence could, and often did, lead to war. Koch speculated that it was fear of violent retaliation and warfare that led the Jalé to develop a social system in which liability for causing injury or death was both strict and collective.

For the Jalé, there were no mitigating circumstances where injury was concerned; the injured party must be indemnified no matter what the circumstances were. Because intent was irrelevant, considerations of negligence, accident, and inadvertence neither aggravated nor mitigated; they simply did not matter. For example, should a man's wife die in childbirth, the husband was liable for her death; had he not impregnated her, the Jalé said, she would not have died (Koch 1974*b*:88). Koch illustrated Jalé reliance on strict liability further with this example concerning a man named Kevel (1974*b*:88):

Kevel was cutting down a large branch of a tree that grew close to a path when the woman approached. Disregarding both the markings that Kevel had placed across the path to warn people of danger and his furious shouts, she hurried on. As the woman passed the tree, the branch broke and killed her and a child she was carrying on her shoulders. My informants insisted that Kevel had to indemify the woman's relatives because "the branch fell down by his hands," even though the accident occurred through the woman's own fault.

Koch was uncertain to what extent the Jalé extended their principle of strict and collective liability to less serious offenses, such as a taboo violation or crop damage caused by one's pigs. It is clear, however, that the principle was sometimes extended to rule violations that did not involve physical injury or death. In fact, the most grave moral and supernatural offense known to the Jalé—their only "crime against society"—was sexual intercourse between members of the same moiety. This form of incest, which they referred to as taking place between "siblings," was so evil that it endangered the survival of all the Jalé. The Jalé believed that unless both culprits were put to death, crops would fail, and pigs and humans would sicken and die (Koch 1974a:87). This "cardinal sin," as Koch referred to it, apparently was rare, but Koch did learn of a few cases in which the death penalty—ideally inflicted by the offenders' own agnates—was in fact carried out (1974a;87).

However, we learn that there could be some exceptions to the penalty. It was possible, under some circumstances at least, for offenders to escape death by submitting to purification in a ritual that required them to consume an intestine filled with human and pig feces. The accused persons might also insist on their innocence and demand an ordeal to clear them. What seems to have mattered most of all was the response of an offender's kinsmen. Their acknowledgment of guilt was a death sentence; their support might literally save the culprit. In this matter, and all others, an individual was completely dependent on his kinsmen to support his rights.

Jalé liability was absolute in its demand for compensation, but while all offenders were compelled to pay compensation, how much was demanded and how immediate the payments were could vary depending on the nature and importance of the social relationships between the interested parties. Residence, kinship, and exchange relationships could come into play to reduce the compensation required or to extend the period of time over which payments were due (Koch 1974b:89, 1974a:86). Only the offended parties could agree to such reduction, and presumably they did so only when their own interests were best served by lenience.[4]

The available ethnographic evidence concerned with Jalé rules and dispute management is not sufficiently detailed to allow us to judge their reliance on strict responsibility with total confidence (the data are especially weak where women are concerned), but Koch's various reports suggest that the Jalé did indeed impose strict responsibility for following many rules, especially those involving personal injury. Compensation was always required, even under circumstances that seem absurd in the light of Western ideas of negligence, accident, precaution, and the like. And when the offended kin group members decided to defer or reduce the compensation, it must be presumed that they did so with a quid pro quo in mind. Actually, rule-based exceptions may not have existed at all: people who violated the most sensitive incest rule might escape the death penalty not so much by entitlement to a rule offering them exemption as by claiming innocence (an arguable plea for an offense that was unlikely to have had an eyewitness) and, more importantly, by receiving the staunch support of their kinsmen.

Jalé reliance on strict responsibility strongly suggests that people may be able to live with a good many very strictly enforced responsibilities for rule following without feeling crushed as a result, but the Jalé evidence leaves enough unanswered questions that we must look further for truly compelling evidence that people *can* live by their rules—strictly.

THE WALBIRI

In any search for societies that live strictly by their rules, it is inevitable that attention is turned to the Australian aborigines of the central desert. In their review of "law and order" among the Australians, Ronald and Catherine Berndt (1964:281) said that they fitted Reisman's concept of a "tradition directed" people. Indeed, many of their rules—especially those dealing with matters of ritual, marriage, and incest—were considered to be sacred, so much so that even their accidental transgression led to the offender's execution; in some instances, there was no need for execution, since supernatural punishment caused the offender to sicken and die (Berndt and Berndt 1964:287).

T. G. H. Strehlow, Australian linguist and former patrol officer in central Australia, observed that sacrilege was punishable—and was, in fact, punished—by death everywhere in central Australia (1970). He recorded several specific cases, some quite recent, in which persons guilty of sacrilege were killed, even though their offenses were sometimes obviously accidental (1970:113):

> All went well at this festival till an unfortunate accident happened one morning. This accident was deemed to constitute a grave act of sacrilege against the grim eagle ancestors. There were cries of alarm from the watching men and shouts of murderous anger from the ceremonial chief and his elders. The young men involved in the accident—there were either two or three of them—were immediately seized. Their necks were twisted around till the vertebrae had been dislocated, and they were probably choked to death as well. Holes were dug at the foot of the eagle totem pole, as a token that it was this symbol itself which had executed the offenders against its sacred dignity. After that the shocked spectators and all other male visitors rushed away from the desecrated ground, taking their wailing women and children with them without further delay. No one dared to lift his voice against the authority exercised by the ceremonial chief or his elders. For an objector to do so would have meant that he would be risking his own execution as well; for the men wielding authority on a ceremonial ground at such times were believed to be acting with the full power of the offended supernatural beings.

Strehlow (1970:114) also reported that within living memory, a thirsty Eastern Aranda woman was speared to death when men discovered from her footprints that her search for water had taken her within sight of some trees where sacred objects were stored. What is more, the strict prohibition of sacrilege could be extended to more secular offenses if the need arose (Strehlow 1970:119):

> Men who held the power of life and death—in this case, for offenses in all religious matters—could not be lightly disregarded in secular matters, or even in private quarrels that were nominally of no concern to any of the old men of authority. Violent-tempered and unruly males, whose arrogant actions would be held as constituting threats against the authority of their elders, or whose intimidatory behavior habitually disturbed the peace of the local community, could, if the need arose, be charged with having committed sacrilege, and then executed on a hunt by young men authorized to do so by the offended elders. Insolent boys could be (and were) killed by the older men themselves.

According to Strehlow, mitigating pleas were few and were seldom honored; for example, even the most feared and powerful ceremonial chiefs could be executed if they were guilty of sacrilege. Strehlow noted that the laws against sacrilege, whether committed accidentally or not, were so strictly enforced that people were sometimes horrified, terrified, and even rebellious, but usually people believed in the rightness of the rules and the penalties that backed them, whether these rules involved sacred rituals or relations between people. For example, among the Aranda, it was unthinkable for a man to revile his father-in-law, much less to kill him. When a man once did so, Strehlow reported that the "whole community was aghast at this crime" and the man was executed (1970:126–127). Modern Australian law and police powers have limited the use of executions even in the remote central desert, but the sacred laws remain in force and, despite the onslaught of European acculturation, many aboriginal peoples hold tenaciously to them, as we saw in Sackett's description of drunkenness in chapter 3.

Reports concerning the adherence of many central Australian peoples to their rules and their insistence on strict accountability in the enforcement of these rules are old and numerous; they strongly influenced Durkheim and Radcliffe-Brown in their development of normative theory. As we have seen, critics of normative theory have doubted that people anywhere actually could and did live under conditions of strict accountability for following many or most of their rules. Was strict accountability among Australian peoples limited to sacrilege and incest regulations, or did it extend throughout these cultures to include more secular aspects of life? The early work on central Australian peoples, such as Spencer and Gillen's writings on the Aranda and Warramunga, provided no definitive answer;[5] later ethnographies, such as W. Lloyd Warner's classic about the Murngin on the coast of Arnhem Land, *A Black Civilization* (1937), likewise left the question open but suggested that strict accountability, when it occurred at all, was indeed limited to certain aspects of sacred ritual and kinship relations. More recent research in Northeast Arnhem Land by L. R. Hiatt (1965) emphasized the complexity, flexibility, and manipulability of Gidjingali rules, a manipulability that Hiatt believed was essential to the viability of their social system.

The first ethnography of a central desert people to provide a concerted examination of this question was Mervyn Meggitt's *Desert People* (1962), a description and analysis of the social organization of the Walbiri. Walbiri rules were exceptionally categorical, and their enforcement was strict. This was true not only for sacred matters but for almost all aspects of life. Although this book was first published in 1962, it seems to have had little impact on the thinking about the possibility that people might be able to live—and might even welcome living—with a great many very strict rules. It should have, for it poses a fundamental challenge to strategic interaction theory.[6] Near neighbors of the Aranda and Warramunga, among other central Australian peoples, Walbiri society and culture were largely intact when Meggitt studied them in 1953–55. Although many of the approximately 1,400 Walbiri in the Northern Territory at this time no longer relied on their traditional hunting-and-gathering practices for year-round subsistence, they remained a vital people who continued to believe that their ways, especially their "laws," were best. Meggitt (1962:34) wrote:

> "There are two kinds of blackfellows," they say, "we who are the Walbiri and those unfortunate people who are not. Our laws are the true laws; other blackfellows have inferior laws which they continually break."

This view summarized the essence of Walbiri culture: the expectation and demand on the part of the Walbiri that their rules be followed. Most Walbiri complied, and those who did not were held strictly accountable for their offenses. Meggitt (1962:251–252) continued:

> Adherence to the law is itself a basic value, for this is thought to distinguish the Walbiri from all other people, who are consequently inferior. As the law originated in the dreamtime, it is beyond critical questioning and conscious change. The totemic philosophy asserts that man, society and nature are interdependent components of one system, whose source is the dreamtime; all are, therefore, amenable to the law, which is co-eval with the system. The law not only embraces ritual, economic, residential and kinship rules and conventions but also what we would call natural laws and technological rules. The care of sacred objects by the men of one patrimoiety, the sexual division of labour, the avoidance of mothers-in-law, the mating of bandicoots, the rising of the sun, and use of fire-ploughs are all forms of behavior that is lawful and proper—they are all *djugaruru*.

Specifically, Walbiri law specified how food was to be shared, certain relatives cared for, gifts exchanged, and educational duties carried out; it prohibited homicide (except as decreed as punishment for another offense), sacrilege, unauthorized sorcery, incest, certain kinds of cohabitation and adultery, abduction of women, and various other acts, including insults (Meggitt 1962:256–257). Walbiri law included all of the types of rules discussed in chapter 2 except for personal routines.

Meggitt assembled a mass of evidence, including his own day-by-day knowledge of life among the Walbiri, to buttress his contention that the Walbiri live in a world of "explicit social rules, which, by and large, everybody obeys; and the people freely characterize each other's behaviour insofar as it conforms to the rules or deviates from them" (1962:251). Time and again, Meggitt described the impressive conformity of the Walbiri (e.g., of 566 marriages, 91.6 percent conformed to the preferred rule, 4.2 percent to the accepted alternate, and only 4.2 were incorrect but still not incestuous).

Some rules, Meggitt believed, were never broken. These included certain rules present in many societies, such as incest with close relatives, avoidance of one's mother-in-law, and avoiding mention of the names of the dead. These proscriptions were hardly unique to the Walbiri or to Australian aborigines but, unlike most societies, Walbiri compliance was total. Compliance was also total for some rules that were not even part of the law. For example, it was a man's duty to defend his wife if she were attacked, and men apparently always did so; also, no one might enter another's shelter without an invitation, and only small children ever violated this rule of privacy.

Needless to say, not all rules, or laws, were followed at all times by everyone. Accidents sometimes led to ritual violations, and hot tempers and sensual desires—for both of which the Walbiri were notable—led to much physical combat and adultery. Camp life among the Walbiri had its full measure of bickering, gossiping, hostilities, accusations, and brawling. Much of this was considered to be a family matter, reprehensible or unfortunate but not a violation of the law. Violations of the law itself were readily identified (Meggitt 1962:257): "Partly as a result of the comparative stereotypy of most social behaviour (including that of offenders) and partly because of the limited number of possible offenses, public opinion is rarely divided on the question of whether or not a person has broken the law." Furthermore, the law was strictly enforced; in general, there were very few exceptions, and for some offenses, there were none at all. Intent was typically irrelevant (Meggitt 1962:255): "Every reasonable man knows that certain behaviour is unlawful and incurs definite penalties. If he has acted in this way, he must have placed present advantage above future punishment; he must have intended to break the law."

No ethnographic account, not even one as rich in detail and as sensitive to Walbiri perspectives as Meggitt's, can provide all the detail one might wish concerning the everyday applications of Walbiri law, but the accumulation of evidence in *Desert People* convincingly demonstrates that rules about exemptions from rules play only a minor role in Walbiri life. Temporary exemptions were few. Sick people were treated with great solicitude, especially by their spouses, but there is no indication that they might have gained advantage by malingering, or that sickness would mitigate the penalty for a violation of the law. Similarly, strong emotions such as rage or a mother's love for her son were understood to produce undesirable conduct, but emotional states did not seem to affect the penalty for serious misconduct (1962:260). And as with other Australian peoples, where sacrilege was concerned, even accident was not a mitigating plea. For example, Meggitt (1962:260) reported an incident in which an old woman named Maisie accidentally committed sacrilege when, while looking for her daughter one night, she inadvertently came upon some men who were preparing sacred shells for use in a ceremony; she withdrew in terror: "Nobody had injured Maisie physically or performed sorcery against her; but within a few days she was insane and had wasted away to skin and bone." She was near death and was, in fact, pronounced dead by a Walbiri medicine man. As her relatives made ready to bury her, Meggitt's wife happened to discover that she was still alive and subsequent attention apparently led to her partial recovery, although she remained insane. Meggitt (1962:260) continued:

> Men with whom I discussed the affair said that Maisie's "trouble" did not surprise them. She had broken an important dreamtime law, the automatic punishment for which should be death; everyone therefore expected her to die. The fact that she had seen the shells accidentally while acting like a good "mother" to help her "daughter" was irrelevant.

Exemptions based on status were also uncommon. Meggitt (1962:257) made this general statement:

> The people rarely permit considerations of intratribal social status to distort their interpretation of the law (except sometimes in the case of women). What is penalized on one occasion is unlikely to be condoned on another.

> A Gadjari (sacred society) leader is not immune from punishment when he attacks another person for private reasons. A medicine-man who "sings" a faithless mistress is as guilty of intended homicide as is any other man who performs sorcery for personal advantage. Indeed, when a medicine-man "sings" an alleged killer in another community, his own countrymen do not justify his action simply in terms of the

superior status of their group; they regard him as the agent of an impartial Walbiri law.

Neither mental retardation, psychosis, nor old age provided exemption from the law, but childhood did excuse some minor offenses. We have already heard that small children were allowed to enter one's shelter without invitation and that fathers tolerated remarkable provocations on the part of their uninitiated sons (1962:116–117). A special exemption from possible intertribal hostility or violence was granted to messengers sent to summon more or less friendly tribes to totemic ceremonies. If such a messenger was decorated with totemic designs and carried a sacred bullroarer, he became sacred and thus immune to attack (1962:46). In a somewhat parallel way, a stranger visiting the Walbiri might do so safely only if he were sponsored by a man who would then be obligated to assist him should he encounter trouble or accept responsibility for his acts should he offend (1962:45).

None of these instances served to modify Meggitt's general assertion that status was largely irrelevant in the determination of penalty. Ceremonial license, like that described for the Murngin Gunabibi, is not reported for the Walbiri (Meggitt 1966). Instead, ceremonial occasions, rather than allowing rule reversals, were so charged with sacred meanings that, if anything, they called for an increase in the strictness of accountability for following the "law." The only setting-based exemption reported was a form of sanctuary sometimes made available to an offender who could escape immediate punishment by fleeing to a neighboring tribe; if he returned after several years of exile, he might face no more than a minor ritual wounding for an offense that would otherwise be punishable by death.

All of this argues strongly for the inflexibility of the Walbiri legal system, but there is some additional evidence that suggests that this view should be tempered, if only slightly. For example, Meggitt had this to say about the role of a person's reputation in the determination of punishment (1962:259):

> When people are taught legal norms, they simultaneously learn of the punishments appropriate to their infraction; consequently, a person who is competent to judge whether certain behaviour transgresses a rule is also able to nominate the punishment due to the offender. It is at this point that considerations of community membership, kinship, and friendship are likely to bias the individual's judgment.

The stated penalty is in effect the maximum that may follow the offense; and people sympathetic to the offender may plead for a lesser punishment. They do not deny his offense, for this is usually patent, but they argue *ad misericordiam* on his behalf, often successfully. Sometimes, however, people (even close relatives) demand that a persistent offender receive the heaviest penalty possible. Thus, a person's reputation, and not his present behaviour alone, may determine the treatment accorded him; very rarely, a chronic recidivist is killed for an offense that, in another man, would occasion a much lighter punishment.

The Walbiri also recognized that some rules, however desirable for most circumstances, might sometimes affect a particular individual with unintended harshness. In such cases, Walbiri belief in generalized equity might lead to an exemption (Meggitt 1962:254). Moreover, there were some rules, principally those relating to every-day domestic matters, over which the ever disputatious Walbiri were free to argue and for which there was no obviously applicable rule. Such an opportunity, and dilemma, arose when a man became psychotic and was taken away to a European hospital. What was to happen to his two wives, since he was permanently "away" but not actually "dead," became a point of long and bitter contention around which rule-based claims and counterclaims swirled without clear direction from Walbiri law (Meggitt 1962:173ff). On other occasions, such as discussions of the obligations "countrymen" owed one another, men might shift the rules upon which their claims against one another were based "with bewildering rapidity" (1962:69).

Strategic interaction did occur, and personal self-interest could often be a factor in Walbiri conduct, but, as Meggitt pointed out, the Walbiri also tried to do the "right" thing (1962:82):

> Most men of my acquaintance genuinely desired to meet their commitments to each other and went to considerable trouble to ensure that they did so. Although calculated self-interest was doubtless an important factor in some situations, there was also present on most occasions the implicit value or ideal of being a Walbiri in good standing with his fellows. And the "decent" Walbiri welcomes the opportunity to act with propriety, for his behaviour then confirms his own high opinion of himself.

Meggitt (1962:219) acknowledged that Walbiri social structure was so complex, especially with regard to the ideal or lawful relations among persons, patrilines, lodges, subsections, and patrimoieties, that there would always be some individuals "who could not, or would not, follow all the rules." Yet these anomalies were "normalized" by the Walbiri so that they could be "fitted into the framework" (1962:219) without perturbing anyone. And such anomalies appear to have been rare as well as untroubling to the Walbiri, for as Meggitt (1962:247) said, "the people did not have to make *ad hoc* plans for action; the norms of the religious and kinship systems constituted an enduring master plan which met most contingencies and to which there were few approved alternatives." Noting the exceptions already discussed, Meggitt (1962:254–255) nevertheless concluded that Walbiri law was remarkably unambiguous. There was, he found, little uncertainty, flexibility, or internal inconsistency in the basic jural rules. His case materials support his conclusion.

How, then, is one to comprehend the Walbiri? As we have noted, clear laws and strict accountability were widely reported among central Australian aboriginal peoples, especially with regard to sacred matters and certain kin relationships. But the Walbiri achieved a singular clarity of rules in many domains of life in addition to these, and, with very few exceptions, the Walbiri followed their rules and held one another strictly accountable for any failure to do so.

Could Meggitt have been wrong in his presentation and interpretation of the Walbiri? Some of the reports from Arnhem Land, such as those of Warner (1937) and of Hiatt (1965), report greater normative flexibility and a less strict approach to accountability, but other reports of Western or Central Desert peoples are more compatible with Meggitt's depiction of the Walbiri. For example, when Gould (1969) traveled with a group of Nyatunyatjara people who were still living by foraging in the desolate Gibson Desert, he found that only three of ninety-four recorded marriages were considered to have violated the rules of the section system and that all three were by people who had come originally from an area 300 miles away. But most persuasive in defense of Meggitt's account is the account itself. It is clear, consistent, detailed, and compelling. It is difficult to believe that matters were greatly different from the report Meggitt made of them. Reviewers of Meggitt's book, while sometimes differing with him on some point or other, have not challenged his description of Walbiri rules and laws, Walbiri compliance with these rules, or the strict penalties that were invoked should persons fail to comply.[7] The Walbiri would appear to prove that people can live with clear rules and strict penalties for their violation without apparent difficulty. Indeed, they appear to derive considerable satisfaction from complying strictly with their "law."

The Walbiri and Jalé, like the Cheyennes and others who follow rules carefully, raise some important questions. In most social theory, rules have been thought of as constraints or controls that are—or are likely to be—felt by people as "restraints," "restrictions," or "burdens." It is this fundamental idea that leads theorists to assume that if a society has many categorical rules for which people are held strictly responsible that they will be "crushed" by the burden, as Albert put it, or that "life could not be lived that way," as Douglas said. Now no one could deny that some rules are felt as burdens; even the Cheyennes and Walbiri complained that some rules were unfairly strict and harsh, and the Jalé apparently agreed. But it is one thing to acknowledge that strict role enforcement can sometimes be burdensome and quite another to conclude that for people to hold one another strictly accountable for following a host of rules is "primitive," "inhumane," or "impossible."

Yet the latter view grew in acceptance not only in social theory but in jurisprudence as well.[8] The opinion expressed by British legal scholar A. L. Goodhart (1926:38) was repeated by many others on both sides of the Atlantic:

> To put it quite plainly, he is liable for every conceivable harm which he inflicts on another. Such a proposition is merely ridiculous. Life would not be worth living on such terms. Life never has been lived on such terms in any age or in any country.

Goodhart did not know about the Jalé or the Walbiri!

It is true that explicit rules, strictly enforced, are in reality often surrounded by exceptions in many societies, including those of the Yurok, the Cheyennes, and the Jalé. But in these and other societies, there are categorical rules that are followed by almost everyone; when these rules are broken, exceptions are granted grudgingly, if at all. These rules, and this strictness of enforcement, are not the inventions of now-discredited advocates of normative theory. Such rules do exist, and among at least a few societies they predominate. The Cheyennes, Jalé, and Walbiri found life worth living in spite of their many strictly enforced rules. Indeed, it could be argued that for these people, life was worth living *because* they held one another so strictly responsible for following rules.

CONCLUSION

There are several assumptions implicit in the rules-as-burdens tradition in Western thought that should be examined. First, the idea that rules are burdens does not distinguish among types of rules; people may feel that some types of rules (secular regulations or taboos, for instance) are burdensome but that other types of rules are not burdensome at all. Second, this way of thinking about rules does not recognize the extent to which people may benefit (and *perceive* themselves as benefiting) by living in a society where everyone—or nearly everyone—conforms to categorical rules. Third, it does not sufficiently acknowledge that exceptions to rules can be granted without weakening the principle of strict liability as long as those exceptions are themselves based on clear rules, and especially if they are generally accepted as reasonable, fair, and just. And, finally, it is by assuming that the locus of responsibility is in the individual rather than in a corporate group that collective enforcement of rules and collective responsibility for rules are seen as oppressive constraints rather than as matters of collectively shared interest.

We have seen that these assumptions do not stand up well to the realities of life in at least some small-scale societies, but we should not conclude that these societies are exotic aberrations in the record of human experience. Some very populous and complex societies outside the Western tradition have made strict rule following central to their way of life. We introduced the Chinese imperial system of law in chapter 1. For the Chinese, collective responsibility for enforcing rules has been the "natural" way of things for millennia. Japanese culture, too, illustrates the ability—and the willingness—of a large population to live strictly by its rules.

From the beginning of Western contact with Japan, European visitors have been struck by the meticulousness of Japanese conformity with many subtle and complex rules. These Europeans wrote about the "iron discipline" of the Japanese people and the "tyrannical strictness" of their rulers; they characterized Japanese society as "regimented," "rigid," "closely ordered," and "oppressively controlled" (Cooper 1965; Kaempfer 1906). For Westerners, the strictness of Japanese rules was little less than amazing. Most of these early visitors recorded their impressions of Japan during the Tokugawa period (1603–1867) when an increasingly centralized and powerful state was enacting and enforcing secular regulations that touched every aspect of life.

Even after the Meiji Restoration, which abolished many laws and regulations and restricted feudal enforcement powers, European visitors continued to be impressed by what they saw as single-minded conformity to rules in all aspects of life. For example, Lafcadio Hearn had traveled widely in Europe, the United States, and the Caribbean before choosing to spend the last fourteen years of his life in Japan, where he married, taught in various schools, and became a naturalized citizen. Before he died in 1904 at the age of fifty-four, he recorded many of his observations about his adopted country. Among his most vivid impressions was what he called the "minute observances" of rules that the Japanese so strictly required of one another. Hearn (1956:100) wrote that in the past "The individual was completely and pitilessly sacrificed to the community. Even now the only safe rule of conduct in a Japanese settlement is to act in all things according to local custom; for the slightest divergence from rule will be observed with disfavour."

Western scholars with an interest in Japan have learned that generalizations about this contradictory and paradoxical culture are likely to come to grief, if not as a result of undiscerned complexity, then because of the many differences having to do with region, rural or urban residence, class or rank within class, caste, or changes over time. Yet the generalization that the Japanese follow their rules very carefully has persisted from earliest European contact to the present day. For example, when John Embree, who did anthropological field research in Japan before World War II, attempted to compare "loosely ordered" societies with others that were more rigorous about following their rules, he chose Japan as his example of a "tight" and "formal" society (Embree 1950). More recent studies of rural Japan have continued to emphasize strict rule following and, despite dramatic socioeconomic change, so have some students of urban Japan.[9] Indeed, some Japanese scholars have agreed with their Western counterparts that a central theme in Japanese culture has been what William Caudill called "compulsive attention" to rules (Norbeck and DeVos 1972:25).

There is evidence for the existence of categorical rules, harshly enforced, very early in Japanese history (Dunn 1969), but it was during the Tokugawa period that secular regulations proliferated, became ever more precise, and were more strictly enforced by the growing power of the state as well as by collectively responsible local communities (Bellah 1957). The laws of Tokugawa times regulated everyday life with greater precision and force than Western observers could comprehend. These sumptuary laws specified exactly how men, women, and children were required to work, build their houses, dress, stand, walk, sit, speak, eat, drink, and smile. They even specified the kind and value of toys that parents were allowed to give to their children. Forms of address were regulated with the same precision as every other form of conventional behavior. Again, we can turn to

Hearn (1956:173): "Demeanour was most elaborately and mercilessly regulated, not merely as to obeisances, of which there were countless grades, varying according to sex as well as class—but even in regard to facial expression, the manner of smiling, the conduct of breath, the way of sitting, standing, walking, rising. Everybody was trained from infancy in this etiquette of expression and deportment." There were also hundreds of moral rules, most of which were regarded as sacred—not Ten Commandments, but hundreds.

It is obvious that some of these rules were felt as burdens. The best evidence for this is the strength and strictness of enforcement that the government imposed (Tsukahira 1966). For one thing, samurai were both a ruling class and roving enforcers of moral law (Storry 1969); they were permitted to kill anyone of lower status whose behavior was "unexpected," which could mean anything from a breach of etiquette to a violation of a moral rule. The government also paid informers to report on rule violations (Dunn 1969). More important, these rules were enforced collectively. Each village community was organized in units of five or more households with an elected leader who was responsible to higher authority. The entire unit was responsible for assuring rule compliance and for punishing wrongdoers; they faced stern collective punishment if they failed in this duty.

Seen through Western eyes, the rules that governed life in Tokugawa times were burdensome in the extreme. Hearn called these regulations "humiliating and vexatious" and was "astonished" by "their implacable minuteness" and "ferocity of detail." He went on to say that (1956:168)

> it is difficult for the Western mind to understand how human beings could patiently submit to laws that regulated not only the size of one's dwelling, and the cost of its furniture, but even the substance and character of clothing . . . not only the price of presents to be made to friends, but the character and the cost of the cheapest toy to be given to a child.

There is little wonder that Westerners often saw these rules as burdensome, and there is no doubt that some Japanese did so as well. There is evidence that the traditional Japanese, especially among the ruling class, were adept at turning rules to their advantage. In larger towns and cities, some people ignored many of the rules; even peasants rebelled from time to time.

Considering that Japan was a complexly stratified society of over 30 million people during this period, none of this should be surprising. Nevertheless, in general, and especially in peasant villages, conformity was remarkable (Asakawa 1929), and the samurai, for all their power, followed countless rules very precisely.

Indeed, it is impossible to read about everyday life in traditional Japan without being struck by how many rules were apparently so deeply internalized that they were uniformly followed without any expression of difficulty or reluctance in doing so.[10] Hearn (1956:174) himself commented: "The strangest fact is that the old-fashioned manners appear natural rather than acquired, instinctive rather than made by training." And when Ruth Benedict (1946:225) attempted to characterize Japanese culture, she emphasized that they lived in a "rigidly charted world" where a person's virtue was measured by his or her success in "carrying out all the rules of good behavior." Some rules, especially some regulations, may have continued to be felt as burdens, but over time a great number of precise conventions, moral rules, and sacred precepts were taken for granted or firmly accepted as right. These rules gave life its meaning, its predictability, and its rewards. When someone failed to follow the rules, people were mystified or horrified, and if the failure was their own or that of a member of their family, they were shamed. They were responsible to a group, and for a group. A person's honor, self-esteem, and shame was shared with his family. One gained virtue by following the rules and lost it by failing to do so. Rules limited, but they also enabled and rewarded—at least they did so in Tokugawa times, and, as we have indicated, to some extent they still do so in modern Japan.

Ruth Benedict noted that some Japanese students and businessmen who traveled to Western countries in the twentieth century were bewildered, angered, or frightened when foreigners were oblivious to the proprieties of conduct that were so important for the Japanese. Obviously, if precise and strict rules of conduct are to be enabling and rewarding, everyone must follow them. Benedict (1946:227) added: "Once Japanese have accepted, to however small a degree, the less codified rules that govern behavior in the United States they find it difficult to imagine their being able to manage the restrictions of their old life in Japan."

This may have been the reaction of some, but many Japanese who were educated in the West prior to World War II returned to Japan without any expressed difficulty; indeed, many of Japan's wartime leaders, including Admiral Yamamoto, were educated in U.S. universities. And many Japanese in more recent times have spent years overseas before returning home apparently as able and willing to conform to Japanese rules as they had been before (Minoura 1979). Indeed, like the Walbiri, they have often expressed contempt for people who do not follow rules as carefully as the Japanese follow theirs. Of course, the reactions of modern Japanese to life in Western societies tells us little about how the Japanese of Tokugawa times felt about their rules, but it is unlikely that they were any less committed to their rules than the modern Japanese have been to theirs.

As there were in earlier times, there are legitimate exceptions to rules in Japan today based on age, gender, intoxication, ceremonies, and various settings. These exceptions are as clearly understood as the rules that they exempt one from following. When someone breaks a rule without a legitimate exception, the traditional Japanese response was often harsh, and it could remain so in modern times (Smith 1961), but the response to some breaches could be flexible, taking into account various aspects of the situation as well as the persons involved. Like the Walbiri, the Japanese could be strict, with no exceptions tolerated, or they could argue for a lesser penalty and urge rehabilitation.

The traditional Japanese are an example of a people who followed many precise rules very carefully and enforced most of them strictly and collectively, yet indisputably found their lives to be worth living. Before we can attempt any explanation of the factors that may underlie the development of strict rules on the one hand or exceptions to them on the other, we must look further at societies such as the Mbuti that are said to avoid categorical rules and strict liability in favor of more flexible and negotiable rules.

CHAPTER 9

Societies with Flexible and Manipulable Rules

According to what I have called strategic interactionism, rules seldom dictate how people must behave but are instead flexible resources for achieving personal goals—flexible because rules are inherently ambiguous, contradictory, uncertain, or arbitrary. As Moore (1978:1) said, "The strategies of individuals are seldom (if ever) consistently committed to reliance on rules and other regularities." Moore was quick to add that "established rules" do exist but that they must manage to coexist with areas of indeterminacy, uncertainty, and manipulability. Robert Murphy's comments about social life also illustrated this view (1971:52): "Each behavioral situation is understood to be unique, and each standard of conduct therefore applies to a multitude of possible interactions. There can be no exact conformity to norms because this is antithetical to the very nature of norms."

As we have just seen, several societies were not like this at all. But we also saw that the Mbuti manipulated many of their rules, ignored some, and reformulated others. In this regard, they fitted the strategic manipulation theory well. But they also articulated some rules very precisely and apparently followed several of these without fail. Other Mbuti rules, including some that defined economic cooperation and religious responsibility, were not clearly stated, but whenever such a rule was broken the Mbuti left no doubt about their disapproval and invoked effective control measure to assure that the rule would be followed in the future. Still, Mbuti rules and their ideas of liability for following them were different from the much more inflexible and absolute rules commonly followed by the Cheyennes, Jalé, Walbiri, or Japanese. The Mbuti were typically less concerned about fitting their behavior to a specific rule, and they were much less inclined to hold one another lastingly accountable for breaking a rule. Yet they sometimes did *both*, so the Mbuti cannot be said to represent a society where the rules are so flexible that they can always be utilized as resources for strategic purposes. Instead, the Mbuti appear to represent an intermediate style between the Walbiri at one extreme and an ideally rule-indifferent or rule-manipulating society on the other. The purpose of this chapter is to examine other small societies whose use of rules may be closer to this ideal.

SOME EXAMPLES

An intriguing illustration of what such a flexible system of rules might look like is offered by the Mehinaku Indians, a very small society in the tropical forest of Brazil. Thomas Gregor, a student of Robert Murphy, employed a dramaturgical perspective largely taken from Erving Goffman to characterize the Mehinaku as "performers" who "staged" their interactions with one another in ways that enhanced their identities as "good citizens": "In the Mehinaku village, everyday conduct—whether gossip, formal speeches, extramarital affairs, or children's play—is shaped by a spatial setting that compels each individual to become a master of stagecraft and the arts of information control" (Gregor 1977:1–2).

The Mehinaku are one of ten single-village tribes living in the Upper Xingu River region of Brazil.[1] The spatial setting Gregor referred to is their circular village, a theater-in-the-round, as he called it, a setting for which Goffman's perspective was made to order. Yet the "stage" was small, and the dramatis personae were limited. There were only seventy-three Mehinaku Indians in the village and some wives from other tribes; all lived in six large houses arranged around a central plaza. In this setting, virtually everything that people did could be seen or heard by others. (The Mbuti, as we have seen, lived with a similar lack of privacy.) Gregor convincingly documented the many ways in which individuals publicly presented themselves to their best advantage. Often they seemed to play with their rules (Gregor termed it "bargaining"), and, as Gregor remarked (1977:30), the Mehinaku "apparently thrive on a measure of ambiguity and playfulness in their relationships and institutions." Yet he warned that this is not all there was to their culture; they also had, as he called it, a "script" of rules and roles that guided and constrained them.

Gregor went on to record various rules, both important and seemingly trivial, that were categorical and strictly enforced. For example, the rules that governed wrestling, a sport the Mehinaku loved, were "strict" (1977:24); taboos involving in-law avoidance were similarly categorical, and the rules that governed initiating and terminating interaction ("hellos" and "goodbyes") were especially inflexible and were very carefully observed (1977:151–152). The Mehinaku also followed strict rules of seclusion at various times, carefully observed incest rules, and articulated and usually observed various clear rules about boasting, sharing, and other behaviors. They also had an extraordinarily elaborate and rule-defined couvade, perhaps because they badly wanted children (Gregor 1977:270). What is more, some of their rules were enforced with no exceptions. For example, any woman, even one from another tribe, was subject to gang rape by Mehinaku men should she, however accidentally, observe them building a men's house or playing sacred flutes; Gregor noted no exceptions (1977:57,314).

The portrait that Gregor skillfully drew of Mehinaku rules and roles is complex. The Mehinaku did manipulate some conveniently flexible rules and played with some others, but some of their social rules could hardly be more explicit and inflexible, so much so that the Mehinaku said that the obligation to follow some rules involving ritual or economic duties was frankly burdensome (1977:252–253).

The complexities of Mehinaku culture cannot easily be summarized, but it seems safe to say that, like the Mbuti, they had some rules which they manipulated in their bargaining for self-interest and others which they enforced strictly and followed carefully. Despite their stagecraft, they would appear to be no nearer than the Mbuti to our polar ideal of rule flexibility and manipulability.[2]

Are there societies that come closer to this ideal? Eleanor Leacock and Richard Lee have asserted that there is a core of features common to "band-living, foraging societies around the world" (1982:7) that includes, inter alia, "great respect for individuality" and "marked flexibility" in living arrangements (1982:8). Leacock and Lee said that egalitarian farmers like the Mehinaku share many of these features, "but what differentiates foragers from egalitarian farmers is the greater informality of their arrangements. Foragers do not 'keep accounts' in as strict a sense" (1982:8). Leacock and Lee placed the Mbuti and San (whom we shall examine later in this chapter), among others, in this category. Earlier, Peter Gardner (1966) came to similar conclusions when he characterized many small hunting-and-gathering societies, including the Mbuti and the San, as markedly "individualistic," and others have referred to such societies as "socially atomistic."[3]

The prototype of a flexible, individualistic and, in fact, "rule-less" society might be found in Claude Lévi-Strauss's famous depiction of the Nambikwara (1961:310): "I had been looking for a society reduced to its simplest expression. The society of the Nambikwara had been reduced to the point at which I found nothing but human beings." Since Lévi-Strauss's own rather scanty account of these nomadic Indians of the Amazonian forests described a good many rules that the Nambikwara appear to have taken quite seriously, he would seem to have been guilty of dramatic license or romantic hyperbole in describing them as "reduced" to a society at its "simplest."[4] Indeed, another society in the forests of the Amazon provides a better example of individuality than the Nambikwara do. Allan Holmberg (1950) studied the Siriono Indians of Eastern Bolivia in 1940 and 1941, before they had experienced disruptive contact with outsiders. The Siriono grew very little food and game was scarce, so although actual starvation was rare, the Siriono were almost always hungry; they spent most of their time either looking for food or resting from the food quest. Periods of abundant food were few; when abundance did occur, the Siriono had no means of food storage, nor did they smoke meat or fish. In fact, they had lost the ability to make fire and had to carry a firebrand with them whenever they moved camp.

By any standard, the Siriono were extremely individualistic. For example, they had no means of mediating a dispute or enforcing rules (Holmberg 1950:60): "The handling of one's affairs is thus largely an individual matter; everyone is expected to stand up for his own rights and to fulfill his own obligations." Among these obligations was a rule calling for food to be shared within the extended family, but "such sharing rarely occurs unless the supply of food is abundant" (Holmberg 1950:60). Even on those few occasions when food was plentiful, it was often hoarded or hidden, and when sharing did take place, reciprocity had to be demanded before it was given, and even then it was given reluctantly. Holmberg wrote (1950:61) that the Siriono constantly complained about the failure of others to share as called for by the rules and accused one another of stealing what food there was, of hiding it, or of eating it alone at night in the forest. One man told Holmberg (1969:155) that "women even push meat up their vaginas to hide it." A successful hunter hid his catch, and an unsuccessful one was derided by his relatives no matter how arduous his efforts had been (1950:95).

What is more, the Siriono displayed remarkable indifference to one another (Holmberg 1950:98): "The apparent unconcern of one individual for another—even within the family—never ceased to amaze me while I was living with the Siriono." Holmberg illustrated this unconcern with the following episode (1950:98):

> Unconcern in one's fellows is manifested on every hand. On one occasion Ekwataia, a cripple who, although he was not married, had made an adjustment to life, went hunting. On his return darkness overcame him about five hundred yards from camp. The night was black as ink, and

Ekwataia lost his way. He began to call for help—for someone to bring him fire or to guide him into camp by calls. No one paid heed to his requests, although by this time he was but a few hundred yards from camp. After about half an hour, his cries ceased, and his sister, Seaci, said, "A jaguar probably got him." When Ekwataia returned the following morning, he told me that he had spent the night sitting on the branch of a tree to avoid being eaten by jaguars. His sister, however, although she manifested a singular unconcern for his survival the night before, complained bitterly that he gave her such a small part of his catch.

Despite their individualism and unconcern for one another, however, the Siriono did recognize and follow some explicit and categorical rules. Holmberg (1969:91–92) reported that after one drank water from a stream with a leaf, the leaf had to be thrown into the forest; otherwise, the evil spirit in the leaf would pollute the water and bring sickness. He said that "all" Siriono followed this rule. For another example, husbands and wives quarreled continually—usually about food—but a rule specified that a man should not beat his wife, and, according to Holmberg (1950:40), the rule was usually followed.[5] Men fought with one another only when they were drunk, and at those times their combat had to be, and almost always was, restricted to wrestling—no fists or weapons were allowed (Holmberg 1950:62).

Except for periods of intense and prolonged hunger, the Siriono made sexual relations their principal preoccupation. Nevertheless, they respected rules concerning the availability of partners, and some of these rules were apparently followed by everyone. A man could not have intercourse with a girl before her puberty initiation; it was believed that an offender would be killed by a supernatural sanction (1950:80). Also, incest was strictly prohibited not only in the nuclear family but also with numerous extended relatives, such as a parallel cousin, the brother, sister, or parallel cousin of one's father or mother, or the child of anyone whom one called "potential spouse." Violations of incest rules, too, were believed to be punished by supernaturally caused death, but Holmberg said (1950:64) that he "never heard of a case of incest among the Siriono, even in mythology."

Holmberg's account of the Siriono leaves no doubt that they sometimes ordered their lives by rules—secular, moral, and supernatural—that were anything but flexible. Their daily activities were also regularized by various implicit rules and routines. Yet the Siriono, as Holmberg described them, usually seemed little concerned with rules. They were so individualistic that rules had little importance in their lives, either as strategic resources or as constraints on their individualism. If Holmberg's description of them is right, they were much less concerned with rules than the Mbuti were and even more "reduced" than the Nambikwara. Whether the Siriono actually "lost" rules that they had enforced in earlier times is arguable, but in their overall rule-lessness, the Siriono offer a dramatic contrast to the Walbiri or the Cheyennes.

What is more, the Siriono were not unique. Peter Gardner (1966) believed that the Siriono were only one example of a widely distributed type of food-gathering peoples who were extremely individualistic, noncooperative, and noncompetitive; he described one of these societies, the Paliyans of southern India, in detail (1965). Most rules among the Paliyans were typically flexible, ambiguous, or unimportant. Like the Siriono, the Paliyans were said to recognize relatively few rules.

Although Gardner's account sometimes lacks relevant detail, it does contain various examples of the flexibility of Paliyan life; the Paliyans often appeared to be a people who typically lived apart from one another in small nuclear families and usually had as little concern for rules as they did for one another. Even rules forbidding incest (supposedly enforced by automatic supernatural sanctions) had little force. Gardner (1966:395) described an incident in which a young man living with his mother and stepfather "frequently" had sexual intercourse with his mother, who became pregnant. The stepfather was angry and left home but, unlike the Mbuti, other people did nothing, and there were no supernatural penalties. In fact, after two weeks the family was reunited.

Still, the Paliyans did have some explicit rules that they followed and enforced. Children were punished for theft or aggression, and adults were subject to direct supernatural punishment for these rule violations irrespective of motive (Gardner 1965:59). The Paliyan proscription of violence was an explicit and fundamental moral rule for them; if, despite the rule, a blow were struck, it could not be returned. This rule was explicitly verbalized and it was categorical. Gardner quoted a Paliyan man as follows (1965:52), "'If we have a single rule by which to live, it is that we do not return a blow.'" This rule was rarely violated. Gardner also reported that some rules were learned by the age of four and after that age were seldom broken. For example, the obligation for everyone to attend the funeral of an adult was strictly followed, as were several rules defining the behavior of kinsmen (1965:31,49).

The Paliyans were a noncooperative people who stressed a meta-rule calling for individual autonomy, and, like the Siriono, they often had little to do with one another. Many of their rules were vague at best, and others were flexible. Most of the time, their lives appeared to be relatively free from the constraint of rules. They could and did follow some rules carefully, but, again like the Siriono, they usually lived without concern for one another or for rules.

The nearby Chenchus, a hunting-and-gathering people described by Christoph von Fürer-Haimendorf (1979), were probably even less constrained by their rules. Like the Paliyans, the Chenchus were very independent, and their freedom to move about in their territory allowed them to avoid conflict—which was just as well, since they had no third-party authority to resolve disputes. Like the Paliyans, they were flexible about most of their rules. Even taboo violations brought misfortune only to the individual offender; the Chenchus did not believe that one person's taboo violation could pollute or endanger others. An occasional rule, such as their explicit regulation prohibiting theft, was apparently never violated, but on the whole, the Chenchus, like the Paliyans and the Siriono—were apparently flexible about following and enforcing most of their rules.

The Ik of Uganda may be an even more extreme example of a people who were reduced to a largely rule-less life.[6] According to Colin Turnbull (1972), the starving Ik had lost every vestige of sociality, becoming so individualized that they did anything to survive, including snatching food out of the mouths of their parents, children, or friends. The Ik retained some rules—more than Turnbull's bleak interpretation of them suggested, in fact—but most of their former rules were no longer observed, and the Ik were indeed highly independent. Turnbull's depiction of the Ik has become controversial on many grounds, including the accuracy of his belief that they had become so individualized that they had no compassion for one another and no surviving social ties. But whatever the merits or defects of Turnbull's book about the Ik, it cannot be said that marked individualism was unknown in other small East African societies. The Hadza of Tanzania were remarkably individualistic, and unlike the Ik, they had suffered no unusual hunger and no starvation. The Hadza were studied by James Woodburn before their traditional way of life was altered by economic programs of the Tanzanian government in 1964. Indeed, in 1958–60, when Woodburn knew them, some 400 Hadza wandered freely in search of animals, plants, and honey, entirely outside the control of governmental taxation or police powers (Woodburn 1964).

The average population of a Hadza camp was only eighteen people. Occasionally as many as a hundred people would camp together, but only for brief periods, and sometimes camps consisted of no more than a handful of people. The most remarkable aspect of Woodburn's report (1972) is that a solitary Hadza could, and did, live independently in need of no cooperation from other Hadza to survive. One man nearly eighty years of age lived alone for three months, and another man, a murderer, lived alone for years (Woodburn 1972:6). The point of this example is not simply that an occasional outcast could survive alone; it was *common* for Hadza to feed themselves alone without help and without difficulty. "Individuals can and do meet their nutritional requirements easily without entering into dependency on others" (Woodburn 1980:103). A Hadza man routinely provided food for himself. While searching for game animals or honey, a man picked berries to satisfy his hunger. If he killed a small animal, he cooked and ate it on the spot. Groups of women, often accompanied by children, left camp every day to gather roots and berries. Each woman collected for herself and her children. Women cooked and ate what they wished before returning to camp, where they fed their small children; there was no obligation for them to feed their husbands (Woodburn 1980:102). The only economic cooperation between a husband and wife involved honey gathering. Food was easily provided, famine was unknown, and the nutritional status of the Hadza was "exceptionally good by East African standards" (Woodburn, 1979:246).

It follows that camp composition was highly unstable. People were free to drift into a camp or leave it as they wished, and at the first sign of conflict, they made a general exodus. What is more, while all Hadza regarded one another as kin and applied kin terms to one another, the bonds between them were weak. As Woodburn said (1979:257), "kinsmen among the Hadza have remarkably few obligations towards each other and display a singular lack of commitment." (This lack of obligation and commitment was also true of husbands and wives, who could end their marriages without ceremony.) Woodburn continued (1979:258):

> The Hadza enjoy a rare invulnerability to whatever might go wrong with the weather, the economy, their friends, or their kin. They are able with ease and without sacrificing vital interests to segregate themselves from all those with whom they are in conflict, a course of action not open to people in societies in which access to crucial goods and services is defined by kinship.

The Hadza would appear to be a people who needed neither one another nor rules. But, in fact, the Hadza did not live without social ties or without rules. Men were inveterate gamblers, and in the dry season they spent more time gambling with one another than they did seeking food (Woodburn 1968a:53); they also took part in an important sacred dance that was supposed to occur every month. Marriage and divorce were accomplished without ritual, but marriage was not without some rule-defined obligations. For example, a man should, and usually did, live in his mother-in-law's camp. In addition to providing bride wealth, he obligated himself to provide his wife and her parents with meat and trade goods (Woodburn 1968b:108–109). The Hadza, whose poisoned arrows were lethal, attempted to avoid conflict; if conflict did occur, their rules called for fighting to take place with staves, not arrows. With a few exceptions, the rule was followed (Woodburn 1979:252).

There was also a social context—the sharing of large game—that was defined by categorical rules that were strictly enforced. These rules, seemingly so anomalous among the Hadza, defined the rights of all initiated men who happened to be in a camp when a large animal was killed. These men had an absolute right to eat the best cuts of meat ("sacred" meat) in secret, away from women and children. They must not be seen, and if asked, they denied to women and children that they had eaten (Woodburn 1979:254). A man who ate any of this sacred meat on his own would be attacked and might be killed; eating such meat inadvertently—by taking the wrong cut from the animal, for example—was not excused. Even if he was not detected in the act, a man who broke this rule would sicken and die, as would any woman or child who consumed sacred meat under any circumstance. Women or children who chanced upon men who were eating sacred meat would be beaten; in the case of women, their property might be destroyed or they would be subject to mass rape. The Hadza took this rule very seriously indeed. The remainder of the meat from a carcass, called "people meat," was shared freely throughout the camp, although explicit rules of etiquette dictated how the meat was actually distributed and eaten.

The Hadza were certainly an extreme, perhaps even unique, case. There was no need for them to cooperate with one another to hunt, gather, or defend themselves. Yet they sought out one another for social reasons, and they defined some of their activities with rules as clear as those found anywhere else. What is more, for one class of activity (eating sacred meat) they apparently imposed absolute liability. By no stretch of the imagination did the Hadza approach the traditional Japanese, the Walbiri, or the Jalé in the number, precision, or stringency of their rules, but they did impose some strict secular, moral, and supernatural rules upon themselves.

Some other very small societies did this, too. Peter Gardner included several Malaysian tropical forest peoples in his typology of societies that were said to be highly individualistic and flexible about their rules. However, descriptions of the Semai by Robert Dentan (1968) and Clayton Robarchek (1977,1979) raise doubts that all Malaysian tropical forest people fitted this mold.[7] In fact, the Chewong, a small aboriginal group of hunters, gatherers, and shifting cultivators in the tropical forest of peninsular Malaysia, could hardly have taken their rules more seriously. As described by social anthropologist Signe Howell (1981), the Chewong organized their lives according to "numerous and complex rules" (1981:135), and liability for following these rules was sometimes collective:

> Mishaps and disease of every kind are a direct result of the transgression of one or more rules. Since the rules cover the acknowledgment or expression of most feelings, the everyday life of the Chewong is largely structured by the all-pervasive presence of them. A significant feature of the rules is that repercussions of transgressions may affect the offender, the person(s) offended against or the society as a whole.

Howell reported that Chewong adults were "extremely diligent" in avoiding transgressions of their many rules and that "the rules are constantly referred to in child-rearing" (1981:141). Many Chewong rules, like those of the Semai (Dentan 1968; Robarchek 1977), had to do with the suppression of emotion, but others referred to everyday matters of etiquette, food, or work. Because the penalty for any transgression of these rules was supernaturally inflicted illness or death, "there is no way a Chewong can safely pass a day without modifying his actions according to one or more rules." Howell (1981:142) added that these rules were not necessarily burdensome:

> Whereas in one sense the rules could be interpreted as a restriction on their lives, it is also valid to say that the rules constitute a body of knowledge by which they can conceive of order. Knowledge of the rules and the implications of their transgression gives them a certain amount of freedom and control over their own lives.

Regrettably, there is little detail available about this small society, but what Howell has written about them is far more similar to accounts of the Walbiri than of the Siriono.

The Eskimo provide another example. Although some features of their social organization have been interpreted as "flexible" (Willmott 1960) and their skill in manipulating apparently inflexible rules has also been noted (Hennigh 1971), there can be little doubt that they were as much constrained by one type of rule—taboos—as were any people on earth (Hoebel 1954). Although there was great variation among the Eskimo bands that stretched from Greenland to Alaska, Eskimo men and women continually modified their behavior to conform with an extraordinary number of taboos that, if broken, would bring illness or death not only to the offender but to the entire community as well. Eskimo people lived in dread of these taboos (Oswalt 1979:182) and, with the help of a shaman, confessed their wrongdoing in an effort to escape more severe supernatural punishment. As Knud Rasmussen's (1929:132–133) justly famous transcript illustrated so well, confession might help to mitigate supernatural punishments, but the violations were deadly serious, and so was the need to confess. Eskimo law left much to be desired in its control of violence, especially of homicides resulting from fights over women, but their taboo system was a model of explicit, categorical rules enforced by collective liability.

AN EXTENDED EXAMPLE: THE SAN[8]

The societies we have considered thus far have illustrated various patterns of reliance on categorical rules and of strict liability. Let us now examine a final hunting-and-gathering society more thoroughly. The San of the Kalahari desert of Botswana and Namibia have been identified by Gardner (1966) and by Leacock and Lee (1982) as a people who were flexible and informal about their rules. Few foraging societies have been described in comparable detail,[9] thanks to the work of Richard Lee, Lorna Marshall, and George Silberbauer, as well as that of Irven DeVore, Nancy Howell, Edward Wilmsen, Patricia Draper, Hans-Joachim Heinz, Miegan Biesele, Nicholas Blurton-Jones, Jiro Tanaka, Philip Tobias, Melvin Konner, Henry Harpending, Polly Wiessner, Richard Katz, and John Yellen, among others. There are also personal documents: Hans-Joachim Heinz wrote about his relationship with a San woman named Nambkwa (Heinz and Lee 1978), and Marjorie Shostak (1981) wrote about a number of San women, particularly Nisa.

Is it correct, as Leacock and Lee (1982) and Gardner (1966) wrote, that the San are flexible and informal about their rules? There are various comments in the works of competent investigators to suggest that such a pattern exists. Nancy Howell (1979:61) commented that the !Kung San tended to be "easygoing" about most restrictions, and Marjorie Shostak (1981:109) wrote: "Adults do not approve of sexual play among children and adolescents, but they do little to keep it from happening." Other investigators have made similar sorts of observations, writing that even very serious kinds of rule violations evoked little overt response. For example, the obligation to share meat was a strong moral rule for the San (Marshall 1976), but some people did not share (Shostak 1981:88). Such people were criticized, but there was apparently little overt pressure to force them to conform to this rule and, in fact, almost all sharing took place among close relatives (Konner 1982).

The ethnographic evidence suggests that the San and Mbuti were alike in many ways. Like the Mbuti, the !Kung San strove for harmony. As Lorna Marshall (1976:286) put it, "Anything other than peace and harmony in human relations makes the !Kung uneasy." Other anthropologists agree that the San abhorred violence. Conflict threatened cooperation, of course, but far more so than it did among the Mbuti; among the San it also threatened life itself, since angry men often grabbed for their poisoned arrows, people took sides, and bystanders were sometimes killed (Lee 1979). Like the Mbuti, the San were highly talkative, and much of their conversation had an argumentative tinge; teasing, accusation, and reliving past grievances were commonplace.

George Silberbauer (1981:171), whose research was with the G/wi San in Botswana, believed that the San were reluctant to attempt forceful coercion of a wrongdoer, since he could easily leave for another band; the loss of a productive hunter would weaken the band, creating more serious consequences than had the original offense. "Grievances must therefore be redressed at an early stage of development, before they become serious enough to cause a lasting breach and before excessive damage is occasioned by the wrong" (Silberbauer 1981:171). For this reason, Silberbauer believed, the San judged right and wrong in terms of rights and obligations clearly set by the rules of the kinship system. He also noted that grievances (often about stinginess, laziness, or deceitfulness) were most commonly aired within the rules of established joking relationships that allowed one partner the right to air "free and trenchant public criticism" while the other partner was obliged to accept the criticism without "resentment that might exacerbate the conflict" (1981:172). Silberbauer provided detailed accounts of the exchange of charges, countercharges, defenses, excuses, and apologies as band members attempted to reconcile differences without worsening the conflict. There can be no doubt that the San were adroit in their use of rules and exceptions to rules to achieve their ends. Silberbauer also described the use of men's feasts and exorcising dances as devices for lessening tension and resolving disputes. When tempers were especially short, cooler heads called for a dance to be held; a strenuous, all-night dance, which everyone eventually joined, apparently reduced tensions (1981:175).

When violence flared, as it often did despite all these efforts, the primary concern of those present was to prevent serious combat by cooling off the situation as quickly as possible. Although Lee (1979) noted that extreme or repeatedly serious offenders might be executed, he also wrote that the San, like the Mbuti, were not primarily concerned with determining guilt or imposing punishment. But the San were not always conciliatory; sometimes they were frankly punitive, and, unlike the Mbuti, the desire for harmonious relations seemed to be forgotten. For example, one of the strictest rules for the !Kung was keeping poisoned arrows out of the hands of children. When Nisa's little brother used one of his father's arrows—luckily, not poisoned—to hit another child, Nisa's father became enraged, blamed his wife for negligence, and then, despite her pregnant condition, kicked her in the stomach so hard that she bled from the mouth and vagina (Shostak 1981:76).

On another occasion, Nisa's husband became furious with her and began to hit her with a branch even though she had their child in her arms. People intervened, telling him he was wrong to hit Nisa when she had the child in her arms. Afterward, the child sickened and died, and a diviner attributed her death to the blows. Nisa accused her husband of having killed the child with malice and threatened him with death in retaliation: she then threatened suicide. The couple later reconciled, but Nisa's first thoughts had been of guilt and retribution, not of harmony. Shostak reported many similar examples, as when Nisa's grandmother berated her daughter for not treating Nisa properly (1981:62), and when Nisa's parents became furious at her first husband for his misconduct. The grandmother's outburst might be construed as an ordinary attempt to correct her daughter, but Nisa's parents not only lost a son-in-law by breaking up the marriage but also made a potential enemy (1981:135–137). They were righteously indignant about misconduct and were surely in no mood to be conciliatory.

A particularly telling and tragic instance occurred later in Nisa's life when her teenage daughter, Nai, was forced by her new husband to have sexual intercourse with him; she struggled to resist him, apparently fell, broke her neck, and died. Nisa was distraught, and she was also incensed. When her daughter's husband and his older sister visited Nisa and her relatives to mourn, Nisa assaulted the woman, beating, kneeing, and kicking her before being pulled away. The husband made no protest (Shostak 1981:312): "Even if Nai's mother seeks revenge, it's justified. I was the one who brought ruin to her." Nisa then grabbed her heavy digging stick and hit him "over and over," avoiding his head (to escape prosecution by the Tswana, whose courts have at least nominal jurisdiction over many !Kung San). When she finally stopped, she said (Shostak 1981:312), "'I'm finished now. I hurt your sister and I hurt you. Now I'm finished.'" But she wasn't; she next accused him to the Tswana headman, who imposed a fine of five goats. Nisa was enraged (1981:313): "'I don't want goats. I want you to take him to prison and kill him there.'" This hardly sounds like a search for peace or harmony; Nisa wanted retribution and lots of it. Talionic revenge was foremost in her mind, and if anyone tried to dissuade her, she did not mention it. It is apparent that the !Kung did not always seek harmony above all.

It is in the nature of most ethnographic writing, even the very high-quality work published about the San, for rules to take on a concreteness, explicitness, and strictness that in reality does not exist. Fortunately, the available material about the San is plentiful and is detailed enough that the reality of rules and their use can usually be discerned. For example, many of the rules (of joking, etiquette, avoidances, incest, sharing, and the like) described in the books of Marshall (1976) and Lee (1979) were said to be categorical, but closer reading indicates that most of these rules did have exceptions. For example, neither the young (Shostak 1981:95) nor the old (Wiessner 1982; Lee 1982:55) were obliged to share. Other statuses, such as those of clown (Biesele and Howell 1981) or healer, could provide special privileges or exemptions (Katz 1982), and so could certain ceremonies. For example, !Kung women were ordinarily very modest about their buttocks, which they refused indignantly to bare for photographs by women of the Marshall expedition despite repeated requests of them to do so (1976:244); but during a girl's first menstruation ceremony, however, older women did bare their buttocks (Biesele and Howell 1981:90).

The San also employed various kinds of disclaimers to transform what otherwise would have been a serious insult into a joke. Their many arguments were filled with serious accusations about laziness, failure to share, and other major wrongs. A joke could break the tension and produce great laughter but, as Richard Lee (1979:372) noted,

> Simply because these arguments happen to be funny does not mean that they lack seriousness. They *are* serious, and they proceed along the knife edge between laughter and anger. Indeed, one of the purposes of this kind of argument is to provoke one's opponent to anger so that one can retort with injured innocence: "What's the matter, we were only kidding."

The San were also skilled at redefining rules, claiming extenuating circumstances, turning an accusation into a counter-accusation, and simply brazening matters out. Adultery is a case in point that illustrates all these and other aspects of the San approach to rules. When Elizabeth Thomas (1959) wrote her popular book *The Harmless People,* she reported that adultery was strongly condemned among the San. Later, Lorna Marshall (1976) summarized years of research among the San by concluding that a San husband was within his right if he killed a man who slept with his wife but that the adulterer was permitted to fight back (Marshall, 1976:280–281): "With poisoned arrows, both men might be killed. Fighting is so dangerous it is feared by the !Kung with a pervading dread." Nevertheless, said Marshall, five cases of adultery came to light between 1951 and 1958. A few years later, Richard Lee (1979:377) reported that adultery was the most common cause of fights among the !Kung, and while he could discover only one instance of a man's intentionally killing his wife over adultery, he found that men did fight and kill other men over adultery (1979:391).

Only when Marjorie Shostak published *Nisa* (1981), with its intimate perspective on !Kung San life, did it become clear that adultery was commonplace, and while it was hardly condoned, the rules governing it were neither as simple nor as categorical as had earlier been reported (Shostak, 1981:266): "Women readily acknowledge their intense emotional involvements with their husbands. Nevertheless, quite early on in marriage, many women start having lovers. Affairs are often long-term, from a few months to a few years, and some continue throughout a lifetime." It goes without saying that many of these lovers were married men. It should also come as no surprise that both husbands and wives were intensely jealous. Accusations of sexual infidelity were an everyday occurrence, and fights among all partners, including the women, in a real or suspected triangle were also common. Yet the San enthusiastically sought sexual pleasure, and the sexual excitement and romantic involvement of adulterous love affairs were almost irresistible.

Still, in one sense Marshall was right. Adultery was wrong, and one must not be caught at it. One's primary obligation was to one's spouse, and open adultery was a profound insult almost sure to result in violence. Adultery had to be discreet or it became dangerous (Shostak 1981:269). For example, Shostak reported that someone saw a woman named Bau with a lover and told Bau's husband, who beat her until, in her own words, she was "almost dead" (1981:19). From then on, Bau was too afraid to have affairs. But this is only one possible outcome, and it is not the most usual one. Many women were found out and beaten, yet their affairs continued, and sometimes a woman might even defy her husband and leave him for her lover, whom she might later marry. When Nisa was a girl, her mother had a lover named Toma. Nisa complained to her mother about this relationship and then told her father about it. She appeared to have done so partly because having a lover was wrong, partly because she was jealous, and partly because she was frustrated at having to wait, tired and unhappy, while the couple made love in the bush. Nisa's father hit his wife, then threatened to kill Toma. Nisa's older brothers also fought with Toma, demanding that he end his indiscreet affair. But Toma persisted, and eventually Nisa's mother went away to live with him.

Discretion was the San ideal, but the strength and persistence of the partners was important in the outcome of an adulterous affair; there were also many other considerations, including the quality of the relationship between husband and wife and the willingness of family and relatives to intervene. Nisa recalled many arguments about adultery in the course of which accusations, claims, and excuses flew with wonderful rapidity and complexity. Rules were referred to and rejected, past wrongs were dredged up, and diversionary tactics were skillfully utilized as various interested parties became involved.

Nisa's romantic affairs were many, overlapping and tempestuous; she had five husbands, serially, and they certainly did not have an easy time living with this passionate, demanding, jealous, and almost fearless woman. Shostak's account of Nisa's life retains so much detail, often in Nisa's own words, that it is impossible not to realize that adultery was an enormously complex human drama for the San, just as it is for people in many other cultures. Sometimes Nisa feared disclosure and tried to be discreet, and she even accepted a beating when she was found out. But usually she avoided this result and used counteraccusations to deny her guilt and prevent punishment. Sometimes she was more brazen, perhaps because she did not love that particular husband or because she felt that she had a right to her lovers. The following exchange between Nisa and her husband Besa illustrates some of these considerations concerning her increasingly open affairs (Shostak 1981:234):

> Besa was angry, "No, you . . . you aren't a woman, maybe that's what it is. Maybe you're a man, because you act like one—one lover and another and another. What kind of woman are you, acting like this?" I said, "Besa, you listen to me. It's because I refuse you. I don't want you. Even when I married you, I did it only because everyone insisted I should. I was afraid to say no, so I married you. You have no right to accuse me with your jealousy. If you do, I'll just leave you. I didn't want to marry you in the beginning, and even now, only a small part of my heart goes out to you. It is not a full heart you have from me. So just leave me alone with my lovers. And if you think someone might be my lover, tell yourself he is. Even so, what will you do?"

Nisa then added that Besa, too, had a lover and even had a child with her, but she denied that she was jealous. She told Besa to have his lovers and she would have hers. Besa plaintively objected, saying that he loved her and wanted her to love him in return. Nisa refused, saying that Besa would become too jealous if love were involved. Besa became furious, and so did Nisa; in the ensuing fight, Besa grabbed a knife and cut her leg severely. Nisa was badly hurt, and Besa's own father criticized him sharply (Shostak 1981:235): "'Have you gone crazy, wanting to kill a woman? A woman has no strength; you don't kill a woman.'" Nisa wanted to leave Besa and go to her mother's camp, but Besa refused. Besa's father urged him to agree (Shostak 1981:235): "How can you want to kill her and then want to be with her right after that?" But Besa insisted, and Nisa remained. She continued to have lovers.

  In this episode and others like it, San men and women accused one another of breaking rules while justifying their own conduct in terms of rules. They felt the pressure of rules, but they also lost their tempers and fought. Others took positions based on their own self-interest. But some people were inflexible about matters of right and wrong, insisting that rules be followed or rule breakers punished, even when their own self-interest could have been served by allowing an exception. For the San, the rules that related to adultery could be manipulable, flexible, and contradictory, but they could also be taken seriously, even strictly, by some people. How rules about adultery were construed among them depended on the circumstances, but it also depended on the individuals involved.

Should we conclude, then, that the San are an example of an ideal type of society in which what is right "depends" on the circumstances, strict rules are social fictions, and people use what rules there are for their own purposes? This does not seem to be the case—not, that is, any more than it was with the Mbuti. We must enter a cautionary note by observing that while the data about the San are unusually good and plentiful, they are not immune to error. For example, it has long been reported, by men and women anthropologists alike, that rape among the !Kung was rare. Nisa's story makes it obvious that it was not (Shostak 1981). After reading Nisa's story, Nancy Howell (1983:187) reexamined her own field notes and "found more evidence that rape is a regular part of !Kung life." This kind of reformulation of an accepted "ethnographic fact" is disquieting, but it is a frequent phenomenon when multiple investigators reexamine their data from a new perspective.

With this caveat firmly in mind, it appears safe to conclude that while the San could be flexible about many of their rules—manipulating, redefining, or even ignoring them—they also took some rules seriously, followed them carefully, and punished breaches harshly. For example, Lorna Marshall (1976) listed numerous explicit rules of deference and avoidance, especially involving joking and respect. She also described a game among these unwarlike people which was called "war," of all things, and which was explicitly rule governed and was unfailingly played according to those rules (1976:333). Marshall reported that some rules, like those that defined incest, were very strict (1976:260). The San also recognized numerous food taboos (Tanaka 1980), and their important healing trance dances were very much rule directed (Katz 1982).

A few of their rules were maintained by force. As we have already seen, a man could assault his wife's lover or his wife, and groups of men could, and did, organize themselves to execute men whose violence could not otherwise be controlled (Lee 1979). Some secular rules had secular enforcement. But other rules were enforced, strictly and collectively, by automatic supernatural sanctions. For example, like many other people, the San took some of their taboos very seriously, believing that their violation would lead to death; Nisa believed that the death of her son was a result of a taboo violation (Shostak 1981:313). The San also feared the malevolence of spirits of the dead, and they believed that the underworld was inhabited by "monsters" who were angered by certain offenses, such as setting fire to a shelter, murder, allowing menstrual blood to fall on the ground, excessive or malicious lying, and flagrant adultery by young wives. When angered, the monsters emerged from the underworld to attack anyone who was luckless enough to encounter them, causing illness, physical injury, blindness, or instant death (Silberbauer 1981:113). Serious wrongdoing put every San in mortal danger, since these monsters imposed both absolute and collective liability.

To avoid these dangers, social pressure was regularly brought to bear on a wrongdoer in the form of subtle criticism, less subtle ridicule, or open insults. For example, Marshall (1976), Lee (1979), and others noted the importance that the San attached to avoiding any indication of boastfulness, competitiveness, or arrogance about one's accomplishments. Patricia Draper (1978:41) made this evaluation:

> Personal success, excellence, achievement, or sheer luck must be handled delicately in this society, for the potential put-down is everywhere. . . . Years and years of this type of conditioning produce a person who is highly sensitive to the evaluation of himself by other people.

In addition to social pressure, then, the San internalized some of their rules, and some of their internal controls were very effective. Silberbauer (1981:164) observed that the San believed that children achieved the age of responsibility by their seventh or eighth year; this early imposition of responsibility referred to important moral rules, not to economic duties, which neither boys nor girls typically undertook until they were at least fifteen years old. Draper (1978:42) reported an instance in which a seventeen-year-old girl flippantly cursed her father, a moral breach; he responded by scolding her, and bystanders joined in a show of shocked criticism. The girl was shamed and withdrew in sulky isolation. Draper concluded that "the way the wrongdoer reacts to the frustration of criticism suggests that the social norms are very well internalized by the individual" (1978:42).

Like the Mbuti, the San lived in small camps, where they enjoyed—and sometimes suffered—continuous close interaction with one another. Observers differ to some degree in their evaluations of how well the San achieved harmony and avoided conflict, but whatever success the San had in coping with their environment and with one another can be attributed only partially to the flexibility or manipulability of their rules. The San did not rival the Jalé, Cheyennes, or

Walbiri when it came to a reliance on categorical rules, strictly enforced, but they did rely on rules, explicit as well as implicit, and they
did enforce them. Draper put it this way (1978:46–47):

> Individuals do strive to avoid angering their co-residents, but they do
> so because the rules about behavior have teeth in them. Furthermore,
> as they live in close, intimate camps, the chances of committing various
> sins and getting away with them are practically negligible. The !Kung,
> in their own way, are as constrained by their culture as we are by our own.

CONCLUSION

Among small-scale foraging societies, said to be so flexible about their
rules, there is marked variation in rule reliance. Some are indeed
highly flexible about many of their rules, but others are far less so.
The Siriono, Paliyans, and Chenchus, for example, paid little apparent heed to rules most of the time. They ignored many, permitted all
manner of exceptions to others, and often considered what was right
or wrong to be dependent on the situation. These extremely individualistic societies had some rules that admitted no exceptions, and
these rules were followed very carefully because failure to do so
resulted in harsh penalties and, in some cases, collective supernatural
punishment. Among the Chewong, most rules were like this. Where
we have the most complete data—for the San—we find a society that
falls somewhere between the Mbuti and the Walbiri. The San were
flexible about some of their rules and sometimes allowed exceptions,
overlooked some wrongdoing while grumbling about it, or disagreed
about which rule should be followed and what should be done if it
were not. But some San rules were categorical; exceptions to these
were rare, and penalties for breaking them were severe. The San were
assuredly not a people who typically managed their affairs without
tough rules, strictly enforced. They were not at all like the Nambikwara that Lévi-Strauss thought he had found.

The findings are clear. Among the world's smallest societies—bands
of foragers in Australia, Southeast Asia, India, Africa, Tierra del
Fuego, the forests of the Amazon Basin, the deserts of North America,
or the tundra of the Far North—there is a range of variation in rule
flexibility that spans our entire proposed continuum, from the Walbiri
at one extreme to the Siriono at the other.[10] There is no need to look

at larger societies with specialists, towns, social classes, or complex economies to find societies that are either extremely flexible about their rules or extremely inflexible. All the variation we had hypothesized might exist is present in the world's smallest, most egalitarian societies. What we face now is the task of explaining why rules sometimes have exceptions and sometimes do not.

PART III

EXPLANATIONS AND IMPLICATIONS

Introduction

The complexity of human rule following should not be painted in chiaroscuro; it should instead have depth, texture, and rich colors. Efforts to portray human rule making and remaking have too often lacked these qualities, and we have had to settle for stick figures. I shall try to do a little better, if only by showing that there are complex forces for exceptions to rules just as there are for strict rules with no exceptions.

This complexity is daunting, and there are practical limits to how much a single work can attempt. Rather than undertaking an exhausting enumeration of all the complexities that I will not address, I shall simply state the goals of the final three chapters. In chapter 10 I will attempt to identify and illustrate the various forces that make exceptions to rules a universal phenomenon, and I will attempt to do the same in chapter 11 for the forces that act against exceptions. In chapter 12, some of the theoretical implications of forces for and against exceptions in various societies will be discussed. These last three chapters are not intended to offer the illusion of completion; they are as much a beginning as an end. The place of rules and exceptions in human affairs will remain a puzzle for some time to come.

CHAPTER 10

Why Exceptions?

From the Paliyans or Siriono at one extreme to the traditional Japanese or Walbiri at the other, there is a world of difference. It would be absurd to suggest that people living in these dramatically different social and cultural systems are similarly constrained by rules or similarly excused from them by rule-based exceptions. That is manifestly not so. The differences between societies such as these are not simply matters of style. At one extreme, categorical rules and strict responsibility are all-important; at the other, categorical rules are sometimes, but only sometimes, important. There is, nevertheless, some common ground among these otherwise very different societies. Even the most "rule-less" people recognize some strikingly strict rules, and even the most "rule-bound" people recognize some exceptions to their rules.

This leads us back to our initial puzzle. If rules are essential for social order, why are there rules for breaking rules? This chapter will suggest that exceptions to rules can be a product of factors such as social incompletion, social stratification, and rapid change or less rapid acculturation that affects some societies more than others, but that exceptions to rules can also result from universal factors present in all societies. The presence of categorical rules, strictly followed and enforced without exceptions, must be achieved in spite of, or at least in disregard of, these many factors.

It is self-evident that many exceptions to rules exist in large, diverse societies. Factors such as ethnic and religious variation, occupational role specialization, inequality in wealth and power, regional or subcultural differences, and rapid economic and technological change all lead to a diversity of laws, morals, and conventions that conflict, compete, overlap, and, inevitably, require exceptions. There is nothing mysterious about any of this. But why do exceptions exist in small-scale, homogeneous societies? Some of the ambiguity, inconsistency, and contradiction in the rules of small societies, as well as in the rule-based exceptions to these rules, may be due to external factors.

All societies are influenced by some external pressures, the very remote and small ones sometimes as much as are some of the nation states. Some, like the Walbiri, may harden their rules in contempt, defiance, or prideful determination not to change, while others, like the Paliyans, retreat into more remote jungles or deserts. But many either may be unable to avoid change or may actively seek it, and with change may come exceptions to rules. War, trade, famine, drought, disease, and new ideologies, among other factors, may force people to make exceptions to their rules in an attempt to accommodate to rapidly changing circumstances. Over time, these accommodations may accumulate, patched together however loosely, in a seemingly inconsistent pattern that exemplifies societal incompletion. The process of rule making to regulate social living can occur ad hoc; there need be no master plan, no integrating mechanism. Some rules may harden, others may be ignored, and new ones will surely emerge. F. G. Bailey discussed these kinds of changes in *Stratagems and Spoils* (1969).

As noted in chapter 7, the Australian aborigines may have hardened their laws in the face of European domination, but other societies in cultural contact allowed exceptions to their rules—temporarily, as the Mbuti did when they were in an African village, or permanently, as the Cheyennes were forced to do when they were overcome by military force. Sometimes terrible environmental conditions compel people to behave as they would ordinarily never do, and however appalling this behavior may be, it may sometimes be defined as an acceptable exception to a rule. For example, prolonged famine, such as that suffered in northern China from 1941 through 1943, can bring about exceptions as appalling as those accepted by the Ik. Starving men sold their children, then their wives; starving mothers, unable to eat their own children, exchanged them, saying, "'You eat mine, I'll eat yours'" (Belden 1949:62).

Examples of societies struggling to maintain their rules or agreeing to allow exceptions to them in the face of changing circumstances are so numerous and well-known that little further detailing of them is required here. David Aberle (1963), along with several other anthropologists, described Navaho social life as "flexible." And with others, he ascribed this flexibility (which he likened to social disorder) to various external environmental factors that led to a rapidly expanding population, monumental cultural change, and growing instability in economic resources. Gary Witherspoon (1975), on the other hand, believed that flexibility was an inherent feature of Navaho culture and social organization.

It hardly needs saying that why one society responds by changing its rules while another resists extreme pressure to do so is still imper-

fectly understood. For example, the sudden and shocking destruction
of their taboo system by Hawaiian royalty was obviously influenced
by the religious, political, and economic considerations when the
Hawaiian Islands came into contact with Western technology and
Christian ideology, but it may also have been influenced by psychological dissatisfaction with the taboo system itself (Davenport, 1969).
Why a society may modify its rules in response to external influences
is as important as it is complex—social survival can be at stake—but
it is a question that goes far beyond the scope of this book. I am
primarily concerned with identifying factors that press for rule exceptions in all societies, including those societies that are the smallest,
most homogeneous, least stratified, and least influenced by external
pressures for change.

Even the smallest, simplest, and most egalitarian of band-level
societies must deal with various social conditions and human attributes
that tend to bring about exceptions to all sorts of rules.[1] These include
temporary conditions that can affect anyone, more enduring ones
that may affect many people, important individual differences, attributes that may be shared by all or most humans, and, not least, the
very nature of rules and social contexts. Some of these phenomena
were introduced in earlier chapters and will require little amplification
here; others will require more extended discussion.

RULES AND CONTEXT

When Robert Murphy (1971:52) wrote: "There can be no exact conformity to norms because this is antithetical to the very nature of
norms," he was right in one sense but wrong in another.[2] People
everywhere *do* conform exactly to some rules (or they try very hard
to do so), and in at least a few societies, people demand and get exact
compliance to *many* rules. But if Murphy was wrong about human
conformity, he was right about rules. Rules usually contain a measure
of ambiguity even when people act as though they do not. The complexities and contradictions of human life tend to work against rules
that attempt to specify exactly what people must or must not do.

As we have already noted, some scholars insist that ambiguity in
the form of "et cetera" phenomena is unavoidable (Shimanoff 1980).
H. L. A. Hart (1961), for example, referred to the "penumbra of
uncertainty" that surrounds any rule. Some rules are ambiguous because they are imprecise, indefinite, or vague, but ambiguity may also
occur because it is so difficult to formulate any rule that will cover

every conceivable contingency that might arise. For example, in his book about the Nazi seizure of power in one German town, William S. Allen (1973:244) mentioned that a memo was sent to all Nazi party members ordering them to appear at a certain time and place for an election-eve meeting; it concluded with the stern dictate, "No excuses will be accepted." There is no doubt that the memo was unambiguous and serious; it meant exactly what it said. But there is also no doubt that if a Nazi had been unable to attend because he was ordered by Hitler to carry out duties elsewhere, his absence would have been excused. Indeed, the exception would probably have become a contingent rule: "No excuses unless ordered by higher authority." There was nothing unclear about the Nazi rule. It was not vague or imprecise; it simply did not anticipate all the contingencies that might arise. Many rules develop exceptions for this reason: the actual situation people face can be more complex than the rule has anticipated.

For rules, then, context is all-important, and as Gregory Bateson (1979) never tired of telling us, context is a complex and changing phenomenon indeed. How people learn about context—*any* context— remains problematic for most scholars; for some, such as Rodney Needham (1972), misunderstanding is the core of human existence. Following Needham's attempts to understand the obscurity and confusion so evident in ordinary communication, he came to doubt that misunderstanding will ever be overcome; instead, he believed that we will remain "opaque" to one another and that "the solitary comprehensible fact about human existence is that it is incomprehensible" (1972:246). From Einstein to Heisenberg to Schutz, it has become obvious that most rules of human conduct are relative to their context, rarely fully certain, often provisional, and usually contingent on circumstances. The complex interpretive procedures by which people assign meaning to their circumstances have been examined in ethnomethodology (Garfinkel 1967; Cicourel 1974) and in the interpretive anthropology of Clifford Geertz (1984). Edward T. Hall (1977), like others who have studied implicit rules, has documented the power of contextual variation in a variety of societies. As circumstances change, the context in which rules are understood to apply also changes, and the pressure to allow exceptions to rules mounts. It is not unreasonable to refer to this pressure as "negotiation," a process by which the meaning of a circumstance—a context—is determined, altered, redetermined, and sometimes agreed upon.[3]

Context is regularly altered by temporal and spatial phenomena. As described in chapters 5 and 6, in certain places and at certain times exceptions to otherwise binding rules may be allowed or even required. These exceptions may be concealed from some people, as in the earlier example by Herdt of homosexuality in the Sambia men's house in Papua New Guinea, where the women and children were deceived but the men knew what was required in one physical context and knew equally well that the same thing was forbidden in all other contexts. And even if the effects of dramatic rule violations during certain ceremonial occasions may serve to reinforce rules and thereby social order,[4] they nevertheless demonstrate that exceptions *can* occur. Societies may succeed in confining rule violations to particular places and occasions, but by doing so they may also establish precedents for other times and other occasions—one exception, that is, can lead to another.

Contextual complexity and indeterminacy are increased by the fact that so many moral and supernatural rules, involving matters such as cooperation, reciprocity, loyalty, self-restraint, and fairness, are imprecise. These principles can be referred to in order to derive more specific, context-relevant rules, but because a moral principle or meta-rule is necessarily general and ambiguous (e.g., "Do unto others . . . "), the possibilities of debate and disagreement over what specific rule should be followed in any given circumstance are, if not limitless, at least plentiful.

Because social living anywhere is, to say the least, always complex, specific rules, too, like meta-rules, may overlap or conflict. As a result, some rules may be construed as hierarchical, with one being more important than another, or they may be seen as context-specific with one relevant now, another then. This complexity and contradiction can lead to legitimate and painful confusion. The tragic plane crash in the Andes discussed in chapter 3 is an example. Donald Tuzin (1982) provided another example in his moving account of the guilt and confusion that Ilahita Arapesh men felt when ritual occasions obliged them to be cruel and sadistic to their wives and children. These men, from the Sepik River area of Papua New Guinea, were ordinarily very affectionate and kind to their wives and children. As Tuzin described their feeling tone, the Western concept of love could be appropriate for describing how they usually felt. However, during certain ceremonies, these same men were required to follow rules that forced them to carry out acts of ritual cruelty against women and children; as Tuzin pointed out, some of the men were confused by this contradiction and felt guilty when they had to behave in so foreign a manner. Feelings such as these may give rise to new rules that provide meaning to the necessity for breaking rules.[5]

Contradiction of this sort is common enough in life, and while it may torment virtuous citizens, it offers ample opportunity for personal gain by those who are less virtuous. Without some imprecision in the jurisdiction and meaning of rules in complex situations, no casuist could be very successful. In real life, however, there are so many opportunities to quibble about issues of right and wrong that casuistry has become disreputable. As George Bernard Shaw wrote in *Caesar and Cleopatra* (1946), "When a stupid man is doing something he is ashamed of, he always declares that it is his duty." Years earlier, La Rochefoucauld (1959:218) noted that "hypocrisy is the homage vice pays to virtue." But sometimes, whether stupid or wise, men are not just hypocritical, they are honestly unsure where their duty lies. As the Comanches told Ralph Linton, which rule ought to be followed sometimes "depends"—and depends on a host of circumstances, many of which are difficult to foresee.

TEMPORARY CONDITIONS AND EXCUSES

As illustrated in chapter 3, every human population must contend with the reality that some conditions will inevitably occur—some regularly, others unpredictably—that will affect peoples' ability to follow rules. Fatigued people must rest and sleep; rules cannot require people to be alert or productive at all times. Rules may determine *when* one may sleep (e.g., only when no enemies are present, only when religious ceremonies are over, only when children are safe), but they cannot forbid sleep altogether. So it is with hunger. Rules may prescribe the most wondrous variations in what may be eaten, how, with which hand, and in what company,[6] but when hunger becomes intense, exceptions to these rules may be necessary (as it was with the famine-tormented Chinese mothers). As we have seen with the Ik, the Eskimo, and the chronically hungry Siriono, very hungry people may not only make exceptions to their rules about what food should be eaten, what food should be shared, who should have priority, and the like but they may ignore such rules altogether.

Illness and injury may not be predictable—at least not within a specifiable rhythm of life in the way that fatigue and hunger are—but no population can escape either one for long. A person who has malaria or a broken leg probably cannot perform ordinary economic or ritual duties, no matter how essential these may be; such a person may or may not be temporarily exempted. Because their subsistence level provided no surplus, the Eskimo and Siriono chose not to exempt such persons; the Sarakatsani shepherds of Greece could afford to feed and indulge a sick adult but seldom did so because they valued strength (Campbell 1964). A person delirious with fever may utter blasphemy or assault a close relative; others must decide whether to treat such conduct with the seriousness that it would ordinarily warrant or to overlook it.

Many societies encourage some or all of their members to experience altered states of consciousness, and some of these states—especially those involving the use of alcohol, cannabis, or other psychotropic drugs—may lead to behaviors that challenge the ordinary forms of propriety. There is nothing imperative about this. Societies may refuse to relax their rules, as the Australian aborigines described by Sackett did with regard to sacrilege while drunk, but the condition— intoxication—challenges existing rules and sets up the possibility that exceptions to rules will occur.

Strong emotions are another example. Some societies may prohibit intoxicants, but strong emotions cannot so easily be mandated out of existence. Grief, sexual passion, rage, jealousy, and other strong emotions are presumably universal, as are many others that may be no less troublesome. Nisa's grief was almost beyond her control, as was her childhood jealousy. People may kill in rage or defy rules as a result of their sexual passion. Men and women often kill themselves in shame or depression. There is much that we do not yet know about the occurrence, meaning, and control of profound emotion in the world's societies, but it seems undeniable that some basic emotions are universal and exist everywhere as states during which ordinary rule following becomes problematic.[7] Societies may allow exceptions for grieving mothers or for jealous husbands, or they may—like the Eskimo, the Semai, and other peoples—enforce rules that suppress the expression and disruptive power of strong emotion. However, as Malinowski observed (1961/1934:lxii), strong emotions (or "passions," as he called them) *are* universal, and rules usually provide only partial control over them. The result is another potential source of challenge to rules and another reason for the development of exceptions—to bring what cannot be legislated out of existence under the sway, if not always the control, of rules. Homicide committed while one is enraged or in fear for one's life need not be excused or even punished less severely, but when a society denies exemption on the basis of strong emotion, it does so despite the presence of a condition (whether that condition is of strong emotion, intoxication, or illness) that makes ordinary rule-governed propriety problematic and creates the possibility that there should be legitimate exceptions to rules for people who are temporarily affected by one of these conditions.

DISABILITY, AGE, AND SEX

As chapter 4 illustrated, some injuries, illnesses, or anomalies of birth may result in permanent physical impairment—for example, deafness, blindness, intersexuality, and mental retardation—or a lesser handicap. Such impairments or disabilities occur everywhere. If physically impaired persons are to remain members of a society, some exceptions to the rules may have to be allowed. It is equally self-evident that rules must take age into account. Infants cannot be responsible for sacrilege, as even the Walbiri recognized, nor can they follow rules of respect or avoidance. Among the San, these very important rules did not apply to children until they were seven or eight (Silberbauer 1981:143); the Mbuti expected their children to behave properly at a younger age. The very elderly pose another problem. Other people may be held responsible for the conduct of the very young or very old, but the very young and very old themselves are everywhere less responsible than they will one day become or in years past used to be. Age is a social imperative that generates pressure for exceptions to rules.

Sex distinction in exceptions to rules is another cultural universal. As recent research on small hunting-and-gathering societies accumulates showing that women can and often do carry out all the economic roles allocated to men, including hunting (Dahlberg 1981), the reasons for so many sex-based differences in rules become increasingly obscure, but there are such differences even among otherwise largely egalitarian peoples, such as the San.[8] Whatever the reasons, every society provides sex-based modifications to its rules. Sometimes women are held to be more strictly responsible for following rules and sometimes less so. It is a far cry from the separation and seclusion of Muslim women (Dwyer 1978) to the relative equality of men and women among the San, but the San nevertheless make sex a consideration in determining responsibility for wrongdoing. For example, women must take great care not to pollute men with their menstrual blood, and they are not permitted to touch poisoned arrows (Howell 1979; Silberbauer 1981). All of these considerations were discussed in chapter 4.

INDIVIDUAL DIFFERENCES

In any society, there may be some people who have personal attributes that exempt them from ordinary punishment. As we have seen earlier, in a prototypically small, egalitarian hunting-and-gathering society, an exceptionally skillful and generous hunter may be excused for certain transgressions. So may an unusually diligent, resourceful, and loving wife. A beautiful and virtuous young woman may have a degree of license in any society. The opposite is also true: persons who are inept, lazy, quarrelsome, or arrogant may be held more strictly to account than all other people, and more serious deviants may suffer still sterner penalties. All this is so richly documented in ethnographic literature that knowledge of it has become commonplace. However, it is true not only that a person's reputation can be a factor in the resolution of disputes or, more generally, in strategic interchanges, although both phenomena are undoubtedly universal, but also that clear—even remarkable—exceptions to rules are sometimes made for certain individuals. The Arapaho dandy Flat-War-Club was a dramatic example, but only one among many.

The effects brought about by psychopaths or sociopaths—in current psychiatric parlance, persons with antisocial personalities—may be more far-reaching and less well recognized. Sociopaths have been reported in many societies; it would not be making a bad guess to say that they probably occur everywhere (Goodman 1967). While the causes of sociopathy are not yet known, sociopathic people are identifiable early in life, and the social mischief they bring about can be devastating. Sociopaths are often violent, repeatedly and impulsively breaking their societies' rules and suffering no remorse for doing so.[9] Ordinary social pressures and appeals to morality have no effect on them. As Robert Lindner (1956) said, they are *in* the world, but not *of* it; they are in perpetual conflict with those about them. In *The Tempest*, Shakespeare had Prospero describe Caliban as a "devil, a born devil, on whose nature, nurture can never stick."

Sometimes people reach consensus that such a person must be exiled (as the Mbuti did) or executed (as the San chose to do). Such outcomes are relatively common even in very small and simple societies, and in this regard, Hoebel (1954) was wrong when he said that lynch law was rare among primitives. When collective action against a repeatedly outrageous offender (who may be a sociopath) is successfully carried out, it may serve to reinforce social order, but it also happens that arrogant, aggressive, even murderous persons sometimes so tyrannize and intimidate their fellows that no action is taken against them. Sometimes an opportunity arises allowing such a one to be killed (Edgerton, 1969), but at other times such people violate rules yet survive and even prosper. A male sociopath might use his strength or audacity to become a war chief, "big man," or the feared possessor of other men's wives; a female might openly flaunt her powers as a witch yet go unpunished. When something like this happens, persons who are not sociopaths could be emboldened to follow the example of one who is by stretching the rules as far as possible and claiming exemption by precedent. If they are too weak, their claims may fail, but the precedent set can be one more force working toward exceptions to the rules.

SOME PSYCHOLOGICAL SOURCES OF EXCEPTIONS

There are additional psychological reasons why people press for the recognition of at least some kinds of exceptions to rules. First, it is self-evident, but no less important because of this, that people usually try to avoid being punished for their rule infractions, claiming entitlement to all manner of exemptions in an effort to reduce their culpability. Where some rules are concerned—and in some societies where many rules are concerned—no claim has much chance of success. But sometimes claims do succeed, because people may respect or fear the claimant, may wish to avoid conflict with the claimant's kinsmen, because something else happens to distract everyone or, occasionally, because the claim really is compelling. The saga of Awaiitigaaj (chapter 4) is instructive here. Sometimes these protective claims are made not only to escape punishment by others but also to protect one's self-esteem against admissions of inadequacy or, as Snyder, Higgins, and Stucky (1983) put it in their book *Excuses*, "bad performance."[10]

Many of these efforts to evade responsibility have an ad lib quality, a desperate grasping at any excuse that might work. These excuses may be highly inventive (as those of young children often are), but they are unlikely to generalize into an accepted rule for breaking other rules. Other excuses, however, may do exactly that. Blaming others, especially newcomers to a society, may become an accepted excuse, and so may possession by a newfound spirit, a newly introduced intoxicant, a newly troubling disease, or some other external factor to which blame can be shifted. In this way, an ad hoc excuse may become accepted as an exception to a rule; the kind of rule that achieves acceptance as a rule-based exception. The acceptance of alcohol as an excuse for *any* mayhem by North American Indians is an example of a new (for them) external agent that was made responsible for human misconduct.

There is another consideration as well. If Western experience is any guide, the necessity for following certain rules strictly with no exceptions can be stressful; if the behavior is difficult and dangerous, it can be even more stressful. Being a child whose father allows no exceptions or an employee whose employer is autocratic are everyday examples of such situations. A single mistake, accidental or not, brings physical punishment or the loss of one's job, respectively. Performing surgery, working as an air traffic controller, or defusing an un-exploded bomb can be still more stressful rule-following activities. It is not uncommon for people who experience such stresses to seek periods of reduced rule-regulation in which "release" or "relaxation" refer partly to escape from the stressful situation where no mistake can be excused and partly to a desire for the suspension of all other rules that might impose demands, either prescriptive or proscriptive. Whether modern societies sanction periods of reduced rule-regula-tion depends, of course, on many factors, but strict rule following can be experienced as intolerably burdensome; as a result, compensatory rule relaxation, including license to break other rules, can be permit-ted. Goffman called this relaxation a "release binge." The drunken escapades of military personnel on leave provide one classic example; the off-duty drinking of some police officers is another (Wambaugh 1975). I must hasten to repeat that not all kinds of strict rules are experienced as stressful: Some moral and supernatural rules are wel-comed and followed with no apparent sign of pressure needing to be released.

Another factor that I believe presses for exceptions to strict rules is the widespread human feeling tht one's intent ought to matter in the determination of responsibility for breaking a rule (Messick and Cook 1983). Just as supernatural powers may punish people who break a rule but are innocent of any intent to do so, humans some-times do the same. We do not know whether Kevel, the Jalé tree cutter, was resentful when he was punished despite his obvious lack of intent to do harm, nor do we know how Maisie, the Walbiri mother, felt when she was supernaturally punished for a completely accidental breach of the sacred laws. But sometimes people can feel resentful—as well as fearful—when a completely innocent rule violation puts them and their family in jeopardy.

An example can be taken from the Hehe of southern Tanzania. The Hehe insisted upon certain formalities of greeting, or at least they did so in 1961–1962, when I did research among them. Like so many peoples throughout the world, when any adult Hehe met another adult under any circumstance, it was necessary to offer a stylized greeting; there were no exceptions. Any failure to comply with this mandatory greeting protocol was considered to be a deliber-ate affront (Winans and Edgerton, 1964) that was likely to be responded to with violence, if the offended person was a man, or with witchcraft, if the offended was a woman. I saw this rule scrupulously followed on thousands of occasions, and I was obliged to follow it myself. I saw it breached only once, when I was walking with a Hehe man along a path and an angry shout halted us. An elderly woman had apparently been sitting in the shade a good fifty yards distant, screened from us by a maize field. She marched toward us, shouting rebukes and accusations. That we had not noticed her—and could not have seen her—was no excuse. She was outraged. The Hehe man I was with was effusively apologetic, but the old woman indignantly rejected his explanations and left us. The errant man was agitated and worried, telling me of his fears for himself and his children. She *could* be a witch, and he had offended her. Even if she were not a witch, she might hire a sorcerer to cause harm. He also lamented over and over that he had not seen her, that he had meant her no offense, and that it was unfair that he should be punished for an unavoidable accident. It was not for two weeks, when further apology to the woman and a favor for her son were accepted, that the man finally relaxed. This degree of compliance with the rules of etiquette and deference was typical of the Hehe, as was their fear whenever a rule was broken, however innocently. The fear was great, but so was the sense of injustice.

Strict rules commonly specify certain routine forms of deference, etiquette, exchange, or sharing or else prohibit such acts as theft, violence, adultery, incest, or sacrilege. It may be tempting to break some of these rules, but if one has the will to follow them, most of them *can* be followed. However, sometimes the intent to follow a rule is not enough. Rules may be broken accidentally, inadvertently, or while following a more important rule. The belief that good intentions should be distinguished from bad ones is well established in Western culture. Hart (1961:155) said that justice requires that we "treat like cases alike and different cases differently," and he added that "evil" should be distinguished from accident (1968:35). This distinction is also made in non-Western cultures and may even be universal. Shweder, Turiel, and Much (1981) have reinforced this idea by suggesting that young children are intuitive moralists who know right from wrong and want them to be treated differently. My point is that if people believe in a principle of fairness, then they must treat similar intent similarly. A person who accidentally kills another should not be punished as severely as one who kills intentionally, in cold blood, or with exceptional cruelty. Many societies, as we have seen, do excuse accidental homicide; others, such as the Yurok, impose a fine for accidental homicide but add to the penalty when malicious intent is present.

It is possible to ignore good intentions or accidents, insisting that intentionality is irrelevant. We do so when we say that "only results matter" or that "the road to hell is paved with good intentions," but it seems likely that in most societies, if not all, a person who intends to follow a rule and yet breaks it by sheer accident or unavoidable circumstances would, *ceteris paribus,* resent having his good intentions ignored. J. G. Peristiany's (1954) now well-known account of an accidental killing among the Pokot of East Africa provides an illustration. When some Pokot were attacked by a neighboring tribe, a Pokot man of one clan accidentally hit a Pokot man from another clan with an arrow, killing him. The death was obviously accidental, one of the unavoidable hazards of combat, but the deceased's clansmen demanded full compensation under the letter of the law, which prohibited interclan homicide. The killer's clan was obliged to pay, but their sense of being wronged was great and was still smoldering when I did research in a nearby Pokot area in 1962. This "injustice" appears to have taken place about eighty years ago.

Grievances such as this would seem to be inimical to social harmony. What, after all, is the point of good intentions if a well-intentioned person who makes an unavoidable mistake is punished as severely as someone who breaks the same rule for personal gain or from sheer malice? The answer is that most social systems do not confound justice in this way. This becomes especially clear when we examine societies like the Jalé and the Walbiri, whose ideas of strict liability are so extreme. Despite their strictness, the Jalé and Walbiri sometimes take a person's reputation into account when deciding on an appropriate penalty for wrongdoing. People who have led exemplary lives have reason to look upon a lifetime of good deeds as a bank account; what is more, their kinsmen, who esteem them highly, will plead their case. The result is familiar: someone with a good reputation will be penalized less severely for the same wrong than someone with a flawed reputation. Meggitt (1962:254) said that the Walbiri believed in a principle of general equity and attempted to reduce the severity of prescribed penalties when they were seen as unfair. The Akamba of Kenya, with whom I did research, clearly imposed more severe penalties on persons with bad reputations (Edgerton 1969); they were fond of saying of such people, "If you need nine men, he is number ten."

The point of these examples is this: people who act with good intentions have reason to expect those intentions to mitigate the seriousness of an offense that they might inadvertently commit, just as persons with a lifetime of virtue behind them have reason to expect that reputation, too, will matter. Even if these expectations that intent should matter are not universal—and this remains an empirical question—they provide a powerful inducement for exceptions in many societies. Some rules can be enforced without any regard for intentions, but to do so without very good reason may well be counterproductive because, as illustrated by the example of the Pokot, those who judge today may be judged tomorrow. Taboos are an enigma. Often imposed without regard for intentionality, an accidental taboo violation brings the same punishment as an intended one. One of the major reasons why people so detest many taboos may be this imperviousness to human intent.

RULES AGAINST HUMAN NATURE

Malinowski (1961/1934) was one of many to observe that some human desires, or passions, could never be curbed completely. Freud often made the same point, insisting that "what nobody desires to do does not have to be forbidden" (1918:91).[11] I take it as beyond serious doubt, if not yet demonstrated to everyone's satisfaction, that in addition to socially cohesive tendencies such as grooming and attachment (Reynolds 1981), the inborn human repertoire includes a capacity for selfishness, jealousy, and aggression, among other potentials that can make for social trouble. Donald Campbell (1975:1114) has written about the evolution of human culture "contra selfish human nature." I am unconvinced by the arguments against the presence of these potentials, although no one can reasonably deny that culture can partially suppress or redirect any or all of them or that humans can convince themselves of their selflessness. Alexander (1975) has gone so far as to suggest that the present-day sincerity of human hypocrisy is a result of natural selection for individuals capable of repressing conscious awareness of their ruthless selfishness. I am aware of no human society that has found it necessary to teach its children to be selfish or jealous of their siblings, nor of any that has needed to teach its young adults to have sexual desires (although it is true that people, females perhaps more easily than males, may of course be taught not to have—or not to acknowledge—such desires). As Max Black once observed, there is no need for rules prohibiting goldfish from eating lamb chops or cats from barking; there is, however, a need for rules that can effectively control behaviors that could lead to socially destructive conflict.

Let us take as one example among many a problem for which all societies must find a solution, namely the universal propensity for men to contest one another for women (the almost equally troublesome role that women often play in these conflicts is another issue). In small-scale societies from Greenland to the Kalahari, men's desire for women, whatever the risk of combat with other men (and also with women), is a reality that calls for the utmost ingenuity in social control mechanisms—including explicit rules. In a good many societies, these mechanisms fail; among the Eskimo and the San, for example, adultery and its sequelae are the principal causes of violence, including homicide. While no society yet described in ethnographic literature has developed rules that have entirely eliminated male contests for women as a source of social tension, some have developed solutions that manage the problem better than others. Some Australian societies, as noted in chapter 5, did not succeed very well in this, despite the attempt to design societal safety valves such as the Gunabibi ceremony of the Murngin.

The Samburu of East Africa did somewhat better. The cattle-herding Samburu were organized in age grades, with the younger grades of men serving as warriors who protected older men, their wives, children, and cattle against the raids of neighboring tribesmen. These young warriors were made physically marginal, being largely segregated from their elders in warrior camps; they were symbolically marginal as well, since they were not permitted to have wives until such time as the elders allowed them to, which may not have occurred before the men of the warrior grade were in their thirties. All the while, the elders were accumulating as many wives as possible, including those young and beautiful women whom the warriors also coveted. As described by Paul Spencer (1965), neither the warriors nor the young women suffered this situation quietly, often approaching the brink of rebellion. The temptation to engage in rebellion or widespread adultery was controlled by a system of belief, shared by all Samburu, that the elders possessed the power to curse to death any warrior who offended. The system was not this simple, of course, but in its essence this rule, enforced by fear of serious illness or death, prevented a potentially explosive societal problem from resulting in violence. But the pressure for exceptions was great, and discreet violations were tolerated.

In fifteenth-century France, the same pressure was also acknowledged, and reduced, by granting to young men—who were also deprived of wives by rich, older men—the rule-based right to collectively rape any but the most virtuous of women (Rossiaud 1976). This widespread pattern of granting young men exemption was not only an excellent social control device, it presumably helped to keep a lid on the id of these young men. And that is the point here. There may be aspects of human nature that are extremely difficult to prohibit. As a result, there is unremitting pressure for exceptions.

A remarkable and instructive chapter in the history of human efforts to devise rules that attempted to prohibit what would *seem* to be natural aspects of male sexuality, including men's desire to have sexual relations with a variety of young women and not to share them, was written in the United States between 1848 and 1879. The Oneida Community was an adventure, to say the least, in communalism; one of the longest-lived utopian experiments of its time and surely one of the most dramatic since it rejected monogamy, the Oneida Community required a form of group marriage, strictly forbade any lasting emotional attachments, and required most men to practice only *coitus reservatus* (Carden 1969). It tried, that is, to legislate against deeply ingrained cultural beliefs and, perhaps, against several aspects of human nature.

The force behind the Oneida Community was an upper-class New Englander, John Humphrey Noyes, whose unconventional early life included his belief in the idea of perfectionism as a religious possibility and in his own perfection as an accomplished fact (Klass 1976). After some serious scrapes that threatened to end his utopian career, Noyes eventually succeeded in attracting enough followers to establish his community. All the Oneidans lived in one great house; everything was required to be shared, including the sexuality of the adults. Requests for sexual intercourse could be made of any woman by any man (women were apparently not the overt initiators of such invitations), and if such a request was accepted—as it usually was—the temporary couple made love for an hour or two in a private room and then separated, forbidden by sternly pronounced rules to develop any lasting affection for each other. If affection was suspected, the couple was kept apart.[12]

This surely was remarkable enough for that time, or for any other, but Noyes soon went much farther. For complicated reasons, it seems difficult to deny, involving Noyes's own psychosexual development and married life, he believed that childbirth should not be imposed on women and that men should and could control many aspects of what was presumed to be their natural sexual desire. In consequence, he formulated the singular idea—soon to become a strict rule for

Oneidans—that sexual intercouse was *more* pleasurable for men if they did not ejaculate. Noyes's son, who lived in the community as a young man, wrote that this remarkable rule requiring *coitus reservatus* was, in fact, carefully followed. Men learned to avoid ejaculation, although their partners were encouraged to experience orgasm; after an hour or so, the men then went back to their rooms apparently satisfied—dutifully, if in no other way (Noyes 1937). That they did, in fact, exercise restraint is evidenced by the fact that very few unplanned births actually occurred (Carden 1969).

Because the community was begun by 85 or so people and grew in its heyday to about 250 adults, there were numerous partners to choose from; but, still, the older members (Noyes was 40 in 1851 and 68 when Oneida collapsed) could be at a disadvantage, if not originally, then surely in the years to come. Accordingly, with an élan reminiscent of the Kapauku headman Awaiitigaaj, Noyes declared a new rule that required one of the partners in any sexual encounter to be a person of greater "perfection"; because perfection was attainable only through experience, this meant an older person—nice touch for Noyes and other older men, and not a bad one for older women who might otherwise have been so neglected that they became the embittered scolds of the Oneida Community. It is not surprising that young men saw an inequity between their lot, restricted to older women, and that of the older men, who now had exclusive access to young women and girls, and they grew restive. Faced with incipient rebellion, Noyes concluded that a desire to ejaculate was natural after all, and he made a new rule (Kephart 1976): only young men having intercourse with postmenopausal women were permitted to ejaculate.

How well this soothed feelings is not clear, although the community seems to have run smoothly enough thanks to some effective forms of social control. What brought its downfall was not this peculiar sexual arrangement but another one. Never at a loss for rules, Noyes decreed that soon after each girl had her first menses, he would become her "first husband," initiating her into full sexuality. This he did, and not without lasting affection from some of the young women, but also not without resentment on the part of some other men, a few of whom finally demanded their rights of defloration. When he refused, Noyes, who was then getting on in years, was reminded of another rule—the statutory rape law in New York. He forthwith fled to Canada, and the Oneida system ended. Noyes had run out of new rules and of new exceptions to old rules. He was unwilling to share the young girls with other men, and so his utopia collapsed.

Oneida was not a single community of interest, despite Noyes's efforts to make it so. It was divided by age and sex, and those members who most objected to the system Noyes developed were the new arrivals, not those who had spent years in Oneida being "socialized" into the system. These differences were exacerbated by Noyes's efforts to focus his rule system on some human desires that proved to be very resistant to control. Sex was one dilemma, but so was sharing scarce and desirable resources. M. E. Spiro's (1978:345) comment about his research in Israel is apposite here:

> Although the Kibbutz children were raised in a totally communal and cooperative system; although their socialization had as its primary aim the inculcation of a cooperative, noncompetitive ethic; although the techniques of socialization were mild, loving, and permissive; although the target responses were properly reinforced; although, in a word, almost all of the culture conditions were designed to exclusively promote cooperation and sharing, the data clearly indicated that Kibbutz children, like other children, do not wish to share scarce and valued goods—they want them for themselves and they resist the attempts of adults to get them to share them.

Human potentials can be, and often are, submerged in a powerful symbolic panoply of rules, and stringent rules may call for punishment when those rules are not adequately internalized. Yet these potentials are seldom, if ever, so fully tamed that they do not lead to behaviors that stretch the rules created to control them. The rules may snap back and become more strict in reaction, but they may also loosen to admit that "boys will be boys," "that's only natural," or "people are just that way; there is nothing we can do about it." When Malinowski wrote that rules could not curb passions, he was only partly right. Rules *can* curb passions, but only with difficulty and usually by allowing some exceptions.

MULTIPLE COMMUNITIES OF INTEREST

A final point is most fundamental. It is rare to find any society, no matter how small, simple, and homogeneous, that truly represents a single community of interest. Individuals among the Mbuti and the San agreed about some things—the need for nonviolence and cooperation, for example—but they disagreed about many others. Indeed, many of the world's small and homogeneous societies have made argumentation into a favorite pastime. Melvin Konner (1982) has referred to a San encampment as a "marathon encounter group."

The Mbuti, too, rarely lacked for an issue to quarrel about. Many other small societies are also notably cranky.[13] People not only disagree—although not always as openly and vigorously as the San and Mbuti do—but they also take sides. Friends, trading partners, brothers, co-wives, spouses, clansmen, neighbors, men, women, and children all have interests that conflict, agree, coalesce, run parallel, or enigmatically disappear, only to reemerge more strongly than ever as a dispute intensifies. Few quarrels really end, and fewer still can involve only two people in societies such as these; instead, many people become involved, often including everyone present at the time, as well as extended kinsmen who join in later because they too have collective rights, interests, and obligations.

Max Gluckman (1967) referred to these multiple relationships as "multiplex," adding that negotiation in search of a compromise solution was the likely outcome when a dispute involved a multiplex relationship. Starr and Yngvesson (1975) showed that not all multiplex relationship disputes are negotiated in this way, but Gluckman's point is true often enough to justify this generalization: In most societies, there are so many compelling and conflicting interests that few solutions to a dispute can please everyone, and when a solution is based on a rule, that rule is likely to be challenged by those who are displeased. In some societies, everyday life is often a continuing round of negotiations about the legitimacy of the various rules that are summoned to support one's claims in complex quarrels—quarrels that not only ramify to involve many other persons and groups but may also extend back in time, through past quarrels and to other rules by which these disputes were resolved or patched over.

In many places and for many purposes, everyday life is not characterized by strict rule following or enforcement but by the balancing of tensions and interests, thus avoiding a more dangerous outcome by accepting a temporary truce in a battle that has no remembered beginning and no foreseeable end. In such a world, while some will demand the strictest interpretation of a rule, others will insist on an exception here and a dispensation there or will appeal to another rule altogether. In a world where compromise is vital, exceptions are sovereign.

CONCLUSION

In conclusion, let us assume that all those theorists who have characterized culture as a control mechanism are right. Clifford Geertz

(1973:44) put the matter squarely when he concluded that "culture is best seen not as complexes of concrete behavior patterns—customs, usages, traditions, habit clusters—as has, by and large, been the case up to now, but as a set of control mechanisms—plans, recipes, rules, instructions (what computer engineers call 'programs')—for the governing of behavior."

What are these rules and instructions governing? Lévi-Strauss said that their purpose was to "say no to nature." Geertz would hardly agree with so bald an assertion about human nature's imperious demands, since for him human nature does not exist independently of culture, within which it evolved. Robin Fox (1980) has even argued that some rules reinforce rather than control natural human tendencies. A few rules may work this way, but most rules *do* control behavior—and culture *is* a control mechanism—yet for rules to achieve clarity and consensus or to be strictly enforced is anything but the "natural" way of things.

As this chapter has attempted to illustrate, there are many factors—in the vicissitudes of life, in human nature, and in rules themselves—that make cultural control by means of clear, strictly enforced rules a most problematic, even implausible, endeavor. For all of the reasons mentioned earlier as well as others, there are always pressures to stretch rules, to bend them, or to recognize some legitimate exceptions to them. In spite of these pressures, seemingly so many and so irresistible, people can and do act *as though* some of their rules are not at all ambiguous, do not conflict with other rules, and are independent of any change in context or any unanticipated contingency. What is more, they can and do enforce some of these rules with deadly seriousness. To act this way is to engage in a kind of cultural make-believe, but this is the essence of culture—defining some things as right, others as wrong, and still others as optional, and then acting as though these things could not be otherwise.

When people in some societies achieve the reality, or the illusion, that their rules are clear and unambiguous and then enforce these rules without exceptions, their accomplishment is notable. If the suggestions made in this chapter are even nearly correct, it follows that when rules exist without exceptions this represents an impressive human accomplishment, one made against imposing odds. In the next chapter, we shall explore some of the reasons why rules without exceptions are a part of human culture in spite of these odds.

CHAPTER 11

Rules with No Exceptions

Anthropologists long ago learned that ethnographic reports about rules that are never broken or rules that must be followed with no exceptions must be treated with considerable skepticism. Very often such assertions refer to an ideal, not to a behavioral actuality; when the supposedly inviolable rule is examined more closely, it is common to find that it *is* broken—sometimes more often than it is followed—and, moreover, that there are some legitimate reasons for its being broken. Nevertheless, after all caution has been duly exercised, there are *some* rules that allow no exceptions and that are rarely, if ever, broken. We have seen some of the evidence on which this conclusion is based; there is more in the many detailed reports by ethnographers who, during long periods of field research, actually saw rules being followed scrupulously or learned firsthand what happened when such rules were violated.

As we have seen in previous chapters, rules that must not be, and usually are not, broken can involve almost every category of human concern and activity: giving birth, preparing food, playing games, offering greetings, avoiding incest or sacrilege, marrying, hunting, planting, exchanging valuable things or services, mourning, fighting, avoiding prohibited foods, making eye contact, performing ritual acts, speaking, sitting, eating, touching, crying, and so on. In spite of the many reasons why rules are likely to have exceptions, there are rules that have none. But as we have also seen, the kinds of rules that are strictly followed or are enforced with no exceptions seem to vary from one society to the next, and so does the emphasis that different societies give to strict liability for rule following.

There are two questions here: Why does *any* human population attempt to regulate its activities by categorical rules, and why do some populations do so more than others? The first question asks what it might be about people anywhere that would lead them to make categorical rules and permit no exceptions to them, why the same group does so for one kind of rule and not for another, or why it is done in one time, place, or circumstance and not in others. There can be, I believe, some answers to the multiple aspects of this question. The second question asks why some societies follow rules more strictly than others do. Answers to this question are more complex, as I shall attempt to show in chapter 12. Gilbert Ryle (1949) once said that many people can talk sense *with* concepts but cannot talk sense *about* them. So it is with rules. People everywhere follow rules, seek exceptions to some of them, and refuse to allow exceptions to others. Why people do these things as they do, here and in other cultural systems, is something we have not yet learned to talk about very sensibly.

"MAN-THE-RULE-MAKER"

The idea that what is uniquely human about mankind is our capacity to make tools has lost some of its appeal in recent years with the discovery that chimpanzees and other nonhuman primates also make tools. But "man the tool-maker," despite Kenneth Oakley's (1950) memorable book title, is not so apt a description for what is quintessentially human as is "man-the-rule-maker." People make many more rules than they do tools, and then they unmake, modify, and remake them for good measure. Marveling at mankind's predeliction for rule making, British philosopher Mary Midgley commented that it makes no sense to imagine that we can do without rules (1978:299): "We cannot ask whether we will have rules, only which rules we will have." The enormous and still growing body of speculation about why this should be the case has suggested two very general answers. First, people classify and name the world of their sensory experience in order to predict, and therefore to avoid, the world's dangers and to better utilize its resources. Second, they make rules to prescribe desirable behavior, such as who should marry whom, and they proscribe unwanted behavior by others with whom they must live.

To begin with the first point, even in their simplest binary form, human classifications are rules (for example, dangerous or not dangerous, bitter or sweet, edible or inedible). And even these binary categories yield meaning in the form of evaluations about this thing or that, what foods to eat, which animals to avoid, or which people to trust. All people classify some people as kin and others as not kin and then attach the most important meanings to these classifications. With evaluations come more and more rules about what to do or not to do and what the meaning of anything or everything is, or ought to be. Indeed, as Ludwig Wittgenstein insisted, *all* human behavior is inherently imbued with meaning, and meaning is both produced by rules and inevitably generates more rules (Wittgenstein 1953).[1] For example, play is often said to be unlike a game in that it lacks rules

(Opie and Opie 1969). That is wrong. Play has meaning—it is fun, it is relaxing, it is exciting—and as Huizinga insisted in *Homo Ludens*, it must have rules, even if they are completely made up by one person on the spur of the moment and change with every succeeding moment. Play also has meta-meaning that distinguishes "play" from "not play," as Bateson observed, and there will always be rules about when and where play is appropriate.[2]

Even an attempt to simulate random activity must follow at least one rule: namely, to avoid any nonrandom pattern or sequence. Computers can be instructed to produce random output (and occasionally do so without instruction), but in so doing, they are instructed to follow a rule. A man lying in the shade might say, if asked, that he is doing nothing. But "nothing" is *some*thing; it is a culturally meaningful category of behavior distinguished from other culturally meaningful categories, such as resting, thinking, planning, scheming, grieving, or worrying—all of which look just the same to an observer: a man lying in the shade of a tree. Anything with meaning—that is, everything—can quickly be made to conform to a rule (children may play here, but not there; it is all right for children to do nothing, but adults should always do something). All of this should be self-evident, but if it is not, familiarity with Geertz's (1973) essay distinguishing a blink from a wink will make it so. Investing the world, shared or private, with meanings and then making rules about those meanings is an incessant human activity.[3]

Humans always create meaning, and meaning presupposes rules, but this axiomatic assertion does not imply that categorical rules are a "natural" result of the universal human search for meaning. Meaning is often produced not by a clear, inflexible rule but by a give-and-take among people, in which a motley of rules and meanings is negotiated back and forth. As Aaron Cicourel (1974:81) commented, this interactive process is likely to be overlooked by those who believe that social rules, like rules for grammar, are produced by determinate neurophysiological mechanisms:

> Despite the fact that the modern linguist's theory of deep structure is an elegant formulation, particularly in contrast with the sociologist's wastebasket usage of latent structure to disguise the inadequacies of his normative theory, both approaches to the idea of rules governing the production of grammatical utterances and social behaviour (treated as analytically distinct for the purposes of this paper) are deficient in their ability to account for the emergent, negotiated nature of meaning over the course of social interaction.

The human search for meaning may be emergent, but it is inseparable from rules, however flexible and negotiable they may seem.

Claude Lévi-Strauss (1969) has insisted as strongly as anyone on the universality and primacy of rule making in human living, saying that humans inevitably make rules, exchange the goods and services they make rules about, and then make more rules to define relationships among people who carry out these exchanges. Few would argue with this, but many would add, as Clifford Geertz (1973) did, that rules have a more primary role to play, the role of providing social control. Geertz is not explicit about what it is that rules are required to control (in this omission he is not alone), but he implies that one reason is the potentially troublesome character of human passions—hunger, sex, jealousy, for example—as well as whatever it is in addition to these passions that people have defined as problematic enough to require control. This latter idea is not a tautology—or should I say, not merely a tautology—because in the process of classifying and evaluating, people make rules that prescribe what they define as good and proscribe what they define as bad, in addition to the need to control the social conflicts brought about by human anger, fear, envy, frustration, greed, and the like.

Now there is nothing very wrong with either of these answers (except for a disquieting vagueness), but neither Lévi-Strauss nor Geertz help us to say which rules will be allowed to have exceptions and which will not. Even the answer about controlling passions fails us here, because there is neither any agreement about which passions require control nor very good evidence from the world's various societies to suggest that one passion requires stricter rule-based control than another.

It is also difficult to say with any confidence how—or even what—children learn about the strictness or flexibility of the rules in their social world. This is so in part because very little research has been done on the natural contexts of children's rule following outside the gaze of adults in non-Western societies[4] and in part because, even in the West, children know more about rules than they can articulate (Shweder, Turiel, and Much 1981), and most research has relied on their articulations. Children's games and play, unsupervised by adults, often mock, challenge, or reverse adults' rules, as Sutton-Smith has pointed out (Schwartzman 1978), but the rules that they mock do not seem to define basic moral issues. Instead, some recent research indicates that contrary to the formulations of Piaget and Kohlberg, children as young as three (at least in the United States) have strong moral feelings (Edwards 1981; Nucci and Nucci 1982). That young children find some rules (such as conventions or regulations) to be arbitrary while firmly insisting on the rightness of others (such as moral rules about the protection of persons, property, and promises) is an intriguing pattern that led Shweder, Turiel, and Much (1981) to characterize children as "intuitive moralists" and, further, to speculate that this intuitive capacity for moral judgment might be innate, like the capacity for language.

If an inherent moral sense exists, it may indicate that children want some rules to be categorical, but it clearly does not exercise any lasting constraint against the development in *all* societies of behavior that violates persons, property, and promises or against the development of exceptions to many moral rules. Even if people everywhere know that it is immoral to harm others, to violate their property, or to break promises, this knowledge, whether innate or tacitly learned from others, is inadequate to prevent immoral behavior. Some people— sociopaths, perhaps—often break moral rules, and it is likely that all people do so once in a while. Relying on people to want to do what is right is never enough;[5] some coercion is always required to force people to follow the rules of their society, although it may be the case that at some stages of life people require less coercion than at others. Older people and latency-age children may be more avid rule followers than are young adults, adolescents, or younger children (Campbell 1975). And, as we saw, people in some societies, such as the Walbiri or the traditional Japanese, are far more willing to follow rules than are people in other societies.

We should also add that the human commitment to morality may be provisional, depending for its strength on certain optimal environmental conditions (Sobesky 1983); under very stressful environmental conditions, such as starvation, brutality, or protracted helplessness, people may become so individualized that they display diminished moral concern for others or none at all. The Ik are one such example, the Siriono, another; the starved and brutalized inmates of Auschwitz are a still more terrifying one (Pawelczynska 1979). Rule enforcement, then, is always needed to supplement human nature and the processes of internalization in the control of human behavior. Why some rules admit no exceptions while others have many and why some societies make more rules about exceptions from rules than others are questions that remain to be answered.

Questions about why some societies more than others enforce rules strictly are so complex that we may never have a satisfactory answer, but this is an issue that will be considered further in the final chapter.

Before turning to that issue, it is necessary to examine some conditions that may tend to produce strict rules in *any* society. The development of strict rules is not likely to have been entirely whimsical, simply another example of human caprice. It is more likely that certain conditions encourage humans to develop categorical rules that allow no exceptions. I suggest that there are at least three such conditions: inequality, the need to cooperate, and the perception of danger. I will also suggest that while these three conditions can be discussed separately, in social life they usually interact.

INEQUALITY

Inequality can produce exceptions to rules, as noted in chapter 3. Slaves, children, and women, for example, are often not held to be as responsible for following rules as free persons, adults, or men would be, but at other times the rules that hold them responsible for their conduct can be very strict indeed. In general, inequality creates conditions conducive to strict rules (Fallers 1973; Roberts and Brintall 1983). When power is unequally distributed, the more powerful are likely to attempt to hold the less powerful strictly responsible for their behavior. The opposite can also be true. Sometimes persons with high social or religious statuses are held more strictly accountable for following rules than ordinary people are. We saw earlier that in the history of imperial China, the most powerful were required to adhere to a principle of *noblesse oblige*. This same principle can sometimes be found in small tribal societies. Thus, the Soara, a hill tribe of Orissa, held their priests and shamans absolutely to account for certain offenses for which ordinary men might escape punishment by appealing to an exception or offering an apology (Elwin 1955).

Usually, however, it is the powerful who impose strict rules on others. In many societies, as we have seen, men use their social or religious dominance to hold women strictly liable for following certain rules. Among the Mehinaku and Walbiri, for example, women were subject to punishment without exception for even accidental intrusion into men's "sacred" activities. The samurai of traditional Japan held their inferiors—that is, all commoners—strictly liable for following many rules.

In relatively egalitarian societies, witches, headmen, shamans, or bullies may demand exceptions to rules for themselves, and they may also attempt to impose strict rules on others. In ranked societies, political leaders, nobles, rich men, popes, samurai, kings, queens, and emperors all have reinforced their prestige and privilege by holding others strictly responsible for following certain rules. For example, Muhammad Tughlak, the sultan of Delhi, was a highly educated and pious ruler who was said by the scholarly fourteenth-century Arab traveler Ibn Batuta to dispense justice absolutely; each offender was punished according to the same law no matter what his status, a practice that enhanced the sultan's power as much as it did the law (Canetti 1962:428).

African kings often enforced their laws—as well as their whims—absolutely. An example can be taken from the rule of terror developed by Shaka, whose expansionist Zulu empire dominated most of southeastern Africa in the early nineteenth century, killing perhaps a million people in the process. Shaka was an absolute monarch in every sense, as the young Englishman Henry Francis Finn learned when he traveled to Shaka's court in 1824. On the first day of his visit, Finn saw ten men executed in response to a flick of Shaka's finger (Stuart and Malcolm 1950:78). During the following years, when Finn was often in Shaka's company and usually under his protection, his journal recorded instance after instance in which Shaka established a new rule, then enforced it without exceptions. One day, Finn saw Shaka order sixty boys under the age of twelve to be "dispatched" before breakfast (Stuart and Malcolm 1950:28).

Many of Shaka's laws had a traditional basis, but others were invented on the spur of the moment, were enforced without any possible exception, and were too ghastly to describe here. Among his less grisly decisions was one that forced his warriors to practice sexual abstinence on pain of death; Shaka tested their resolve by lining the men up nude, while executioners with their clubs at the ready stood behind them. Shaka then ordered young women to approach the warriors and dance erotically; any man who developed an erection was instantly clubbed to death (Ritter 1957:320). And when Shaka's mother died, he saw to it that thousands died with her, including ten young women who were buried alive in her grave. While Shaka may sincerely have mourned his mother, he ordered these killings not from grief but from his expressed belief that it was only possible to rule through terror (Ritter 1957:319).

Donald Black (1976:13), defining stratification as inequality of wealth, concluded that "the more stratification a society has, the more law it has." Black explained the reason for this increase in law by calling attention to Jean-Jacques Rousseau's words from 1762 (1968:68): "The universal spirit of Laws, in all countries, is to favor the strong in opposition to the weak, and to assist those who have possessions against those who have none. This inconveniency is inevitable, and without exception." Marshall Sahlins (1963) agreed, finding in Polynesia that where differences in wealth were greatest, the authority of chiefs was strongest and strict laws were harshly enforced. Black (1976) has provided an excellent discussion of the many ways in which rules of all kinds, from law to etiquette, have been produced to favor persons of higher rank. These rules are often enforced on persons of lower rank with no exceptions. When autocrats do pardon their subjects, or masters their slaves, or when kings and chiefs provide sanctuary, it seems to be because a position of power can sometimes be protected best by a show of mercy or compassion (McKnight 1981) or a show of power—the power to provide an exception to an otherwise strict rule.

Strict laws can sometimes be imposed arbitrarily, as done by Shaka Zulu and other absolute monarchs; at other times, however, the very powerful find themselves constrained by the very laws that they created in an effort to control others. British historian E. P. Thompson (1975) analyzed the notorious English Black Act of 1723, which overnight created at least 50, and perhaps as many as 250, new capital crimes. The law was ostensibly enacted to control poaching in the king's forests, but there can be little doubt that it was actually intended to extend the power of the landed gentry and aristocracy. Because the English upper classes at this time maintained their dominance through the rule of law rather than through overt military, religious, or economic means, it was essential that any new law, especially one as bloodthirsty as this one, appear to be legitimate and just (Thompson, 1975:265). The law was drafted and enforced by some utterly ruthless men, including Sir Robert Walpole, who scoffed at any pretense of justice.

Yet Thompson stated that while this strict law, like others, was created by a callous political oligarchy to protect its own self-interests, the law did not just oppress the weak but also constrained the powerful. Despite every effort to bend the law to their purposes, the powerful were trapped by it; they could no longer act arbitrarily. Thompson tartly concluded (1975:267) that the Black Act was a "bad law" made by "bad legislators" and enlarged by "bad judges," and he added: "Even this law bound the rulers to act only in the ways which its forms permitted; they had difficulties with these forms; they could not always override the sense of natural justice of the jurors; and we may imagine how Walpole would have acted . . . if he had been subject to no forms of law at all." Cesare Beccaria would have been pleased, for he also wrote in the eighteenth century that laws must be clear and precise to protect common people (Maestro 1973:22).

Inequality, then, creates conditions that are likely to lead to strict rule making. So, too, does the need for cooperation.

COOPERATION

The need to cooperate in order to achieve an important goal can lead to the imposition of inflexible rules even in small-scale societies whose rules are typically flexible. Cephu's comeuppance (chapter 7) when he set up his net in front of other Mbuti hunters was harsh, but where this rule was concerned, there were no exceptions. The need to cooperate for military reasons can also bring into effect strict rules that would be quite out of keeping with ordinary occasions. This was true of some small-scale societies such as the Jivaro of the Amazon forest (Turney-High 1971), among whom, during times of war, otherwise unruly young men had to obey a chief whose powers ended as soon as the military foray did. Even citizens of foreign powers ordinarily contemptuous of—or downright hostile toward—one another could cooperate in following strict rules if the need were great enough. In turn-of-the-century China, when the so-called Boxers, supported by imperial Chinese troops, besieged the foreign legations in Peking, the American, Belgian, British, French, Italian, German, Japanese, and Russian soldiers, sailors, marines, missionaries, diplomats, and merchants and their wives overcame their considerable distaste for one another to follow strict rules of food and water rationing and to accept military orders for their mutual survival. They did survive, but barely (O'Connor 1973).[6]

The cooperation necessary to conduct ceremonies likewise could call into effect very strict rules. Australians of the Central Desert were accustomed to strict rules, but the power of ceremonial leaders to impose and enforce life-and-death rules was absolute; the Cheyennes, too, had their strict rules, but during such ceremonies as the Sun Dance, for example, their rules became even stricter. The Mbuti were ordinarily flexible about their rules, but where the Molimo ceremony was concerned, men were strictly required to contribute food, to stay awake, and to sing, while women were required to stay out of sight of the Molimo (Schebesta 1936; Putnam 1954).

The cooperation necessary for some kinds of games can also lead to explicit rules that must be followed exactly. These rules are often markedly more exact than those that appear to govern nongame aspects of everyday behavior. In his provocative essay on trust as a condition of stable, concerted action, Harold Garfinkel (1963) asserted that he was unable to find any game, even chess, whose explicit rules covered all the legitimate possibilities that might arise or that could be made to arise by "only a slight exercise of wit." However, as Garfinkel also observed, when he intentionally employed his wit to make these non–rule-covered possibilities arise, his opponents were less than pleased. It is plausible—although it has not yet been shown—that all games have some ambiguous rules and some unstated et cetera phenomena, but the point is that players usually demand that games be played as though no ambiguities exist. They *want* the rules to be followed exactly.

For example, Opie and Opie (1969) described many children's games, played out of the sight of adults, that required participants to follow explicit rules without fail. So it was among the San, where some children's games, such as the one called "war," had rules that were followed exactly (Marshall 1976:333). Thomas Gregor described a game called "wasp" played by Mehinaku children. The game began with several older children carefully making a spiral design of a wasp's nest on the ground. Then a younger child tried to trace the design as closely as possible, while the other children stood by watching, their hands full of sand: "Should one child fail to trace the line exactly as it is drawn, all shout and throw sand at him" (1977:111).

Adults' gambling games often follow rules very carefully also. The game of *bau* as played in East Africa has rules as complicated as any gambling game played in a Las Vegas casino. Although bau is often played for entertainment rather than for profit, its rules must be followed to the letter or, as I frequently observed, the audience will protest, and the offended player may become quite angry. The rules of bau, often called "African chess," are far more complex than those of poker, and no gambling casino in the West takes the rules of poker more seriously than bau players take their rules. In societies with dramaturgical entertainment, the rules that direct performers and audience alike can be similarly binding.[7] For some kinds of entertainment, humans appear willing to accept strict rules, if only temporarily.

Collective hunting provides another dramatic example of the tightening of rules when cooperation is perceived to be essential. Robert H. Lowie (1927) was among the first to observe that North American Indian tribes, especially those of the Great Plains, appointed warriors as police during collective hunts to avoid premature attacks on the herd. The practice was at least 200 years old, Lowie wrote, and almost identical among some dozen tribes in the nineteenth century. Because the practice of temporarily appointing police to enforce hunting rules strictly was so radically different from ordinary life in these tribes, where people were, according to Lowie, generally "wholly free," he

saw regulation of the hunt as a precursor to the origin of the state
(1927:104). Control of impetuous hunters who could drive away a
herd of buffalo before it could be hunted was indeed a problem for
all of the North American Plains tribes, and when food was short, the
problem could become acute. Still, as we saw in chapter 7, the
Cheyenne police recognized some exceptions to the rule based on
such factors as reputation, age, and relationship. And all the Plains
tribes seem to have reduced the punishment if the offender were
deferential to the police and apologized politely (Ewers 1955). Apparently, this admission of wrongdoing was, as is often true of apology
in general, a tacit promise not to repeat the wrongful act. Exceptions
for good cause might be granted, but cooperation during collective
hunts was important enough for these societies to establish unusually
clear rules and to authorize members of warrior societies to enforce
these rules with unusual strictness.

The need for people to cooperate can establish conditions conducive to the enforcement of absolute liability, but the need to cooperate
may not be sufficient in itself to insure that no exceptions will be
permitted. To take another example, sometimes even the most em-
phatic rules calling for the sharing of animal food—a form of cooperation *par excellence,* in which game that is killed by one person must
be divided among many—are broken, and penalties are not imposed.
In many small societies, sharing a large animal kill is vital; hunters
cannot know which one of them will kill an animal, or when, and the
meat cannot be preserved. As essential as sharing may be (and many
social theorists believe that the need to share is the very basis of
culture), and as strongly as rules demand it—and such rules are often
said to have no exceptions—people sometimes share only reluctantly.
Among the San, for example, a moral rule called for everyone in a
band to share, but as we have seen, almost all sharing was among
close relatives (Konner 1982:9), and a few "stingy" people refused to
share altogether. These people were criticized, and others were reluctant to share with them in the future, but otherwise there was no
penalty. Among the Mbuti net-hunters, where sharing was equally
important, women routinely hid some food for themselves and their
families. Although they hid their actions because these were wrong,
among the Siriono, people sometimes simply refused to share, with
impunity.

It appears, then, that people may cooperate by following rules
without exceptions when their lives are in danger or when their
entertainment calls for it, but when self-interest appears to be served

by ignoring the rules of cooperation, self-interest may prevail, even at times in the face of third-party rule enforcement.

DANGER

An important factor in the creation of strict rules is the perception of danger. All people must learn to avoid the obvious hazards of their environment, and this often requires rules. Sometimes a danger is so great that it will generate a rule so strict that it has no exceptions. Keeping poisoned arrows out of the reach of children was such a rule among the San. In our society, the dangers of high-speed auto traffic and, increasingly, of air traffic have led us to develop progressively stricter rules for our self-protection, just as we have passed laws and regulations to protect the safety of our food and water, to prevent industrial injury, and to prevent the accidental detonation of nuclear weapons. In our search for safety, we have created governmental agencies to protect us against just about everything that we are seriously fearful about. Despite our cultural commitment to exceptions of all kinds as mitigating pleas in law, we continue to apply strict liability to many regulatory offenses. We are fearful of botulism in canned salmon, tuberculosis in milk, and carcinogens in many things we eat and drink.

At the start of this section I referred to perceived danger rather than to fear because the awareness of threat may initially be cognitive rather than emotional and may result in a dispassionately calculated decision, but the perception of danger can evoke emotions ranging from a vague sense of unease to stark terror. As Carroll Izard wrote, "There is no human emotion more toxic than fear" (1977:355).[8] Its effects on the sympathetic portion of the autonomic nervous system prepare animals, including humans, for flight; in extreme degree, however, fear constricts perception, cognition, and action and may immobilize, or "freeze," a person (Izard 1977:365). Survivors of the disastrous 1972 Buffalo Creek flood in West Virginia reported that their fear was so great that they lost control of their legs or could not move at all (Erikson 1976), a reaction all too familiar to soldiers in battle. Some fears may be innate; if not, they are learned very early in life. These include fears of strange objects or persons, especially when they approach rapidly; of being lost or alone; of sudden noises or movements; of animals; of heights; and of darkness (Bowlby 1973; Lewis and Rosenblum 1974). Humans may even share an inborn fear of snakes with some great apes and Old World monkeys, although this fear has not been demonstrated universally (Morris and Morris 1965). Fears such as these almost certainly came to be part of the human experience because they once had adaptive value, but the rules that humans may make about strangers, animals, the dark, or cliffs may have no ontogenetic basis. The great herpetologist Ionides (whom I several times had the opportunity to watch catching deadly snakes in Kenya) followed strict rules of safety in trapping and handling snakes (Lane 1963). But these were prudential rules that he had come to find essential (and that I was happy to follow); they had no necessary relationship to a panhuman fear of snakes. A fear of leopards is another example. Chimpanzees fear leopards, who prey upon them, and John Bowlby (1973:143) has speculated that leopard predation upon evolving humans may have left them with a similar fear. As we saw in chapter 7, the Mbuti feared leopards greatly, so much so that they had rules forbidding people to eat leopards or even to touch a dead one (Turnbull 1965*b*). But this fear and avoidance is more likely to be a cultural response to the contemporary danger that leopards posed to the lives of Mbuti than it is a reflection of evolution.

It is probable that humans everywhere share certain fears as a consequence of their evolutionary past, but most human fear is a product of culturally constructed dangers that can involve threats to honor, respect, or dignity as much as to life and limb. Danger is principally defined by culture, and what terrifies one group of people may not cause any concern among another. For example, as Sir James Frazer (1933) noted, many societies regard the dead as terribly dangerous: Their bodies must be treated with great caution, their names must never be uttered, and various rules must be followed to avoid angering their spirits. In some societies, however, the dead are not feared; instead, they are thought to protect crops, bring rain, serve as oracles, or otherwise aid the living. The San followed many categorical rules to avoid the dangers posed by spirits of the dead; the Mbuti, on the other hand, grieved for the dead and did not wish to die, but saw nothing dangerous about the bodies or spirits of those who were dead.

What is perceived to be dangerous, then, differs from one society to the next. It may also differ within a society. Some foods, behaviors, or places are dangerous to children but not to adults, to women but not to men, or to great hunters but not to ordinary ones. For instance, a Cheyenne warrior often had to observe very strict rules of dress, diet, or ritual if he was to survive his next battle. And in many societies, there are very strict rules that apply only to particular individuals; such rules include the avoidance of certain foods, places, or activities. Sometimes individuals attempt to assure their safety in a perilous situation by imposing absolutely strict rules on themselves, as Admiral Byrd did in order to survive in Antarctica (Byrd 1938). And, as Freud wrote in *Totem and Taboo,* "compulsive neurotics" individually create prohibitions for themselves "which they follow as strictly as savages observe the taboos common to their tribe or society" (1918:36). They do so to protect themselves against dangers, or, in Freud's chilling words, "unconquerable anxiety."

Strict rules sometimes appear to result from the belief that other people are so dangerous that any failure to appease them, respect them, or avoid them will provoke their most malevolent response. When it is believed, as it so often is, that some people (witches or sorcerers, for example) possess the inherent or acquired power to harm others, the fear that they will cause injury, illness, or death often amounts to nothing less than terror. Recall the example of the Hehe man (chapter 10) who lived in terror until his breach of etiquette had been neutralized and then forgiven. A. I. Hallowell noted the constraining fear of supernatural malevolence among the Saulteaux Indians, as Clyde Kluckhohn did among the Navaho; one never knew who might be a witch, so it was best not to offend anyone. Elizabeth Colson (1974) observed the same pattern among the Tonga of Zambia. This fear of the potential malignancy of others—through gossip, rumor, or witchcraft—can be an astoundingly effective means of assuring rule compliance, as anthropologists have recognized for many years. So much has been written about this source of rule following that it is unnecessary to add more than this comment by Colson (1974:45): "Fear, to most of us, seems a poor basis on which to found a society or develop a system of law. But we are unrealistic if we ignore the fear and concentrate solely on the advantages people see in their associations."[9]

We in industrial and postindustrial societies are not as free as we would like to be of the fear that others may wish to use their malevolent powers against us, but this danger is at least no longer central in the lives of most of us. However, we still rely on ritual procedures—some of which, like those employed by professional athletes, can be very strict indeed—that are thought to be necessary (or at least very helpful) in preventing bad luck, in reducing fear, and in lessening the dangers of problematic role performance. Some of our most important ritual rules involve greetings and related etiquette of deference and demeanor. As noted by many observers of the Far West in its wildest days and of the Deep South in antebellum times, men were most remarkably polite to one another because any offense—real or suspected—could lead to armed conflict or to a duel, and various scholars have speculated that the strict rules of Japanese etiquette originated in the fear of the samurai's swords.[10]

That the rules of etiquette, including those governing greetings, were often very binding indeed did not escape the notice of Erving Goffman, who frequently described the strict constraint of these rules over behaviors in public life. An example from a much earlier period may explain why such rules were sometimes followed so sedulously. An anonymous author of a book of etiquette in England took great pains to specify every imaginable rule of procedure to be followed in providing proper deference to titled and untitled persons at a proper dinner. There were ranks of priority specifying the order in which guests should be escorted into the dining room, with all aristocrats preceding mere country gentlemen, and among these lesser ranks, barristers' wives brought up the rear, just behind military officers and their wives. There were equally precise rules about who sat with whom and how the meal was to be eaten. The author added this telling comment (Anon. 1872:16): "These rules appear doubtless to many unnecessary and absurd, but they are not really so; and perhaps there is no truer sign of good breeding than to know how to render 'honour to whom honour is due.' Assuredly they are of great use to prevent personal piques at supposed preferences and neglects." The value of rules so clear that no host or hostess need worry about offending a guest would be great indeed, and not only in Victorian England.

Fear of another person's malevolence, like the need for etiquette, can involve a few people or many, but in general, it appears that the greater the number of people who perceive themselves to be endangered, the greater the likelihood that categorical rules will develop to reduce that danger. Sometimes the perceived danger threatens a society from without. For example, the Black Death and cholera epidemics in Europe created such widespread terror that citizens and governments alike imposed harsh rules of separation and quarantine in an effort to escape death (Tuchman 1978; McGrew 1965). Sometimes when populations meet, the desire of one population to maintain the integrity and superiority of its culture vis-à-vis the cultures of others causes rules to tighten, as may have happened for the Walbiri and the Mbuti. It certainly has done so historically for many societies that have insisted on their foods, dress, religion, or rules of etiquette, the more so because others around them have different customs that threaten to become dominant. Kai Erikson (1966) described this phenomenon of rule tightening to maintain social boundaries among the Puritans of seventeenth-century Massachusetts, and the Hopi of Oraibi are a modern example (Thompson 1950).

Among the dangers that threaten societies from within, few have been more widely feared than feuding. A common reason for strict rules and adherence to absolute liability is to prevent the violent and socially disruptive retaliation of the feud. The Cheyenne rule against killing another Cheyenne was explicitly spoken of as a way to prevent the feuds they so greatly feared, and the Eskimo said the same thing (Hennigh 1971). As Moore (1972) cogently argued over a decade ago, if everyone concerned is certain that a serious offense will be punished without exception, delay, equivocation, or intimidation, they may be less inclined to take retribution into their own hands, and feud may thus be avoided. In his study of feud in the Mediterranean and the Middle East, Jacob Black-Michaud (1975) emphasized that the prevention of feud was especially important when it was essential for coresidents to cooperate; in such circumstances, Black-Michaud found that serious offenses were dealt with at once. Austin Kennett (1925) reported that the Sinai Bedouin, among whom responsibility for injury was absolute and collective, employed "wound assessors" (a hereditary status) to quickly examine any wounded person and to assess the exact monetary compensation called for by law and dependent on the nature of the wound. Like exact penalties for a killing, this practice helped to avoid retaliation by preventing any bickering that might otherwise have taken place about the severity of an injury or the amount of compensation due.

Sometimes the danger of feud is controlled by a third-party adjudicator, as was the case among the Tarahumara Indians. The Tarahumara recognized and articulated many explicit rules but, in the ordinary course of events, treated these rules as if they were elastic rather than strict. According to Jacob Fried (1953), there were good ecological reasons why the Tarahumara could not follow all of their rigid rules, and exceptions were usually honored. Occasionally, however, people engaged in serious disputes that were referred to the *Gobernadores*—the authorities—who, as everyone knew, would enforce rules absolutely. The danger for the Tarahumara was that disputes would escalate, and to prevent violence from occurring and recurring, the Gobernadores intepreted rules strictly.

When assurance of prompt and equitable justice is lacking, the danger of feud mounts, as it did among the Nuer (whose temporary use of sanctuary to delay retaliation was described in chapter 5).

Evans-Pritchard wrote that even after the blood debt for homicide had been paid in full, the hostility simmered (Evans-Pritchard 1940:154–155):

> Indeed, all Nuer recognize that in spite of payments and sacrifices a feud goes on forever, for the dead man's kin never cease "to have war in their hearts." For years after cattle have been paid close agnates of the slayer avoid close agnates of the dead man, especially at dances, for in the excitement they engender the mere knocking against a man whose kinsman has been slain may cause a fight to break out, because the offence is never forgiven and the score must finally be paid with a life. Nuer know that "a feud never ends."

The rules prohibiting homicide are often strict, but in all but a few societies, killings occur nevertheless. Given this ineluctable reality, societies that wish to avoid violent retaliation, perhaps with no end in sight, must develop absolutely categorical rules requiring the exile of a murderer (as the Cheyennes did), his collective execution (as the San did), immediate payment of full compensation (as the Bedouin did), or third-party adjudication (as the Tarahumara did). The alternative is an endless cycle of blood vengeance that can eventually reduce a society to an embattled, embittered, fearful remnant of a once substantial population. This was the fate of the Kaingáng Indians of Brazil, whose history took this tragically self-destructive course (Henry 1941).

We can also hypothesize that rules tend to become most categorical when the actions of a single person can endanger the lives of a larger collectivity. For example, we might all be in terror for our lives (greater terror, that is) if we did not believe that the rules governing the codes and practices that must be followed by political leaders and military officers were not so explicitly written and strictly enforced that neither "mistakes" nor madness could detonate nuclear weapons. On a smaller scale, the lives of many soldiers may depend on the vigilance of a single sentry; he *must* be responsible. When the penalty for a rule violation is both terribly dangerous and *automatic,* the strictness of rules is likely to increase still further. As we saw in earlier examples, supernatural rules—that is, taboos or sacred proscriptions—are widespread phenomena. When such a rule is broken, however innocently, all members of a corporate group or society may be in danger of death. For example, the Chetris, a high Hindu caste of Nepal, demanded "rigid" observance of caste rules (Fürer-Haimendorf 1967:169). While they admired individuals who followed these rules exactly, they did not rely on individual conscience but instead all monitored one another's compliance. This was essential because, as Fürer-Haimendorf (1967:169) added:

> A breach of customary law by a single individual can have a pernicious chain effect on many others. By incurring pollution a man in turn pollutes the innocent members of his household, or even kinsmen and friends who, ignorant of his guilt, have partaken of food cooked in his house. The pollution which results from such caste-offenses as social contact with low-caste persons is automatic and contagious.

It is not surprising that Chetris watched one another carefully for signs of possible rule breaking, and someone who was even suspected of such a dangerous violation might be boycotted and discredited. Personal feelings could not be allowed to jeopardize a family's ritual purity, and parents did "not hesitate" to expel a daughter who had a premarital love affair; a Chetri husband was required to take the "same unbending attitude" toward an unfaithful wife, no matter how much he might have wished to forgive her (Fürer-Haimendorf 1967:170). Ritual impurity was not a direct threat to life, it was a cultural danger that destroyed the respect, honor, and status of a group of kinsmen. This was danger enough, because the Chetris cherished their ritual purity above all else, and they allowed no exceptions to the rules that were essential to ensure that purity.[11]

DANGER, COOPERATION, AND INEQUALITY

It is sometimes possible to see rules being followed and enforced more strictly almost exclusively as a response to the perception of danger. This happened in World War II, for example, as troops moved from the relative safety of rear areas into combat (Smith 1949). But although the perception of danger, the need to cooperate, and the presence of inequality (especially in authority) can each conduce toward the imposition of strict rules, these factors seldom occur independently of one another. Instead, they combine, recombine, and shift in their emphasis, and so do the countervailing pressures for exceptions to rules. The following two examples illustrate some aspects of the complexity involved in governance by strict rules under changing conditions of danger, cooperation, and inequality. First, let us consider fire prevention in medieval times, then the organization of men aboard warships at sea.

In medieval times, one of humankind's greatest fears—perhaps *the* greatest fear—was of fire. In towns and large cities alike, roofs were typically thatched and walls and floors were made of wood (or, in Asia, bamboo). People often slept on straw pallets near open fires, which were routinely used for heating or cooking; candles and lanterns were used for light, and torches and bonfires were common in many ceremonies or ordinary celebrations. It is little wonder that fires were so common or that they were devastating, especially in larger, densely packed settlements. Once a fire began, there was little that fire fighters could do, because they had no means of delivering much water to the flames. If fire prevention regulations were to be effective, they had to concentrate on preventing ignition, either by requiring nonflammable building materials or by controlling the use of fire itself. After great fires swept through European communities, laws of both kinds were enacted (Blackstone 1957), and sometimes they were enforced with no exceptions. Usually, however, after the sense of urgency and horror passed, the laws were circumvented (Salusbury-Jones 1939). Without an immediate sense of danger, people resisted the laws created to protect them, and the government lacked the means to coerce compliance, as Pendrill (1925) documented for the city of London in 1302.

The medieval Chinese were also plagued by conflagrations in their vast cities, but with their much greater governmental authority, they were able to enforce far stricter laws. For example, by A.D. 1275, Hangchou (south of Shanghai) was the largest city in the world, with over one million inhabitants; it was also, by Marco Polo's ecstatic accounts, the world's richest city, with greater wealth and luxury than was known anywhere in Europe (Gernet 1962). Unlike some older Chinese cities that were partially protected against fires by enormously wide avenues and high stone walls, Hangchou was a firetrap. Its houses were multistory tinderboxes, packed together with no firebreaks. Its vast population, including many impoverished immigrants from the countryside, could neither be expected to live without fire or, given the flammability of the city, to avoid all accidents. Great fires were common, occurring almost yearly; one that occurred in A.D. 1137 burned over 10,000 houses (Gernet 1962:34).

Hangchou was the capitol of China and, even more so than the rest of the country, had access to an autocratic central government that was able to enforce laws much more strictly than was possible in medieval Europe. According to Marco Polo (Yule 1929), this government was sufficiently concerned about fires to enact an extraordinary program of fire prevention. First, tall observation towers were built and manned by soldiers who signaled the first sign of fire to other soldiers, who then rushed to the fire with all manner of fire-fighting equipment, including fireproof clothing. In addition, other soldiers patrolled the streets to prevent the outbreak of fire. Fires inside homes were prohibited by law after an evening curfew, and offenders were arrested, as was anyone who went into the streets at night with a torch or lantern. These laws were written without exceptions and were enforced with rigor, as Gernet (1962:36) observed: "These severe measures must have seemed extremely harsh to the inhabitants of a town where the night life had always been extremely lively." Such strict laws were a response to a profound sense of danger, the need for considerable cooperation (more than one million people could have thwarted a few thousand soldier fire fighters had they wished), and inequality in authority (allowing effective taxation and governmental force).

A similar organizational problem was posed by the need to man warships during the nineteenth century. Following the Roman precept that soldiers and sailors should fear their officers more than they should the enemy, U.S. and British warships (as well as those of other nations) of the eighteenth and nineteenth centuries were ruled by captains who possessed autocratic, almost absolute powers. They imposed "iron discipline" based on written regulations—the "Articles of War" and "King's Regulations," respectively—that specified crimes and their penalties without exceptions. Boards of appeal or judicial review existed in the home countries, but while a ship was at sea, especially under conditions of war, the captain was all-powerful. His rule was harsh, particularly in the U.S. Navy, where discipline was described as the strictest and most oppressive in any nineteenth-century fleet (Valle 1980:18–19)—a remarkable fact, considering the strict regulations that were also enforced on British ships (Pope 1963).

A nineteenth-century warship such as the frigate *United States,* which Herman Melville (1892) described from his personal knowledge as a seaman aboard her in 1843–44, was a "city afloat," with all the facilities and stores necessary to maintain a crew of 357 enlisted seamen, 50 marines, and 23 officers. The seamen lived a crowded existence, with no privacy; below decks they were intimidated by a gang called "the mob," whose members stole what they wished and were not averse to sodomy.[12] Some crew members were professional seamen and a few were educated men, but the majority were neither educated nor solid citizens, an outcome made certain by barely tolerable shipboard living conditions, many dangers, and low pay. Every U.S. crew at that time was polyglot, with numerous Germans, Dutch,

Danes, Spaniards, Portuguese, and Chinese, as well as many Britons, joining Americans, some of whom were slaves or Black freedmen.

The officers looked upon their crews as a dangerous underclass (some were violent criminals) and even as animals, in need of the strictest regulations to control them. The Articles of War were strict enough to provide these controls, and violations of them were punished by the liberal use of flogging. Because there was no jail space on these crowded ships, physical punishment was the preferred alternative, and on some ships, flogging—to be witnessed by all hands, without exception—was an almost daily occurrence. Ships were run like penal colonies; order was maintained by armed marines, who served more as police than as a military force.

Except for officers, who were usually immune to shipboard punishment, there were few exceptions granted to the inflexible rules that constituted shipboard discipline. Melville (1892) reported that a seaman of exemplary record might be spared full punishment if other respected seamen spoke for him, but in general such men stayed away from rule violations and needed no one to plead for them; he also noted one instance in which a Black seaman on the *United States* was exempted, probably due to his status as a slave. There was also some relaxing of discipline, called skylarking, on quiet watches when there was no danger, but on the whole, there were few exceptions for any reason. These ships were highly stratified, from senior officers (who were sometimes Virginia aristocrats and who always acted as autocrats, whatever their true social rank) through junior officers, midshipmen, and marines to the "sons of adversity" who served as the crew. All these men faced common dangers, but there was little sense of cooperation except that imposed by occasional necessity and the pressure of the marines. The crewmen were alienated at best and mutinous at worst, and they regularly deserted at any friendly port. Under these dangerous conditions, cooperation could only be achieved by the imposition of rules of almost unprecedented severity and inflexibility.

U.S. naval discipline moderated over the years, of course, but as recently as 1949, a U.S. naval court could still prescribe death for twenty-two separate offenses, while in England, by 1900, there were only two capital crimes, murder and treason. Shipboard discipline in the various navies of World War II varied, but it could be severe and inflexible.[13]

Yet in the most dangerous service, submarines, strict rules were the least in evidence. The dangers on board submarines could hardly be exceeded in any other form of military service. For example, 75 percent (30,000) of all the men who served in the German U-boats during World War II were killed. All men who served in U.S. Navy submarines were volunteers who received extra, hazardous-duty pay. Submarines were indeed hazardous, and they were also uncomfortable, with little space and, especially when submerged, extreme temperatures and foul air (Frank and Horan 1945).

The difference between submarine crews of the 1940s and crews of the surface vessels of the 1840s lay in the sense of the former of belonging to an elite corps, specially trained and privileged, and of sharing a common duty and danger. Such crews certainly squabbled, especially when danger was *not* present, but crewmen knew that any man's mistake could mean death for them all (Casey 1945); in that recognition, they achieved a remarkable symbiosis—a consensus that made explicit rules largely unnecessary. Their rules were often tacit, and penalties became ad hoc or irrelevant; it was unthinkable that the basic rules would, or could, be broken by intent. Accidents happened, but training eliminated most of them. Officers, especially the captain, still had power (the Articles of War were still harsh and inflexible), but a captain's power was based on respect—respect earned not by his rank but by his performance under the close-quartered, critical scrutiny of his crew (Gasaway 1970; Schaeffer 1952).

Aboard a wartime submarine, inequality lessened, cooperation increased, a complementarity of roles grew (crewmen and officers had to know several jobs in case they needed to replace one another), and rules became largely implicit. Of absolute necessity, the rules were carefully followed; enforcement was rarely an issue. The harsh realities of submarine existence made it obvious to all that liability was collective. After careful selection of personnel and rigorous training, submarines in combat conditions achieved what ordinary societies seldom do—the creation of a society of men who *want* to do what they *must* do to survive. This example can be misleading, because a submarine is a very special society; it is one of great danger, where mistakes cannot be made. But the example of submarines makes the point that danger, cooperation, and inequality are general phenomena, so general that specific circumstances always give them special meaning. Strict rules on nineteenth-century warships were coercive and punitive; they were so intended and so perceived by all who served on those unhappy ships. Strict rules on a twentieth-century submarine were seen as necessary for survival. The difference was vast. In the first instance, a minority of men had the power to use force to impose strict rules on a resentful majority; in the second, all men agreed that strict rules were essential for their welfare.

CONCLUSION

The conditions that call for exceptions to rules are so numerous and so compelling in all societies that all rules *should* have exceptions. But they do not. All the societies examined here have some rules that are meant to be followed without exceptions. If the rule is broken, the penalty follows; no pleas, no apologies, no negotiations. It is very likely that rules like these are found in all societies, just as they were among the Siriono or Paliyans. As we have seen, some societies have many strict rules that allow no exceptions. Since the press of conditions for exceptions is so strong, this chapter has explored some of the reasons why strict rule making and enforcement may occur.

I have suggested that three general conditions are often associated with the development of strict rules that must be followed without exception. When two or more of these conditions occur together, the probability that strict liability will exist increases, but there is nothing mechanical about this increased probability. In his acclaimed book *The Sociology of Law* (1976), Donald Black concluded that the "behavior" of law, as he called it, was "mechanistically" and "quantifiably" linked to specifiable social and cultural conditions, including inequality and the need to cooperate. I believe that strict liability for rule following, whether the rules are laws or taboos, is more complexly determined. That is so, in part, because the same condition—inequality, for example—that can bring about strict rules can also call for exceptions. What is more, how these conditions interact with one another depends on their cultural meaning and, most of all, on the extent to which they are perceived as being dangerous. Again, unlike Black whose approach attempts to explain the quantity and style of law without any regard for individual experience or motivation, I find that a necessary, if not sufficient explanation for why people sometimes make strict rules and enforce them without exception is psychological—specifically, it is because people perceive danger and experience fear. But, as I have tried to show, there is nothing inevitable about the relationship between the perception of danger and the development of rules without exceptions.

It can be argued that some environments are less dangerous than others (the Mbuti forest, for example, is relatively danger-free), but all environments do present some manifest dangers (animals, enemies, disease, weather, famine, etc.) for humans, and all human societies create cultural dangers of their own that threaten their respect, honor, purity, humanity, masculinity, and the like.[14] But many of these environmental and culturally defined dangers do not lead to categorical rules. One reason why this is so may be that fear is simply too toxic an emotion. If all dangers in human existence were recognized and dwelled upon, people might well be immobilized by fear. Also, people sometimes react to perceived danger not by tightening their rules but by withdrawing from the source of danger, either by living more separate lives, as the Paliyans or Siriono did, or by retreating into a refuge, as the timid Tasaday did in their remote Philippine forest (Nance 1975).

And many people in many societies habituate to fear, greatly limiting the kinds of situations that will be defined as dangerous. John Bowlby (1973:192) described this phenomenon in the development of children who eventually learn to accept as familiar and safe what was once strange and frightening. Sometimes, the rules that reduce danger become so routinized, so taken for granted, that the perception of danger virtually disappears, creating an illusion of safety.[15] For example, the rules of the road that make driving automobiles more or less safe are undeniably vital if we are to survive even an ordinary excursion on a crowded city street. Yet with experience, most drivers become so familiar with the rules and laws that regulate driving that they can—almost literally—drive to and from work without conscious attention to any of these regulations or any sense of fear. Only if something untoward occurs—for example, another car drives through a red light or crosses over the center line—will a driver be likely to become aware of the dangers of driving. If every driver were to think of every hazard of driving, it is not too farfetched to imagine that the resulting fear would become so oppressive that one's driving would be impaired. Indeed, one might refuse to drive at all. As an experiment, think of the trust we place in oncoming motorists not to cross over the center line and smash into us head-on. The next time you drive on a winding road, try suspending this trust by imagining that oncoming motorists may not stay on their side of the road. The result will be heightened arousal, if not stark terror.[16]

Many dangers, then, are neutralized by routines that reduce fear. But, too, most dangers are not constant; they wax and wane, and when they wane, rules may relax until exceptions are permitted. Of course, there are likely to be individual differences in people's susceptibility to fears and their consequent acceptance of strict rules to reduce perceived danger. People who suffer from phobias illustrate how extreme fears can become. It should also be emphasized that extremes of danger such as invasions, plagues, famines, and the like may result not in strict rules at all but rather in social breakdown, in the loosening of rules to the point of individualism (Barton 1969).

Kai Erickson (1976) documented this breakdown among the survivors of a flood in a West Virginia community. Travelers to East Africa in the late nineteenth century found many villages abandoned, their inhabitants scattered and terrified by slave raids. We saw earlier how hunger led many societies to break their rules of sharing, and in some societies, like the famished Siriono and Ik, people abandoned many of their rules. In other societies, historical experience with social chaos increases people's willingness to accept strict laws and governmental controls, as the following traditional Islamic saying illustrates (Dwyer 1978:139): "'Sixty years of tyranny are better than one hour of civil strife.'"

The relationship between danger and strict rules is not only complex but also can be paradoxical. As we noted earlier, in many societies some of the strictest rules are both trivial and seemingly unrelated to any danger. For example, the Mbuti must wash themselves whenever they cross a stream and cannot hunt unless children cause the campfire to smoke in a prescribed way; fish cannot be eaten by adults but is acceptable food for children. A San woman's milk must not touch her husband, or his success as a hunter will be affected; neither men nor women may sit where someone of the opposite sex has recently sat; and the name of an absent child must not be mentioned. Some of these rules are terrifying taboos and others are said to be necessary because it is thought to be vaguely dangerous not to have them, but often, people can give no reason for these rules. They are simply followed.

Perhaps such rules reflect past dangers, now long fogotten. Of course, rules can be conservative: Why risk danger by abandoning rules that have held danger in abeyance in the past? What is more, in all societies, certain rules that are followed without exceptions, or virtually no exceptions, would seem to be remote from any direct perception of danger. Terms for kinsmen, avoidance of certain persons, joking with others, ways of covering the genitalia, among others, are commonly specified by very clear and strict rules. Rules like these obviously ease everyday life, making behavior more predictable and meaningful, yet it is stretching a point to attribute these rules primarily to perceived danger.

Although there is nothing inevitable about the perception of danger and the development of strict rules, the two phenomena are nevertheless related. However, as a cautionary principle, we must guard against making danger a *deus ex machina,* rather like announcing that there is a dormitive principle in opium. Fear is manifestly a varied emotion, being specific and diffuse, intense and mild, chronic and momentary. If something as diverse as this were used to explain everything, it would explain nothing. I do not mean fear to be understood in so global or reductionistic a fashion.[17] What I do mean is that categorical rules, those rules that must be followed without exception, very often come into being because the people who make and enforce them believe that they personally, or their corporate group collectively, would suffer death, serious illness or injury, or disastrous loss of property or honor if such a rule were not followed.

I am not suggesting that fear is the central emotion in human living, in the evolution of rules, or in the organization of society. Joy is important, and so are envy, boredom, hopefulness, empathy, and other feeling states. But I am making an empirical generalization, based on the materials reviewed in previous chapters, that before people will establish strict rules, they must usually believe that they would be in grave danger if they did not do so. People do not usually enforce strict rules out of a sense of joy, envy, boredom, or hopefulness; strict rules are primarily a product of perceived danger, and that people develop strict rules as often as they do reflects the extent to which they perceive danger in their lives. But as I have attempted to show, the issues are complex, and although perceived danger may be the best explanation for why strict rules come into being and persist, it is not yet the equivalent of a quark as a basic building block for rule making; while fear may be necessary for the development of strict rules, it is not sufficient.

CHAPTER 12

Rules, Exceptions, and Social Order

We have now illustrated and discussed various types of rules and exceptions, and we have identified factors that press for exceptions in all societies and others that militate against them. We have also contrasted societies that treat most of their rules flexibly with other societies that specify many of their rules precisely and enforce them strictly. We should now return to the basic question of this book: If rules are essential for social order, then why should exceptions to these rules be allowed? My answer is that exceptions are allowed because there are many factors that pressure people to grant them and, moreover, because exceptions that are defined by rules do not weaken social order but maintain it in the same ways that other rules do.

The reasons for this conclusion will be presented later in this chapter, but first we should return to the unanswered question that was posed in chapter 10: Why do some societies more than others follow their rules carefully and enforce them strictly? Why, that is, are the Siriono so different from the Walbiri? This is an inordinately difficult question, and it is not the question that this book set out to answer. However, it is an intriguing puzzle, and explaining why it cannot easily be solved will help to provide the background necessary to explain why allowing rule-defined exceptions is not inconsistent with maintaining social order.

We can begin by asking whether the factors identified in the preceding two chapters can provide a basis for predicting whether a particular society or type of society will treat its rules flexibly or inflexibly. The answer is that they may, but only to a limited extent. One of the reasons that the identification of factors pressing for or against exceptions does not translate into accurate intercultural predictions about societies' relative flexibility is conceptual. What *is* flexibility or inflexibility? John Embree (1950) attempted to compare social types that differed in flexibility when he contrasted what he called the "tight" rule system of the Japanese with the "loose" system of the Thais, whom he believed differed from the Japanese in their marked individuation and lack of regularity, discipline, and regimentation. But Embree did not identify the causes of "tight" or "loose" systems, nor did he specify any procedures for measuring differential tightness or looseness.

Intuitively, the Japanese are "tighter" about their rules than all the Thais, just as the Walbiri are "tighter" than the Siriono, but are the Mbuti more or less "tight" than the Paliyans? The Mbuti have more rules that are followed without exception and are strictly enforced than do the Paliyans, but the Paliyans have one moral rule— nonaggression—that is both central to their way of life and very strictly followed and enforced. Is a society's inflexibility an additive product of how many strict rules they follow and enforce, or is inflexibility better thought of in terms of the importance of the rules that are strictly followed? The Mbuti followed many rules strictly, but Turnbull wrote that these often seemed trivial, and the Mbuti themselves offered no compelling reasons for conforming to them. The Paliyans, on the other hand, explicitly emphasized that nonaggression was the most important rule in their lives. If we were to decide that importance was to be the criterion, how would we judge a rule's importance? Would we rely on our intepretations or on a people's own views? The dilemma is both serious and commonplace in intercultural comparisons.

In addition to this kind of conceptual issue, there are measurement problems. Whether one wishes to define a society's tightness in terms of the number or relative importance of rules that are enforced strictly, intercultural comparisons must rely on ethnographic data that seldom permit reliable measurement of rule following or rule enforcement. This problem plagued Bryce Ryan and Murray Straus (1954) when they attempted to define "looseness" among the Sinhalese of Ceylon in terms of their many alternatives to rules and their tolerance of rule violation. Indeed, when Pertti Pelto (1968) attempted to measure these same two variables in a sample of twenty-one societies, he was unable to do so with acceptable interrater reliability. As a result, he was forced to utilize social variables that could be more reliably measured, such as the presence of a theocracy or the corporate ownership of stored food, in lieu of direct measures of rule following or enforcement. The variable that best predicted a "tight" society in Pelto's research was high population density. There may be a correlation between a population's density and the kind of social organization, rules, and rule enforcement needed to maintain that population, but keep in mind that among hunting-and-gathering societies with very low population density (reviewed in chapter 9) there was a great range in rule flexibility, from the Siriono at one extreme to the Walbiri at the other. To further emphasize the limited usefulness of high population density as a predictor of inflexible rule systems, one might think of high-density cities such as New York or San Francisco, with their tolerance for alternative rules. Another example is the Chinese section of Hong Kong, whose density—more than twenty times that of New York City—may be the highest ever recorded. The Chinese families who lived in such close quarters followed some rules strictly, but it would be difficult to find any basis for equating the strictness of their rule system with that of the Walbiri (Anderson 1972).

Strong rule systems, then, would appear to develop for more complicated reasons than population density alone. Black's (1976) recent attempt to identify purely social factors that are related to an increase in law offers a set of social conditions that may have relevance for this issue, but because Black defined law as "governmental social control" he dealt with a somewhat different phenomenon than the relative strictness or tightness of rule systems. A more valuable approach for this purpose is Peter M. Gardner's (1966) characterization of a particular type of foraging society as individualistic, atomistic, noncooperative, and noncompetitive; exemplified by the Paliyans, this type of society was flexible about rules, few of which were clear, carefully followed, or strictly enforced. Gardner believed that this type of society represented an adaptation that for various ecological reasons stressed economic self-sufficiency, psychological autonomy, and the avoidance of conflict. There may indeed be a relationship between flexible rules and the opportunity both for people to move away from conflict and for nuclear family economic self-sufficiency. Unfortunately for the force of Gardner's thesis, he included in his individualistic, noncooperative, foraging type of society both the Mbuti and the San, societies that would appear to be strongly cooperative by any criterion.[1]

Efforts such as these to identify social conditions that effectively predict the relative flexibility of societies have encountered difficulties on conceptual grounds, in the unreliability of rule-compliance measures, and in matters of sample selection. But even if all these problems were resolved, still other, perhaps more important, problems would remain. For example, the approaches discussed have relied on social, cultural, and ecological variables to the exclusion of psychological and historical ones. A key psychological variable appears to be the perception of danger, but as we have seen, what is culturally perceived as dangerous is highly variable. Only occasionally is danger defined as a direct threat to life (poisoned arrows, for example) that could be measured adequately in any society. More often, danger is defined as a fear of witches or forbidden foods or as moral breaches that threaten the harmony between man and the supernatural worlds. All these are dangers, to be sure, but they are difficult to compare from one society to the next. As difficult as these psychological factors are to measure, historical influences are even more difficult. This is especially true in nonliterate societies, where no records survive of past events, great or not so great, that might have influenced the development and enforcement of rules of all kinds. When psychological and historical factors are not made a part of the equation, what remains is certain to lose a good part of its predictive power. Inequality of authority and the need to cooperate (whether in my formulation or in Black's) are important, but they are only part of the causal nexus. The difficulties involved in specifying interculturally valid predictors of relative rule strictness can best be seen by looking again at the societies we examined earlier whose rules are particularly strict.

Let us begin with the Jalé and their emphasis on categorical rules, very strictly and collectively enforced. Koch believed that the Jalé developed their reliance on strict and collective responsibility because they lacked any binding third-party authority to prevent conflict from leading to feud or warfare. The Jalé were not alone in this fear; the Cheyennes shared it and tried to enforce their law against homicide strictly. Many other societies did the same. Sally Moore (1972) pointed out the advantage of strict and collective responsibility as a guarantee to any injured party and to his corporate group that compensation would be made without the need for violent retaliation. This principle may indeed be the reason why the Jalé developed their system of rules with no exceptions, but other quite similar societies in the western highlands of Papua New Guinea also feared feuding and warfare, also had only weak third-party authority to resolve disputes, and yet did not develop either strict or collective responsibility. For example, the Kapauku, described in detail by Leopold Pospisil (1958a), disliked feuding and warfare too, and like the Jalé, they lacked strong third-party authority to resolve disputes. The Kapauku recognized, and actually recited, many abstract rules and laws (Pospisil cites 121 of these), but when disputes—including violent ones—occurred, the Kapauku allowed a variety of mitigating and aggravating circumstances. For them, some exceptions were legitimate (1958a:250–251); for the Jalé, none was typically permitted.

How might we explain the Cheyennes' virtual obsession with rules and governance? Well, for one thing, they were compelled to cooper-

ate to survive. The Plains were subject to extremes of heat and cold,
with hot summer winds that could drive people and animals to madness and winter blizzards that could kill anyone who did not reach
shelter in time (Webb 1931). The quest for food was continuous and
often unavailing. Vast herds of buffalo and lesser ones of antelope
were rich resources, but they were not always available; to exploit
these animals, the Cheyennes had to move their camps through
drought and blizzard, often contending with enemy tribes who sought
the same herds. Sometimes the herds were not found, and the
Cheyennes were reduced to scrounging after prairie dogs or skunks
(Limbaugh 1973:9). Their environment had many dangers in addition to weather and an uncertain food supply. The warfare that
pervaded Plains life was not a game in which honor was achieved by
bloodless feats of bravery, it was a deadly serious business, albeit one
in which bravery and honor were essential (Oliver 1962). Plains warfare was often bloody, and sometimes many lives were lost; some who
survived lost their wives and children as captives or lost their wealth
in horses. In addition to the need to cooperate and to so many
perceived dangers, the Cheyennes recognized inequality in authority
in the form of powerful chiefs and military societies with full police
powers. All the necessary ingredients for a system of strict rules and
laws were there. However, if the Cheyenne concern with governing
by strict laws was a response to these—and only to these—exigencies,
then it is difficult to understand why other Plains societies did not
develop similarly strict rule systems. Some Plains societies were larger
and richer than the Cheyennes, but others were smaller, weaker in
number of warriors, and poorer in horses and access to buffalo.
All these societies had to cooperate in order to cope with the same
environment and the same enemies. All had very similar economic
and political systems, yet none of these societies—whether larger or
smaller, weaker or stronger—was as obsessed by law and governance
as were the Cheyennes (Hoebel 1954). In fact, as Linton observed,
the Comanches, as warlike as any Plains society, had little use for law
or strict liability.

   Treated as a single case, the Cheyenne rule system can be explained
plausibly enough, but once the Cheyennes are compared with their
neighbors, this explanation evanesces, and the Cheyennes become as
enigmatic as the Jalé. The Walbiri are equally puzzling. Was their
extremely categorical rule system, which was so strictly enforced,
widespread among central Australian societies before European contact? There is no convincing answer to this, but if the Walbiri system
was formerly shared by neighboring societies whose rules were equally

strict, how could that be explained? Were they in greater need of rules to create harmony than were societies in other parts of the world? Did they have a greater need for cooperation? Were they in greater danger from intratribal violence or feuding? It is impossible to answer any of these questions affirmatively. And why did they develop their beliefs in the unchanging and unchallengeable "dreamtime" law? Again, no plausible answer is forthcoming. If the Walbiri represent a traditional retention of what was once widespread in central Australia and perhaps elsewhere among Australian aboriginal peoples, there is no obvious reason why this pattern should have arisen in such extreme form.

Another explanation might be that the Walbiri, who have been eating European food since the 1920s and living in government settlements since World War II, have recently exaggerated their earlier pattern of adherence to tradition and law. As Meggitt (1962:333) recognized, life in government settlements or on cattle stations relieved them of the necessity to rely on hunting or gathering for their subsistence. It also allowed them to remain congregated in sizable groups rather than having to split up into smaller foraging bands to exploit their desert resources. As a result, their social life intensified and, perhaps, so did their need for strict accountability to their law. Robert Tonkinson (1974) has noted a related phenomenon among the aborigines at Jigalong Mission in Western Australia. These aborigines clung fiercely to their "law," followed their rules carefully, and explicitly saw themselves as needing traditional law. Tonkinson (1974) believed that these people, who witnessed the cultural disintegration of aboriginal populations elsewhere in Australia, held so tenaciously to their law as a conscious defense against the perceived danger of cultural disintegration and perhaps of the loss of self-esteem as well.

But this explanation, too, is speculative. Over the course of modern history, many small, foraging societies have been at times permanently forced to settle in larger than usual groups as the economic dependents of a state government. The Walbiri and the people of Jigalong Mission may have enforced their rules more strictly as a result, but when other small societies have undergone comparable changes, their systems of rules have loosened or have disintegrated altogether. The context of change is important, as context always is, but context is a product of the past as well as of the present, and without a knowledge of history, any explanation will be incomplete.

It is unlikely that anyone would have the temerity to suggest that even the availability of centuries of written history is sufficient to

explain fully the development of strict rule compliance in traditional
Japan, but historical information about the importance of early Chinese influence or governmental changes during the later Tokugawa
period is certainly helpful. However, it is not only the historical impact
of great events or vast political changes that directly affects the
development of strict rule systems but also the history of attitudes
about rules, responsibility, and, most of all, about people. For example, the belief that strict rules are necessary in order to control human
behavior can be related to beliefs about human nature. In many
Western societies, the belief arose that human nature was evil, requiring strict controls to avoid social disorder (Stevenson 1974). Various
influences, including that of Durkheimian sociology, extended this
distrust of human nature into modern social theory. For example, in
Moral Education, Durkheim (1961:42) wrote: "The totality of moral
regulations really forms about each person an imaginary wall, at the
foot of which a multitude of human passions simply die without being
able to go further." But, he warned, if the barrier "weakens," the
passions "pour through," finding "no limits where they can or must
stop." Perhaps even more than other Europeans, Russians feared the
dark aspects of man's nature, concluding that disorder (*besporiadok*)
would result if man were not ruled by strong authority (Connor
1972). Dostoyevski's novels brilliantly explore the Russians' fear of
chaos and their search for an absolute form of authority (Jones 1976).[2]
Beliefs about human nature may themselves be epiphenomena of
various environmental, economic, or demographic factors, but they
may nevertheless be a legacy of the past that continues to influence
the development of rule systems. I emphasize the relevance of beliefs
such as these because, as noted earlier, any search for the causes of
inflexibility in rule systems must look to the past as well as to the
present.

Efforts to predict the relative flexibility of rules in various societies
are difficult because of a complex of largely incommensurable factors,
such as attitudes about danger that were developed in the past and
then modified by successive social and cultural changes. This does not
mean, however, that whether a society's rules will be flexible or inflexible is wholly indeterminate, only that predictions should be prob-
abilistic in nature and cautious in their claims. With these strictures
in mind, it is probable that societies in which the need for economic
cooperation does not extend beyond the nuclear family, where opportunities for mobility are such that families can move away from others
with whom there is actual or potential conflict, and where there is no
inequality that grants one class economic, religious, or kin-group

power over another will tend to have more flexible rules (and fewer inflexible ones) than societies in which there is no opportunity to move away from conflict, where the economic system requires cooperation, and where there is inequality.[3]

This formulation refers only to the relative inflexibility of rules, not to exceptions to rules. Whether exceptions to rules will be permitted, or required, is another issue, and we will now turn to it.

WHY RULES ABOUT EXCEPTIONS TO RULES?

The central questions that have organized this inquiry into rules and exceptions are these: If rules are so important for the creation and maintenance of social order, then why allow exceptions to them? Why not state these rules explicitly and unambiguously, follow them, and penalize anyone who fails to do so? If the answer to the first question— whether rules are indeed vital for social order—is pursued in a global way, it can become the epistemological equivalent of gardening in a nuclear-waste dump. Only if we keep in mind that there are different kinds of rules and that some rules help to solve problems for people while others create problems—at least for some people—can we avoid the hazards of global assertions about the role of rules in human affairs. With this cautionary note in mind, it must nevertheless be repeated that no society has done without rules altogether and that all societies have taken some of their rules very seriously.

Social order is a complex concept imposed on a great deal of disorderly human behavior, but if what we mean by it is the regularity of social life, then much of this kind of order is the product of implicit rules or routines rather than of explicit rules. But social order also refers to the control of conflict, and some explicit rules do regulate behaviors that might otherwise lead to conflict; for example, moral rules, by defining what ought to be or what must be, may prevent unwanted behavior from taking place at all. Sometimes, however, rules work against one another, representing not the interest of a band, village, or society but those of a particular family, kinship group, gender, age set, or economic specialization. Still other kinds of rules, especially supernatural ones, can create such fear that individuals or groups may turn against one another in accusations of witchcraft or of other malevolence.

Different kinds of rules, then, have different social consequences, intended and unintended. Some of these consequences may increase the regularity of life and decrease conflict. Others offer meaning and morality, and some provide safety. In the most general sense, humans everywhere make rules that regularize their behavior, and in all societies some of these rules are followed as though any failure to do so would jeopardize social order.

In fact, we have found no society in which people did not believe that some rules were so vital that they had to be followed without fail and enforced without exceptions. Sometimes these rules without exceptions are only enforced for brief periods, on special occasions or in particular settings, but in some societies, rules without exceptions may come to outnumber more flexible rules. And so it is possible, as we have illustrated, for people in some societies to see their rules as so important that they do require one another to follow them without exceptions. But despite the success of some societies in enforcing rules strictly, there are many reasons (as I have indicated) why people may want exceptions to be permitted. None of the societies we have examined enforced *all* of its rules strictly, and it is virtually certain that no society has ever done so.

Indeed, there is one kind of exception that must be granted if any society is to survive: young children cannot be held responsible for rule following, not even for following those rules for which everyone else is held to strictly, such as the avoidance of sacrilege among the Walbiri or of pollution among the Chetris. If, like adults, young children were executed or ostracized for an accidental act of sacrilege, there might soon be no more young children. Adults can be held responsible for seeing to it that children do not behave in ways that endanger themselves or others, but the children themselves cannot be blamed. The question then becomes, At what age is a child responsible? The age at which a child is determined to be a culturally responsible person is one example of the many pressures for exceptions to rules that exist in any society. Every society must compromise strict rule enforcement in at least this way, and all in fact do so in other ways as well, but if a society makes exceptions to its rules in terms of other rules that are equally clear and accepted, then it can accommodate to pressures for exceptions without compromising the viability of its system of rules and responsibilities.

First, consider all of those factors discussed in chapter 10 that make strict enforcement of categorical rules difficult to maintain. Factors such as illness, injury, intoxication, age, sex, individual differences, ideas of equity and intent, reputational considerations, human nature, context, and "et cetera" phenomena can create powerful pressures against rules that permit no exceptions. One outcome is the development of many alternatives to rules, with each alternative as acceptable as the next. Flexible rules like these are subject to negotiation and redefinition, not to mention argumentation and dispute. Another outcome is for rule violations, however offensive they may be, to be overlooked; offended parties in many societies have no choice but to "lump it" (Nader and Todd 1978). Ambiguous rules, alternatives to rules, and weak rule enforcement can easily increase the probability of conflict, as individuals and groups pursue their interests without concern for what is required or right. And some societies that lack clear rules, including clear exceptions to rules, must cope with anger, confusion, resentment, and open aggression as individuals or groups conflict with one another.

No rules, no matter how clear or how strictly enforced, can prevent deviance or conflict altogether, but clear rules that provide exceptions to rules can serve to restrict deviance and conflict in two ways. First, they can relieve the pressure for exceptions that some people may feel and express by allowing age, illness, intent, or good reputation to reduce responsibility for rule following; second, by being defined as rules, these exceptions can reinforce the principle of clearly defined responsibility. A rule that requires everyone to behave in a certain way, *unless* one or more specific conditions exists, is still a rule that can be enforced as strictly as a rule without any "unless" provisions.

The fundamental problem in bringing about social order is to make behavior predictable and controllable. People everywhere have done this by persuading or compelling one another to behave in predictable and acceptable ways and then holding one another responsible for their behavior. If the conditions that press against these regular ways of behaving are not brought under the sway of rules, then prediction is lessened and control is weakened.

Exceptions defined by rules occur worldwide. Whether these exceptions are the result of temporary conditions, special kinds of people, occasions, or settings, they can be defined with the same clarity and enforced with the same stringency as rules that permit no exceptions. To bring human behavior under the sway of rules is a social necessity. When a society succeeds in redefining as a legitimate exception behavior that would otherwise be objectionable and disruptive, the sway of rules is extended, not diminished. Rules, and rules about exceptions to rules, can never control all behavior effectively; there will always be some disruptive behavior that is neither regulated nor punished, and as a result, there will always be some conflict. But to bring most behavior under the regulation of rules, including rules about exceptions to rules, is a necessary step toward the creation of social order—and even imperfect social order is a supreme human achievement.

RULES, FREEDOM, AND SECURITY: AN IRONY

For Westerners, the idea of freedom is often related to escape from the constraints of society and thus of rules. For the Greeks, individualism was framed by the Homeric ideal of personal fame, and it often led to lawless self-seeking (Muller 1961). Americans have also thought of freedom in "lawless" ways, envying the lone frontiersman—free to come and go as he pleased and hunting, sleeping, and eating when he chose—and lamenting everything that caused this freedom to be replaced by the constraint of rules. The imagined antinomy between individual freedom and social constraint is a master metaphor of Western thought.[4] There may be some analogies to this opposition between freedom and security in the experiences of small populations who ordinarily live in small, mobile bands, coming together in larger groups only for certain times of the year. When such bands come together, it is common for some strict rules to emerge in an attempt to prevent conflict, with the rules loosening when the large band again splits into smaller ones.[5] But size is not the only consideration. As populations grow larger, new organizational forms emerge so that people in large cities may become less bound by strict rules than are people in smaller towns and villages and in tribal societies.[6]

The opposition between freedom and security is central to Western thought, but when it is applied to non-Western societies it can be misleading. Some rules are probably felt to be constraining everywhere. These are often secular regulations, but they may include some explicit conventions, supernatural injunctions, or even more rules. Even in societies where there is no concept of freedom as such (for example, among the Pokot of Kenya or the Kuma of Papua New Guinea), some people may nevertheless insist on their right to choice and may resist efforts to remove that right from them. In both societies mentioned, young women fell in love with—or at least became strongly attached to—young men and wanted to marry the young men of their choice; older persons denied them this freedom to choose, imposing their right to choose whom girls should marry, and when. This was a rule, a right of parents and kin, and it was backed by the right to use coercion. In both societies, girls resented this rule so much that they often attempted suicide in protest, sometimes succeeding in the attempt (Edgerton and Conant 1964; Reay 1959).

Some other rules, including taboos, may be experienced as equally burdensome. But many rules are probably not seen as constraints on one's freedom. Moral rules, for example, may create freedom by defining what freedom ought to be, and even some secular regulations, by providing safety, may be seen as giving people freedom by giving them the security to live. And implicit rules may not be consciously perceived at all. The view that there is opposition between freedom and the constraint of rules can be misleading, then, because it overlooks rules that create freedom to make choices or to live without fear and also because it implies that strict rules and exceptions to these rules, like Victor Turner's (1969) "structure" and "communitas," oppose one another and alternate over time in a dialectical process.[7]

Factors that press for and against exceptions to rules exist in any society, and they may sometimes interact dialectically when, for instance, a time of very strict regulation becomes burdensome and is followed by a period of relaxed rule enforcement, or when too many exceptions lead to a sense of anarchy and martial law is imposed. But the essential point is that most of the time, strict rules and exceptions to rules do not coexist in a Janus-faced social reality primarily because they are reciprocals of one another but more because the conditions that create them exist in all societies; these conditions emerge from different social and psychological realities.

Rather than conceptualizing these realities in dialectical terms, we can view them more easily by imagining them as an elastic and discontinuous double helix, usually separate but interacting at certain points. It is even misleading to conceptualize the two sets of forces as being in disequilibrium or as representing social tension. People do seek exceptions to rules for many reasons, and they can feel thwarted when rules remain strict, but they can also experience tension when they believe that exceptions create danger or confusion or else contradict their sense of what is right and natural. There can be tension, but it exists in people, not in social equilibrium.

There is an irony to this. There are exceptions to rules that are themselves rules. By seeking this kind of exception in order to escape responsibility for following some rules, people do not escape responsibility altogether; they only accept a different responsibility. There is another irony as well: by making and enforcing strict rules, people sometimes constrain themselves, but they may also achieve a more valuable freedom—from danger, dishonor, or uncertainty. The search for exceptions to rules or for rules without exceptions, then, entails a double irony. As long as people live together, they will have rules. Some of these rules will have exceptions, and some will not. Both kinds of rules constrain people in some ways and free them in others. There is no escape from rules or responsibility by establishing exceptions based on rules.

CONCLUSION

The most general conclusion that all of this material suggests is that neither normative theory nor strategic interaction theory offers an accurate model of rules and their uses in the world's societies. What is more, these two theories are so hypostasized and polarized that neither can easily accommodate relevant aspects of the other. In the world of social reality everywhere, some kinds of rules are strictly enforced while others are manipulated, bent, or redefined for strategic purposes. Many rules and their exceptions are subject to strategic rule manipulation, bargaining, and negotiating for personal advantage. In pursuit of their self-interests, people use apologies as promissory notes for better behavior in the future, adroitly employ excuses to confirm their devotion to virtuous rule following, and fervently insist that an apparent violation of one rule was brought about by the necessity of following another, more important one. Strategic rule manipulations like these occur in small-scale societies as well as in urban centers. People everywhere bargain and maneuver for advantage, using rules for their own interests when they can. This kind of behavior, so central to the strategic interaction perspective, certainly takes place everywhere, but—and this is a large but—it does not always take place anywhere. Try as people may to stretch rules, some rules are not elastic. Sometimes people follow rules very carefully, seeking no exceptions and receiving none should they inadvertently break a rule. They may even want to be punished if they break a rule.

Our proverb that "rules are made to be broken" is only a part of social reality, the part comprehended by strategic interaction ideas. Other rules are made to be followed, and they are followed, usually, even when it is difficult to do so. And some rules are not seen at all, even though they direct our lives in many ways. Perhaps it is not dramatic enough, this statement of social reality, to bring about a change in our social theories, but any theory of rules and their uses that does not represent these multiple realities is more a simulacrum than it is a useful social theory.

Notes

1: Rules and Exceptions

1. Not everyone grants rules such sovereignty over human behavior. Wittgenstein (1953), for example, called attention to behavior that to an observer seemed to follow no rule and in which the actor can explicate no rule. For a subtle and ironic view of social order as well as a scholarly review of the issues involved in various theories of social action, I recommend Alan Dawe (1978).

2. Robin Fox (1977) has summarized much of this evidence, as has Phyllis Dolhinow (1972), along with many others, such as Hamburg and McCown (1979) and Reynolds (1981).

3. The history of normative theory, or functionalism, has generated endless volumes. Much of this material is noted by Wrong (1961), Blake and Davis (1964), Moore (1978), and Zeitlin (1973). For a particularly lively, even impassioned interpretation, see Gouldner (1970). Rule-centered theory in legal anthropology is discussed by Comaroff and Roberts (1981).

4. It is impossible and unnecessary to summarize these fields here. Useful reviews are available by Wilson (1970), Giddens (1979), and Bottomore and Nisbet (1978). For a review of the impact of these perspectives on anthropology, I recommend Evens (1977).

5. I believe that an essential feature of related perspectives—such as symbolic interactionism (Weinstein 1982), Goffman's dramaturgical variant (Wilshire 1982), or process models of adjudication—is the assumption that individuals routinely calculate their self-interest, then strategically manipulate roles to serve those interests. The study of "symbolic interaction," pioneered by G. H. Mead and developed by Herbert Blumer, became a school at the University of Chicago (Fisher and Strauss 1978) and there is a journal called *Symbolic Interaction*. Reviews of the practicalities of rule use are available in Goffman (1959, 1963, 1969), Cicourel (1964), Garfinkel (1967), Douglas (1970b), and Schlenker (1980); Lyman and Scott (1970) review the development of the strategic interaction perspective from various angles, and coin their own term, "the sociology of the absurd," for a part of it. Habermas (1971) looks at strategic interaction in therapy. For some strategic interaction perspectives in anthropology, see Berreman (1962), Bailey (1969), Goldschmidt (1969), and Murphy (1971). When I refer to this perspective as "strategic interactionism," I acknowledge Goffman's central role in the development of the perspective and the influence of his book *Strategic Interaction*

(1969), but my use of the term is not restricted to Goffman or to his particular definitions of strategic interaction.

6. An early analysis of strategic interaction in the Himalayas was provided by Gerald Berreman (1962). A more recent example, which we shall examine further in chapter 8, is available in Gregor (1977). For a discussion of the phenomenon from another point of view, see Robert LeVine (1973).

7. LeVine (1973) has also stressed the flexibility and ambiguity of rules. What is more, he has offered a typology of rules that emphasizes the importance of different rule types. His typology differs from the one I shall propose in chapter 2.

8. For a discussion of this undeniably important topic, see Pelto and Pelto (1975).

2: Rules, Responsibility, and Exceptions

1. A good exploration of this issue is provided by John Haviland (1977) in his discussion of gossip and reputation among the Zinacanteco Indians of Oaxaca.

2. For an introduction to aspects of rule use and interpretation, see Garfinkel (1967), Denzin (1970), Cicourel (1972), and Hawkins and Tiedeman (1975).

3. Examples of Eskimo suicide are summarized in Hoebel (1954) and Oswalt (1979). For firsthand accounts, see Amundson (1908), Freuchen (1961), Jenness (1922), Rasmussen (1929), Stefansson (1922), and Weyer (1932).

4. An influential article by Gardner Murphy (1954) is a case in point. For a general review of internalization, see Scott (1971).

5. For a discussion on the concept in law, see Howard (1963). Strict liability is sometimes distinguished from absolute liability, but I shall not distinguish between the two.

6. For an early discussion of the social factors that lead to the development of collective liability, see Yehudi Cohen (1964); the more recent perspective of Sally Moore (1972) is more plausible, in my view.

7. As I have noted elsewhere (Edgerton 1971*b*), some Akamba rules can be explicit, inflexible, and broadly acknowledged as right or necessary. Some rules, mostly secular regulations, can be flexible, but some moral and supernatural rules can be quite rigid. For another example, see Fallers (1969).

8. For a sampling of these typologies, I recommend Black (1962), Goffman (1963), Denzin (1970), Collett (1977), Shimanoff (1980), and Gibbs (1981).

9. For an early discussion of "alternatives" in anthropology, see Kluckhohn (1941), and for a famous discussion of habit, see John Dewey (1922).

10. See, for example, Birdwhistell (1970), Hall (1977), and Douglas (1975).

11. For an overview, see Sommer (1969), Hall (1959, 1963, 1966), Mehrabian (1976), and Ashcraft and Scheflen (1976).

12. For a variety of examples of these phenomena see Douglas (1970*b*), Garfinkel (1967), Mehan and Wood (1974), and Edgerton (1979).

13. Denzin's (1970) discussion of polite-interactional rules is relevant here, and so is Youssouf, Grimshaw, and Bird's (1976) discussion of greetings among the Tuareg. Tuareg rules of the encounter are strict and elaborate.

14. For more extended discussion, see Black (1962) and Shweder, Turiel, and Much (1981).

15. Jerry Jacobs (1962) has explored this phenomenon, especially with regard to teenage suicide; see also Fürer-Haimendorf for a discussion of the concept of sin (1974).

16. See, for example, Rappeport (1974) and Millon (1981).

17. For reviews of the natural law concept, see Battaglia (1981), Benditt (1978), and Tuck (1979).

18. Mary Douglas has made this point in *Purity and Danger* (1966).

19. There has been a recent controversy about whether—and if so, to what extent—water was withheld from Australian aborigine taboo violators (Eastwell 1982, 1984*a*, 1984*b*; Reid and Williams 1984).

20. Harris (1977; 1979) has attempted to locate adaptive reasons for various taboos.

21. Kennedy (1970) has made a parallel argument about the role of witchcraft accusations.

3: Conditions That Temporarily Exempt

1. The subject of emotion is both extremely complex and poorly studied in non-Western societies. For a general discussion, see Izard (1977) and Rosaldo (1983).

2. Graffam and Turner (1984) describe the strategic uses of dream content in a sheltered workshop for developmentally disabled persons. For a general discussion of dreams, see Lincoln (1970).

3. *Los Angeles Herald-Examiner,* October 29, 1981.

4. See Stoller (1984) and Crapanzano and Garrison (1977) for additional examples.

5. Further details are available in Harris (1978).

6. As Hill (1978) correctly observed, it should not be concluded that people drink only, or even solely, to take advantage of the excuse drunkenness may confer.

7. In a series of balanced-placebo studies, Marlatt and Rohsenow have offered convincing evidence that people who believe they are drinking alcohol (but are not) behave as though they were drunk; similarly, those who believe they are drinking nonalcoholic beverages behave as though they were sober, even though they have ingested alcohol.

8. Personal communication, J. G. Kennedy (1984).

9. Conducted in Uganda, Kenya, and Tanzania, 1961–62 (Edgerton 1971*b*).

10. For an extended discussion of this issue, see Pospisil (1971).

11. *Los Angeles Times*, September 14, 1981.

12. Several recent law review articles have considered PMS as a mitigating plea, noting among other things that without a clear and valid medical test for PMS as an *exceptional* condition, all premenopausal women (or none at all) must be eligible for the excuse (Taylor and Dalton 1983; Press 1983). Other exemptions may lose their force over time. For example, throughout Europe in the Middle Ages, the idea of a "sporting chance" was widespread and gave even convicted criminals a chance to escape punishment. As medieval scholar G. G. Coulton (1925) recorded, if a criminal on the way to prison could evade his guards long enough to seize a monk by his cowl, he would be granted six weeks and three days of freedom. A contemporary malefactor who escaped his guards and managed to seize the Archbishop of Canterbury would be very likely to have his sentence extended rather than reduced. This form of exception differs from other temporary conditions, but it was temporary, and it *was* a rule.

4: Statuses That Exempt

1. For this and related arguments, see Black (1976).

2. I use the concept of status rather than of role to indicate the relatively long-lasting character of exemptions based on status. Following Linton (1936), status refers to the rights and duties of a person who occupies a particular social position. The same, to be sure, can be said of the concept of role, but I prefer, following Cicourel (1972), to use that of role for more temporary phenomena.

3. A person could be hanged for the theft of a shilling in Elizabethan England (Samaha 1974).

4. Surgical procedures to change sex are recent and are limited to a few societies.

5. The spelling of "Navajo" is now preferred by many persons of this ethnic group. I recognize the legitimacy of this preference but will use the spelling of the author to whom I refer.

6. Many Eskimo prefer to be known as Inuit. In addition to the reason mentioned in the preceding note, I retain *Eskimo* here because it is so well-known and, to my knowledge, should carry no stigma in the context of this book.

7. As far as I know, there is no ethnographic evidence on this point.

8. A review of the place of strangers in African societies is available in Shack and Skinner (1979); the dramatic portrayal of shipwrecked Europeans in seventeenth-century Japan fascinated many readers of James Clavell's novel *Shogun* (Smith 1980).

9. This epic of status inequality can be better appreciated in light of Alan MacFarlane's (1978) thesis about the origins of English individualism.

10. For a more extended look at sex roles, including berdache, see Kessler

and McKenna (1978). Other useful examples are found in Callender and Kochems (1983) and Biersack (1984).

11. For a comparable example from Java, see Peacock (1978).

12. As I reported elsewhere, among the Pokot of East Africa, severely mentally retarded (Edgerton 1970) or intersexual children (Edgerton 1964) were supposed to be killed shortly after birth, but some parents were emotionally unable to do this.

5: Occasions That Exempt

1. A recent review of this varied subject is available in Barbara Babcock's edited volume *The Reversible World* (1978) and in Fried and Fried (1980); some of the problems of definition are examined by Huber (1980).

2. See especially *Secular Ritual* (1978), edited by Sally Moore and Barbara Myerhoff, and *Studies in Festivity and Ritual* (1982), edited by Victor Turner.

3. For a discussion of this ceremonial cycle among Australian aborigines, see Berndt (1951).

4. Although many Kikuyu would prefer the spelling Gikuyu, I am retaining Kikuyu here because it is more familiar and, to my knowledge, not pejorative. The materials describing Mau Mau oathing ceremonies come from colonial interviews with Africans employed in "cleansing" Mau Mau detainees, as well as from British police and administrative officers in 1961–62. These practices are described in various confidential reports of the Kenya Colony Information Department and in some books, such as Henderson (1958).

5. A sense of the importance of initiation experiences for the Kikuyu is provided in a novel, *The River Between* (1965), by Ngugi Wa Thiongo, and in ethnographic reports by Father C. Cagnolo (1933) and Jomo Kenyatta (1965).

6. In 1962, I met a European filmmaker who claimed to have witnessed the ceremonies, but to the best of my knowledge, he has still provided no evidence of having done so.

6: Settings That Exempt

1. For an overview, especially of ethnomethodology, see Mehan and Wood (1974).

2. A useful review of this history is available in Cox (1911).

3. We need hardly be reminded that the Iranian takeover of the U.S. Embassy in Teheran in 1979 was considered by many to be an act of war.

4. Various examples are provided by Spencer and Gillen (1899; 1927) for the Central Desert peoples.

5. Forms of Eskimo sanctuary, usually involving any dwelling (either tent or ice house), are described by Hennigh (1971).

6. Khalaf (1979), 21.
7. Ibid., 21–22.
8. For a general discussion, see Oliver (1974).
9. See Kelly (1957).
10. For discussions of these issues, see Kelly (1957) and Ellis (1829), IV: 161.

7: A Societal Contrast in Rules and Responsibility

1. Linton's contrast between the Comanches and Polynesians is an intriguing one. Others have confirmed Linton's report about the flexibility of rules in Comanche culture (Hoebel 1954; Wallace and Hoebel 1952), but it is also clear, as Linton acknowledged, that the Comanches followed some rules very strictly. A compelling example of this aspect of Comanche life was provided by Nelson Lee (1957), who had the misfortune, along with three other white men, to be captured. While Lee and one other man watched in terror, the remaining two were ceremonially scalped and tortured before finally being killed. Lee and the other survivor later learned that they were spared because the Comanche supernatural rules permitted only two persons to be sacrificed in this manner at one time. Polynesia is difficult to analyze because of the diversity within the culture area and the lack of information about commoners who made up the bulk of the population. It is clear that chiefs could and did impose secular and religious rules upon commoners with the utmost severity (Sahlins 1958; Gifford 1929), but it is also reported—from, in Tonga, for example—that exceptions were sometimes made (Mariner 1920).

2. The most complete bibliographies I know are in Turnbull (1965a, 1965b).

3. There are different ecological zones within the Ituri Forest, and Mbuti bands vary in their means of exploiting these zones. Some, for example, rely on cooperative net hunting, while others are primarily archers who hunt without nets (Tanno 1976). The net hunters are more successful than the archers in providing meat (Harako 1976:78). As Turnbull was at pains to point out in his debates with Schebesta, there is great variation in beliefs and behavior from one Mbuti band to another. Therefore, while some of the discussion that is offered here may apply more generally to the Mbuti, it is prudent to assume that most of the information applies only to the Epulu band of net hunters with whom Turnbull most often stayed.

4. Although there was a summer period when honey was plentiful and the band could split into smaller groups and still subsist quite well, for most of the year band fission posed a danger to successful net hunting (Turnbull 1968: Harako 1976).

5. Schebesta (1933, 1936) insisted that although the Mbuti had borrowed their ideas about taboos, sorcery, and witchcraft from African villages, they took some of these beliefs seriously. Turnbull denied that this was the case, at least for the band he knew.

6. For a description of the explicit rules for the initial distribution of game, see Harako (1976), 76.

7. Turnbull does not explain what the circumstances might be that would lead to such a dire outcome. There *were* physically handicapped children and adults in the band he studied, and among other net hunters, as Harako (1976:85 ff.) reported, elderly men seldom hunted, yet their survival was apparently never in doubt.

8. Some examples of useful accounts by military men are those of Clark (1885), Dodge (1882), Cooke (1857), Utley (1977), and especially Abert (1847); among explorers, traders, scouts and the like, see Collins (1928), Garrard (1955), James (1823), Lavender (1954), and Seger (1924).

9. There are numerous valuable accounts by Cheyennes or part-Cheyennes, especially Hyde (1968), Marquis (1931), Cohoe (1964), Peterson (1968), Stands-in-Timber and Liberty (1967), and Storm (1972); accounts by Cheyenne women are available in Michelson (1932), Limbaugh (1973), and Marriott and Rachlin (1977).

10. Secondary analyses of Cheyenne culture and history continue to appear. Among the more valuable are Eggan (1937), Provinse (1937), Anderson (1951), Berthrong (1963), Powell (1969), Strauss (1977), Hoig (1980), and Moore (1984).

11. This point has been discussed by Moore (1974), who correctly pointed to certain biases in the ethnography of the Cheyennes. It is likely that the Cheyennes themselves, and some non-Cheyennes who wrote about them, attempted to describe their culture primarily in positive terms. Some, especially older Cheyennes themselves, may sometimes have spoken of ideals as though these were behavioral realities. Still, there is enough material available from enough sources to compensate for most of these kinds of distortions. (I am grateful to E. A. Hoebel for going over some of his trouble-cases with me when I was a student at the University of Minnesota in 1954).

Based on research in the 1960s, Weist (1970) went even farther by referring to the Northern Cheyennes as a diverse and "loosely structured" society in which norms were not clearly specified. If this is a correct description of the modern Cheyenne, it may be a result of the deculturation and demoralization of reservation living (Berthrong 1976). Compared to most other tribal societies, the Cheyennes gave little evidence of normative looseness prior to the reservation period. Instead, there is a great deal of firsthand evidence that the Cheyennes made clear rules and often enforced them quite strictly.

8: Explicit Rules, Strictly Enforced

1. I must number myself among those who have contributed to this belief. See MacAndrew and Edgerton (1969: 167), where it is argued that exceptions to rules are to society as a lubricant is to an engine.

2. In Western law, intent alone without an act (*actus reus*) usually cannot be punished (Hart 1961).

3. For a more extended discussion of this issue, see the various comments following the article by Kessel (1981).

4. Koch et al. (1976) reported that disputes between agnatic kin could sometimes be resolved by rituals of avoidance and reconciliation.

5. Readers interested in this question may wish to read Spencer and Gillen (1899; 1927) or a secondary source such as Berndt and Berndt (1964) or Tindale (1974).

6. Gluckman's (1972) review of the evidence for strict liability noted Meggitt's work with the Walbiri but paid no particular attention to the strictness of their system of rules and accountability.

7. For a sample of these reviews, consult Goodale (1963) and Beckett (1963). Readers might also wish to consult Munn (1973), Meggitt (1966), and Hamilton (1980).

8. For further discussion see Moore (1972), Hart (1968), and Howard (1963).

9. Among the many relevant examples of rural research are Beardsley, Hall, and Ward (1959), Smith (1961), and Ames (1981); urban research can be represented by Dore (1958) and Clifford (1976). For an overview, see Befu (1971).

10. Bellah (1957) has written an admirable review of Tokugawa beliefs and practices; Storry (1978) has done equally well for the samurai. Everyday life in this period has often been documented in English; for examples, see Dunn (1969), Cooper (1965), Frederic (1972), and especially Kaempfer (1903), a German doctor who wrote acutely about his experiences in Japan, including his audiences with the Shogun, in the late seventeenth century.

9: Societies with Flexible and Manipulable Rules

1. Ellen Basso (1973) has described another of these small villages.

2. Gregor's (1977) account of the Mehinaku is a most valuable one for present purposes, and anyone interested in looking more carefully at the issues raised by rules and exceptions could profit by reading it.

3. Gardner did distinguish among various types of foraging societies in terms of the kinds of rules they followed.

4. Gardner (1966) cites this interpretation with apparent approval.

5. There were two major exceptions in which a wife was killed; both men left the band voluntarily, but returned later.

6. The Ik were not principally hunters or foragers when Turnbull knew them, but they probably had been before they were forced out of their hunting territory by the government of Uganda (Turnbull 1972).

7. Many reports of Southeast Asian tropical forest societies are so sketchy that they are difficult to evaluate. For example, see Evans (1937), Schebesta (1927), and Bernatzik (1951).

8. There continues to be some dispute about the pejorative implications of the earlier term *Bushman* versus the term *San*. Some South African scholars,

such as George Silberbauer (1981), still prefer "Bushman," but I shall follow common U.S. usage and call them "San." For the most part, I shall not distinguish between groups of San, such as the !Kung or G/wi.

9. There is also considerable material available on the Chippewa Indians, but there is also controversy about the nature of their "atomistic" way of life (Barnouw 1961; Hickerson 1967). And, of course, there is an enormous amount of ethnographic description about the Eskimo; some interpreters of Eskimo culture stressed its flexibility (Willmot, 1960; Balikci, 1970), but others noted the stringency of some rules, especially their taboos. And W. R. Rivers's classic ethnography of the Todas (1906) is a treasure chest of information.

10. If I had discussed more of these small societies, more patterns of rule reliance might have emerged; greater extremes than those of the Walbiri or Siriono may exist. Anyone wishing to examine more band-level societies should consult the bibliography in Gardner (1966), Lee and DeVore (1968), Gellner (1980), Dahlberg (1981), and Leacock and Lee (1982). I also recommend Chapman (1982) and Nance (1975).

10: Why Exceptions?

1. For a discussion of some relevant features of band-egalitarian societies, see Fried (1967) and Leacock and Lea (1982).

2. I do not intend to single out Murphy for criticism. Others have been more adamant than he was about the situational variability of rules, and Murphy did occasionally acknowledge that some rules were "rigidly followed" (1971:242), even though this recognition played little part in his theory of norms. His views on strategic uses of rules are exemplary of that perspective.

3. This process by which meaning is sought in an appeal to rules has been discussed at length by Cicourel (1974); some relevant views on the negotiation of meaning are also available in Basso and Selby (1976) and Douglas (1973).

4. A good discussion of ritual as opposing the indeterminacy of ordinary life is provided by Moore and Myerhoff (1977).

5. In this respect, Cicourel's (1974) discussion of the procedures children use to assign meaning to events by referring to rules is excellent.

6. For a catalog of these rules, see Simoons (1961).

7. This long-neglected field is now beginning to develop. Two valuable examples are contained in special issues of *Ethos*, vol. 11, "Self and Emotion," edited by R. I. Levy, Fall 1983, and "The Socialization of Affect," edited by S. Harkness and P. L. Kilbride, Winter 1983.

8. For a thorough and challenging review of the evidence concerning strength, capacity for work, reproductive capacity, and the division of labor, see Conant (1982). A useful review of gender role is provided by Kessler and McKenna (1978).

9. The literature on this phenomenon is very large. For an introduction, I recommend McCord and McCord (1964), Rappeport (1974), Cloninger, Reich, and Guze (1975), Smith (1978), and Millon (1981).

10. This book presents a wealth of materials concerning the variety of excuses that certain people make, the self-protective purposes these excuses serve, and even some therapeutic interventions that are recommended when excuse-making becomes counterproductive. It is richly illustrated and includes many introductions to the psychological literature, but it differs from the present book by being almost entirely concerned with the psychological world of the excuse-maker; the book's view is summarized by its subtitle, "Masquerades in Search of Grace."

11. Robin Fox's (1977, 1980) contention that many rules, such as those that control incest and aggression, do not oppose natural desires but simply label naturally occurring aversions, is ingenious but unconvincing. Even if Fox is right about incest, his argument would not explain human rules against various other human desires.

12. Hostetler (1974:29) believes that older women belonging to the central committee monitored and approved all such invitations, effectively controlling the sexual behavior of the Oneidans.

13. See Leacock and Lee (1982).

11: Rules with No Exceptions

1. For a useful introduction to some of Wittgenstein's views on meaning, Peter Winch (1958) is still worth consulting. Gregory Bateson (1979) is required reading. Roland Barthes's (1967) introduction to semiology is also useful.

2. For a review of play in various societies, see Schwartzman (1978).

3. Geertz's most recent views (1984) on interpreting meaning in other cultures should also be consulted.

4. There are, nevertheless, some useful beginnings, such as Rawls (1955), Opie and Opie (1959), Cicourel (1974), Damon (1977), and Youniss (1980).

5. This strong assertion refers to natural societies, not too small, ad hoc groups such as total institutions, where the power of internalized rules may indeed prevent deviance, at least for a time.

6. Speaking of the cooperation between elite French units and their Vietnamese allies at the siege of Dien Bien Phu, Paratroop Major Bigeard said, "Our comradeship was excellent—after all, we were fighting for our skins" (Fall 1967:237).

7. Goffman has discussed some of these rules in *Frame Analysis* (1974), as has Richard Sennett in his often brilliant book *The Fall of Public Man* (1977).

8. General discussions are available in Gray (1971) and Rachman (1974) as well as in Izard (1977) and Tuan (1979).

9. There are so many compelling examples of these fears from societies all over the world that further documentation is unnecessary. Nevertheless, Edward Winter (1959) did an admirable job of capturing the fear of witchcraft in everyday life in his book *Beyond the Mountains of the Moon.*

10. For example, see W. J. Cash's classic book *The Mind of the South* (1941) or *Violence in America*, by Graham and Gurr (1974); for discussions of the samurai, see Storry (1978) or Dunn (1969).

11. For further discussion of collective responsibility, see Moore (1972).

12. Melville is circumspect about this point, but he seems to mean that a crew member who could not defend himself might be raped.

13. For a useful sociological account of life aboard a U.S. Navy destroyer, see Johnson (1972); for submarines, see Earls (1969).

14. Freud saw these cultural constructed fears as irrational, but as psychoanalyst John Bowlby (1973) has insisted, they are real and rational within their cultural context.

15. For examples of human responses to fear in various societies, see Tuan (1979).

16. In a class project conducted at UCLA in 1974, students who lost their trust in oncoming motorists experienced fear, and some were unable to drive at all until they reestablished trust.

17. With Spiro (1978), I see nothing wrong with seeking scientific explanations at the most fundamental, and hence explanatory, level possible. No one has yet found a molecular basis for intellectual creativity, but there is evidence that neurons must be involved, and the basis of neuronal excitability is the presence of voltage-sensitive ion channels in the neuronal plasma membrane (Catterall 1984). For a more general discussion of reductionism, see Johnson (1982).

12: Rules, Exceptions, and Social Order

1. Gardner contrasted his individualistic type with another that was defined as cooperative; in this type he placed the Walbiri. In my opinion, the net-hunting Mbuti would have to be considered more cooperative than the Walbiri.

2. For views of human nature in other societies, see Chan (1960) and Stevenson (1974).

3. This formulation draws on the work of Gardner (1966) and on the earlier Culture and Ecology in East Africa Project directed by Walter Goldschmidt (Edgerton 1971).

4. Belief in the freedom on the frontier was well developed among the Russians, too, as they looked to the Caucausus for freedom from social constraint (Tolstoy 1961). Herbert Muller (1961) has reviewed concepts of freedom and constraint in modern sociological texts. See also *Freedom and Control in Modern Society* (Berger, Abel, and Page 1954). Needless to say, this vast subject is beyond the scope of the present work and may well be beyond the scope of any work.

5. Lowie (1948) noted this phenomenon years ago, citing the Yaghan of Tierra del Fuego as well as the Plains Indians of North America. Ewers

(1958:96) confirmed that Plains Indians tightened their rules during their large summer encampments, loosening them again when band size was reduced.

6. The evidence here varies throughout the history of urban living, but see Barth (1978) and Berreman (1978).

7. There are many other examples of perspectives that see strict rules and exceptions to them—that is, constraint and freedom—as opposing each other in dialectical fashion. See, for example, Comaroff and Roberts (1981) and Gulliver (1979).

References

Aberle, D. F.
    1963   "Some Sources of Flexibility in Navaho Social Organization." *Southwestern Journal of Anthropology* 19:1–18.

Abert, J. W.
    1847   *Report of Lieut. J. W. Abert of His Examination of New Mexico in the Years 1846–47.* 30th U.S. Congress, 1st sess., 1847, House Executive Document no. 23.

Ackerman, S. E., and R. L. M. Lee.
    1981   "Structure and Anti-Structure in the Culture-Bound Syndromes: The Malay Case." *Culture, Medicine, and Psychiatry* 5:233–248.

Albert, E. M.
    1963   "Women of Burundi: A Study of Social Values." In *Women of Tropical Africa,* edited by D. Paulme, pp. 179–215. Berkeley and Los Angeles: University of California Press.

Alexander, F. G., and S. T. Selesnick
    1966   *The History of Psychiatry: An Evolution of Psychiatric Thought and Practice from Prehistoric Times to the Present.* New York: Harper & Row.

Alexander, R. D.
    1975   "The Search for a General Theory of Behavior." *Behavioral Science* 20:77–100.

Allen, W. S.
    1973   *The Nazi Seizure of Power: The Experience of a Single German Town 1930–1935.* New York: New Viewpoints.

Ames, W. L.
    1981   *Police and Community in Japan.* Berkeley, Los Angeles, London: University of California Press.

Amundsen, R.
    1908   *The North West Passage.* Vol. 1. London: Archibald Constable and Co.

Anderson, E. N., Jr.
    1972   "Some Chinese Methods of Dealing with Crowding." *Urban Anthropology* 1:141–150.

Anderson, R.
    1951   *A Study of Cheyenne Culture History, with Special Reference to the Northern Cheyennes.* Ann Arbor: University Microfilms.

Anonymous
    1872   *Modern Etiquette in Private and Public.* London: Frederick Warne.

273

Ardener, S.
 1973 "Sexual Insult and Female Militancy." *Man* 8:422–440.
Arensberg, C.
 1959 *The Irish Countryman*. Gloucester, Mass.: Peter Smith.
Ariès, P.
 1965 *Centuries of Childhood: A Social History of Family Life*. New York: Alfred A. Knopf.
Asakawa, K., ed.
 1929 *The Documents of Iriki*. New Haven: Yale University Press.
Ashcraft, N., and A. E. Scheflen
 1976 *People Space: The Making and Breaking of Human Boundaries*. Garden City, N.Y.: Anchor Books, Doubleday.
Babcock, B., ed.
 1978 *The Reversible World: Symbolic Inversion in Art and Society*. Ithaca, N.Y.: Cornell University Press.
Bailey, F. G.
 1969 *Stratagems and Spoils: A Social Anthropology of Politics*. Oxford: Blackwell.
Balikci, A.
 1970 *The Netsilik Eskimo*. Garden City, N.Y.: The Natural History Press.
Barnett, D. L., and K. Njama
 1966 *Mau Mau From Within: Autobiography and Analysis of Kenya's Peasant Revolt*. London: MacGibbon and Kee.
Barnouw, V.
 1961 "Chippewa Social Atomism." *American Anthropologist* 63:1006–1113.
Barrere, D.
 1957 "A Reconstruction of the History and Function of the Puuhonau and the Hale O Keawe at Honaunau." In *The Natural and Cultural History of Honaunau, Kona, Hawaii*. The Cultural History of Honaunau, Vol. 2, edited by K. P. Emory, J. F. G. Stokes, D. B. Barrere, and M. A. Kelly, pp. 38–67. Honolulu: Bernice P. Bishop Museum.
Barth, F.
 1966 *Models of Social Organization*. Occasional Paper no. 23. London: Royal Anthropological Institute.
Barth, F., ed.
 1978 *Scale and Social Organization*. Oslo: Universitetsforlaget.
Barthes, R.
 1967 *Elements of Semiology*. Translated by A. Lavers and C. Smith. London: Jonathan Cape.
Barton, A. H.
 1969 *Communities in Disaster: A Sociological Study of Collective Stress Situations*. New York: Doubleday.
Basso, E. B.
 1973 *The Kalapalo Indians of Central Brazil*. New York: Holt, Rinehart and Winston.

Basso, K. H., and H. A. Selby, eds.
  1976   *Meaning in Anthropology*. Albuquerque: University of New Mexico Press.
Bateson, G.
  1958   *Naven: A Survey of the Problems Suggested by a Composite Picture of the Culture of a New Guinea Tribe Drawn from Three Points of View*. 2d rev. ed. Stanford: Stanford University Press (1st ed. Cambridge University Press, 1936).
  1979   *Mind and Nature*. New York: Dutton.
Battaglia, A.
  1981   *Toward a Reformulation of Natural Law*. New York: The Seabury Press.
Beardsley, R. K., J. W. Hall, and R. E. Ward
  1959   *Village Japan*. Chicago: University of Chicago Press.
Beaubrun, M. H.
  1975   "Cannabis or Alcohol: The Jamaican Experience." In *Cannabis and Culture*, edited by V. Rubin, pp. 485–494. The Hague: Mouton.
Beckett, J.
  1963   Review of *Desert People*, by M. J. Meggitt. In *Journal of the Polynesian Society* 72:428–430.
Befu, H.
  1971   *Japan: An Anthropological Introduction*. San Francisco: Chandler.
Belden, J.
  1949   *China Shakes the World*. New York: Harper and Brothers.
Bellah, R. N.
  1957   *Tokugawa Religion: The Values of Pre-Industrial Japan*. Glencoe: The Free Press.
Bellamy, J.
  1973   *Crime and Public Order in England in the Later Middle Ages*. London: Routledge & Kegan Paul.
Benditt, T. M.
  1978   *Law as Rule and Principle: Problems of Legal Philosophy*. Stanford: Stanford University Press.
Benedict, R.
  1946   *The Crysanthemum and the Sword: Patterns of Japanese Culture*. Cleveland: World.
Berger, M., T. Abel, and C. H. Page, eds.
  1954   *Freedom and Control in Modern Society*. New York: D. Van Nostrand.
Bernatzik, H. A.
  1951   *The Spirits of the Yellow Leaves*. London: Robert Hale.
Berndt, R. M.
  1951   *Kunapipi: A Study of an Australian Aboriginal Religious Cult*. Melbourne: F. W. Cheshire.
Berndt, R. M., and C. H. Berndt
  1964   *The World of the First Australians: An Introduction to the Traditional Life of the Australian Aborigines*. Sydney: Ure Smith.

Berreman, G.
   1962   *Behind Many Masks: Ethnography and Impression Management in a Himalayan Village:* Monograph no. 8. Ithaca, N.Y.: Society for Applied Anthropology.
   1978   "Scale and Social Relations." *Current Anthropology* 19:225–245.
   1979   *Caste and Other Inequities: Essays on Inequality.* Kirpa Dai Series in Folklore and Anthropology, no. 2. Meerat, India: Folklore Institute.
Berthrong, D. J.
   1963   *The Southern Cheyennes.* Norman: University of Oklahoma Press.
   1976   *The Cheyenne and Arapaho Ordeal: Reservation and Agency Life in the Indian Territory, 1875–1907.* Norman: University of Oklahoma Press.
Bierce, A.
   1911   "The Devil's Dictionary." In *The Collected Works of Ambrose Bierce,* vol. 7. New York: Neale Publishing Company.
Biersack, A.
   1984   "Paiela 'Women-Men': The Reflexive Foundations of Gender Ideology." *American Ethnologist* 11:118–138.
Biesele, M., and N. Howell
   1981   "'The Old People Give You Life': Aging Among !Kung Hunter-Gatherers." In *Other Ways of Growing Old: Anthropological Perspectives,* edited by P. T. Amoss and S. Harrell, pp. 77–98. Stanford: Stanford University Press.
Bilby, J. W.
   1923   *Among Unknown Eskimo.* London: Seeley Service.
Birdwhistell, R. L.
   1970   *Kinesics and Context: Essays on Body Motion Communication.* Philadelphia: University of Pennsylvania Press.
Black, D.
   1976   *The Behavior of Law.* New York: Academic Press.
Black, M.
   1962   *Models and Metaphors: Studies in Language and Philosophy.* Ithaca, N.Y.: Cornell University Press.
Black-Michaud, J.
   1975   *Cohesive Force: Feud in the Mediterranean and the Middle East.* New York: St. Martin's Press.
Blackstone, B. V.
   1957   *A History of the British Fire Service.* London: Routledge & Kegan Paul.
Blake, J., and K. Davis
   1964   "Norms, Values and Sanctions." In *Handbook of Modern Sociology,* edited by R. E. L. Faris, pp. 456–484. Chicago: Rand McNally.
Bligh, W.
   1937   *The Log of the Bounty.* Edited by Owen Rutter. 2 vols. London: Golden Cockerel Press.

Bodde, D.
  1938   *China's First Unifier: A Study of the Ch'in Dynasty as Seen in the Life of Li Ssu.* Leiden: E. J. Brill.
  1975   *Festivals in Classical China: New Year and Other Annual Observances During the Han Dynasty 206 B.C.–A.D. 220.* Princeton: Princeton University Press.

Bodde, D., and C. Morris
  1967   *Law in Imperial China: Exemplified by 190 Ch'ing Dynasty Cases* (translated from the Hsing-an hui-lan), *with Historical, Social, and Juridical Commentaries.* Cambridge, Mass.: Harvard University Press.

Bohannan, P.
  1960   *African Homicide and Suicide.* Princeton: Princeton University Press.
  1965   "The Differing Realms of the Law." In *The Ethnography of Law.* Edited by L. Nader. Vol. 67, no. 6, pt. 2. Special Publication. Washington, D.C.: American Anthropological Association.

Bonnie, R. J., and C. H. Whitebread.
  1974   *The Marihuana Conviction: A History of Marihuana Prohibitions in the United States.* Charlottesville: University of Virginia Press.

Bottomore, T., and R. Nisbet, eds.
  1978   *A History of Sociological Analysis.* New York: Basic Books.

Bourdieu, P.
  1977   *Outline of a Theory of Practice.* Translated by Richard Nice. Cambridge: Cambridge University Press.

Bourgignon, E.
  1976   *Possession.* San Francisco: Chandler and Sharp Publishers, Inc.

Bowlby, J.
  1973   *Attachment and Loss.* Vol. 2. *Separation: Anxiety and Anger.* New York: Basic Books.

Bowles, P.
  1962   *A Hundred Camels in the Courtyard.* San Francisco: City Lights Bookshop.

Brandt, R. B.
  1954   *Hopi Ethics: A Theoretical Analysis.* Chicago: University of Chicago Press.

Bronfenbrenner, U.
  1970   *Two Worlds of Childhood: U.S. and U.S.S.R.* New York: Russell Sage.

Bullough, V.
  1974   "Transvestites in the Middle Ages." *American Journal of Sociology* 79:1381–1394.

Bunzel, R.
  1929– *Introduction to Zuni Ceremonialism.* Washington, D.C.: U.S. Government
    30   Printing Office, Smithsonian Institution Bureau of American Ethnology Bulletin 47.

Burney, C.
  1977   *The Ancient Near East.* Ithaca, N.Y.: Cornell University Press.

Byrd, R. E.
1938   *Alone.* New York: G. P. Putnam's Sons.

Cabral, S. L.
1980   "'Time-Out': The Recreational Use of Drugs by Portuguese-American Immigrants in Southeastern New England." *Journal of Drug Issues* 10:287–299.

Cagnolo, C.
1933   *The Akikuyu.* Nyeri, Kenya: Printed by Akikuyu in the Mission Printing School.

Callender, C., and L. M. Kochems
1983   "The North American Berdache." *Current Anthropology* 24:443–470.

Campbell, D. T.
1975   "On the Conflicts between Biological and Social Evolution and between Psychology and Moral Tradition." *American Psychologist* 30:1103–1126.

Campbell, J. K.
1964   *Honour, Family and Patronage: A Study of Institutions and Moral Values in a Greek Mountain Community.* Oxford: Clarendon Press.

Cancian, F.
1975   *What are Norms? A Study of Beliefs and Action in a Maya Community.* London: Cambridge University Press.

Canetti, E.
1962   *Crowds and Power.* Translated by Carol Stewart. New York: The Viking Press.

Carden, M. L.
1969   *Oneida: Utopian Community to Modern Corporation.* Baltimore: The Johns Hopkins Press.

Carstairs, G. M.
1954   "Daru and Bhang: Cultural Factors in the Choice of Intoxicant." *Quarterly Journal of Studies on Alcohol* 15:220–237.

Casey, R. J.
1945   *Battle Below: The War of the Submarines.* Indianapolis: Bobbs-Merrill.

Cash, W. J.
1941   *The Mind of the South.* New York: Alfred A. Knopf.

Castle, R. M.
1974   "Ash Meadows: A Fly-In Brothel." In *Deviance: Field Studies and Self-Disclosures,* edited by J. Jacobs, pp. 41–58. Palo Alto, Calif.: National Press.

Catterall, W. A.
1984   "The Molecular Basis of Neural Excitability." *Science* 223:653–661.

Cavan, S.
1966   *Liquor License: An Ethnography of Bar Behavior.* Chicago: Aldine.

Cawadias, A. P.
1943   *Hermaphroditos: The Human Intersex.* London: William Heineman.

Chan, W. T.

1960   "The Concept of Man in Chinese Thought." In *The Concept of Man: A Study in Comparative Philosophy,* edited by S. Radhakrishnan and P. T. Raju, pp. 172–219. Lincoln, Neb.: Johnsen.

Chapman, A.
1982   *Drama and Power in a Hunting Society: The Selk'nam of Tierra del Fuego.* Cambridge: Cambridge University Press.

Cicourel, A. V.
1964   *Method and Measurement in Sociology.* New York: Free Press.
1972   "Basic and Normative Rules in the Negotiation of Status and Role." In *Studies in Social Interaction,* edited by D. Sudnow, pp. 229–258. New York: Free Press.
1974   *Cognitive Sociology: Language and Meaning in Social Interaction.* New York: Free Press.

Clark, W. P.
1885   *The Indian Sign Language.* Philadelphia: L. R. Hamersly and Co.

Clifford, W.
1976   *Crime Control in Japan.* Lexington, Mass.: D. C. Heath.

Cloninger, C. R., T. Reich, and S. B. Guze
1975   "The Multifactorial Model of Disease Transmission of Sociopathy (Antisocial Personality)." *British Journal of Psychiatry* 127:11–22.

Codere, H.
1975   "The Social and Cultural Context of Cannabis Use in Rwanda." In *Cannabis and Culture,* edited by V. Rubin, pp. 217–226. The Hague: Mouton.

Cohen, Y.A.
1964   *The Transition from Childhood to Adolescence: Cross-Cultural Studies of Initiation Ceremonies, Legal Systems and Incest Taboos.* Chicago: Aldine.

Cohoe, W.
1964   *The Cheyenne Sketchbook.* Commentary by E. A. Hoebel and Karen D. Peterson. Norman: University of Oklahoma Press.

Collett, P., ed.
1977   *Social Roles and Social Behaviour.* Totowa, N.J.: Rowman and Littlefield.

Collins, H. E.
1928   *Warpath and Cattle Trail.* New York: William Morrow & Co.

Collins, R.
1975   *Conflict Sociology: Toward an Explanatory Science.* New York: Academic Press.

Colson, E.
1974   *Tradition and Contract: The Problem of Order.* Chicago: Aldine.

Comaroff, J. L., and S. Roberts
1981   *Rules and Processes: The Cultural Logic of Dispute in an African Context.* Chicago: University of Chicago Press.

Conant, F. P.
1966   "The External Coherence of Pokot Ritual Behavior." *Philosophical Transactions of the Royal Society of London* (ser. B) 251:505–519.

1982   "Strength, Reproductive Capacity, and the Division of Labor in
        East Africa." In *Culture and Ecology: Eclectic Perspectives*, edited by
        J. G. Kennedy and R. B. Edgerton, pp. 26–55. Special Publication
        no. 15. Washington, D.C.: American Anthropological Association.
Connor, W. D.
1972   *Deviance in Soviet Society: Crime, Delinquency, and Alcoholism.* New
        York: Columbia University Press.
Cooke, P. S.
1857   *Scenes and Adventures in the Army: or, Romance of Military Life.*
        Philadelphia: Lindsay and Blakiston.
Cooper, M., ed.
1965   *They Came to Japan: An Anthology of European Reports on Japan,
        1543–1640.* Berkeley and Los Angeles: University of California
        Press.
Coulton, G. G., ed.
1925   *The Medieval Village.* London: Cambridge University Press.
Coyne, J. C.
1976   "Toward an Interactional Description of Depression." *Psychiatry*
        39:28–40.
Cox, C. J.
1911   *The Sanctuaries and Sanctuary Seekers of Medieval England.* London:
        George Allen and Sons.
Crapanzano, V., and V. Garrison, eds.
1977   *Case Studies in Spirit Possession.* New York: Wiley.
Creel, H. G.
1953   *Chinese Thought: From Confucius to Mao Tse-Tung.* Chicago: Univer-
        sity of Chicago Press.
Crumrine, N. R.
1969   "Capakoba, The Mayo Easter Ceremonial Impersonator: Explana-
        tions of Ritual Clowning." *Journal for the Scientific Study of Religion*
        8:1–22.
Dahlberg, F., ed.
1981   *Woman the Gatherer.* New Haven, Conn.: Yale University Press.
Damon, W.
1977   *The Social World of the Child.* San Francisco: Jossey-Bass.
Davenport, W.
1969   "The 'Hawaiian Cultural Revolution': Some Political and Economic
        Considerations." *American Anthropologist* 71:1–20.
Davis, N. Z.
1975   *Society and Culture in Early Modern France.* Stanford: Stanford Uni-
        versity Press.
Dawe, A.
1978   "Theories of Social Action," In *A History of Sociological Analysis*,
        edited by T. Bottomore and R. Nisbet, pp. 362–417. New York:
        Basic Books.

Dentan, R. K.
1968   *The Semai: A Nonviolent People of Malaya.* New York: Holt, Rinehart and Winston.

Denys, N.
1908   *The Description and Natural History of the Coasts of North America (Acadia).* Edited by W. Ganong. Toronto: The Champlain Society.

Denzin, N. K.
1970   "Rules of Conduct and the Study of Deviant Behavior: Notes on the Social Relationship." In *Deviance and Respectability,* edited by J. O. Douglas, pp. 120–159. New York: Basic Books.

Devereux, G.
1963   "Primitive Psychiatric Diagnosis: A General Theory of the Diagnostic Process. In *Man's Image in Medicine and Anthropology,* edited by I. Galdston. New York: International Universities Press.

Dewey, J.
1922   *Human Nature and Conduct.* New York: H. Holt and Co.

Diamond, A. S.
1951   *The Evolution of Law and Order.* London: Watts and Co.
1957   "An Eye for an Eye." *Iraq* 19:151–155.

Dickson, H. R. P.
1949   *The Arab of the Desert: A Glimpse into Badawin Life in Kuwait and Sau'di Arabia.* London: George Allen and Unwin.

Dirks, R.
1978   "Resource Fluctuations and Competitive Transformations in West Indian Slave Societies." In *Extinction and Survival in Human Populations,* edited by C. D. Laughlin and I. A. Brady, pp. 122–180. New York: Columbia University Press.

Dodge, R. I.
1882   *Our Wild Indians: Thirty-three Years Personal Experience.* Hartford, Conn.: A. D. Worthington.

Dolhinow, P., ed.
1972   *Primate Patterns.* New York: Holt, Rinehart and Winston.

Dore, R. P.
1958   *City Life in Japan.* Berkeley and Los Angeles: University of California Press.

Dorsey, G. A.
1905   *The Cheyenne. I. Ceremonial Organization. II. The Sun Dance.* Chicago: Field Columbian Museum Publications 99, 103; Anthropological Series IX, nos. 1,2.

Douglas, J. D., ed.
1970a *Deviance and Respectability: The Social Construction of Moral Meanings.* New York: Basic Books.
1970b *Understanding Everyday Life.* Chicago: Aldine.

Douglas, J. D., P. K. Rasmussen, and C. A. Flanagan
1977   *The Nude Beach.* Beverly Hills, Calif.: Sage.

Douglas, M.
  1966   *Purity and Danger: An Analysis of Concepts of Pollution and Taboo.*
         London: Routledge & Kegan Paul.
  1973   *Rules and Meanings: The Anthropology of Everyday Knowledge.* Balti-
         more: Penguin.
  1975   *Implicit Meanings: Essays in Anthropology.* London: Routledge &
         Kegan Paul.
Draper, P.
  1978   "The Learning Environment for Aggression and Anti-Social Be-
         havior among the !Kung." In *Learning Non-Aggression: The Experi-
         ence of Non-Literate Societies,* edited by A. Montagu, pp. 31–53.
         Oxford: Oxford University Press.
Dreher, M.
  1982   *Working Men and Ganja.* Philadelphia: ISHI Publications.
Dubois, J. A.
  1897   *Hindu Manners, Customs and Ceremonies.* 3d ed. Edited by H. D.
         Beauchamp. Oxford: Clarendon Press.
Dumont, L.
  1960   "World Renunciations in Indian Religions." *Contributions to Indian
         Sociology* 4:33–61.
Dundas, C.
  1921   "Native Laws of Some Bantu Tribes of East Africa." *Journal of the
         Royal Anthropological Institute* 51:217–278.
Dunn, C. J.
  1969   *Everyday Life in Traditional Japan.* London: Batsford.
Durkheim, E.
  1961   *Moral Education.* New York: Free Press.
Dwyer, D. H.
  1978   *Images and Self-Images: Male and Female in Morocco.* New York:
         Columbia University Press.
Earls, J. H.
  1969   "Human Adjustment to an Exotic Environment." *Archives of General
         Psychiatry* 20:117–123.
Eastwell, H. D.
  1982   "Voodoo Death and the Mechanism for Dispatch of the Dying in
         East Arnhem, Australia." *American Anthropologist* 84:5–18.
  1984a "Death Watch in East Arnhem, Australia." *American Anthropologist*
         86:119–121.
  1984b "The Forefather Needs No Fluids: Voodoo Death and Its
         Simulacra." *American Anthropologist* 86:133–136.
Edgerton, R. B.
  1964   "Pokot Intersexuality: An East African Example of Sexual Incon-
         gruity." *American Anthropologist* 66:1288–1299.
  1969   "On the 'Recognition' of Mental Illness." In *Changing Perspectives
         in Mental Illness,* edited by S. Plog and R. Edgerton, pp. 49–72.
         New York: Holt, Rinehart and Winston.
  1970   "Mental Retardation in Non-Western Societies: Toward a Cross-

Cultural Perspective on Incompetence." In *Social-Cultural Aspects of Mental Retardation,* edited by H. C. Haywood, pp. 523–539. New York: Appleton-Century-Crofts.

1971*a*   "A Traditional African Psychiatrist." *Southwestern Journal of Anthropology* 27:259–278.

1971*b*   *The Individual in Cultural Adaptation: A Study of Four East African Societies.* Berkeley, Los Angeles, London: University of California Press.

1976   *Deviance: A Cross-Cultural Perspective.* Menlo Park, Calif.: Cummings.

1979   *Alone Together: Social Order on an Urban Beach.* Berkeley, Los Angeles, London: University of California Press.

Edgerton, R. B., and F. P. Conant
1964   "Kilapat: The 'Shaming Party' Among the Pokot of East Africa." *Southwestern Journal of Anthropology* 20:406–418.

Edwards, C. P.
1981   "The Comparative Study of the Development of Moral Judgment and Reasoning." In *Handbook of Cross-Cultural Human Development,* edited by R. H. Munroe, R. L. Munroe, and B. B. Whiting, pp. 501–528. New York: Garland STPM Press.

Eggan, F.
1937   "The Cheyenne and Arapaho Kinship System." In *Social Anthropology of the North American Indian Tribes,* edited by F. Eggan, pp. 35–98. Chicago: University of Chicago Press.

Eliade, M.
1958   *Patterns in Comparative Religion.* New York: Meridian.
1959   *The Sacred and the Profane: The Nature of Religion.* New York: Harcourt, Brace and Company.

Elias, T. O.
1956   *The Nature of African Customary Law.* Manchester: Manchester University Press.

Ellis, W.
1829   *Polynesian Researches.* 4 vols. London: Fisher, Son and Jackson.

Elwin, V.
1955   *The Religion of an Indian Tribe.* Bombay: Oxford University Press.

Emboden, W. A.
1972   "Ritual Use of *Cannabis sativa L.*: A Historical-Ethnographic Survey." In *Flesh of the Gods: The Ritual Use of Hallucinogens,* edited by P. T. Furst, pp. 214–236. New York: Praeger.

Embree, J.
1950   "Thailand—A Loosely Structured Social System." *American Anthropologist* 52:181–193.

Emmet, D.
1966   *Rules, Roles, and Relations.* London: Macmillan.

Erikson, E.
1977   *Toys and Reasons: Stages in the Ritualization of Experience.* New York: Norton.

Erikson, K. T.
  1966   *Wayward Puritans: A Study in the Sociology of Deviance.* New York: John Wiley.
  1976   *Everything in its Path: Destruction of Community in the Buffalo Creek Flood.* New York: Simon and Schuster.
Estroff, S. E.
  1981   *Making It Crazy: An Ethnography of Psychiatric Clients in an American Community.* Berkeley, Los Angeles, London: University of California Press.
Evans, I. H. N.
  1937   *The Negritos of Malaya.* Cambridge: Cambridge University Press.
Evans-Pritchard, E. E.
  1929   "Some Collective Expressions of Obscenity in Africa." *Journal of the Royal Anthropological Institute* 59:311–331.
  1940   *The Nuer: A Description of the Modes of Livelihood and Political Institutions of a Nilotic People.* Oxford: Clarendon Press.
Evens, T. S. M.
  1977   "The Prediction of the Individual in Anthropological Interactionism." *American Anthropologist* 79:579–597.
Ewers, J. C.
  1955   *The Horse in Blackfoot Indian Culture: With Comparative Material from Other Western Tribes.* Smithsonian Institution, Bureau of American Ethnology Bulletin 159, Washington, D.C.: U.S. Government Printing Office.
  1958   *The Blackfeet: Raiders of the Northwestern Plains.* Norman: University of Oklahoma Press.
Fall, B. B.
  1967   *Hell in a Very Small Place: The Siege of Dien Bien Phu.* Philadelphia: Lippincott.
Fallers, L. A.
  1969   *Law Without Precedent: Legal Ideas in Action in the Courts of Colonial Busoga.* Chicago: University of Chicago Press.
  1973   *Inequality: Social Stratification Reconsidered.* Chicago: University of Chicago Press.
Faris, J. C.
  1969   "Mumming in an Outport Fishing Settlement: A Description and Suggestions on the Cognitive Complex." In *Christmas Mumming in Newfoundland: Essays in Anthropology, Folklore and History,* edited by H. Halpert and G. Story, pp. 128–144. Toronto: University of Toronto Press.
Fingarette, H., and A. F. Hasse
  1979   *Mental Disabilities and Criminal Responsibility.* Berkeley, Los Angeles, London: University of California Press.
Firth, R.
  1961   "Suicide and Risk-Taking in Tikopia Society." *Psychiatry* 24:1–17.

Fisher, B. M., and A. L. Strauss
  1978   "Interactionism." In *A History of Sociological Analysis,* edited by
          T. Bottomore and R. Nisbet, pp. 457–498. New York: Basic Books.
Fisher, J. D., and D. Byrne
  1975   "Too Close for Comfort: Sex Differences in Response to Invasions
          of Personal Space." *Journal of Personal and Social Psychology* 32:15–
          21.
Fox, R.
  1977   "The Inherent Rules of Violence." In *Social Rules and Social Be-
          haviour,* edited by P. Collett, pp. 132–149. Totowa, N.J.: Rowman
          and Littlefield.
  1980   *The Red Lamp of Incest.* New York: E. P. Dutton.
Frank, G., and J. P. Horan, with J. M. Eckberg
  1945   *U.S.S. Seawolf: Submarine Raider of the Pacific.* New York: G. P.
          Putnam's Sons.
Fraser, H. A.
  1974   "The Law and Cannabis in the West Indies." *Social and Economic
          Studies* 23:361–385.
Frazer. J. G.
  1933   *The Fear of the Dead in Primitive Religion.* London: Macmillan.
Frederic, L.
  1972   *Daily Life in Japan at the Time of the Samurai.* Translated by E. Lowe.
          London: Allen & Unwin.
Freuchen, P.
  1961   *Book of the Eskimos.* Edited and preface written by D. Freuchen.
          Greenwich, Conn.: Fawcett Publications.
Freud, S.
  1918   *Totem and Taboo: Resemblances between the Psychic Lives of Savages and
          Neurotics.* Translated by A. A. Brill. New York: Random House.
Fried, J.
  1953   "The Relation of Ideal Norms to Actual Behavior in Tarahumara
          Society." *Southwestern Journal of Anthropology* 9:286–295.
Fried, M. H.
  1967   *The Evolution of Political Society: An Essay in Political Anthropology.*
          New York: Random House.
Fried, M. N., and M. H. Fried
  1980   *Transitions: Four Rituals in Eight Cultures.* New York: Norton.
Fuchs, P.
  1955   *The Land of Veiled Men.* Translated by B. Fawcett. London: Weiden-
          feld and Nicholson.
Fürer-Haimendorf, C. von
  1967   *Morals and Merit: A Study of Values and Social Controls in South Asian
          Societies.* London: Weidenfeld and Nicolson.
  1974   "The Sense of Sin in Cross-Cultural Perspective." *Man* 9:539–556.
  1979   *South Asia Societies: A Study of Values and Social Controls.* London:

East-West Publications.

Galloway, K. B., and R. B. Johnson
  1973   *West Point: America's Power Fraternity.* New York: Simon and Schuster.

Gardner, P. M.
  1965   "Ecology and Social Structure in Refugee Populations: The Paliyans of South India." Ph.D. dissertation, University of Pennsylvania.
  1966   "Symmetric Respect and Memorate Knowledge: The Structure and Ecology of Individualistic Culture." *Southwestern Journal of Anthropology* 22:389–415.

Garfinkel, H.
  1963   "A Conception of, and Experiments with, 'Trust' as a Condition of Stable Concerted Action." In *Motivation and Social Interaction,* edited by D. J. Harvey, pp. 187–238. New York: Ronald Press.
  1967   *Studies in Ethnomethodology.* New York: Prentice-Hall.

Garrard, L. H.
  1955   *Wah-To-Yah and the Taos Trail.* Norman: University of Oklahoma Press.

Gaster, T.
  1955   *New Year: Its History, Customs and Superstitions.* New York: Abelard-Schuman.

Gasaway, E. B.
  1970   *Grey Wolf, Grey Sea.* New York: Ballantine.

Geertz, C.
  1973   *The Interpretation of Cultures.* New York: Basic Books.
  1984   *Local Knowledge: Further Essays in Interpretive Anthropology.* New York: Basic Books.

Gellner, E., ed.
  1980   *Soviet and Western Anthropology.* London: Duckworth.

Gernet, J.
  1962   *Daily Life in China on the Eve of the Mongol Invasion, 1250–1276.* Stanford: Stanford University Press.

Gibbs, J.
  1965   "Norms: The Problem of Definition and Classification." *American Journal of Sociology* 60:586–594.
  1981   *Norms, Deviance, and Social Control: Conceptual Matters.* New York: Elsevier.

Giddens, A.
  1979   *Central Problems in Social Theory: Action, Structure and Contradiction in Social Analysis.* Berkeley, Los Angeles, London: University of California Press.

Gifford, E. W.
  1929   *Tongan Society.* Bulletin 61. Honolulu: Bernice P. Bishop Museum.

Gladwin. T.

1957   "Personality Structure in the Plains." *Anthropological Quarterly* 30:111–124.

Gluckman, M.

1949   "The Role of the Sexes in Wiko Circumcision Ceremonies." In *Social Structure: Studies Presented to A. R. Radcliffe-Brown,* edited by M. Fortes. Oxford: Clarendon Press.

1954   *Rituals of Rebellion in Southeast Africa.* Manchester: Manchester University Press.

1959   *Custom and Conflict in Africa.* Glencoe: The Free Press.

1965   *The Ideas in Barotse Jurisprudence.* New Haven, Conn.: Yale University Press.

1967   *The Judicial Process Among the Barotse of Northern Rhodesia.* 2d ed. with two additional chapters. Manchester: Manchester University Press (orig. published 1955).

Gluckman, M., ed.

1972   *The Allocation of Responsibility.* Manchester: University of Manchester Press.

Goffman, E.

1963   *Behavior in Public Places.* New York: The Free Press.

1969   *Strategic Interaction.* Philadelphia: University of Pennsylvania Press.

1974   *Frame Analysis.* New York: Harper & Row.

Goldschmidt, W.

1969   *Kambuya's Cattle: The Legacy of an African Herdsman.* Berkeley and Los Angeles: University of California Press.

Goodale, J. C.

1963   Review of *Desert People,* by M. J. Meggitt. *American Anthropologist* 65:928–931.

Goodhart, A. L.

1926   "The Myth of Absolute Liability." *The Law Quarterly Review* 42:37–51.

Goodman, M. E.

1967   *The Individual and Culture.* Homewood, Ill.: Dorsey.

Gould, R. A.

1969   *Yiwara: Foragers of the Australian Desert.* New York: Charles Scribner's Sons.

Gouldner, A. W.

1970   *The Coming Crisis of Western Sociology.* New York: Basic Books.

Graffam, J., and J. L. Turner

1984   "Escape from Boredom: The Meaning of Eventfulness in the Lives of Clients at a Sheltered Workshop." In *Lives in Process: Mildly Retarded Adults in a Large City,* edited by R. B. Edgerton, pp. 121–144. Monograph no. 6. Washington, D.C.: American Association on Mental Deficiency.

Graham, H. D., and T. R. Gurr

1974   *Violence in America: Historical and Comparative Perspectives.* New

York: Bantam.

Granet, M.
   1934   *La Pensée Chinoise*. Paris: La Renaissance du livre.
Gray, J. A.
   1971   *The Psychology of Fear and Stress*. London: Weidenfeld and Nicholson.
Green, R.
   1974   *Sexual Identity and Conflict in Children and Adults*. New York: Basic Books.
Gregor, T.
   1977   *Mehinaku: The Drama of Daily Life in a Brazilian Indian Village*. Chicago: University of Chicago Press.
Gregory, S. W., Jr.
   1982   "Accounts as Assembled from Breaching Experiments." *Symbolic Interaction* 5:49–63.
Grinnell, G. B.
   1902   "Cheyenne Woman Customs." *American Anthropologist* 4:13–16.
   1915   "The Fighting Cheyennes." New York: Scribner.
   1923   *The Cheyenne Indians: Their History and Ways of Life*. 2 vols. New Haven, Conn.: Yale University Press.
   1962   *The Cheyenne Indians: Their History and Ways of Life*. 2 vols. New introduction by Mari Sandoz. New York: Cooper Square Publishers.
Gulliver, P. H.
   1963   *Social Control in an African Society*. London: Routledge & Kegan Paul.
   1979   *Disputes and Negotiations: A Cross-Cultural Perspective*. New York: Academic Press.
Gwaltney, J. L.
   1970   *The Thrice Shy: Cultural Accommodation to Blindness and Other Disasters in a Mexican Community*. New York: Columbia University Press.
Habermas, J.
   1971   *Knowledge and Human Interests*. Translated by J. J. Shapiro. Boston: Beacon Press.
Hall, E. T.
   1959   *The Silent Language*. Garden City, N.Y.: Doubleday & Co.
   1963   "A System for the Notation of Proxemic Behavior." *American Anthropologist* 65:1003–1026.
   1966   *The Hidden Dimension*. Garden City, N.Y.: Doubleday & Co.
   1977   *Beyond Culture*. Garden City, N.Y.: Anchor Press, Doubleday.
Hallowell, A. I.
   1976   *Contributions to Anthropology: Selected Papers of A. Irving Hallowell*. Chicago: University of Chicago Press.
Halpert, H.
   1969   "A Typology of Mumming." In *Christmas Mumming in Newfoundland: Essays in Anthropology, Folklore and History*, edited by H. Halpert

& G. M. Story, pp. 35–61. Toronto: University of Toronto Press.

Hamburg, D., and E. McCown, eds.
1979   *The Great Apes.* Menlo Park, Calif.: Benjamin-Cummings.

Hamilton, A.
1980   "Dual Social Systems: Technology, Labour and Woman's Secret Rites in the Eastern Western Desert of Australia." *Oceania* 51:4–19.

Hara, T., with F. Saito and R. Pineau
1961   *Japanese Destroyer Captain.* New York: Ballantine Books.

Harako, R.
1976   "The Mbuti as Hunters: A Study of Ecological Anthropology of the Mbuti Pygmies." *Kyoto University African Studies* 10:37–100.

Harris, G.
1957   "Possession 'Hysteria' in a Kenya Tribe." *American Anthropologist* 59:1046–1066.
1978   *Casting Out Anger: Religion among the Taita of Kenya.* New York: Cambridge University Press.

Harris, M.
1977   *Cannibals and Kings: The Origins of Culture.* New York: Vintage Books.
1979   *Cultural Materialism: The Struggle for a Science of Culture.* New York: Random House.

Hart, H. L. A.
1961   *The Concept of Law.* Oxford: Clarendon Press.
1964   *The Morality of the Criminal Law: Two Lectures.* Jerusalem: The Magnes Press, The Hebrew University.
1968   *Punishment and Responsibility.* Oxford: Basil Blackwell.

Hasan, K. A.
1975   "Social Aspects of the Use of Cannabis in India." In *Cannabis and Culture,* edited by V. Rubin, pp. 235–246. The Hague: Mouton.

Haviland, J. B.
1977   *Gossip, Reputation and Knowledge in Zinacantan.* Chicago: University of Chicago Press.

Hawes, C. H.
1903   *In the Uttermost East.* New York: Harper & Row.

Hawkins, R., and G. Tiedeman
1975   *The Creation of Deviance: Interpersonal and Organizational Determinants.* Columbus, Ohio: Charles E. Merritt.

Hearn, L.
1956   *Japan: An Attempt at Interpretation.* Tokyo: Charles E. Tuttle.

Heath, D.
1958   "Drinking Patterns of the Bolivian Kamba." *Quarterly Journal of Studies on Alcohol* 19:491–508.
1964   "Prohibition and Post-Repeal Drinking Patterns Among the Navaho." *Quarterly Journal of Studies on Alcohol* 25:119–135.

Heinz, H-J., and M. Lee.
1978   *Nambkwa: Life Among the Bushmen.* London: Jonathan Cape.

Henderson, I., with P. Goodhart
1958　*Man Hunt in Kenya.* Garden City, N.Y.: Doubleday & Co.
Hennigh, L.
1971　"You Have to Be a Good Lawyer to Be an Eskimo." In *Alliance in Eskimo Society,* edited by L. Guemple, pp. 89–109. Seattle: American Ethnological Society.
Henry, J.
1941　*Jungle People: A Kaingáng Tribe of the Highlands of Brazil.* Richmond, Va.: J. J. Augustin.
Herdt, G. H.
1981　*Guardians of the Flutes: Idioms of Masculinity.* New York: McGraw-Hill.
Hiatt, L. R.
1965　*Kinship and Conflict: A Study of the Aboriginal Community in Northern Arnhemland.* Canberra: Australia National University Press.
Hickerson, H.
1967　"Some Implications of the Theory of Particularity or 'Atomism' of Northern Algonkians." *Current Anthropology* 8:313–343.
Hill, E.
1972　*The Trinidad Carnival.* Austin: University of Texas Press.
Hill, T. W.
1978　"Drunken Comportment of Urban Indians: 'Time-Out' Behavior?" *Journal of Anthropological Research* 34:442–467.
Hill, W. W.
1935　"The Status of the Hermaphrodite and Transvestite in Navaho Culture." *American Anthropologist* 37:273–279.
Hobley, C. W.
1922　*Bantu Beliefs and Magic.* London: H. F. & G. Witherby.
Hoebel, E. A.
1954　*The Law of Primitive Man.* Cambridge, Mass.: Harvard University Press.
1960　*The Cheyennes: Indians of the Great Plains.* New York: Henry Holt.
Hogbin, H. I.
1961　*Law and Order in Polynesia: A Study of Primitive Legal Institutions.* Hamden, Conn.: The Shoe String Press.
Hoig, S.
1980　*The Peace Chiefs of the Cheyennes.* Norman: University of Oklahoma Press.
Hollis, M.
1977　*Models of Man: Philosophical Thoughts on Social Action.* Cambridge: Cambridge University Press.
Holm, B.
1972　*Crooked Beak of Heaven: Masks and Other Ceremonial Art of the Northwest Coast.* Seattle: University of Washington Press.
Holmberg, A. R.
1950　*Nomads of the Long Bow: The Siriono of Eastern Bolivia.* The Smithsonian Institution. Washington, D.C.: U.S. Government Printing

Office.
1969   *Nomads of the Long Bow: The Siriono of Eastern Bolivia.* 2d rev. ed. Garden City, N.Y.: The Natural History Press.

Horton, D.
1943   "The Functions of Alcohol in Primitive Societies: A Cross-Cultural Study." *Journal of Studies on Alcohol* 4:199–320.

Hostetler, J. A.
1974   *Communitarian Societies.* New York: Holt, Rinehart and Winston.

Howard, A.
1974   *Ain't No Big Thing: Coping Strategies in a Hawaiian-American Community.* Honolulu: The University Press of Hawaii.

Howard, C.
1963   *Strict Liability.* London: Sweet & Maxwell.

Howell, N.
1979   *Demography of the Dobe !Kung.* New York: Academic Press.
1983   Review of *Nisa: The Life and Words of a !Kung Woman,* by M. Shostak. *American Ethnologist* 10:187–188.

Howell, P. P.
1954   *A Manual of Nuer Law: Being an Account of Customary Law, Its Evolution and Development in the Courts Established by the Sudan Government.* London: Oxford University Press.

Howell, S.
1981   "Rules, Not Words." In *Indigenous Psychologies: The Anthropology of the Self,* edited by P. Heelas and A. Lock, pp. 133–143. London: Academic Press.

Huber, P. B.
1980   "The Anggor Bowman: Ritual and Society in Melanesia." *American Ethnologist* 7:43–57.

Hulsewé, A. F. P.
1955   *Remnants of Han Law.* Vol 1. Leiden: E. J. Brill.

Hunt, D.
1970   *Parents and Children in History: The Psychology of Family Life in Early Modern France.* New York: Basic Books.

Huntington, R., and P. Metcalf
1979   *Celebrations of Death: The Anthropology of Mortuary Ritual.* Cambridge: Cambridge University Press.

Huntsman, J., and A. Hooper
1975   "Male and Female in Tokelau Culture." *The Journal of the Polynesian Society* 84:415–430.

Hyde, G. E.
1968   *Life of George Bent: Written From His Letters.* Norman: University of Oklahoma Press.

Izard, C. E.
1977   *Human Emotions.* New York: Plenum Press.

Jacobs, D. R.
1961   "The Culture Themes and Puberty Rites of the Akamba." Ph.D. dissertation, New York University.

Jacobs, J.
1982   *The Moral Justification of Suicide.* Springfield, Ill.: Charles C Thomas.
Jacobs, S-E.
1968   "Berdache: A Brief Review of the Literature." *Colorado Anthropologist* 1:25–40.
James, E.
1823   *Account of an Expedition from Pittsburgh to the Rocky Mountains, Performed in the Years 1819 and '20, by Order of the Hon. J. C. Calhoun, Secretary of War: Under the Command of Major Stephen H. Long.* Philadelphia: H. C. Carey and I. Lea.
Jarves, J. J.
1847   *History of the Hawaiian Islands.* Honolulu: Charles Edwin Hitchcock.
Jenness, D.
1922   *The Life of the Copper Eskimos.* Report of the Canadian Arctic Expedition, 1913–1918. Vol. 12, pt. A. Ottawa: King's Printer.
Johnson, A.
1982   "Reductionism in Cultural Ecology: The Amazon Case." *Current Anthropology* 23:413–428.
Johnson, J. M.
1972   "The Practical Uses of Rules." In *Theoretical Perspectives in Deviance,* edited by R. A. Scott and J. D. Douglas, pp. 215–248. New York: Basic Books.
Jones, M. V.
1976   *Dostoyevsky: The Novel of Discord.* London: Paul Elek.
Jones, R. T.
1971   "Marihuana-Induced 'High': Influence of Expectation, Setting and Previous Drug Experience." *Pharmacological Reviews* 23:359–369.
Joseph, R.
1975   "Economic Significance of *Cannabis sativa* in the Moroccan Rif." In *Cannabis and Culture,* edited by V. Rubin, pp. 185–194. The Hague: Mouton.
Junod, H. A.
1962   *The Life of a South African Tribe.* Vol. 1. New Hyde Park, N.Y.: University Books.
Kaempfer, E.
1906   *The History of Japan.* 3 vols. Glasgow: James MacLehose and Sons.
Kapferer, B., ed.
1976   *Transaction and Meaning: Directions in the Anthropology of Exchange and Symbolic Behavior.* Philadelphia: Institute for the Study of Human Issues.
Katz, R.
1982   *Boiling Energy: Community Healing Among the Kalahari Kung.* Cambridge, Mass.: Harvard University Press.
Keesing, R. M.
1974   "Theories of Culture." In *Annual Review of Anthropology.* Vol. 3, edited by B. J. Siegel, A. R. Beals, and S. A. Tyler, pp. 73–97. Palo

Alto, Calif.: Annual Reviews.

1982   "Introduction." In *Rituals of Manhood: Male Initiation in Papua New Guinea,* edited by G. H. Herdt, pp. 1–43. Berkeley, Los Angeles, London: University of California Press.

Kelly, M. A.

1957   "The Concept of Asylum." In *The Natural and Cultural History of Honaunau, Kona, Hawaii.* The Cultural History of Honaunau, vol. 2, edited by K. P. Emory, J. F. G. Stokes, D. B. Barrere, and M. A. Kelly, pp. 81–136. Honolulu: Bernice P. Bishop Museum.

Kennedy, J. G.

1967   "Mushahara: A Nubian Concept of Supernatural Danger and the Theory of Taboo." *American Anthropologist* 69:685–702.

1970   "Bonds of Laughter Among the Tarahumara Indians: Toward a Rethinking of Joking Relationship Theory." In *The Social Anthropology of Latin America,* edited by W. Goldschmidt and H. Hoijer. Los Angeles: University of California, Latin American Center.

1984   Personal Communication.

Kennedy, J., J. Teague, and L. Fairbanks

1980   "Qat Use in North Yemen and the Problem of Addiction: A Study in Medical Anthropology." *Culture, Medicine and Psychiatry* 4:311–344.

Kennett, A.

1925   *Bedouin Justice: Law & Customs Among the Egyptian Bedouin,* Cambridge: Cambridge University Press.

Kenyatta, J.

1965   *Facing Mount Kenya: The Tribal Life of the Gikuyu.* Introduction by B. Malinowski. New York: Vintage Books.

Kephart, W. M.

1976   *Extraordinary Groups: The Sociology of Unconventional Lifestyles.* New York: St. Martin's Press.

Kessel, G. M.

1981   "Sororicide/Filiacide: Homicide for Family Honour." *Current Anthropology* 22:141–158.

Kessler, S. J., and W. McKenna

1978   *Gender: An Ethnomethodological Approach.* New York: John Wiley & Sons.

Khalaf, S.

1979   "Violence and Its Control in Tribal Bedouin Society." Seminar paper. Department of Anthropology, UCLA.

Khalifa, A. M.

1975   "Traditional Patterns of Hashish Use in Egypt." In *Cannabis and Culture,* edited by V. Rubin, pp. 195–206. The Hague: Mouton.

Khan, M. A.; A. Abbas; and K. Jensen

1975   "Cannabis Usage in Pakistan: A Pilot Study of Long-Term Effects on Social Status and Physical Health." In *Cannabis and Culture,* edited by V. Rubin, pp. 345–354. The Hague: Mouton.

Kitsinger, S.
    1971   "The Rastafarian Brethren of Jamaica." In *Peoples and Cultures of the Caribbean: An Anthropological Reader,* edited by M. M. Horowitz, pp. 580–588. Garden City, N.Y.: Natural History Press.

Klass, D.
    1976   "Psychohistory and Communal Patterns: John Humphrey Noyes and the Oneida Community." In *The Biographical Process: Studies in the History and Psychology of Religion,* edited by F. E. Reynold and D. Capps, pp. 273–296. The Hague: Mouton.

Kleinman, A.
    1980   *Patients and Healers in the Context of Culture.* Berkeley, Los Angeles, and London: University of California Press.

Kluckhohn, C.
    1941   "Patterning in Navaho Culture." In *Language, Culture and Personality,* edited by L. Spier, pp. 109–130. Menasha, Wis.: Sapir Memorial Publication Fund.

Köbben, A. J. F.
    1979   "Unity and Disunity: Cottica Djuka Society as a Kinship System." In *Maroon Societies: Rebel Slave Communities in the Americas,* 2d ed., edited by R. Price. Baltimore: Johns Hopkins University Press.

Koch, K-F.
    1974a   "Incest and Its Punishment in Jalé Society." *The Journal of the Polynesia Society* 83:84–91.
    1974b   *War and Peace in Jalémo: The Management of Conflict in Highland New Guinea.* Cambridge, Mass.: Harvard University Press.

Koch, K-F., S. Altorki, A. Arno, and L. Hickson
    1976   "Ritual Reconciliation and the Obviation of Grievances: A Comparative Study in the Ethnography of Law." *Ethnology* 41:269–284.

Konner, M.
    1982   *The Tangled Wing: Biological Constraints on the Human Spirit.* New York: Holt, Rinehart and Winston.

Kracke, W. H.
    1978   *Force and Persuasion: Leadership in an Amazonian Society.* Chicago: University of Chicago Press.

Kroeber, A. L.
    1925   *Handbook of the Indians of California* (chap. 2, "Yurok Law and Custom"). Smithsonian Institution, Bureau of American Ethnology, Bulletin 78. Washington, D.C.: U.S. Government Printing Office.

LaBarre, W.
    1969   *They Shall Take Up Serpents: Psychology of a Southern Snake-Handling Cult.* New York: Schocken.

Ladurie, E. L.
    1979   *Carnival in Romans.* Translated by M. Feeney. New York: George Braziller.

Laird, C.

1979   *Limbo: A Memoir About Life in a Nursing Home by a Survivor.* Novato, Calif.: Chandler & Sharp Publishers, Inc.

Lane, M.
   1963   *Life with Ionides.* New York: Viking Press.

Langness, L. L.
   1965   "Hysterical Psychosis in the New Guinea Highlands: A Bena Bena Example." *Psychiatry* 28:259–277.

La Rochefoucauld, F.
   1959   "Les Maximes." In *The Maxims of La Rochefoucauld,* edited by L. Kronenberger. New York: Random House Vintage Books (orig. published 1665–1678).

Laurence, J.
   1960   *A History of Capital Punishment.* New York: The Citadel Press.

Lavender, D.
   1954   *Bent's Fort.* New York: Doubleday.

Leach, E. R.
   1961   *Pul Eliya: A Village in Ceylon.* London: Cambridge University Press.
   1964   *Political Systems of Highland Burma: A Study of Kachin Social Structure (with a new introductory note).* Boston: Beacon Press.
   1982   *Social Anthropology.* New York: Oxford University Press.

Leacock, E., and R. Lee, eds.
   1982   *Politics and History in Band Societies.* Cambridge: Cambridge University Press.

Leakey, L. S. B.
   1954   *Defeating Mau-Mau.* London: Methuen.

Lee, N.
   1957   *Three Years among the Comanches: The Narrative of Nelson Lee, the Texas Ranger.* Norman: University of Oklahoma Press.

Lee, R. B.
   1979   *The !Kung San: Men, Women, and Work in a Foraging Society.* Cambridge: Cambridge University Press.
   1982   "Politics, Sexual and Non-Sexual, in an Egalitarian Society." In *Politics and History in Band Societies,* edited by E. Leacock and R. Lee, pp. 37–59. Cambridge: Cambridge University Press.

Lee, R. B., and I. DeVore, eds.
   1968   *Man the Hunter.* Chicago: Aldine.

Lessa, W. A.
   1966   *Ulithi: A Micronesian Design for Living.* New York: Holt, Rinehart and Winston.

LeVine, R. A.
   1973   *Culture, Behavior and Personality.* Chicago: Aldine.
   1982   "Gusii Funerals: Meanings of Life and Death in an African Community." *Ethos* 10:26–65.

Lévi-Strauss, C.
   1961   *Tristes Tropiques.* Translated by John Russell. New York: Atheneum.

1969   *Elementary Structures of Kinship.* Edited by J. R. von Sturmer and R. Needham. Translated by J. H. Bell. Boston: Beacon Press.

Levy, R.
1973   *Tahitians: Mind and Experience in the Society Islands.* Chicago: University of Chicago Press.

Lewis, I. M.
1971   *Ecstatic Religion: An Anthropological Study of Spirit Possession and Shamanism.* Baltimore: Penguin.

Lewis, M., and L. A. Rosenblum, eds.
1974   *The Origins of Fear.* New York: John Wiley & Sons.

Li, V. H.
1978   *Law without Lawyers: A Comparative View of Law in China and the United States.* Boulder, Colo.: Westview Press.

Li, Y-N., ed.
1975   *The First Emperor of China.* White Plains, N.Y.: International Arts and Sciences Press.

Limbaugh, R. H., ed.
1973   *Cheyenne and Sioux: The Reminiscences of Four Indians and a White Soldier.* Compiled by Thomas B. Marquis. Monograph no. 3. Stockton, Cal.: Pacific Center for Western Historical Studies.

Lincoln, J. S.
1970   *The Dream in Primitive Cultures.* New York: Johnson Reprint Corporation (orig. published 1935).

Lindblom, G.
1920   *The Akamba in British East Africa.* Uppsala: Appelbergs Boktryckeri Aktiebolag.

Lindner, R.
1956   *Must You Conform?* New York: Rinehart and Co.

Linton, R.
1936   *The Study of Man.* New York: Appleton-Century-Crofts.
1949   "Problems of Status Personality." In *Culture and Personality,* edited by S. S. Sargent and M. W. Smith, pp. 163–174. New York: The Viking Fund.

Llewellyn, K. N., and E. A. Hoebel
1941   *The Cheyenne Way: Conflict and Case Law in Primitive Jurisprudence.* Norman: University of Oklahoma Press.

Lowie, R. H.
1927   *The Origin of the State.* New York: Harcourt, Brace and Company.
1948   "Some Aspects of Political Organization Among American Aborigines." *Journal of the Royal Anthropological Institute of Great Britain and Ireland* 78:11–24.
1954   *Indians of the Plains.* New York: McGraw-Hill.

Ludwig, A.
1971   *Treating the Treatment Failures: The Challenge of Chronic Schizophrenia.* New York: Grune and Stratton.

Lyman, S. M., and M. B. Scott

1970   *A Sociology of the Absurd.* New York: Appleton-Century-Crofts.

MacAndrew, C., and R. B. Edgerton
1969   *Drunken Comportment: A Social Explanation.* Chicago: Aldine.

MacFarlane, A.
1978   *The Origins of English Individualism: The Family, Property and Social Transition.* New York: Cambridge University Press.

MacLeod, W. C.
1937   "Police and Punishment Among Native Americans of the Plains." *Journal of the American Institute of Criminal Law and Criminology* 28:181–201.

Maestro, M.
1973   *Cesare Beccaria and the Origins of Penal Reform.* Philadelphia: Temple University Press.

Maine, Sir H.
1861   *Ancient Law: Its Connection with the Early History of Society and Its Relation to Modern Ideas.* London: J. Murray.

Mair, L.
1965   *An Introduction to Social Anthropology.* Oxford: Clarendon Press.

Maitland, F. W.
1911   *The Collected Papers of Frederic William Maitland.* Cambridge: Cambridge University Press.

Malinowski, B.
1926   *Crime and Custom in Savage Society.* London: Kegan Paul, Trench, Trubner.
1961   "Introduction." In *Law and Order in Polynesia: A Study of Primitive Legal Institutions,* edited by H. Ian Hogbin, Hamden, Conn.: The Shoe String Press (orig. published 1934).

Marett, R. R.
1912   *Anthropology.* London: Macmillan.

Mariner, W.
1820   *An Account of the Natives of the Tonga Islands in the South Pacific.* Compiled and arranged by J. Martin. Boston: Charles Ewer.

Marlatt, G. A., and D. J. Rohsenow
1980   "Cognitive Processes in Alcohol Use: Expectancy and the Balanced Placebo Design." In *Advances in Substance Abuse: Behavioral and Biological Research,* vol. 1, edited by N. K. Mello, pp. 159–199. Greenwich, Conn.: J. A. I. Press.

Marquis, T. B.
1931   *Wooden Leg: A Warrior Who Fought Custer.* Lincoln: University of Nebraska Press.

Marriott, A., and C. K. Rachlin
1977   *Dance around the Sun. The Life of Mary Little Bear Inkanish: Cheyenne.* New York: Thomas Y. Crowell.

Marshall, L.
1976   *The !Kung of Nyae Nyae.* Cambridge, Mass.: Harvard University Press.

Marshall, M.
   1979   *Weekend Warriors: Alcohol in a Micronesian Culture.* Palo Alto, Calif.:
           Mayfield.
Martin, M. A.
   1975   "Ethnobotanical Aspects of Cannabis in Southeast Asia." In *Can-
           nabis and Culture,* edited by V. Rubin, pp. 63–76. The Hague:
           Mouton.
Matson, F. W.
   1976   *The Idea of Man.* New York: Delta.
McCord, W., and J. McCord
   1964   *The Psychopath: An Essay on the Criminal Mind.* New York: Van
           Nostrand Reinhard.
McGrew, R.
   1965   *Russia and the Cholera 1823–1832.* Madison: University of Wisconsin
           Press.
McHugh, P.
   1968   *Defining the Situation: The Organization of Meaning in Social Interac-
           tion.* Indianapolis: Bobbs-Merrill.
McKnight, B. E.
   1981   *The Quality of Mercy: Amnesties and Traditional Chinese Justice.* Hono-
           lulu: The University Press of Hawaii.
Mead, M., ed.
   1937   *Cooperation and Competition Among Primitive Peoples.* New York:
           McGraw-Hill.
Meggitt, M. J.
   1962   *Desert People: A Study of the Walbiri Aborigines of Central Australia.*
           Sydney: Angus and Robertson.
   1966   *Gadjari Among the Walbiri Aborigines of Central Australia.* The Oceania
           Monographs, no. 14. Sydney: The University of Sydney.
Mehan, H., and H. Wood.
   1974   *The Reality of Ethnomethodology.* New York: John Wiley & Sons.
Mehrabian, A.
   1976   *Public Places and Private Spaces: The Psychology of Work, Play, and
           Living Environments.* New York: Basic Books.
Melville, H.
   1892   *White-Jacket, or, The World in a Man-of-War.* New York: United
           States Book Company.
Messick, D. M., and K. S. Cook, eds.
   1983   *Equity Theory: Psychological and Sociological Theory.* New York:
           Praeger.
Michelson, T.
   1932   *The Narrative of a Southern Cheyenne Woman.* Smithsonian Miscel-
           laneous Collections, vol. 87, no. 9. Washington, D.C.: Government
           Printing Office.
Midgley, M.
   1978   *Beast and Man: The Roots of Human Nature.* Ithaca, N.Y.: Cornell

University Press.

Miller, D. M., and D. C. Wertz
1976 *Hindu Monastic Life: The Monks and Monasteries of Bhubaneswar.* Montreal: McGill–Queen's University Press.

Millon, T.
1981 *Disorders of Personality, DSM-III: Axis II.* New York: John Wiley & Sons.

Mills, C. W.
1940 "Situated Action and the Vocabulary of Motives." *American Sociological Review* 6:904–913.
1959 *The Sociological Imagination.* New York: Oxford University Press.

Mischel, W., and F. Mischel
1958 "Psychological Aspects of Spirit Possession." *American Anthropologist* 60:249–260.

Minoura, Y.
1979 "Life In-Between: The Acquisition of Cultural Identity among Japanese Children Living in the United States." Ph.D. dissertation, University of California, Los Angeles.

Mooney, J.
1907 *The Cheyenne Indians.* Lancaster, Pa.: Memoirs of the American Anthropological Association, vol. 1, pt. 6.

Moore, J. H.
1974 "A Study of Religious Symbolism Among the Cheyenne Indians." Ph.D. dissertation, New York University.
1984 "Cheyenne Norms and Cosmology." *American Ethnologist* 11:291–312.

Moore, S. F.
1972 "Legal Liability and Evolutionary Interpretation: Some Aspects of Strict Liability, Self-Help and Collective Responsibility." In *The Allocation of Responsibility,* edited by M. Gluckman, pp. 51–108. Manchester: University of Manchester Press.
1978 *Law as Process: An Anthropological Approach.* London: Routledge & Kegan Paul.

Moore, S. F., and B. G. Myerhoff, eds.
1977 *Secular Ritual.* Assen/Amsterdam: Van Gorcum.

Moore, W. E.
1978 "Functionalism." In *A History of Sociological Analysis,* edited by T. Bottomore and R. Nisbet, pp. 321–361. New York: Basic Books.

Morris, H.
1976 *On Guilt and Innocence: Essays in Legal Philosophy and Moral Philosophy.* Berkeley, Los Angeles, London: University of California Press.

Morris, R., and D. Morris
1965 *Men and Snakes.* London: Hutchinson.

Morris, R. T.
1956 "A Typology of Norms." *American Sociological Review* 21:610–613.

Morrison, J.
  1935   *The Journal of James Morrison*. London: Golden Cockerel Press.
Muller, H. J.
  1961   *Freedom in the Ancient World*. New York: Harper.
Munn, N.
  1973   *Walbiri Iconography*. Ithaca, N.Y.: Cornell University Press.
Muriithi, J. K., and P. N. Ndoria
  1971   *War in the Forest*. Nairobi: East African Publishing House.
Murphy, G.
  1954   "The Internalization of Social Controls." In *Freedom and Control in Modern Society*, edited by M. Berger, T. Abel, and C. H. Page, pp. 3–17. New York: Van Nostrand.
Murphy, R. F.
  1963   "Social Distance and the Veil." *American Anthropologist* 66:1257–1274.
  1971   *The Dialectics of Social Life: Alarms and Excursions in Anthropological Theory*. New York: Basic Books.
Musil, A.
  1928   *The Manners and Customs of the Rwala Bedouins*. Oriental Explorations and Studies, no. 6. New York: American Geographical Society.
Muthiani, J.
  1973   *Akamba from Within: Egalitarianism in Social Relations*. New York: Exposition Press.
Nader, L., and H. F. Todd, Jr., eds.
  1978   *The Disputing Process—Law in Ten Societies*. New York: Columbia University Press.
Nance, J.
  1975   *The Gentle Tasaday: A Stone Age People in the Philippine Rain Forest*. New York: Harcourt Brace Jovanovich.
Ndeti, K.
  1972   *Elements of Akamba Life*. Nairobi: East African Publishing House.
Needham, J.
  1951   *Human Law and the Laws of Nature in China and the West*. London: Oxford University Press.
Needham, R.
  1963   Introduction. In *Primitive Classification*, edited by E. Durkheim and M. Mauss. Chicago: University of Chicago Press.
  1972   *Belief, Language and Experience*. Chicago: University of Chicago Press.
Nettleford, R.
  1978   *Caribbean Cultural Identity: The Case of Jamaica*. Los Angeles: University of California, Center for Afro-American Studies.
Newman, P. L.
  1964   "Wild Man Behavior in a New Guinea Highlands Community." *American Anthropologist* 66:1–19.

Ngugi, wa T.
1965   *The River Between.* London: Heidemann.
Nida, E. A.
1962   "Akamba Initiation Rites and Culture Themes." *Practical Anthropology* 9:145–150, 153–155.
Nisbet, R.
1973   *The Social Philosophers: Community and Conflict in Western Thought.* New York: Crowell.
Norbeck, E.
1954   *Takashima: A Japanese Fishing Community.* Salt Lake City: University of Utah Press.
1963   "African Rituals of Conflict." *American Anthropologist* 65:1254–1279.
1974   *Religion in Human Life.* New York: Holt, Rinehart & Winston.
Norbeck, E., and G. DeVos
1972   "Culture and Personality: The Japanese." In *Psychology Anthropology*, edited by F. L. K. Hsu, pp. 21–70. Cambridge: Schenkman.
Noyes, P.
1937   *My Father's House: An Oneida Boyhood.* New York: Farrar & Rinehart.
Nucci, L. P., and M. S. Nucci
1982   "Children's Social Interactions in the Context of Moral and Conventional Transgressions." *Child Development* 53:403–412.
Oakley, K. P.
1950   *Man-the-Tool-Maker.* London: British Museum.
O'Connor, R.
1973   *The Boxer Rebellion.* London: Robert Hale.
Oliver, D.
1974   *Ancient Tahitian Society.* 3 vols. Honolulu: University Press of Hawaii.
Oliver, S. C.
1962   *Ecology and Cultural Continuity as Contributing Factors in the Social Organization of the Plains Indians.* Berkeley and Los Angeles: University of California Press.
1965   "Individuality, Freedom of Choice, and Cultural Flexibility of the Kamba." *American Anthropologist* 67:421–428.
1982   "The Hills and Plains: A Comparison of Two Kamba Communities." In *Culture and Ecology: Eclectic Perspectives,* edited by J. G. Kennedy and R. B. Edgerton, pp. 142–157. Special Publication no. 15. Washington, D.C.: American Anthropological Association.
Opie, P., and I. Opie
1969   *Children's Games in Street and Playground.* London: Oxford University Press.
Ortiz, A.
1972   *The Tewa World: Space, Time, Being, and Becoming in a Pueblo Society.* Chicago: University of Chicago Press.
Oswalt, W. H.

1979   *Eskimos and Explorers.* Novato, Calif.: Chandler and Sharp.

Parsons, T.
1953   "Illness and the Role of the Physician." In *Personality in Nature, Society and Culture*, 2d ed., edited by C. Kluckhohn and H. Murray. New York: Alfred A. Knopf.

Pawelczynska, A.
1979   *Values and Violence in Auschwitz: A Sociological Analysis.* Berkeley, Los Angeles, London: University of California Press.

Peacock, J. L.
1978   "Symbolic Reversal and Social History: Transvestites and Clowns of Java." In *The Reversible World,* edited by B. A. Babcock. Ithaca, N.Y.: Cornell University Press.

Pease, T. C., and R. C. Werner, eds.
1934   *The French Foundations, 1680–1693.* Collections of the Illinois State Historical Library, vol. 23. Springfield, Ill.: Illinois State Historical Library.

Pelto, P. J.
1968   "The Difference Between 'Tight' and 'Loose' Societies." *Trans-Action,* April:37–40.

Pelto, P. J., and G. H. Pelto
1975   "Intra-Cultural Diversity: Some Theoretical Issues." *American Ethnologist* 2:1–18.

Pendrill, C.
1925   *London Life in the 14th Century.* London: George Allen and Unwin.

Penwill, D. J.
1951   *Kamba Customary Law: Notes Taken in the Machakos District of Kenya Colony.* London: Macmillan.

Peristiany, J. G.
1954   "Pokot Sanctions and Structure." *Africa* 24:17–25.

Peterson, K. D.
1964   "Cheyenne Soldier Societies." *Plains Anthropologist* 9:146–172.

1968   *Howling Wolf: A Cheyenne Warrior's Graphic Interpretation of His People.* Palo Alto, Calif.: American West Publishing Co.

Petter, R. C.
1907   *Sketch of the Cheyenne Grammar.* Lancaster, Pa.: Memoirs of the American Anthropological Association, vol. 1, pt. 6.

Pope, P.
1963   *The Black Ship.* London: Weidenfeld and Nicholson.

Pospisil, L.
1958a   *Kapauku Papuans and Their Law.* New Haven, Conn.: Yale University Publications in Anthropology, no. 67.

1958b   "Social Change and Primitive Law: Consequences of a Papuan Legal Case." *American Anthropologist* 60:832–837.

1971   *Anthropology of Law: A Comparative Theory.* New York: Harper & Row.

Pound, R.

1921   *The Spirit of the Common Law.* Boston: Beacon Press.
Powell, P. J.
1969   *Sweet Medicine: The Continuing Role of the Sacred Arrows, the Sun Dance, and the Sacred Buffalo Hat in Northern Cheyenne History.* 2 vols. Norman: University of Oklahoma Press.
1981   *The People of the Sacred Mountain.* New York: Harper & Row.
Press, M. P.
1983   "Premenstrual Stress Syndrome as a Defense in Criminal Cases." *Duke Law Journal* 1983:176–195.
Provinse, J. H.
1937   "The Underlying Sanctions of Plains Indian Culture." In *Social Anthropology of the North American Indian Tribes,* edited by F. Eggan, pp. 341–376. Chicago: University of Chicago Press.
Pruess, J. B.
1979   "Merit and Misconduct: Venerating the Bo Tree at a Buddhist Shrine." *American Ethnologist* 6:261–273.
Putnam, A. E.
1954   *Eight Years With Congo Pygmies.* New York: Prentice-Hall.
Rachman, S.
1974   *The Meaning of Fear.* Baltimore: Penguin.
Radcliffe-Brown, A. R.
1939   *Taboo.* Cambridge: Cambridge University Press.
1940   "On Joking Relationships." *Africa* 13:195–210.
Rappeport, J. R.
1974   "Antisocial Behavior." In *American Handbook of Psychiatry,* 2d. ed., edited by S. Arieti, pp. 237–269. New York: Basic Books.
Rasmussen, K.
1929   *Intellectual Culture of the Iglulik Eskimos.* Copenhagen: Gyldendalske Boghandel, Nordisk Forlag.
1931   *The Netsilik Eskimos: Social Life and Spiritual Culture.* Copenhagen: Gyldendalske Boghandel, Nordisk Forlag.
Rattray, R. S.
1929   *Ashanti Law and Constitution.* Oxford: Clarendon.
Rawls, J.
1955   "Two Concepts of Rules." *Philosophical Review* 64:3–32.
Ray, V. F.
1945   "The Contrary Pattern in American Indian Ceremonialism." *Southwestern Journal of Anthropology* 1:75–113.
Read, K. E.
1980   *Other Voices: The Style of a Male Homosexual Tavern.* Novato, Calif.: Chandler and Sharp.
Read, P. P.
1974   *Alive.* New York: Avon.
Reay, M.
1959   *The Kuma: Freedom and Conformity in the New Guinea Highlands.* Melbourne: Melbourne University Press.

1974   "Changing Conventions of Dispute Settlement in the Minj Area." In *Contention and Dispute: Aspects of Law and Social Control in Melanesia*, edited by A. L. Epstein, pp. 198–239. Canberra: Australian National University.

Reid, J., and N. Williams
1984   "'Voodoo Death' in Arnhemland: Whose Reality?" *American Anthropologist* 86:121–133.

Reynolds, P. C.
1981   *On the Evolution of Human Behavior: The Argument from Animals to Man*. Berkeley, Los Angeles, London: University of California Press.

Ritter, E. A.
1957   *Shaka Zulu: The Rise of the Zulu Empire*. London: Longmans.

Rivers, W. H. R.
1906   *The Todas*. London: Macmillan.

Robarchek, C. A.
1977   "Frustration, Aggression, and the Nonviolent Semai." *American Ethnologist* 4:762–779.
1979   "Conflict, Emotion, and Abreaction: Resolution of Conflict among the Semai Senoi." *Ethos* 7:104–123.

Roberts, R. E., and D. Brintnall
1983   *Reinventing Inequality: An Inquiry into Society and Stratification*. Cambridge: Schenkman.

Robson, W. A.
1935   *Civilisation and the Growth of Law*. New York: Macmillan.

Romney, K., and R. Romney
1963   "The Mixtecans of Juxtlahuaca, Mexico." In *Six Cultures: Studies of Child Rearing*, edited by B. B. Whiting, pp. 541–691. New York: Wiley.

Rosaldo, M. Z.
1980   *Knowledge and Passion: Ilongot Notions of Self and Social Life*. Cambridge: Cambridge University Press.
1983   "The Shame of Headhunters and the Autonomy of Self." *Ethos* 11:135–151.

Rossiaud, J.
1976   "Prostitution, Youth, and Society in the Towns of Southeastern France in the Fifteenth Century." *Annales, Economies, Sociétés, Civilisations* 31:289–325.

Rousseau, J-J.
1968   *The Social Contract: or, Principles of Political Right*. Middlesex: Penguin Books (orig. published 1762).

Rubin, V., and L. Comitas
1976   *Ganja in Jamaica: The Effects of Marijuana Use*. New York: Anchor Books.

Ryan, B. F., and M. A. Straus
1954   "The Integration of Sinhalese Society." *Research Studies of the State*

College of Washington 22:179–227.

Ryle, G.
1949   *The Concept of Mind.* New York: Barnes & Noble.

Sackett, L.
1977   "Liquor and the Law: Wiluna, Western Australia." In *Aborigines and Change: Australia in the '70s,* edited by R. M. Berndt, pp. 90–99. Social Anthropology Series, no. 11. Canberra: Australian Institute of Aboriginal Studies.

Sagan, E.
1974   *Cannibalism: Human Aggression and Cultural Form.* New York: Harper & Row.

Sahlins, M. D.
1963   "Poor Man, Rich Man, Big-Man, Chief: Political Types in Melanesia and Polynesia." *Comparative Studies in Society and History* 5:285–303.

Salusbury-Jones, G. T.
1939   *Street Life in Medieval England.* London: Pen-in-Hand.

Samaha, J.
1974   *Law and Order in Historical Perspective: The Case of Elizabethan Essex.* New York: Academic Press.

Sandoz, M.
1953   *Cheyenne Autumn.* New York: McGraw-Hill.

Sankhdher, L. M.
1974   *Caste Interaction in a Village Tribe.* New Delhi: K. B. Publications.

Schaeffer, H.
1952   *U-Boat 977.* London: William Kimber.

Scharfstein, B-A.
1974   *The Mind of China: The Culture, Customs, and Beliefs of Traditional China.* New York: Basic Books.

Schebesta, P.
1927   *Among the Forest Dwarfs of Malaya.* Translated by Arthur Chambers. London: Hutchinson & Co.
1933   *Among Congo Pygmies.* Translated by Gerald Griffin. London: Hutchinson & Co.
1936   *Revisiting My Pygmy Hosts.* Translated by Gerald Griffin. London: Hutchinson & Co.

Scheffler, H.
1965   *Choiseul Island Social Structure.* Berkeley and Los Angeles: University of California Press.

Schegloff, E. A.
1968   "Sequencing in Conversational Openings." *American Anthropologist* 70:1075–1095.

Scheper-Hughes, N.
1979   *Saints, Scholars, and Schizophrenics: Mental Illness in Rural Ireland.* Berkeley and Los Angeles: University of California Press.

Schlegel, A., and H. Barry, III
1980   "The Evolutionary Significance of Adolescent Initiation Cere-

monies." *American Ethnologist* 7:696–715.

Schlenker, B. R.
1980 *Impression Management: The Self-Concept, Social Identity, and Interpersonal Relations.* Monterey, Calif.: Brooks/Cole.

Schutz, A.
1967 *The Phenomenology of the Social World.* Translated by G. Walsh and F. Lehnert. Introduction by G. Walsh. Chicago: Northwestern University Press.

Schwartzman, H. B.
1978 *Transformations: The Anthropology of Children's Play.* New York: Plenum.

Scott, J. F.
1971 *Internalization of Norms: A Sociological Theory of Moral Commitment.* Englewood Cliffs, N.J.: Prentice-Hall.

Scott, M. B., and S. M. Lyman
1968 "Accounts." *American Sociological Review* 33:46–61.

Scott, R. A.
1969 *The Making of Blind Men.* New York: Russell Sage.

Seger, J. H.
1924 "Early Days Among the Cheyenne and Arapaho Indians." University of Oklahoma Bulletin No. 19, March.

Sennett, R.
1977 *The Fall of Public Man.* New York: Alfred A. Knopf.

Service, E. R.
1962 *Primitive Social Organization: An Evolutionary Perspective.* New York: Random House.

Shack, W. A., and E. P. Skinner, eds.
1979 *Strangers in African Societies.* Berkeley, Los Angeles, London: University of California Press.

Sharani, M. N.
1981 "Growing in Respect: Aging Among the Kirghiz of Afghanistan." In *Other Ways of Growing Old: Anthropological Perspectives,* edited by P. T. Amoss and S. Harrell, pp. 175–191. Stanford: Stanford University Press.

Shaw, G. B.
1946 *Three Plays for Puritans.* London: Penguin (orig. published 1901).

Shimanoff, S. B.
1980 *Communication Rules: Theory and Research.* Beverly Hills, Calif.: Sage Publications.

Shore, B.
1978 "Ghosts and Government: A Structural Analysis of Alternative Institutions for Conflict Management in Samoa." *Man* 13:175–199.

Shostak, M.
1981 *Nisa: The Life and Words of a !Kung Woman.* Cambridge, Mass.: Harvard University Press.

Shweder, R. A., E. Turiel, and N. C. Much

1981 "The Moral Intuitions of the Child." In *Social Cognitive Development: Frontiers and Possible Futures,* edited by J. H. Flavell and L. Ross, pp. 288–305. Cambridge: Cambridge University Press.

Sigerist, H.
1977 "The Special Position of the Sick." In *Culture, Disease, and Healing: Studies in Medical Anthropology,* edited by D. Landy, pp. 388–394. New York: Macmillan.

Silberbauer, G. B.
1981 *Hunter and Habitat in the Central Kalahari Desert.* Cambridge University Press.

Simmel, G.
1950 *The Sociology of Georg Simmel.* Edited and translated by K. H. Wolff. New York: The Free Press.

Simoons, F. J.
1961 *Eat Not This Flesh: Food Avoidances in the Old World.* Madison: University of Wisconsin Press.

Skinner, A. B.
1912 *Notes on the Eastern Cree and Northern Saulteaux.* New York: Anthropological Papers of the American Museum of Natural History 9 (Part 1):1–177.

Smith, H.
1980 "The Paradoxes of the Japanese Samurai." In *Learning from Shogun: Japanese History and Western Fantasy,* edited by H. Smith, pp. 99–112. Program in Asian Studies. Santa Barbara, Calif.: University of California, Santa Barbara.

Smith, H. W.
1978 "Effects of Set on Subject's Interpretation of Placebo Marihuana Effects." *Social Science and Medicine* 12:107–109.

Smith, M. B.
1949 "Combat Motivations Among Ground Troops." In *The American Soldier,* edited by S. A. Stouffer, pp. 105–191. Princeton: Princeton University Press.

Smith, R. J.
1961 "The Japanese Rural Community: Norms, Sanctions, and Ostracism." *American Anthropologist* 63:522–533.
1978 *The Psychopath in Society.* New York: Academic Press.

Snyder, C. R., R. L. Higgins, and R. J. Stucky
1983 *Excuses: Masquerades in Search of Grace.* New York: John Wiley & Sons.

Sobesky, W. E.
1983 "The Effects of Situational Factors on Moral Development." *Child Development* 54:575–584.

Sommer, R.
1969 *Personal Space.* Englewood Cliffs, N. J.: Prentice-Hall.

Spencer, B., and F. J. Gillen
1899 *The Native Tribes of Central Australia.* London: Macmillan.

1927   *The Arunta: A Study of a Stone Age People.* 2 vols. London: Macmillan.

Spencer, P.
1965   *The Samburu: A Study of Gerontocracy in a Nomadic Tribe.* Berkeley and Los Angeles: University of California Press.

Spiro, M. E.
1978   "Culture and Human Nature." In *The Making of Psychological Anthropology,* edited by G. D. Spindler, pp. 331–360. Berkeley, Los Angeles, London: University of California Press.

Spradley, J. P., and B. J. Mann
1975   *The Cocktail Waitress: Woman's Work in a Man's World.* New York: John Wiley & Sons.

Stands-in-Timber, J., and M. Liberty
1967   *Cheyenne Memories.* New Haven, Conn.: Yale University Press.

Stanner, W. E. H.
1959   "Continuity and Schism in an African Tribe." *Oceania* 29:208–217.

Starr, J., and B. Yngvesson
1975   "Scarcity and Disputing: Zeroing-in on Compromise Decisions." *American Ethnologist* 12:553–566.

Stefansson, V.
1922   *The Friendly Arctic.* New York: Macmillan.
1951   *My Life With The Eskimo.* New York: Macmillan.

Stephen, Sir J. F.
1883   *A History of the Criminal Law of England.* Vol. 1. New York: Burt Franklin.

Stevenson, L.
1974   *Seven Theories of Human Nature.* Oxford: The Clarendon Press.

Stewart, K.
1969   "Dream Therapy in Malaya." In *Altered States of Consciousness,* edited by C. T. Tart, pp. 161–170. Garden City, N.Y.: Doubleday.

Stoller, P.
1984   "Horrific Comedy: Cultural Resistance and the Hauka Movement in Niger." *Ethos* 12:165–188.

Storm, H.
1972   *Seven Arrows.* New York: Harper & Row.

Storry, R.
1978   *The Way of the Samurai.* New York: Putnam.

Story, G. M.
1969   "Mummers in Newfoundland History: A Survey of the Printed Record." In *Christmas Mumming in Newfoundland: Essays in Anthropology, Folklore and History,* edited by H. Halpert and G. Story, pp. 165–185. Toronto: University of Toronto Press.

Strauss, A. S.
1977   "Northern Cheyenne Ethnopsychology." *Ethos* 5:326–57.

Strehlow, T. G. H.
1970   "Geography and the Totemic Landscape in Central Australia: A

Functional Study." In *Australian Aboriginal Anthropology: Modern Studies in the Social Anthropology of the Australian Aborigines,* edited by R. M. Berndt, pp. 92–140. Nedlands: University of Western Australia Press.

Stuart, J., and D. M. Malcolm, eds.
1950   *The Diary of Henry Francis Fynn.* Pietermartizburg: Shuter and Shooter.

Sztompka, P.
1974   *System and Function: Toward a Theory of Society.* New York: Academic Press.

Tanaka, J.
1980   *The San Hunter-Gatherers of the Kalahari: A Study in Ecological Anthropology.* Translated by D. W. Hughes. Tokyo: University of Tokyo Press.

Tanno, T.
1976   "The Mbuti Net-Hunters in the Ituri Forest, Eastern Zaire—Their Hunting Activities and Band Composition." *Kyoto University African Studies* 10:101–136.

Taylor, L., and K. Dalton
1983   "Premenstrual Syndrome: A New Criminal Defense?" *California Western Law Review* 19:269–287.

Thesiger, W.
1964   *The Marsh Arabs.* London: Alfred A. Knopf.

Thomas, E. M.
1959   *The Harmless People.* New York: Alfred A. Knopf.

Thompson, D.
1916   *David Thompson's Narrative of His Explorations in Western America, 1784–1812.* Edited by J. B. Tyrell. Publication no. 12. Toronto: The Champlain Society.

Thompson, E. P.
1975   *Whigs and Hunters: The Origin of the Black Act.* London: Allen Lane.

Thompson, L.
1950   *Culture in Crisis: A Study of the Hopi Indians.* New York: Russell & Russell.

Thwaites, R. G., ed.
1896   *Jesuit Relations and Allied Documents.* Vols. 17 and 46. Cleveland: Burrows Bros.

Tindale, N. B.
1974   *Aboriginal Tribes of Australia: Their Terrain, Environmental Controls, Distribution, Limits, and Proper Names.* Berkeley, Los Angeles, London: University of California Press.

Tinklenberg, J. R., W. T. Roth, B. S. Kopell, and P. Murphy
1977   "Cannabis and Alcohol Effects on Assaultiveness in Adolescent Delinquents." *Annals of the New York Academy of Sciences* 282:85–94.

Tolstoy, L.
1961   *The Cossacks and the Raid.* Translated by A. R. MacAndrew. New

York: Signet.

Tonkinson, R.
1974   *The Jigalong Mob: Aboriginal Victors of the Desert Crusade.* Menlo Park, Calif.: Cummings.

Tooker, E.
1970   *The Iroquois Ceremonial of Midwinter.* Syracuse, N.Y.: Syracuse University Press.

Tsukahira, T. G.
1966   *Feudal Control in Tokugawa Japan.* Cambridge, Mass.: Harvard University Press.

Tuan, Y-F.
1979   *Landscapes of Fear.* Minneapolis: University of Minnesota Press.

Tuchman, B. W.
1978   *A Distant Mirror: The Calamitous 14th Century.* New York: Ballantine Books.

Tuck, R.
1979   *Natural Rights Theories: Their Origin and Development.* Cambridge: Cambridge University Press.

Turnbull, C.
1961   *The Forest People.* New York: Simon and Schuster.
1965a   *The Mbuti Pygmies: An Ethnographic Survey.* New York: Anthropological Papers of the Museum of Natural History. Vol. 50, pt. 3.
1965b   *Wayward Servants: The Two Worlds of the African Pygmies.* Garden City, N.Y.: Natural History Press.
1968   "The Importance of Flux in Two Hunting Societies." In *Man the Hunter,* edited by R. B. Lee and I. DeVore, pp. 132–137. Chicago: Aldine.
1972   *The Mountain People.* New York: Simon and Schuster.
1978   "The Politics of Non-Aggression (Zaire)." In *Learning Non-Aggression: The Experience of Non-Literate Societies,* edited by A. Montagu, pp. 161–221. Oxford: Oxford University Press.
1981   "Mbuti Womanhood." In *Woman the Gatherer,* edited by F. Dahlberg, pp. 205–220. New Haven, Conn.: Yale University Press.
1983   *The Human Cycle.* New York: Simon and Schuster.

Turnbull, J.
1813   *A Voyage round the World.* London: T. Maxwell.

Turner, V.
1957   *Schism and Continuity in an African Society.* Manchester: Manchester University Press.
1969   *The Ritual Process: Structure and Anti-Structure.* Chicago: Aldine.
1974   *Dramas, Fields, and Metaphors: Symbolic Action in Human Society.* Ithaca, N.Y.: Cornell University Press.
1978   "Comments and Conclusions." In *The Reversible World,* edited by B. Babcock, pp. 276–296. Ithaca, N.Y.: Cornell University Press.

Turner, V., ed.
1982   *Studies in Festivity and Ritual.* Washington, D.C.: Smithsonian In-

stitution Press.

Turney-High, H. H.
   1971   *Primitive War: Its Practice and Concepts.* 2d ed. Columbia, S.C.: University of South Carolina Press.

Tuzin, D. F.
   1982   "Ritual Violence among the Ilahita Arapesh: The Dynamics of Moral and Religious Uncertainty." In *Rituals of Manhood: Male Initiation in Papua New Guinea,* edited by G. H. Herdt, pp. 321–355. Berkeley, Los Angeles, London: University of California Press.

Underhill, R. M.
   1953   *Red Man's America: A History of Indians in the United States.* Chicago: University of Chicago Press.

Utley, R. M., ed.
   1977   *Life in Custer's Cavalry: Diaries and Letters of Albert and Jennie Barnitz 1867–1868.* New Haven, Conn.: Yale University Press.

Uzzell, D.
   1974   "Susto Revisited: Illness as Strategic Role." *American Ethnologist* 1:369–378.

Valle, J. E.
   1980   *Rocks and Shoals: Order and Discipline in the Old Navy, 1800–1861.* Annapolis, Md.: Naval Institute Press.

Van Allen, J.
   1972   "'Sitting On a Man': Colonialism and the Lost Political Institutions of Igbo Women." *Canadian Journal of African Studies* 6:165–181.

Van Gennep, A.
   1909   *Les Rites de Passage.* Paris: Librairie Critique, Emil Moury.

Vansina, J.
   1955   "Initiation Rituals of Bushong." *Africa* 25:138–152.

Wagatsuma, H.
   1970   "Study of Personality and Behavior in Japanese Society and Culture." In *The Study of Japan in the Behavioral Sciences,* edited by E. Norbeck and S. Parman. Rice University Studies. Vol. 56, no. 4.

Wallace, E., and E. A. Hoebel
   1952   *The Comanches: Lords of the South Plains.* Norman: University of Oklahoma Press.

Wambaugh, J.
   1975   *The Choirboys.* New York: Delacorte.

Warner, W. L.
   1937   *A Black Civilization: A Social Study of an Australian Tribe.* New York: Harper.

Washburne, C.
   1961   *Primitive Drinking: A Study of the Uses and Functions of Alcohol in Preliterate Societies.* New York: College and University Press.

Webb, W. P.
   1931   *The Great Plains.* Boston: Ginn.

Weil, A. T.

1972   *The Natural Mind.* Boston: Houghton Mifflin.

Weinberg, M. S.
1970   "The Nudist Management of Respectability: Strategy for, and Consequences of, the Construction of a Situated Morality." In *Deviance and Respectability: The Social Construction of Moral Meanings,* edited by J. D. Douglas, pp. 375–403. New York: Basic Books.

Weinstein, D.
1982   "Versions of SI." *Symbolic Interaction* 5:149–156.

Weist, K. M.
1970   "The Northern Cheyennes: Diversity in a Loosely Structured Society." Ann Arbor: University Microfilms.

Welch, C. E.
1966   "'Oh, dem Golden Slippers': The Philadelphia Mummers Parade." *Journal of American Folklore* 79:533–535.

Welsford, E.
1936   *The Fool: His Social and Literary History.* New York: Farrar & Rinehart.

Weyer, E. M.
1932   *The Eskimos.* New Haven, Conn.: Yale University Press.

White, T. H.
1960   *The Once and Future King.* New York: Dell.

Wiessner, P.
1982   "Risk, Reciprocity and Social Influences on !Kung San Economics." In *Politics and History in Band Societies,* edited by E. Leacock and R. Lee, pp. 61–84. Cambridge: Cambridge University Press.

Willmott, W. E.
1960   "The Flexibility of Eskimo Social Organization." *Anthropologica* 2:48–57.

Wilshire, B.
1982   "The Dramaturgical Model of Behavior: Its Strengths and Weaknesses." *Symbolic Interaction* 5:287–297.

Wilson, J.
1799   *A Missionary Voyage to the Southern Pacific Ocean, Performed in the Years 1796, 1797, 1798 in the Ship Duff. . . .* London: T. Chapman.

Wilson, M.
1959   *Divine Kings and the "Breath of Men."* Cambridge: Cambridge University Press.

Wilson, P. J.
1967   "Status Ambiguity and Spirit Possession." *Man* 3:366–378.

Wilson, T. P.
1970   "Conceptions of Interaction and Forms of Sociological Explanation." *American Sociological Review* 35:697–710.

Winans, E. V., and R. B. Edgerton
1964   "Hehe Magical Justice." *American Anthropologist* 66:745–764.

Winch, P.
1958 *The Idea of a Social Science and Its Relation to Philosophy.* London: Routledge & Kegan Paul.
Winter, E.
1959 *Beyond the Mountains of the Moon.* London: Routledge & Kegan Paul.
Witherspoon. G.
1975 *Navajo Kinship and Marriage.* Chicago: University of Chicago Press.
Wittgenstein, L.
1953 *Philosophical Investigations.* Translated by G. E. M. Anscombe. New York: Macmillan.
Woodburn, J. C.
1964 "The Social Organization of the Hadza of North Tanzania." Ph.D. dissertation, Cambridge University.
1968*a* "An Introduction of Hadza Ecology." In *Man the Hunter,* edited by R. B. Lee and I. DeVore, pp. 49–55. Chicago: Aldine.
1968*b* "Stability and Flexibility in Hadza Residential Groupings." In *Man the Hunter,* edited by R. B. Lee and I. DeVore, pp. 103–110. Chicago: Aldine.
1972 "Ecology, Nomadic Movement and the Composition of the Local Group among Hunters and Gatherers: An East African Example and Its Implications." In *Man, Settlement and Urbanism,* edited by P. J. Ucko, R. Tringham, and G. W. Dimbleby, pp. 192–206. London: Gerald Duckworth.
1979 "Minimal Politics: The Political Organization of the Hadza of North Tanzania." In *Politics in Leadership: A Comparative Perspective,* edited by W. A. Shack and P. S. Cohen, pp. 244–266. Oxford: Clarendon Press.
1980 "Hunters and Gatherers Today and Reconstruction of the Past." In *Soviet and Western Anthropology,* edited by E. Gellner, pp. 95–117. London: Gerald Duckworth.
Wrong, D.
1961 "The Oversocialized Conception of Man in Modern Sociology." *American Sociological Review* 26:183–193.
Yaron, R.
1969 *The Laws of Eshnunna.* Jerusalem: Magnes Press, The Hebrew University.
Youniss, J.
1980 *Parents and Peers in Social Development.* Chicago: University of Chicago Press.
Youssouf, I. A., A. P. Grimshaw, and C. S. Bird
1976 "Greetings in the Desert." *American Ethnologist* 3:797–824.
Yule, Henry, ed.
1929 *The Book of Marco Polo the Venetian, Concerning the Kingdoms and Marvels of the East.* 3d ed., Vol. 1. Translated by H. Yule. London:

John Murray.

Zborowski, M.

   1952   "Cultural Components in Response to Pain." *Journal of Social Issues*
           8:16–30.

Zeitlin, I. M.

   1973   *Rethinking Sociology: A Critique of Contemporary Theory.* New York:
           Appleton-Century-Crofts.

Name Index

Aberle, D. F., 203, 273
Ackerman, S. E., and R. L. M. Lee, 71, 273
Albert, Ethel, 157, 172, 267n, 273
Alexander, F. G., and S. T. Selesnick, 70, 273
Alexander, R. D., 215, 273
Allen, William S., 205, 273
Ames, W. L., 268n, 273
Amundsen, R., 262n, 273
Andersen, R., 267n, 273
Anderson, E. N., Jr., 250, 273
Ardener, Shirley, 111, 274
Arensberg, C., 76, 274
Ariés, P., 76, 274
Aristotle, 23
Asakawa, K., 176, 274
Ashcraft, N., and A. E. Scheflen, 262n, 274

Babcock, Barbara, 265n, 274
Bailey, F. G., 203, 261n, 274
Balicki, A., 269n, 274
Barker, Roger, 113
Barnett, D. L., and K. Njama, 103, 274
Barnouw, V., 269n, 274
Barrere, Dorothy, 125, 274
Barth, F., 12, 272, 274
Barthes, R., 270, 274
Basso, Ellen B., 268n, 274
Basso, K. H., 269, 275
Bateson, Gregory, 10, 95, 205, 224, 270, 275
Battaglia, A., 263n, 275
Beardsley, R. K., J. W. Hall, and R. E. Ward, 268n, 275
Beaubrun, M. H., 68, 69, 275

Beccaria, Cesare, 229
Beckett, J., 268n, 275
Befu, H., 268n, 275
Belden, J., 203, 275
Bellah, R. N., 174, 268n, 275
Bellamy, John, 119–120, 275
Benditt, T. M., 263n, 275
Benedict, Ruth, 63, 77, 176, 275
Bent, George, 145, 147, 150
Berger, M., T. Abel, and C. H. Page, 271, 275
Bernatzik, H. A., 268n, 275
Berndt, R. M., 265n, 275
Berndt, R. M., and C. Berndt, 163, 268n, 275
Berreman, Gerald, 87–88, 117, 261n, 262n, 272, 276
Berthrong, D. J., 146, 153–154, 267n, 276
Bierce, Ambrose, 42, 276
Biersack, A., 265n, 276
Biesele, Miegan, 188, 191, 276
Bilby, J. W., 79, 276
Birdwhistell, R., 262n, 276
Black, Donald, 228, 229, 244, 250–251, 264n, 276
Black, Max, 24, 29, 73, 130, 215, 262n, 263n, 276
Black-Michaud, Jacob, 237, 276
Blackstone, B. V., 240, 276
Blake, J., and K. Davis, 8, 261n, 276
Bligh, Capt. William, 91–92, 276
Blurton-Jones, Nicholas, 188
Bodde, D., 17, 18, 96, 277
Bodde, D., and C. Morris, 17, 18, 19, 20, 277
Bohannan, Paul, 5–6, 14, 22, 62, 277
Bonnie, R. J., and C. H. Whitebread, 67, 277

315

Subject Index

324

chronic illness, 69; disability, 209 (*See* Intersexuality); mental illness, 69–72, 81, 169
temporary conditions, 33, 49–74, 140, 155, 168, 207, 257; illness, 54, 55–58, 73–74, 138, 168, 256–257; intoxication, 54–55, 61–69, 73–74, 97, 138, 153, 177, 208, 256; personal attributes, 209; reputation, 210, 214–215, 256, 257; strong emotions, 52, 55, 138, 168, 208; unconsciousness, 53–54, 55. *See also* Qat; Cannabis sativa
defined, 33
biologically, 75, 76–82; age: childhood, 75, 76, 138, 150, 169, 177, 191; the elderly, 75, 76–77, 138, 169, 177, 191; blindness, 76, 79–80; epilepsy, 76; MR 76, 81–82, 169; paraplegia, 76
culturally, 82–93; clergy, 82–83; clowns, 90–93, 137, 138–139, 191; contraries, 148; "escape hatch" statuses, 87–89, 148; "half-men half-women," 148; joking relationships, 89–90; strangers, 82; wealthy & influential persons, 82–87
factors, for, 3, 201, 202, 256–257, 259
acculturation, 202
external, 202–204; environmental conditions, 203, 226, 252; famine, 184, 203
rapid change, 202
social incompletion, 202–203
social stratification, 202
factors against, 227, 259
inequality, 227–230
need to cooperate, 227, 230–233
perception of danger, 227, 233 (*see also* Fear)

occasions, 94–112, 139, 140, 147, 155, 169, 257
ceremonies, 94–112, 139, 147, 149, 155, 177, 191, 206, 230
cyclical-calendrical, 95–102
rituals, 94–112, 139–140
status change, 95, 102–107, 139; initiation, 95, 102–106; "life crisis," 95, 106–107
women's rights, 95, 107–112
settings, 113–126, 139, 140, 148, 155, 169, 177, 257
bars, 113–114
"portable settings," 115
possession of sacred materials, 121, 149
sanctuary, 118–126, 148–149, 169 (*see* Asylum)
statuses, 33, 75–93, 138, 140, 148, 155, 168–169, 191, 227, 257
Excuses, 33, 61, 70, 87, 207, 211

Fear, 233–239, 244–247, 255
Female vigilantism, 107–112
Feuding, 237–238
Fire prevention, medieval, 240–241
Flat-War-Club, 147
Fools, 90
Funerals, 106–107, 183

Game theory, 12
Gidjingali, 165
Gilyak, 81
Greeks, 78, 118, 258
Gunabibi ceremony, 100–102, 169, 216
Gururumba, 88–89
Gusii, 15, 25

Hadza, 184–187
Hammurabi, code of, 30, 158
Hawaiian, 106–107, 123–126, 204
Hehe, 53–54, 212–213, 235
Hindus, 45
Homosexual behavior, 78, 116–117, 135, 206

Designer: U.C. Press Staff
Compositor: Prestige Typography
Printer: Thomson-Shore, Inc.
Binder: John H. Dekker & Sons
Text: 10/12 Baskerville Roman
Display: Baskerville